WISDOM, WIT, AND PATHOS

SELECTED FROM THE WORKS

OF

OUIDA

Bi

PHILADELPHIA
J. B. LIPPINCOTT & CO.
1884

Printing Statement:

Due to the very old age and scarcity of this book,
many of the pages may be hard to read due to the
blurring of the original text, possible missing pages,
missing text, dark backgrounds and other issues
beyond our control.

Because this is such an important and rare work, we
believe it is best to reproduce this book regardless of
its original condition.

Thank you for your understanding.

CONTENTS.

SELECTIONS FROM—

ARIADNE.

ONE grows to love the Roman fountains as sea-born men the sea. Go where you will there is the water; whether it foams by Trevi, where the green moss grows in it like ocean weed about the feet of the ocean god, or whether it rushes reddened by the evening light, from the mouth of an old lion that once saw Cleopatra; whether it leaps high in air, trying to reach the gold cross on St. Peter's or pours its triple cascade over the Pauline granite; whether it spouts out of a great barrel in a wall in old Trastevere, or throws up into the air a gossamer as fine as Arachne's web in a green garden way where the lizards run, or in a crowded corner where the fruit-sellers sit against the wall;—in all its shapes one grows to love the water that fills Rome with an unchanging melody all through the year.

AND indeed I do believe all things and all traditions. History is like that old stag that Charles of France found out hunting in the woods once, with the bronze collar round its neck on which was written, "Cæsar mihi hoc donavit." How one's fancy loves to linger about that old stag, and what a crowd of mighty shades come thronging at the very thought of him! How wonderful it is to think of—that quiet grey beast leading his lovely

A

life under the shadows of the woods, with his hinds and their fawns about him, whilst Cæsar after Cæsar fell and generation on generation passed away and perished! But the sciolist taps you on the arm. "Deer average fifty years of life; it was some mere court trick of course —how easy to have such a collar made!" Well, what have we gained? The stag was better than the sciolist.

L IFE costs but little on these sunny, silent shores; four walls of loose stones, a roof of furze and brambles, a fare of fish and fruit and millet-bread, a fire of driftwood easily gathered—and all is told. For a feast pluck the violet cactus; for a holiday push the old red boat to sea, and set the brown sail square against the sun—nothing can be cheaper, perhaps few things can be better.

To feel the western breezes blow over that sapphire sea, laden with the fragrance of a score of blossoming isles. To lie under the hollow rocks, where centuries before the fisher folk put up that painted tablet to the dear Madonna, for all poor shipwrecked souls. To climb the high hills through the tangle of myrtle and tamarisk, and the tufted rosemary, with the kids bleating above upon some unseen height. To watch the soft night close in, and the warning lights shine out over shoals and sunken rocks, and the moon hang low and golden in the blue dusk at the end there under the arch of the boughs. To spend long hours in the cool, fresh, break of day, drifting with the tide, and leaping with bare free limbs into the waves, and lying outstretched upon them, glancing down to the depths below, where silvery fish are gliding and coral branches are growing, and pink shells are floating like roseleaves, five fathoms low and more. Oh! a good life, and none better, abroad in the winds and weather, as Nature meant that every living thing should be, only, alas, the devil put it into the mind of man to build cities ! A good life for the soul and the body : and from it this sea-born Joy came to seek the Ghetto !

WITH a visible and physical ill one can deal ; one can thrust a knife into a man at need, one can give a woman money for bread or masses, one can run for medicine or a priest. But for a creature with a face like Ariadnê's, who had believed in the old gods and found them fables, who had sought for the old altars and found them ruins, who had dreamed of Imperial Rome and found the Ghetto—for such a sorrow as this, what could one do ?

SOME said I might have been a learned man, had I taken more pains. But I think it was only their kindness. I have that twist in my brain, which is the curse of my countrymen—a sort of devilish quickness at doing well, that prevents us ever doing best ; just the same sort of thing that makes our goatherds rhyme perfect sonnets, and keeps them dunces before the alphabet.

IF our beloved Leopardi, instead of bemoaning his fate in his despair and sickening of his narrow home, had tried to see how many fair strange things there lay at his house door, had tried to care for the troubles of the men that hung the nets on the trees, and the innocent woes of the girl that carried the grass to the cow, and the obscure martyrdom of maternity and widowhood that the old woman had gone through who sat spinning on the top of the stairs, he would have found that his little borgo that he hated so for its dulness had

all the comedies and tragedies of life lying under the
sound of its tolling bells. He would not have been less
sorrowful, for the greater the soul the sadder it is for the
unutterable waste, the unending pain of life. But he
would never have been dull : he would never have despised, and despising missed, the stories and the poems
that were round him in the millet fields and the olive
orchards. There is only one lamp which we can carry
in our hand, and which will burn through the darkest
night, and make the light of a home for us in a desert
place : it is sympathy with everything that breathes.

INTO other lands I wandered, then, and sought full
half the world. When one wants but little, and has
a useful tongue, and knows how to be merry with the
young folk, and sorrowful with the old, and can take the
fair weather with the foul, and wear one's philosophy like
an easy boot, treading with it on no man's toe, and no
dog's tail ; why, if one be of this sort, I say, one is, in
a great manner, independent of fortune ; and the very
little that one needs one can usually obtain. Many years
I strayed about, seeing many cities and many minds, like
Odysseus ; being no saint, but, at the same time, being no
thief and no liar.

ART was dear to me. Wandering through many
lands, I had come to know the charm of quiet
cloisters ; the delight of a strange, rare volume ; the
interest of a quaint bit of pottery ; the unutterable loveliness of some perfect painter's vision, making a glory in
some dusky, world-forgotten church : and so my life was
full of gladness here in Rome, where the ass's hoof ringing on a stone may show you that Vitruvius was right,

where you had doubted him ; or the sun shining down upon a cabbage garden, or a coppersmith's shreds of metal, may gleam on a signet ring of the Flavian women, or a broken vase that may have served vile Tullia for drink.

ART is, after nature, the only consolation that one has at all for living.

I HAVE been all my life blown on by all sorts of weather, and I know there is nothing so good as the sun and the wind for driving ill-nature and selfishness out of one.

ANYTHING in the open air is always well ; it is because men now-a-days shut themselves up so much in rooms and pen themselves in stifling styes, where never the wind comes or the clouds are looked at, that puling discontent and plague-struck envy are the note of all modern politics and philosophies. The open air breeds Leonidas, the factory room Felix Pyat.

I LIT my pipe. A pipe is a pocket philosopher, a truer one than Socrates. For it never asks questions. Socrates must have been very tiresome when one thinks of it.

I HAVE had some skill in managing the minds of crowds ; it is a mere knack, like any other ; it belongs to no particular character or culture. Arnold of

Brescia had it, and so had Masaniello.   Lamartine had it, and so had Jack Cade.

IT is of use to have a reputation for queerness; it gains one many solitary moments of peace.

ERSILIA was a good soul, and full of kindliness; but charity is a flower not naturally of earthly growth, and it needs manuring with a promise of profit.

THE soul of the poet is like a mirror of an astrologer: it bears the reflection of the past and of the future, and can show the secrets of men and gods; but all the same it is dimmed by the breath of those who stand by and gaze into it.

"YOU are not unhappy now?" I said to her in farewell.

She looked at me with a smile.

"You have given me hope; and I am in Rome, and I am young."

She was right. Rome may be only a ruin, and Hope but another name for deception and disappointment; but Youth is supreme happiness in itself, because all possibilities lie in it, and nothing in it is as yet irrevocable.

THERE never was an Æneas; there never was a Numa; well, what the better are we? We only lose the Trojan ship gliding into Tiber's mouth, when the

woodland thickets that bloomed by Ostia were reddening
with the first warmth of the day's sun ; we only lose the
Sabine lover going by the Sacred Way at night, and
sweet Egeria weeping in the woods of Nemi ; and are—
by their loss—how much the poorer !

Perhaps all these things never were.

The little stone of truth, rolling through the many
ages of the world, has gathered and grown grey with the
thick mosses of romance and superstition. But tradition
must always have that little stone of truth as its kernel ;
and perhaps he who rejects all, is likelier to be wrong
than even foolish folk like myself who love to believe all,
and who tread the new paths, thinking ever of the ancient
stories.

T HERE can be hardly any life more lovely upon
earth than that of a young student of art in Rome.
With the morning, to rise to the sound of countless bells
and of innumerable streams, and see the silver lines of the
snow new fallen on the mountains against the deep rose of
the dawn, and the shadows of the night steal away softly
from off the city, releasing, one by one, dome and spire, and
cupola and roof, till all the wide white wonder of the place
discloses itself under the broad brightness of full day ; to
go down into the dark cool streets, with the pigeons fluttering in the fountains, and the sounds of the morning
chants coming from many a church door and convent
window, and little scholars and singing children going by
with white clothes on, or scarlet robes, as though walking
forth from the canvas of Botticelli or Garofalo ; to eat
frugally, sitting close by some shop of flowers and birds,
and watching all the while the humours and the pageants
of the streets by quaint corners, rich with sculptures of
the Renaissance, and spanned by arches of architects
that builded for Agrippa, under grated windows with

arms of Frangipanni or Colonna, and pillars that Apollo-
dorus raised ; to go into the great courts of palaces, mur-
murous with the fall of water, and fresh with green leaves
and golden fruit, that rob the colossal statues of their
gloom and gauntness, and thence into the vast chambers
where the greatest dreams that men have ever had, are
written on panel and on canvas, and the immensity and
the silence of them all are beautiful and eloquent with
dead men's legacies to the living, where the Hours and
the Seasons frolic beside the Maries at the Sepulchre, and
Adonis bares his lovely limbs, in nowise ashamed because
S. Jerome and S. Mark are there ; to study and muse,
and wonder and be still, and be full of the peace which
passes all understanding, because the earth is lovely as
Adonis is, and life is yet unspent ; to come out of the
sacred light, half golden, and half dusky, and full of many
blended colours, where the marbles and the pictures live,
sole dwellers in the deserted dwellings of princes ; to
come out where the oranges are all aglow in the sunshine,
and the red camellias are pushing against the hoary head
of the old stone Hermes, and to go down the width of the
mighty steps into the gay piazza, alive with bells tolling,
and crowds laughing, and drums abeat, and the flutter of
carnival banners in the wind ; and to get away from it all
with a full heart, and ascend to see the sun set from the
terrace of the Medici, or the Pamfili, or the Borghese
woods, and watch the flame-like clouds stream homewards behind S. Peter's, and the pines of Monte Mario
grow black against the west, till the pale green of evening
spreads itself above them, and the stars arise ; and then,
with a prayer—be your faith what it will—a prayer to the
Unknown God, to go down again through the violet-
scented air and the dreamful twilight, and so, with unspeakable thankfulness, simply because you live, and this
is Rome—so homeward.

THE strong instinctive veracity in her weighed the
measure of her days, and gave them their right
name. She was content, her life was full of the sweetness
and strength of the arts, and of the peace of noble occupa-
tion and endeavour. But some true instinct in her taught
her that this is peace, but is not more than peace. Happiness comes but from the beating of one heart upon
another.

THERE was a high wall near, covered with peach-
trees, and topped with wistaria and valerian, and
the handsome wild caperplant; and against the wall
stood rows of tall golden sunflowers late in their blooming;
the sun they seldom could see for the wall, and it was
pathetic always to me, as the day wore on, to watch
the poor stately amber heads turn straining to greet their
god, and only meeting the stones and the cobwebs, and
the peach-leaves of their inexorable barrier.

They were so like us!—straining after the light, and
only finding bricks and gossamer and wasps'-nests! But
the sunflowers never made mistakes as we do: they never
took the broken edge of a glass bottle or the glimmer of
a stable lanthorn for the glory of Helios, and comforted
themselves with it—as we can do.

DEAR, where we love much we always forgive, because
we ourselves are nothing, and what we love is all.

THERE is something in the silence of an empty room
that sometimes has a terrible eloquence: it is like
the look of coming death in the eyes of a dumb animal;
it beggars words and makes them needless.

WHEN you have said to yourself that you will kill any one, the world only seems to hold yourself and him, and God—who will see the justice done.

WHAT is it that love does to a woman?—without it she only sleeps; with it, alone, she lives.

A GREAT love is an absolute isolation, and an absolute absorption. Nothing lives or moves or breathes, save one life: for one life alone the sun rises and sets, the seasons revolve, the clouds bear rain, and the stars ride on high; the multitudes around cease to exist, or seem but ghostly shades; of all the sounds of earth there is but one voice audible; all past ages have been but the herald of one soul; all eternity can be but its heritage alone.

IS Nature kind or cruel? Who can tell?
The cyclone comes, or the earthquake; the great wave rises and swallows the cities and the villages, and goes back whence it came; the earth yawns, and devours the pretty towns and the sleeping children, the gardens where the lovers were sitting, and the churches where women prayed, and then the morass dries up and the gulf unites again. Men build afresh, and the grass grows, and the trees, and all the flowering seasons come back as of old. But the dead are dead: nothing changes that!

As it is with the earth, so it is with our life; our own poor, short, little life, that is all we can really call our own.

Calamities shatter, and despair engulfs it; and yet after a time the chasm seems to close; the storm wave seems to roll back; the leaves and the grass return; and we make new dwellings. That is, the daily ways of living are resumed, and the common tricks of our speech and act are as they used to be before disaster came upon us. Then wise people say, he or she has "got over it." Alas, alas! the drowned children will not come back to us; the love that was struck down, the prayer that was silenced, the altar that was ruined, the garden that was ravished, they are all gone for ever,— for ever, for ever! Yet we live; because grief does not always kill, and often does not speak.

I CREPT through the myrtles downward, away from the house where the statue lay shattered. The earliest of the nightingales of the year was beginning her lay in some leafy covert hard by, but never would he hear music in their piping again; never, never: any more than I should hear the song of the Faun in the fountain.

For the song that we hear with our ears is only the song that is sung in our hearts.

And his heart, I knew, would be for ever empty and silent, like a temple that has been burned with fire, and left standing, pitiful and terrible, in mockery of a lost religion, and of a forsaken god.

MEN and women, losing the thing they love, lose much, but the artist loses far more; for him are slaughtered all the children of his dreams, and from him are driven all the fair companions of his solitude.

LOVE art alone, forsaking all other loves, and she will make you happy, with a happiness that shall defy the seasons and the sorrows of time, the pains of the vulgar and the changes of fortune, and be with you day and night, a light that is never dim. But mingle with it any human love—and art will look for ever at you with the eyes of Christ when he looked at the faithless follower as the cock crew.

AND, indeed, there are always the poor: the vast throngs born century after century, only to know the pangs of life and of death, and nothing more. Methinks that human life is, after all, but like a human body, with a fair and smiling face, but all the limbs ulcered and cramped and racked with pain. No surgery of statecraft has ever known how to keep the fair head erect, yet give the trunk and the limbs health.

FOR in a great love there is a self-sustaining strength by which it lives, deprived of everything, as there are plants that live upon our barren ruins burned by the sun, and parched and shelterless, yet ever lifting green leaves to the light.

AND indeed after all there is nothing more cruel than the impotence of genius to hold and keep those commonest joys and mere natural affections which dullards and worse than dullards rejoice in at their pleasure; the common human things, whose loss makes the great possessions of its imperial powers all valueless and vain as harps unstrung, or as lutes that are broken.

" THIS world of our own immediate day is weak and
weary, because it is no longer young; yet it
possesses one noble attribute—it has an acute and almost
universal sympathy, which does indeed often degenerate
into a false and illogical sentiment, yet serves to redeem
an age of egotism. We have escaped both the gem-like
hardness of the Pagan, and the narrowing selfishness of
the Christian and the Israelite. We are sick for the woe
of creation, and we wonder why such woe is ours, and
why it is entailed on the innocent dumb beasts, that
perish in millions for us, unpitied, day and night. Rome
had no altar to Pity: it is the one God that we own.
When that pity in us for all things is perfected, perhaps
we shall have reached a religion of sympathy that will
be purer than any religion the world has yet seen, and
more productive. ' Save my country !' cried the Pagan
to his deities. ' Save my soul !' cries the Christian at
his altars. We, who are without a god, murmur to the
great unknown forces of Nature: ' Let me save others
some little portion of this pain entailed on all simple and
guileless things, that are forced to live, without any fault
of their own at their birth, or any will of their own in
their begetting.'"

HOW should we have great Art in our day? We
have no faith. Belief of some sort is the lifeblood of Art. When Athene and Zeus ceased to excite
any veneration in the minds of men, sculpture and architecture both lost their greatness. When the Madonna
and her son lost that mystery and divinity, which for the
simple minds of the early painters they possessed, the
soul went out of canvas and of wood. When we carve a
Venus now, she is but a light woman ; when we paint a
Jesus now, it is but a little suckling, or a sorrowful
prisoner. We want a great inspiration. We ought to

find it in the things that are really beautiful, but we are not sure enough, perhaps, what is so. What does dominate us is a passion for nature ; for the sea, for the sky, for the mountain, for the forest, for the evening storm, for the break of day. Perhaps when we are thoroughly steeped in this we shall reach greatness once more. But the artificiality of all modern life is against it ; so is its cynicism. Sadness and sarcasm make a great Lucretius as a great Juvenal, and scorn makes a strong Aristophanes ; but they do not make a Praxiteles and an Apelles ; they do not even make a Raffaelle, or a Flaxman.

Art, if it be anything, is the perpetual uplifting of what is beautiful in the sight of the multitudes—the perpetual adoration of that loveliness, material and moral, which men in the haste and the greed of their lives are everlastingly forgetting : unless it be that it is empty and useless as a child's reed-pipe when the reed is snapt and the child's breath spent. Genius is obligation.

"NO woman, I think, ever loved you as this woman does, whom you have left as I would not leave a dog," said Maryx, and something of his old ardent eloquence returned to him, and his voice rose and rang clearer as the courage in him consummated the self-sacrifice that he had set himself for her sake. "Have you ever thought what you have done? When you have killed Art in an artist, you have done the cruellest murder that earth can behold. Other and weaker natures than hers might forget, but she never. Her fame will be short-lived as that rose, for she sees but your face, and the world will tire of that, but she will not. She can dream no more. She can only remember. Do you know what that is to the artist?—it is to be blind and to weary the world ; the

world that has no more pity than you have ! You think
her consoled because her genius has not left her ; are
you a poet and yet do not know that genius is only a
power to suffer more and to remember longer ?—nothing
else. You say to yourself that she will have fame, that
will beguile her as the god came to Ariadnê ; perhaps ;
but across that fame, let it become what it may, there
will settle for ever the shadow of the world's dishonour ;
it will be for ever poisoned, and cursed, and embittered
by the scorn of fools, and the reproach of women, since
by you they have been given their lashes of nettles, and
by you have been given their by-word to hoot. She
will walk in the light of triumph, you say, and therefore
you have not hurt her ; do you not see that the fiercer
that light may beat on her, the sharper will the eyes of
the world search out the brand with which you have
burned her. For when do men forgive force in the
woman ? and when do women ever forgive the woman's
greatness ? and when does every cur fail to snarl at the life
that is higher than its fellows ? It is by the very genius
in her that you have had such power to wound, such
power to blight and to destroy. By so long as her name
shall be spoken, so long will the wrong you have done
her cling round it, to make it meet for reproach. A mere
woman dies, and her woe and her shame die with her,
and the earth covers her and them ; but such shelter is
denied for ever to the woman who has genius and fame ;
long after she is dead she will lie out on common soil,
naked and unhouselled, for all the winds to blow on her
and all the carrion birds to tear."

" NO, no. That is accursed ! To touch Art without a
    right to touch it, merely as a means to find bread
—you are too honest to think of such a thing. Unless

Art be adored for its own sake and purely, it must be left
alone. Philip of Macedon had every free man's child
taught Art! I would have every boy and girl taught its
sacredness ; so, we might in time get back some accuracy
of taste in the public, some conscientiousness of production in the artist. If artistic creation be not a joy, an imperious necessity, an instinct of all the forces of the mind,
let the boy go and plough, and the girl go and spin."

MAYBE you turn your back on happiness. I have
heard that wise people often do that. They look
up so at the sun and the stars, that they set their foot on
the lark that would have sung to them and woke them
brightly in the morning—and kill it.

LANDSCAPE painting is the only original form of
painting that modern times can boast. It has
not exhausted itself yet ; it is capable of infinite de-
velopment. Ruysdael, Rembrandt, and the rest, did
great scenes, it is true, but it has been left to our
painters to put soul into the sunshine of a cornfield, and
suggest a whole life of labour in a dull evening sky hanging over a brown ploughed upland, with the horses going
tired homewards, and one grey figure trudging after them,
to the hut on the edge of the moor. Of course the modern
fancy of making nature answer to all human moods, like
an Eölian harp, is morbid and exaggerated, but it has a
beauty in it, and a certain truth. Our tenderer souls
take refuge in the country now, as they used to do in the
cloister.

I THINK if people oftener saw the break of day they would vow oftener to keep that dawning day holy, and would not so often let its fair hours drift away with nothing done that were not best left undone.

WE are the sons of our Time : it is not for us to slay our mother.   Let us cover her dishonour if we see it, lest we should provoke the Erinyes.

HOW one loves Canova the man, and how one exe-crates Canova the artist ! Surely never was a great repute achieved by so false a talent and so perfect a character.   One would think he had been born and bred in Versailles instead of Treviso.   He is called a natural-ist ! Look at his Graces ! He is always Coysevax and Coustou at heart.   Never purely classic, never frankly modern.   Louis XIV. would have loved him better than Bernini.

IF Alexander had believed himself a bubble of gas in-stead of the son of a god, he would not have changed the face of the world.   Negation cannot be the parent of heroism, though it will produce an indifference that coun-terfeits it not ill, since Petronius died quite as serenely as ever did the martyrs of the Church.

GENIUS cannot escape the taint of its time more than a child the influence of its begetting.   Augustus could have Horace and Ovid ; he could never have had Homer and Milton.

B

I DO not think with you. Talent takes the mark of its generation; genius stamps its time with its own impression. Virgil had the sentiment of an united Italy.

TELL her that past she thinks so great was only very like the Serapis which men worshipped so many ages in Theophilis, and which, when the soldiers struck it down at last, proved itself only a hollow Colossus with a colony of rats in its head that scampered right and left.

FALCONET struck the death-note of the plastic arts when he said, "Our marbles have *almost* colour." That is just where we err. We are incessantly striving to make Sculpture at once a romance-writer and a painter, and of course she loses all dignity and does but seem the jay in borrowed plumes of sable. Conceits are altogether out of keeping with marble. They suit a cabinet painting or a piece of china. Bernini was the first to show the disease when he veiled the head of his Nile to indicate that the source was unknown.

WHOSOEVER has any sort of fame has lighted a beacon that is always shining upon him, and can never more return into the cool twilight of privacy even when most he wishes. It is of these retributions—some call them compensations—of which life is full.

MEN have forgotten the virile Pyrrhic dance, and have become incapable of the grace of the Ionian; their only dance is a Danse Macabre, and they are always hand in hand with a skeleton.

BY night Rome is still a city for the gods ; the shadows
veil its wounds, the lustre silvers all its stones ; its
silence is haunted as no other silence is ; if you have
faith, there where the dark gloss of the laurel brushes
the marble as in Agrippa's time, you will see the Immortals passing by chained with dead leaves and weeping.

A GREAT love is an absolute isolation and an absolute absorption. Nothing lives or moves or
breathes save one life ; for one life alone the sun rises
and sets, the seasons revolve, the clouds bear rain, and
the stars ride on high ; the multitudes around cease to
exist, or seem but ghostly shades ; of all the sounds of
earth there is but one voice audible ; all past ages have
been but the herald of one soul ; all eternity can be but
its heritage alone.

PERHAPS she was right : for a few hours of joy one
owes the debt of years, and should give a pardon
wide and deep as the deep sea.

This Love which she had made in his likeness, the
tyrant and compeller of the world, was to her as the
angel which brings perfect dreams and lets the tired
sleeper visit heaven.

" AND when the ship sails away without you ? " I said
brutally, and laughing still, because the mention
of the schooner had broken the bonds of the silence that
had held me against my will half paralysed, and I seemed
to be again upon the Tyrrhene shore, seeing the white
sail fade against the sky.

"And when that ship sails without you ? The day will
come. It always comes. You are my Ariadnê ; yet you
forget Naxos ! Oh, the day will come ! you will kiss the

feet of your idol then, and they will not stay; they will
go away, away, away, and they will not tarry for your
prayers or your tears—ay, it is always so. Two love,
and one tires. And you know nothing of that; you who
would have love immortal."

And I laughed again, for it seemed to me so horrible,
and I was half mad.

No doubt it would have been kinder had I struck my
knife down into her breast with her words unspoken.

All shade of colour forsook her face; only the soft
azure of the veins remained, and changed to an ashen
grey. She shook with a sudden shiver from head to foot
as the name she hated, the name of Ariadnê, fell upon
her ear. The icebolt had fallen in her paradise. A
scared and terrible fear dilated her eyes, that opened
wide in the amaze of some suddenly stricken creature.

"And when he leaves you?" I said, with cruel iteration.
"Do you remember what you told me once of the woman
by the marshes by the sea, who had nothing left by which
to remember love save wounds that never healed? That
is all his love will leave you by-and-by."

"Ah, never!"

She spoke rather to herself than me. The terror was
fading out of her eyes, the blood returning to her face;
she was in the sweet bewildered trance of that blind faith
which goes wherever it is led, and never asks the end nor
dreads the fate. Her love was deathless: how could she
know that his was mortal?

"You are cruel," she said, with her mouth quivering,
but the old, soft, grand courage in her eyes. "We are
together for ever; he has said so. But even if—if—I
only remembered him by wounds, what would that change
in me? He would *have* loved me. If he would wish to
wound me, so he should. I am his own as the dogs are.
Think!—he looked at me, and all the world grew beautiful; he touched me, and I was happy—I, who never had

been happy in my life. You look at me strangely; you speak harshly. Why? I used to think, surely you would be glad——"

I gripped my knife and cursed him in my soul.

How could one say to her the thing that he had made her in man's and woman's sight?

"I thought you would be glad," she said, wistfully, "and I would have told you long ago—myself. I do not know why you should look so. Perhaps you are angered because I seemed ungrateful to you and Maryx. Perhaps I was so. I have no thought—only of him. What he wished, that I did. Even Rome itself was for me nothing, and the gods—there is only one for me; and he is with me always. And I think the serpents and the apes are gone for ever from the tree, and he only hears the nightingales — now. He tells me so often. Very often. Do you remember I used to dream of greatness for myself—ah, what does it matter! I want nothing now. When he looks at me—the gods themselves could give me nothing more."

And the sweet tranquil radiance came back into her eyes, and her thoughts wandered into the memories of this perfect passion which possessed her, and she forgot that I was there.

My throat was choking; my eyes felt blind; my tongue clove to my mouth. I, who knew what that end would be as surely as I knew the day then shining would sink into the earth, I was dumb, like a brute beast—I, who had gone to take his life.

Before this love which knew nothing of the laws of mankind, how poor and trite and trivial looked 'hose laws! What could I dare to say to her of shame? Ah! if it had only been for any other's sake! But he,—perhaps he did not lie to her; perhaps he did only hear the nightingales with her beside him; but how soon their song would pall upon his ear, how soon would he sigh for the poisonous kiss of the serpents! I knew! I knew!

I stood heart-broken in the warm light that was falling through the casement and streaming towards her face. What could I say to her? Men harder and sterner and surer in every way of their own judgment than I was of mine no doubt would have shaken her with harsh hands from that dream in which she had wandered to her own destruction.

No doubt a sterner moralist than I would have had no pity, and would have hurled on her all the weight of those bitter truths of which she was so ignorant; would have shown her that pit of earthly scorn upon whose brink she stood; would have torn down all that perfect, credulous faith of hers, which could have no longer life nor any more lasting root than the flowering creeper born of a summer's sun, and gorgeous as the sunset's hues, and clinging about a ruin-mantling decay. Oh yes, no doubt. But I am only weak, and of little wisdom, and never certain that the laws and ways of the world are just, and never capable of long giving pain to any harmless creature, least of all to her.

She seemed to rouse herself with effort to remember I was there, and turned on me her eyes that were suffused and dreamful with happiness, like a young child's with sleep.

"I must have seemed so thankless to you: you were so very good to me," she said, with that serious sweetness of her rare smile that I had used to watch for, as an old dog watches for his young owner's—an old dog that is used to be forgotten, but does not himself forget, though he is old. "I must have seemed so thankless; but he bade me be silent, and I have no law but him. After that night when we walked in Nero's fields, and I went home and learned he loved me;—do you not see I forgot that there was any one in all the world except himself and me? It must always be so—at least, so I think. Oh, how true that poem was! Do you remember how he read it that night after Mozart amongst the roses by the fire? What use was endless life and all the lore of the spirits and seers to Sospitra? I was like Sospitra, till he came; always thinking of the stars and the heavens in the desert all alone, and always wishing for life eternal, when it is only life *together* that is worth a wish or a prayer. But why do you look at me so? Perhaps you do not understand. Perhaps I am selfish."

This was all that it seemed to her—that I did not understand. Could she see the tears of blood that welled up in my eyes? Could she see the blank despair that blinded my sight? Could she see the frozen hand that I felt clutching at my heart and benumbing it? I did not understand; that was all that it seemed to her.

She was my Ariadnê, born again to suffer the same fate. I saw the future : she could not. I knew that he would leave her as surely as the night succeeds the day. I knew that his passion—if passion, indeed, it were, and not only the mere common vanity of subjugation and possession—would pall on him and fade out little by little, as the stars fade out of the grey morning skies. I knew, but I had not the courage to tell her.

Men were faithful only to the faithless. But what could she know of this?

"Thinking of the stars and of the heavens in the desert all alone! Yes!" I cried; and the bonds of my silence were unloosed, and the words rushed from my lips like a torrent from between the hills.

"Yes ; and never to see the stars any more, and to lose for ever the peace of the desert—that, you think, is gain! Oh, my dear! what can I say to you? What can I say? You will not believe if I tell you. I shall seem a liar and a prophet of false woe. I shall curse when I would bless. What can I say to you? Athene watched over you. You were of those who dwell alone,

but whom the gods are with. You had the clue and the
sword, and they are nothing to you; you lose them both
at his word, at the mere breath of his lips, and know no
god but his idle law, that shifts as the winds of the sea.
And you count that gain? Oh, just Heaven! Oh, my
dear, my heart is broken; how can I tell you? One man
loved you who was great and good, to whom you were a
sacred thing, who would have lifted you up in heaven,
and never have touched too roughly a single hair of
your head; and you saw him no more than the very
earth that you trod; he was less to you than the marbles
he wrought in; and he suffers: and what do you care?
You have had the greatest wrong that a woman can
have, and you think it the greatest good, the sweetest
gift! He has torn your whole life down as a cruel
hand tears a rose in the morning light, and you rejoice!
For what do you know? He will kill your soul, and
still you will kiss his hand. Some women are so. When
he leaves you, what will you do? For you there will
only be death. The weak are consoled, but the strong
never. What will you do? What will you do? You
are like a child that culls flowers at the edge of a snake's
breeding-pit. He waked you—yes!—to send you in a
deeper sleep, blind and dumb to everything but his will.
Nay, nay! that is not your fault. Love does not come
at will; and of goodness it is not born, nor of gratitude,
nor of any right or reason on the earth. Only that you
should have had no thought of us—no thought at all—
only of him by whom your ruin comes; that seems hard!
Ay, it is hard. You stood just so in my dream, and you
hesitated between the flower of passion and the flower of
death. Ah, well might Love laugh. They grow on the
same bough; Love knows that. Oh, my dear, my dear,
I come too late! Look! he has done worse than murder,
for that only kills the body; but he has killed the soul in
you. He will crush out all that came to you from heaven;

all your mind and your hopes and your dreams, and all the
mystery in you, that we poor half-dumb fools call genius,
and that made the common daylight above you full of all
beautiful shapes and visions that our duller eyes could not
see as you went. He has done worse than murder, and
I came to take his life. Ay, I would slay him now as I
would strangle the snake in my path. And even for this
I come too late. I cannot do you even this poor last
service. To strike him dead would only be to strike you
too. I come too late ! Take my knife, lest I should see
him—take it. Till he leaves you I will wait."

I drew the fine, thin blade across my knee and broke
it in two pieces, and threw the two halves at her feet.

Then I turned without looking once at her, and went
away.

I do not know how the day waned and passed ; the skies
seemed red with fire, and the canals with blood. I do
not know how I found my road over the marble floors
and out into the air. I only remember that I felt my
way feebly with my hands, as though the golden sunlight
were all darkness, and that I groped my way down the
steps and out under an angle of the masonry, staring
stupidly upon the gliding waters.

I do not know whether a minute had gone by or many
hours, when some shivering sense of sound made me look
up at the casement above, a high, vast casement fretted
with dusky gold and many colours, and all kinds of
sculptured stone. The sun was making a glory as of
jewels on its painted panes. Some of them were open ;
I could see within the chamber Hilarion's fair and delicate head, and his face drooped with a soft smile. I
could see her, with all her loveliness, melting, as it were,
into his embrace, and see her mouth meet his.

If I had not broken the steel !——

I rose from the stones and cursed them, and departed
from the place as the moon rose.

HE was silent; the moonlight poured down between us white and wide; there lay a little dead bird on the stones, I remember, a redbreast, stiff and cold. The people traffic in such things here, in the square of Agrippa; it had fallen, doubtless, off some market stall.

Poor little robin! All the innocent sweet woodland singing-life of it was over, over in agony, and not a soul in all the wide earth was the better for its pain; not even the huckster who had missed making his copper coin by it. Woe is me; the sorrow of the world is great.

I pointed to it where it lay, poor little soft huddled heap of bright feathers; there is no sadder sight than a dead bird, for what lovelier life can there be than a bird's life, free in the sun and the rain, in the blossom and foliage?

"Make the little cold throat sing at sunrise," I said to him. "When you can do that, then think to undo what you have done."

"She will forget:—"

"You know she never will forget. There is your crime."

"She will have her art——"

"Will the dead bird sing?"

HERE, if anywhere in the "divine city of the Vatican"—for in truth a city and divine it is, and well has it been called so—here, if anywhere, will wake the soul of the artist; here, where the very pavement bears the story of Odysseus, and each passage-way is a Via Sacra, and every stone is old with years whose tale is told by hundreds or by thousands, and the wounded Adonis can be adored beside the tempted Christ of Sistine, and the serious beauty of the Erythean Sibyl lives beside the laughing grace of ivy-crowned Thalia, and the Jupiter

Maximus frowns on the mortals made of earth's dust,
and the Jehovah who has called forth woman meets the
first smile of Eve. A Divine City indeed, holding in its
innumerable chambers and its courts of granite and of
porphyry all that man has ever dreamed of, in his hope
and in his terror, of the Unknown God.

THE days of joyous, foolish mumming came—the
carnival mumming that as a boy I had loved so
well, and that, ever since I had come and stitched under
my Apollo and Crispin, I had never been loth to meddle
and mix in, going mad with my lit taper, like the rest,
and my whistle of the Befana, and all the salt and sport
of a war of wits such as old Rome has always heard in
midwinter since the seven nights of the Saturnalia.

Dear Lord! to think that twice a thousand years ago
and more, along these banks of Tiber, and down in the
Velabrum and up the Sacred Way, men and women and
children were leaping, and dancing, and shouting, and
electing their festal king, and exchanging their new-year
gifts of wax candles and little clay figures: and that
now-a-days we are doing just the same thing in the same
season, in the same places, only with all the real faunic
joyfulness gone out of it with the old slain Saturn, and a
great deal of empty and luxurious show come in instead !
It makes one sad, mankind looks such a fool.

Better be Heine's fool on the seashore, who asks the
winds their "wherefore" and their "whence." You remember Heine's poem—that one in the "North Sea"
series, that speaks of the man by the shore, and asks
what is Man, and what shall become of him, and who
lives on high in the stars? and tells how the waves keep
on murmuring and the winds rising, the clouds scudding
before the breeze, and the planets shining so cold and so

far, and how on the shore a fool waits for an answer, and waits in vain. It is a terrible poem, and terrible because it is true.

Every one of us stands on the brink of the endless sea that is Time and is Death; and all the blind, beautiful, mute, majestic forces of creation move around us and yet tell us nothing.

It is wonderful that, with this awful mystery always about us, we can go on on our little lives as cheerfully as we do; that on the edge of that mystical shore we yet can think so much about the crab in the lobster-pot, the eel in the sand, the sail in the distance, the child's face at home.

Well, no doubt it is heaven's mercy that we can do so; it saves from madness such thinking souls as are amongst us.

"MY dear, of love there is very little in the world. There are many things that take its likeness: fierce unstable passions and poor egotisms of all sorts, vanities too, and many other follies—Apatê and Philotês in a thousand masquerading characters that gain great Love discredit. The loves of men, and women too, my dear, are hardly better very often than Minos' love for Skylla; you remember how he threw her down from the stern of his vessel when he had made the use of her he wished, and she had cut the curls of Nisias. A great love does not of necessity imply a great intelligence, but it must spring out of a great nature, that is certain; and where the heart has spent itself in much base petty commerce, it has no deep treasury of gold on which to draw; it is bankrupt from its very over-trading. A noble passion is very rare; believe me; as rare as any other very noble thing."

"DO you call him a poet because he has the trick of a sonorous cadence and of words that fall with the measure of music, so that youths and maidens recite them for the vain charm of their mere empty sound? It is a lie—it is a blasphemy. A poet! A poet suffers for the meanest thing that lives; the feeblest creature dead in the dust is pain to him; his joy and his sorrow alike outweigh tenfold the joys and the sorrows of men; he looks on the world as Christ looked on Jerusalem, and weeps; he loves, and all heaven and all hell are in his love; he is faithful unto death, because fidelity alone can give to love the grandeur and the promise of eternity; he is like the martyrs of the church who lay upon the wheel with their limbs racked, yet held the roses of Paradise in their hands and heard the angels in the air. That is a poet; that is what Dante was, and Shelley and Milton and Petrarca. But this man? this singer of the senses, whose sole lament is that the appetites of the body are too soon exhausted; this languid and curious analysist who rends the soul aside with merciless cruelty, and puts away the quivering nerves with cold indifference, once he has seen their secrets?—this a poet? Then so was Nero harping! Accursed be the book and all the polished vileness that his verses ever palmed off on men by their mere tricks of sound. This a poet! As soon are the swine that rout the garbage, the lions of the Apocalypse by the throne of God!"

THE glad water sparkles and ripples everywhere; above the broad porphyry basins butterflies of every colour flutter, and swallows fly; lovers and children swing balls of flowers, made as only our Romans know how to make them; the wide lawns under the deep-shadowed avenues are full of blossoms; the air is full of fragrance; the palms rise against a cloudless sky;

the nights are lustrous; in the cool of the great galleries the statues seem to smile: so spring had been to me always; but now the season was without joy, and the scent of the flowers on the wind hurt me as it smote my nostrils.

For a great darkness seemed always between me and the sun, and I wondered that the birds could sing, and the children run amongst the blossoms—the world being so vile.

WOMEN hope that the dead love may revive; but men know that of all dead things none are so past recall as a dead passion.

The courtesan may scourge it with a whip of nettles back into life; but the innocent woman may wet it for ever with her tears, she will find no resurrection.

ART is an angel of God, but when Love has entered the soul, the angel unfolds its plumes and takes flight, and the wind of its wings withers as it passes. He whom it has left misses the angel at his ear, but he is alone for ever. Sometimes it will seem to him then that it had been no angel ever, but a fiend that lied, making him waste his years in a barren toil, and his nights in a joyless passion; for there are two things beside which all Art is but a mockery and a curse: they are a child that is dying and a love that is lost.

LOVE art alone, forsaking all other loves, and she will make you happy, with a happiness that shall defy the seasons and the sorrows of time, the pains of the vulgar and the changes of fortune, and be with you day and night, a light that is never dim. But mingle with

it any human love—and art will look for ever at you with
the eyes of Christ when he looked at the faithless follower as
the cock crew.

THE little garden of the Rospigliosi seems to have all
mediæval Rome shut in it, as you go up the winding
stairs with all their lichens and water-plants and broken
marbles, into the garden itself, with its smooth emerald
turf and spreading magnolias, and broad fish-ponds, and
orange and citron trees, and the frescoed building at the
end where Guido's Aurora floats in unchanging youth,
and the buoyant Hours run before the sun.

Myself I own I care not very much for that Aurora;
she is no incarnation of the morning, and though she
floats wonderfully and does truly seem to move, yet is
she in nowise ethereal nor suggestive of the dawn either
of day or life. When he painted her, he must have been
in love with some lusty taverner's buxom wife busked in
her holiday attire.

But whatever one may think of the famed Aurora, of
the loveliness of her quiet garden home, safe in the shelter
of the stately palace walls, there can be no question; the
little place is beautiful, and sitting in its solitude with
the brown magnolia fruit falling on the grass, and the
blackbirds pecking between the primroses, all the courtly
and superb pageant of the dead ages will come trooping by
you, and you will fancy that the boy Metastasio is reciting
strophes under yonder Spanish chestnut-tree, and cardinals,
and nobles, and gracious ladies, and pretty pages are all
listening, leaning against the stone rail of the central water.

For this is the especial charm and sorcery of Rome,
that, sitting idly in her beautiful garden-ways, you can
turn over a score of centuries and summon all their
pomp and pain before you, as easily as little children
can turn over the pages of a coloured picture-book until
their eyes are dazzled.

CHANDOS.

IT is so easy for the preacher, when he has entered the days of darkness, to tell us to find no flavour in the golden fruit, no music in the song of the charmer, no spell in eyes that look love, no delirium in the soft dreams of the lotus—so easy when these things are dead and barren for himself, to say they are forbidden! But men must be far more or far less than mortal ere they can blind their eyes, and dull their senses, and forswear their nature, and obey the dreariness of the commandment; and there is little need to force the sackcloth and the serge upon us. The roses wither long before the wassail is over, and there is no magic that will make them bloom again, for there is none that renews us—youth. The Helots had their one short, joyous festival in their long year of labour; life may leave us ours. It will be surely to us, long before its close, a harder tyrant and a more remorseless taskmaster than ever was the Lacedemonian to his bond-slaves,—bidding us make bricks without straw, breaking the bowed back, and leaving us as our sole chance of freedom the hour when we shall turn our faces to the wall—and die.

SOCIETY, that smooth and sparkling sea, is excessively difficult to navigate; its surf looks no more than champagne foam, but a thousand quicksands and

shoals lie beneath : there are breakers ahead for more
than half the dainty pleasure-boats that skim their hour
upon it ; and the foundered lie by millions, forgotten,
five fathoms deep below. The only safe ballast upon it
is gold dust ; and if stress of weather come on you, it will
swallow you without remorse. Trevenna had none of
this ballast ; he had come out to sea in as ticklish a
cockle-shell as might be ; he might go down any moment,
and he carried no commission, being a sort of nameless,
unchartered rover : yet float he did, securely.

CORALS, pink and delicate, rivet continents together ;
ivy tendrils, that a child may break, hold Norman
walls with bonds of iron ; a little ring, a toy of gold, a
jeweller's bagatelle, forges chains heavier than the galley-
slave's : so a woman's look may fetter a lifetime.

HE had passed through life having escaped singularly
all the shadows that lie on it for most men ; and
he had, far more than most, what may be termed the
faculty for happiness—a gift, in any temperament, whose
wisdom and whose beauty the world too little recognises.

A TEMPERAMENT that is *never* earnest is at times
well-nigh as wearisome as a temperament that is
never gay ; there comes a time when, if you can never
touch to any depth, the ceaseless froth and brightness of
the surface will create a certain sense of impatience, a
certain sense of want.

A STRAW misplaced will make us enemies; a mill-stone of benefits hung about his neck may fail to anchor down by us a single friend. We may lavish what we will—kindly thought, loyal service, untiring aid, and generous deed—and they are all but as oil to the burning, as fuel to the flame, when spent upon those who are jealous of us.

TRUTH is a rough, honest, helter-skelter terrier, that none like to see brought into their drawing-rooms, throwing over all their dainty little ornaments, upsetting their choicest Dresden, that nobody guessed was cracked till it fell with the mended side uppermost, and keeping every one in incessant tremor lest the next snap should be at their braids or their boots, of which neither the varnish nor the luxuriance will stand rough usage.

WHEN will men learn to know that the power of genius, and the human shell in which it chances to be harboured, are as distinct as is the diamond from the quartz-bed in which they find it?

HAD he embraced dishonour, and accepted the rescue that a lie would have lent him, this misery in its greatest share had never been upon him. He would have come hither with riches about him, and the loveliness he had worshipped would have been his own beyond the touch of any rival's hand. Choosing to cleave to the old creeds of his race, and passing, without a backward glance, into the paths of honour and of justice, it was thus with him now. Verily, virtue must be her own reward, as in the

Socratic creed; for she will bring no other dower than
peace of conscience in her gift to whosoever weds her.
"I have loved justice, and fled from iniquity; wherefore
here I die in exile," said Hildebrand upon his death-bed.
They will be the closing words of most lives that have
followed truth.

THERE are liberties sweeter than love; there are
goals higher than happiness.

Some memory of them stirred in him there, with the
noiseless flow of the lingering water at his feet, and above
the quiet of the stars; the thoughts of his youth came
back to him, and his heart ached with their longing.

Out of the salt depths of their calamity men had
gathered the heroisms of their future; out of the desert
of their exile they had learned the power to return as
conquerors. The greater things within him awakened
from their lethargy; the innate strength so long untried,
so long lulled to dreamy indolence and rest, uncoiled from
its prostration; the force that would resist and, it might
be, survive, slowly came upon him, with the taunts of his
foe. It was possible that there was that still in him which
might be grander and truer to the ambitions of his imaginative childhood under adversity, than in the voluptuous
sweetness of his rich and careless life. It was possible, if
—if he could once meet the fate he shuddered from, once
look at the bitterness of the life that waited for him, and
enter on its desolate and arid waste without going back
to the closed gates of his forfeited paradise to stretch his
limbs within their shadow once more ere he died.

There is more courage needed oftentimes to accept the
onward flow of existence, bitter as the waters of Marah,
black and narrow as the channel of Jordan, than there is
ever needed to bow down the neck to the sweep of the
death-angel's sword.

HE accepted the desolation of his life, for the sake of all beyond life, greater than life, which looked down on him from the silence of the night.

IT was sunset in Venice,—that supreme moment when the magical flush of light transfigures all, and wanderers whose eyes have long ached with the greyness and the glare of northward cities gaze and think themselves in heaven. The still waters of the lagunes, the marbles and the porphyry and the jasper of the mighty palaces, the soft grey of the ruins all covered with clinging green and the glowing blossoms of creepers, the hidden antique nooks where some woman's head leaned out of an arched casement, like a dream of the Dandolo time when the Adriatic swarmed with the returning galleys laden with Byzantine spoil, the dim, mystic, majestic walls that towered above the gliding surface of the eternal water, once alive with flowers, and music, and the gleam of golden tresses, and the laughter of careless revellers in the Venice of Goldoni, in the Venice of the Past ;—everywhere the sunset glowed with the marvel of its colour, with the wonder of its warmth.

Then a moment, and it was gone. Night fell with the hushed shadowy stillness that belongs to Venice alone ; and in the place of the riot and luxuriance of colour there was the tremulous darkness of the young night, with the beat of an oar on the water, the scent of unclosing carnation-buds, the white gleam of moonlight, and the odour of lilies-of-the-valley blossoming in the dark archway of some mosaic-lined window.

THE ruin that had stripped him of all else taught him to fathom the depths of his own attainments. He had in him the gifts of a Goethe; but it was only under adversity that these reached their stature and bore their fruit.

THE words were true. The bread of bitterness is the food on which men grow to their fullest stature ; the waters of bitterness are the debatable ford through which they reach the shores of wisdom ; the ashes boldly grasped and eaten without faltering are the price that must be paid for the golden fruit of knowledge. The swimmer cannot tell his strength till he has gone through the wild force of opposing waves; the great man cannot tell the might of his hand and the power of his resistance till he has wrestled with the angel of adversity, and held it close till it has blessed him.

THE artist was true to his genius; he knew it a greater gift than happiness; and as his hands wandered by instinct over the familiar notes, the power of his kingdom came to him, the passion of his mistress was on him, and the grandeur of the melody swelled out to mingle with the night, divine as consolation, supreme as victory.

THE man who puts chains on another's limbs is only one shade worse than he who puts fetters on another's free thoughts and on another's free conscience.

ONE fetter of tradition loosened, one web of super-stition broken, one ray of light let in on dark-ness, one principle of liberty secured, are worth the living for, he mused. Fame !—it is the flower of a day, that dies when the next sun rises. But to do some-thing, however little, to free men from their chains, to aid something, however faintly, the rights of reason and of truth, to be unvanquished through all and against all, these may bring one nearer the pure ambitions of youth.

Happiness dies as age comes to us; it sets for ever, with the suns of early years: yet perhaps we may keep a higher thing beside which it holds but a brief loyalty, if to ourselves we can rest true, if for the liberty of the world we can do anything.

DO not believe that happiness makes us selfish; it is a treason to the sweetest gift of life. It is when it has deserted us that it grows hard to keep all the better things in us from dying in the blight.

"COLERIDGE cried, 'O God, how glorious it is to live!' Renan asks, 'O God, when will it be worth while to live?' In nature we echo the poet; in the world we echo the thinker."

"YET you are greater than you were then," he said, slowly. "I know it,—I who am but a wine-cup rioter and love nothing but my summer-day fooling. You are greater; but the harvest you sow will only be reaped over your grave."

"I should be content could I believe it would be reaped then."

"Be content then. You may be so."

"God knows! Do you not think Marsy and Delisle de Sales and Linguet believed, as they suffered in their dungeons for mere truth of speech, that the remembrance of future generations would solace them? Bichât gave himself to premature death for science' sake; does the world once in a year speak his name? Yet how near those men are to us, to be forgotten! A century, and history will scarce chronicle them."

"Then why give the wealth of your intellect to men?"

"Are there not higher things than present reward and the mere talk of tongues? The *monstrari digito* were scarce a lofty goal. We may love Truth and strive to serve her, disregarding what she brings us. Those who need a bribe from her are not her true believers."

Philippe d'Orvâle tossed his silvery hair from his eyes, —eyes of such sunny lustre still.

"Ay! And those who held that sublime code of yours, that cleaving to truth for truth's sake, where are they? How have they fared in every climate and in every age? Stoned, crucified, burned, fettered, broken on the vast black granite mass of the blind multitude's brutality, of the priesthood's curse and craft!"

"True! Yet if through us, ever so slightly, the bondage of the creeds' traditions be loosened from the lives they stifle, and those multitudes—so weary, so feverish, so much more to be pitied than condemned—become less blind, less brute, the sacrifice is not in vain."

"In your sense, no. But the world reels back again into darkness as soon as a hand has lifted it for a while into light. Men hold themselves purified, civilised; a year of war,—and lust and bloodthirst rage untamed in all their barbarism; a taste of slaughter,—and they are wolves again! There was truth in the old feudal saying, 'Oignez vilain, il vous poindra; poignez vilain, il vous oindra.' Beat the multitudes you talk of with a despot's sword, and they will lick your feet; touch them with a Christ-like pity, and they will nail you to the cross."

There was terrible truth in the words: this man of princely blood, who disdained all sceptres and wanted nothing of the world, could look through and through it with his bold sunlit eyes, and see its rottenness to the core.

Chandos sighed as he heard.

"You are right,—only too right. Yet even while they crouch to the tyrant's sabre, how bitterly they need release ! even while they crucify their teachers and their saviours, how little they know what they do ! They may forsake themselves ; but they should not be forsaken."

Philippe d'Orvâle looked on him with a light soft as woman's tears in his eyes, and dashed his hand down on the alabaster.

"Chandos, you live twenty centuries too late. You would have been crowned in Athens, and throned in Asia. But here, as a saving grace, they will call you— 'mad !'"

"Well, if they do ? The title has its honours. It was hooted against Solon and Socrates."

"I WOULD do all in the world to please *you*, monseigneur," he answered, sadly ; "but I cannot change my nature. The little aziola loves the shade, and shrinks from noise and glare and all the ways of men ; I am like it. You cannot make the aziola a bird for sunlight ; you cannot make me as others are."

Chandos looked down on him with an almost tender compassion. To him, whose years were so rich in every pleasure and every delight that men can enjoy, the loneliness and pain of Lulli's life, divorced from all the living world, made it a marvel profoundly melancholy, profoundly formed to claim the utmost gentleness and sympathy.

"I would not have you as others are, Lulli," he said, softly. "If in all the selfishness and pleasures of our world there were not some here and there to give their lives to high thoughts and to unselfish things, as you give yours, we should soon, I fear, forget that such existed. But for such recluse's devotion to an art as yours, the classics would have perished; without the cloister-pen-men, the laws of science would never have broken the bondage of tradition."

Lulli looked up eagerly; then his head drooped again with the inexpressible weariness of that vain longing which "toils to reach the stars."

"Ah, what is the best that I reach?—the breath of the wind which passes, and sighs, and is heard no more."

"HOW crabbed a scroll!" he went on, throwing him-self down a moment on the thyme and grass. "The characters must baffle even you; the years that have yellowed the vellum have altered the fashion. Whose is it?"

"An old Elizabethan musician's," answered Lulli, as he looked up. "Yes; the years take all,—our youth, our work, our life, even our graves."

Something in his Provençal cadence gave a rhythm to his simplest speech: the words fell sadly on his listener's ear, though on the sensuous luxuriance of his own exist-ence no shadow ever rested, no skeleton ever crouched.

"Yes: the years take all," he said, with a certain sad-ness on him. "How many unperfected resolves, un-achieved careers, unaccomplished ambitions, immatured discoveries, perish under the rapidity of time, as unripe fruits fall before their season! Bichât died at thirty-one:—if he had lived, his name would now have outshone Aristotle's."

"We live too little time to do anything even for the art we give our life to," murmured Lulli. "When we die, our work dies with us: our better self must perish

with our bodies ; the first change of fashion will sweep it
into oblivion."

"Yet something may last of it," suggested Chandos,
while his hand wandered among the blue bells of the
curling hyacinths. "Because few save scholars read the
'*Defensio Populi*' now, the work it did for free thought
cannot die. None the less does the cathedral enrich
Cologne because the name of the man who begot its
beauty has passed unrecorded. None the less is the
world aided by the effort of every true and daring mind
because the thinker himself has been crushed down in
the rush of unthinking crowds."

"No, if *it* could live!" murmured Lulli, softly, with a
musing pain in the broken words. "But look! the scroll
was as dear to its writer as his score to Beethoven,—the
child of his love, cradled in his thoughts night and day,
cherished as never mother cherished her first-born, beloved as wife or mistress, son or daughter, never were.
Perhaps he denied himself much to give his time more to
his labour ; and when he died, lonely and in want, because he had pursued that for which men called him a
dreamer, his latest thought was of the work which never
could speak to others as it spoke to him, which he must
die and leave, in anguish that none ever felt to sever from
a human thing. Yet what remains of his love and his toil?
It is gone, as a laugh or a sob dies off the ear, leaving no
echo behind. His name signed here tells nothing to the
men for whom he laboured, adds nothing to the art for
which he lived. As it is with him, so will it be with me."

His voice, that had risen in sudden and untutored
eloquence, sank suddenly into the sadness and the weariness of the man whose highest joy is but relief from pain ;
and in it was a keener pang still,—the grief of one who
strives for what incessantly escapes him.

"Wait," said Chandos, gently. "Are we sure that
nothing lives of the music you mourn? It may live on

the lips of the people, in those Old-World songs whose
cause we cannot trace, yet which come sweet and fresh
transmitted to every generation. How often we hear
some nameless melody echo down a country-side! the
singers cannot tell you whence it came; they only know
their mothers sang it by their cradles, and they will sing
it by their children's. But in the past the song had its
birth in genius."

Guido Lulli bent his head.

"True: such an immortality were all-sufficient: we
could well afford to have our names forgotten——"

"LET that fellow alone, Cos," laughed Chandos, to
avert the stormy element which seemed to threaten
the serenity of his breakfast-party. "Trevenna will beat
us all with his tongue, if we tempt him to try conclusions.
He should be a Chancellor of the Exchequer or a Cheap
John; I am not quite clear which as yet."

"Identically the same things!" cried Trevenna. "The
only difference is the scale they are on; one talks from
the bench, and the other from the benches; one cheapens
tins, and the other cheapens taxes; one has a salve for
an incurable disease, and the other a salve for the national
debt; one rounds his periods to put off a watch that won't
go, and the other to cover a deficit that won't close; but
they radically drive the same trade, and both are successful if the spavined mare trots out looking sound, and the
people pay up. 'Look what I save you,' cry Cheap John
and Chancellor; and while they shout their economics,
they pocket their shillings. Ah, if I were sure I could
bamboozle a village, I should know I was qualified to
make up a Budget."

"MOST impudent of men! When will you learn the first lesson of society, and decently and discreetly *apprendre à vous effacer?*"

"*A m'effacer?* The advice Lady Harriet Vandeleur gave Cecil. Very good for mediocre people, I dare say; but it wouldn't suit *me.* There are some people, you know, that won't iron down for the hardest rollers. *M'effacer?* No! I'd rather any day be an ill-bred originality than a well-bred nonentity."

"Then you succeed perfectly in being what you wish! Don't you know, monsieur, that to set yourself against conventionalities is like talking too loud?—an impertinence and an under-breeding that society resents by exclusion "

"Yes, I know it. But a duke may bawl, and nobody shuts out *him;* a prince might hop on one leg, and everybody would begin to hop too. Now, what the ducal lungs and the princely legs might do with impunity, I declare I've a right to do, if I like."

"*Bécasse!* no one can declare his rights till he can do much more, and—purchase them. Have a million, and we may perhaps give you a little license to be unlike other persons: without the million it is an ill-bred *gaucherie.*"

"Ah, I know! Only a nobleman may be original; a poor penniless wretch upon town must be humbly and insignificantly commonplace. What a pity for the success of the aristocratic monopolists that nature puts clever fellows and fools just in the reverse order! But then nature's a shocking socialist."

"And so are you."

Trevenna laughed.

"Hush, madame. Pray don't destroy me with such a whisper."

TALENT wears well; genius wears itself out; talent drives a brougham in fact, genius a sun-chariot in fancy; talent keeps to earth and fattens there, genius soars to the empyrean, to get picked by every kite that flies; talent is the part and the venison, genius the seltzer and souffle of life. The man who has talent sails successfully on the top of the wave; the man with genius beats himself to pieces, fifty to one, on the first rock he meets.

ONE innocent may be wrongly suspected until he is made the thing that the libel called him.

MEN shut out happiness from their schemes for the world's happiness. They might as well try to bring flowers to bloom without the sun.

THE most dastardly sin on earth is the desertion of the fallen.

LET the world abandon you, but to yourself be true.

THE bread of bitterness is the food on which men grow to their fullest stature.

YOUTH without faith is a day without sun.

I DETEST posterity—every king hates his heir.

SCANDALS are like dandelion seeds; they are arrow-headed and stick when they fall, and bring forth and multiply fourfold.

THE puff perfect is the puff personal — adroitly masked.

I WEAR the Bonnet Rouge discreetly weighed down with a fine tassel of British prudence.

HE was a master of the great art of banter. It is a marvellous force; it kills sanctity, unveils sophistry, travesties wisdom, cuts through the finest shield, and turns the noblest impulses to hopeless ridicule.

IMMORTALITY is dull work—a hideous statue that gets black as soot in no time; funeral sermons that make you out a vial of revelations and discuss the probabilities of your being in the realms of Satan; a bust that slants you off at the shoulders and sticks you up on a bracket; a tombstone for the canes of the curious to poke at; an occasional attention in the way of withered immortelles or biographical Billingsgate, and a partial preservation shared in common with mummies, auks' eggs, snakes in bottles, and deformities in spirits of wine:—that's posthumous fame. I must say I don't see much fun in it.

IT were hard not to be wrong in philosophies when the
body starves on a pinch of oatmeal. It is the law of
necessity, the balance of economy; human fuel must be
used up that the machine of the world may spin on; but
it is not, perhaps, marvellous that the living fuel is sometimes unreconciled to that symmetrical rule of waste and
repair, of consumer and consumed.

IT is many centuries since Caius Gracchus called the
mercantile classes to aid the people against the
patricians, and found too late that they were deadlier
oppressors than all the optimates; but the error still
goes on, and the moneymakers churn it into gold, as
they churned it then into the Asiatic revenues and the
senatorial amulets.

THE love of a people is the most sublime crown that
can rest on the brow of any man, but the love of a
mob is a mongrel that fawns and slavers one moment, to
rend and tear the next.

FOLLE-FARINE.

IN this old-world district, amidst the pastures and
corn-lands of Normandy, superstition had taken a
hold which the passage of centuries and the advent of
revolution had done very little to lessen. Few of the
people could read, and fewer still could write. They
knew nothing but what their priests and politicians told
them to believe. They went to their beds with the
poultry, and rose as the cock crew: they went to mass,
as their ducks to the osier and weed ponds; and to the
conscription as their lambs to the slaughter. They
understood that there was a world beyond them, but
they remembered it only as the best market for their
fruit, their fowls, their lace, their skins. Their brains
were as dim as were their oil-lit streets at night; though
their lives were content and mirthful, and for the most
part pious. They went out into the summer meadows
chanting aves, in seasons of drought to pray for rain
on their parching orchards, in the same credulity with
which they groped through the winter-fog bearing torches,
and chanting dirges to gain a blessing at seed-time on
their bleak, black fallows.

The beauty and the faith of the old mediæval life were
with them still; and with its beauty and its faith were its
bigotry and cruelty likewise.

They led simple and contented lives; for the most

part honest, and amongst themselves cheerful and
kindly : preserving much grace of colour, of costume, of
idiosyncrasy, because apart from the hueless communism
and characterless monotony of modern cities.

But they believed in sorcery and in devilry : they were
brutal to their beasts, and could be as brutal to their
foes : they were steeped in legend and tradition from
their cradles ; and all the darkest superstitions of dead
ages still found home and treasury in their hearts and at
their hearths.

They had always been a religious people in this birth
country of the Flamma race : the strong poetic reverence
of their forefathers, which had symbolised itself in the
carving of every lintel, corbel or buttress in their streets,
and the fashion of every spire on which a weather-
vane could gleam against the sun, was still in their
blood ; the poetry had departed, but the bigotry remained.

"THE earth and the air are good," she thought, as
she lay there watching the dark leaves sway in
the foam and the wind, and the bright-bosomed birds
float from blossom to blossom. For there was latent in
her, all untaught, that old pantheistic instinct of the
divine age, when the world was young, to behold a
sentient consciousness in every leaf unfolded to the light ;
to see a soul in every created thing the day shines on ;
to feel the presence of an eternal life in every breeze that
moves, in every grass that grows ; in every flame that
lifts itself to heaven ; in every bell that vibrates on the
air ; in every moth that soars to reach the stars.

Pantheism is the religion of the poet ; and nature had
made her a poet, though man as yet had but made of her
an outcast, a slave, and a beast of burden.

"The earth and the air are good," she thought, watching

D

the sun-rays pierce the purple hearts of a passion-flower, the shadows move across the deep brown water, the radiant butterfly alight upon a lily, the scarlet-throated birds dart in and out through the yellow feathery blossoms of the limes.

WHEN a man clings to life for life's sake, because it is fair and sweet, and good in the sight and the senses, there may be weakness in his shudder at its threatening loss.   But when a man is loth to lose life although it be hard, and joyless, and barren of all delights, because this life gives him power to accomplish things greater than he, which yet without him must perish, there is the strength in him, as there is the agony of Prometheus.

With him it must die also : that deep dim greatness within him, which moves him, despite himself ; that nameless unspeakable force which compels him to create and to achieve ; that vision by which he beholds worlds beyond him not seen by his fellows.

Weary of life he may be ; of life material, and full of subtlety ; of passion, of pleasure, of pain ; of the kisses that burn, of the laugh that rings hollow, of the honey that so soon turns to gall, of the sickly fatigues, and the tired, cloyed hunger, that are the portion of men upon earth.   Weary of these he may be ; but still if the gods have breathed on him, and made him mad with the madness that men have called genius, there will be that in him greater than himself, which he knows,—and cannot know without some fierce wrench and pang,—will be numbed and made impotent, and drift away, lost for evermore, into that eternal night, which is all that men behold of death.

THE grass of the Holy River gathers perfume from the marvellous suns, and the moonless nights, and the gorgeous bloom of the east, from the aromatic breath of the leopard, and the perfume of the fallen pomegranate, and the sacred oil that floats in the lamps, and the caress of the girl-bather's feet, and the myrrh-dropping unguents that glide from the maiden's bare limbs in the moonlight,—the grass holds and feeds on them all. But not till the grass has been torn from the roots, and been crushed, and been bruised and destroyed, can the full odours exhale of all it has tasted and treasured.

Even thus the imagination of man may be great, but it can never be at its greatest until one serpent, with merciless fangs, has bitten it through and through, and impregnated it with passion and with poison,—that one deathless serpent which is memory.

AND, indeed, to those who are alive to the nameless, universal, Eternal Soul which breathes in all the grasses of the fields, and beams in the eyes of all creatures of earth and air, and throbs in the living light of palpitating stars, and thrills through the young sap of forest trees, and stirs in the strange loves of wind-borne plants, and hums in every song of the bee, and burns in every quiver of the flame, and peoples with sentient myriads every drop of dew that gathers on a hare-bell, every bead of water that ripples in a brook—to them the mortal life of man can seem but little, save at once the fiercest and the feeblest thing that does exist ; at once the most cruel and the most impotent ; tyrants of direst destruction, and bondsmen of lowest captivity.

THE earth has always most charm, and least pain, to the poet or the artist when men are hidden away under their roofs. Then they do not break its calm with either their mirth or their brutality; then the vile and revolting coarseness of their works, that blot it with so much deformity, is softened and obscured in the purple breaths of shadow, and the dim tender gleam of stars.

WHEN the world was in its youth, it had leisure to treasure its recollections; even to pause and look back; to see what flower of a fair thought, what fruit of a noble art, it might have overlooked or left down-trodden. But now it is so old, and is so tired; it is purblind, and heavy of foot; it does not notice what it destroys; it desires rest and can find none; nothing can matter greatly to it; its dead are so many that it cannot count them; and being thus worn and dulled with age, and suffocated under the weight of its innumerable memories, it is very slow to be moved, and swift—terribly swift—to forget.

Why should it not be?

It has known the best, it has known the worst that ever can befall it.

And the prayer that to the heart of man seems so freshly born from his own desire, what is it on the weary ear of the world, save the same old, old cry which it has heard through all the ages, empty as the sound of the wind, and for ever—for ever—unanswered?

FOR there is nothing so cruel in life as a Faith;—the Faith, whatever its name may be, that draws a man on all his years through on one narrow path, by one tremulous light, and then at the last, with a laugh—drowns him.

I THINK I see!—the great God walked by the edge
of the river, and he mused on a gift to give man,
on a joy that should be a joy on the earth for ever ; and
he passed by the lily white as snow, by the thyme that
fed the bees, by the gold heart in the arum flower, by
the orange flame of the tall sandrush, by all the great
water-blossoms which the sun kissed and the swallows
loved, and he came to the one little reed pierced with the
snake's-tongues, and all alone amidst millions. Then he
took it up, and cut it to the root, and killed it ; killed it
as a reed—but breathed into it a song audible and beautiful to all the ears of men. Was that death to the reed?
—or life ? Would a thousand summers of life by the
waterside have been worth that one thrill of song when
a god first spoke through it ?

IT is odd that you should live in a palace, and he
should want for bread ; but then he can create
things, and you can only buy them. So it is even,
perhaps.

A WORD that needs compelling is broken by the
heart before the lips give it. It is to plant a tree
without a root to put faith in a man that needs a bond.

"YOU are glad since you sing !" said the old man
to her as she passed him again on her homeward
way and paused again beside him.

"The birds in cages sing," she answered him, "but
think you they are glad ?"

"Are they not ?"

She sat down a moment beside him, on the bank which
was soft with moss, and odorous with wild flowers curling

up the stems of the poplars and straying over into the
corn beyond.

"Are they? Look. Yesterday I passed a cottage, it
is on the Great South Road ; far away from here. The
house was empty ; the people no doubt were gone to
labour in the fields ; there was a wicker cage hanging to
the wall, and in the cage there was a blackbird. The
sun beat on his head ; his square of sod was a dry clod
of bare earth ; the heat had dried every drop of water in
his pan ; and yet the bird was singing. Singing how ?
In torment, beating his breast against the bars till the
blood started, crying to the skies to have mercy on him
and to let the rain fall. His song was shrill ; it had a
scream in it ; still he sang. Do you say the merle was
glad ? "

"What did you do ? " asked the old man, still breaking
his stones with a monotonous rise and fall of his hammer.

" I took the cage down and opened the door."

"And he ? "

"He shot up in the air first, then dropped down amidst
the grasses, where a little brook which the drought had
not dried was still running ; and he bathed and drank,
and bathed again, seeming mad with the joy of the water.
When I lost him from sight he was swaying among the
leaves on a bough over the river ; but then he was silent."

"And what do you mean by that ? "

Her eyes clouded ; she was mute. She vaguely knew
the meaning it bore to herself, but it was beyond her to
express it. All things of nature had voices and parables
for her, because her fancy was vivid, and her mind was
still too dark, and too profoundly ignorant, for her to be
able to shape her thoughts into metaphor or deduction.
The bird had spoken to her ; by his silence as by his
song ; but what he had uttered she could not well utter
again. Save indeed that song was not gladness, and
neither was silence pain.

"THE future?" she said at last, "that means something that one has not, and that is to come—is it
so?" "Something that one never has, and that never
comes," muttered the old man, wearily cracking the flints
in two; "something that one possesses in one's sleep,
and that is farther off each time that one awakes; and
yet a thing that one sees always, sees even when one
lies a dying they say—for men are fools."

IN one of the most fertile and most fair districts of
northern France there was a little Norman town,
very, very old, and beautiful exceedingly by reason of its
ancient streets, its high peaked roofs, its marvellous
galleries and carvings, its exquisite greys and browns, its
silence and its colour, and its rich still life.

Its centre was a great cathedral, noble as York or
Chartres; a cathedral, whose spire shot to the clouds,
and whose innumerable towers and pinnacles were all
pierced to the day, so that the blue sky shone and the
birds of the air flew all through them. A slow brown
river, broad enough for market boats and for corn barges,
stole through the place to the sea, lapping as it went the
wooden piles of the houses, and reflecting the quaint
shapes of the carvings, the hues of the signs and the
draperies, the dark spaces of the dormer windows, the
bright heads of some casement-cluster of carnations, the
laughing face of a girl leaning out to smile on her lover.

All around it lay the deep grass unshaven, the leagues
on leagues of fruitful orchards, the low blue hills tenderly
interlacing one another, the fields of colza, where the
white head-dress of the women-workers flashed in the
sun like a silvery pigeon's wing. To the west there were
the deep green woods, and the wide plains golden with
gorse of Arthur's and of Merlin's lands; and beyond, to

the northward, was the dim stretch of the ocean breaking
on a yellow shore, whither the river ran, and whither led
straight shady roads, hidden with linden and with poplar
trees, and marked ever and anon by a wayside wooden
Christ, or by a little murmuring well crowned with a
crucifix.

A beautiful, old, shadowy, ancient place : picturesque
everywhere; often silent, with a sweet sad silence that
was chiefly broken by the sound of bells or the chaunting
of choristers. A place of the Middle Ages still. With
lanterns swinging on cords from house to house as the
only light ; with wondrous scroll-works and quaint signs
at the doors of all its traders ; with monks' cowls and
golden croziers and white-robed acolytes in its streets ;
with the subtle smoke of incense coming out from the
cathedral door to mingle with the odours of the fruits and
flowers in the market-place ; with great flat-bottomed
boats drifting down the river under the leaning eaves of
its dwellings ; and with the galleries of its opposing
houses touching so nearly that a girl leaning in one could
stretch a Provence rose or toss an Easter egg across to
her neighbour in the other.

Doubtless there were often squalor, poverty, dust, filth,
and uncomeliness within these old and beautiful homes.
Doubtless often the dwellers therein were housed like
cattle and slept like pigs, and looked but once out to the
woods and waters of the landscapes round for one hundred times that they looked at their hidden silver in an
old delf jug, or at their tawdry coloured prints of St. Vic-
torian or St. Scævola.

But yet much of the beauty and the nobility of the old,
simple, restful, rich-hued life of the past still abode there,
and remained with them. In the straight, lithe form of
their maidens, untrammelled by modern garb, and moving
with the free majestic grace of forest does. In the vast,
dim, sculptured chambers, where the grandam span by

the wood fire, and the little children played in the shadows,
and the lovers whispered in the embrasured window. In
the broad market-place, where the mules cropped the
clover, and the tawny awnings caught the sunlight, and
the white caps of the girls framed faces fitted for the
pencils of missal painters, and the flush of colour from
mellow wall-fruits and grape-clusters glanced amidst the
shelter of deepest, freshest green. In the perpetual presence of their cathedral, which, through sun and storm,
through frost and summer, through noon and midnight,
stood there amidst them, and watched the galled oxen
tread their painful way, and the scourged mules droop
their humble heads, and the helpless, harmless flocks go
forth to the slaughter, and the old weary lives of the men
and women pass through hunger and cold to the grave,
and the sun and the moon rise and set, and the flowers
and the children blossom and fade, and the endless years
come and go, bringing peace, bringing war; bringing
harvest, bringing famine; bringing life, bringing death;
and, beholding these, still said to the multitude in its
terrible irony, " Lo ! your God is Love."

This little town lay far from the great Paris highway
and all greatly frequented tracks. It was but a short
distance from the coast, but near no harbour of greater
extent than such as some small fishing village had made
in the rocks for the trawlers. Few strangers ever came
to it, except some wandering painters or antiquaries.
It sent its apples and eggs, its poultry and honey, its
colza and corn to the use of the great cities; but it was
rarely that any of its own people went thither.

Now and then some one of the oval-faced, blue-eyed,
lithe-limbed maidens of its little homely households would
sigh and flush and grow restless, and murmur of Paris;
and would steal out in the break of a warm grey morning
whilst only the birds were still waking ; and would patter
away in her wooden shoes over the broad, white, southern

road, with a stick over her shoulder, and a bundle of all
her worldly goods upon the stick. And she would look
back often, often, as she went ; and when all was lost in
the blue haze of distance save the lofty spire which she
still saw through her tears, she would say in her heart,
with her lips parched and trembling, " I will come back
again. I will come back again."

But none such ever did come back.

They came back no more than did the white sweet
sheaves of the lilies which the women gathered and sent
to be bought and sold in the city—to gleam one faint
summer night in a gilded balcony, and to be flung out
the next morning, withered and dead.

One amongst the few who had thus gone whither the
lilies went, and of whom the people would still talk as
their mules paced homewards through the lanes at twilight,
had been Reine Flamma, the daughter of the miller of
Yprés.

"THERE are only two trades in a city," said the actors
to her, with a smile as bitter as her own, "only
two trades—to buy souls and to sell them. What business
have you here, who do neither the one nor the other ?"

There was music still in this trampled reed of the
river, into which the gods had once bidden the stray
winds and the wandering waters breathe their melody ;
but there, in the press, the buyers and sellers only saw in
it a frail thing of the sand and the stream, only made to
be woven for barter, or bind together the sheaves of the
roses of pleasure.

ART was to him as mother, brethren, mistress, offspring, religion — all that other men hold dear.
He had none of these, he desired none of them ; and his
genius sufficed to him in their stead.

It was an intense and reckless egotism, made alike
cruel and sublime by its intensity and purity, like the
egotism of a mother in her child. To it, as the mother
to her child, he would have sacrificed every living creature; but to it also, like her, he would have sacrified his
very existence as unhesitatingly. But it was an egotism
which, though merciless in its tyranny, was as pure as
snow in its impersonality; it was untainted by any grain
of avarice, of vanity, of selfish desire; it was independent
of all sympathy; it was simply and intensely the passion
for immortality :—that sublime selfishness, that superb
madness, of all great minds.

Art had taken him for its own, as Demeter, in the days
of her desolation, took the child Demophoon to nurture
him as her own on the food of gods, and to plunge
him through the flames of a fire that would give him immortal life. As the pusillanimous and sordid fears of the
mortal mother lost to the child for evermore the possession of Olympian joys and of perpetual youth, so did the
craven and earthly cares of bodily needs hold the artist
back from the radiance of the life of the soul, and drag
him from the purifying fires. Yet he had not been utterly
discouraged; he strove against the Metanira of circumstance; he did his best to struggle free from the mortal
bonds that bound him; and, as the child Demophoon
mourned for the great goddess that had nurtured him,
refusing to be comforted, so did he turn from the base
consolations of the senses and the appetites, and beheld
ever before his sight the ineffable majesty of that Mater
Dolorosa who once and for ever had anointed him as her
own.

MEN did not believe in him; what he wrought saddened and terrified them; they turned aside to
those who fed them on simpler and on sweeter food.

His works were great, but they were such as the public mind deems impious. They unveiled human corruption too nakedly, and they shadowed forth visions too exalted, and satires too unsparing, for them to be acceptable to the multitude. They were compounded of an idealism clear and cold as crystal, and of a reality cruel and voluptuous as love. They were penetrated with an acrid satire and an intense despair: the world caring only for a honied falsehood and a gilded gloss in every art, would have none of them.

"SEE you—what he lacks is only the sinew that gold gives. What he has done is great. The world rightly seeing must fear it; and fear is the highest homage the world ever gives. But he is penniless; and he has many foes; and jealousy can with so much ease thrust aside the greatness which it fears into obscurity, when that greatness is marred by the failures and the feebleness of poverty. Genius scorns the power of gold: it is wrong; gold is the war-scythe on its chariot, which mows down the millions of its foes and gives free passage to the sun-coursers with which it leaves those heavenly fields of light for the gross battle-fields of earth."

IT is true that the great artist is as a fallen god who remembers a time when worlds arose at his breath, and at his bidding the barren lands blossomed into fruitfulness; the sorcery of the thyrsus is still his, though weakened.

The powers of lost dominions haunt his memory; the remembered glory of an eternal sun is in his eyes, and makes the light of common day seem darkness; the heart sickness of a long exile weighs on him; incessantly he

labours to overtake the mirage of a loveliness which fades
as he pursues it. In the poetic creation by which the
bondage of his material life is redeemed, he finds at once
ecstasy and disgust, because he feels at once his strength
and weakness. For him all things of earth and air, and
sea and cloud, have beauty; and to his ear all voices of
the forest land and water world are audible.

He is as a god, since he can call into palpable shape
dreams born of impalpable thought; as a god, since he
has known the truth divested of lies, and has stood face
to face with it, and been not afraid; a god thus. But
a cripple inasmuch as his hand can never fashion the
shapes that his vision beholds; an alien because he has
lost what he never will find upon earth; a beast, since
ever and again his passions will drag him to wallow in
the filth of sensual indulgence; a slave, since oftentimes
the divinity that is in him breaks and bends under the
devilry that also is in him, and he obeys the instincts of
vileness, and when he would fain bless the nations he
curses them.

" I DO not know," she said, wearily afresh. " Marcellin
says that every God is deaf. He must be deaf—
or very cruel. Look; everything lives in pain; and yet
no God pities and makes an end of the earth. I would
—if I were He. Look—at dawn, the other day, I was
out in the wood. I came upon a little rabbit in a trap;
a little, pretty, soft black-and-white thing, quite young.
It was screaming in its horrible misery; it had been
screaming all night. Its thighs were broken in the iron
teeth; the trap held it tight; it could not escape, it could
only scream—scream—scream. All in vain. When I
had set it free it was mangled as if a wolf had gnawed
it; the iron teeth had bitten through the fur, and the
flesh, and the bone; it had lost so much blood, and it

was in so much pain, that it could not live. I laid it
down in the bracken, and put water to its mouth, and
did what I could; but it was of no use. It had been too
much hurt. It died as the sun rose; a little, harmless,
shy, happy thing, you know, that never killed any creature,
and only asked to nibble a leaf or two, or sleep in a little
round hole, and run about merry and free. How can one
care for a God since He lets these things be?"

Arslàn smiled as he heard.

"Child,—men care for a god only as a god means a
good to them. Men are heirs of heaven, they say; and,
in right of their heritage, they make life hell to every
living thing that dares dispute the world with them. You
do not understand that,—tut! You are not human then.
If you were human, you would begrudge a blade of grass
to a rabbit, and arrogate to yourself a lease of immortality."

"OF a winter night," she said, slowly, "I have heard
old Pitchou read aloud to Flamma, and she reads
of their God, the one they hang everywhere on the crosses
here; and the story ran that the populace scourged and
nailed to death the one whom they knew afterwards, when
too late, to have been the great man that they looked for,
and that, being bidden to make their choice of one to
save, they chose to ransom and honour a thief: one
called Barabbas. Is it true?—if the world's choice were
wrong once, why not twice?"

Arslàn smiled; the smile she knew so well, and which
had no more warmth than the ice floes of his native seas.

"Why not twice? Why not a thousand times? A
thief has the world's sympathies always. It is always
the Barabbas—the trickster in talent, the forger of stolen
wisdom, the bravo of political crime, the huckster of
plundered thoughts, the charlatan of false art, whom the

vox populi elects and sets free, and sends on his way
rejoicing. 'Will ye have Christ or Barabbas?' Every
generation is asked the same question, and every generation gives the same answer; and scourges the divinity
out of its midst, and finds its idol in brute force and low
greed."

She only dimly comprehended, not well knowing why
her words had thus roused him. She pondered awhile,
then her face cleared.

"But the end?" she asked. "The dead God is the
God of all these people round us now, and they have
built great places in His honour, and they bow when they
pass His likeness in the highway or the marketplace.
But with Barabbas—what was the end? It seems that
they loathe and despise him?"

Arslàn laughed a little.

"His end? In Syria may be the vultures picked his
bones, where they lay whitening on the plains—those
times were primitive, the world was young. But in our
day Barabbas lives and dies in honour, and has a tomb
that stares all men in the face, setting forth his virtues,
so that all who run may read. In our day Barabbas—
the Barabbas of money-greeds and delicate cunning, and
the theft which has risen to science, and the assassination that kills souls and not bodies, and the crime that
deals moral death and not material death—our Barabbas,
who is crowned Fraud in the place of mailed Force, lives
always in purple and fine linen, and ends in the odours of
sanctity with the prayers of priests over his corpse."

He spoke with a certain fierce passion that rose in him
whenever he thought of that world which had rejected
him, and had accepted so many others, weaker in brain
and nerve, but stronger in one sense, because more dishonest; and as he spoke he went straight to a wall on
his right, where a great sea of grey paper was stretched,
untouched and ready to his hand.

She would have spoken, but he made a motion to silence.

"Hush! be quiet," he said to her, almost harshly, "I have thought of something."

And he took the charcoal and swept rapidly with it over the dull blank surface till the vacancy glowed with life. A thought had kindled in him; a vision had arisen before him.

The scene around him vanished utterly from his sight. The grey stone walls, the square windows through which the fading sun-rays fell; the level pastures and sullen streams, and paled skies without, all faded away as though they had existed only in a dream.

All the empty space about him became peopled with many human shapes that for him had breath and being, though no other eye could have beheld them. The old Syrian world of eighteen hundred years before arose and glowed before him. The things of his own life died away, and in their stead he saw the fierce flame of eastern suns, the gleaming range of marble palaces, the purple flush of pomegranate flowers, the deep colour of oriental robes, the soft silver of hills olive crested, the tumult of a city at high festival. And he could not rest until all he thus saw in his vision he had rendered as far as his hand could render it; and what he drew was this.

A great thirsty, heated, seething crowd; a crowd that had manhood and womanhood, age and infancy, youths and maidens within its ranks; a crowd in whose faces every animal lust and every human passion were let loose; a crowd on which a noon sun without shadow streamed; a sun which parched and festered and engendered all corruption in the land on which it looked. This crowd was in a city, a city on whose flat roofs the myrtle and the cistus bloomed; above whose walls the plumes of olives waved; upon whose distant slopes the darkling cedar groves rose straight against the sky,

and on whose lofty temple plates of gold glistened against
the shining heavens. This crowd had scourges, and stones,
and goads in their hands; and in their midst they led
one clothed in white, whose head was thorn-crowned,
and whose eyes were filled with a god's pity and a
man's reproach; and him they stoned, and lashed, and
hooted.

And triumphant in the throng, whose choice he was,
seated aloft upon men's shoulders, with a purple robe
thrown on his shoulders, there sat a brawny, grinning,
bloated, jibbering thing, with curled lips and savage
eyes, and satyr's leer: the creature of greed, of lust, of
obscenity, of brutality, of avarice, of desire. This thing
the people followed, rejoicing exceedingly, content in the
guide whom they had chosen, victorious in the fiend for
whom they spurned a deity; crying, with wide open
throats and brazen lungs,—"Barabbas !"

There was not a form in all this close-packed throng
which had not a terrible irony in it, which was not in
itself a symbol of some appetite or of some vice, for
which women and men abjure the godhead in them.

A gorged drunkard lay asleep with his amphora broken
beneath him, the stream of the purple wine lapped eagerly
by ragged children. A money-changer had left the receipt
of custom, eager to watch and shout, and a thief clutched
both hands full of the forsaken coins and fled.

A miser had dropped a bag of gold, and stopped to
catch at all the rolling pieces, regardless in his greed
how the crowd trampled and trod on him. A mother
chid and struck her little brown curly child, because he
stretched his arms and turned his face towards the thorn-
crowned captive.

A priest of the temple, with a blood-stained knife thrust
in his girdle, dragged beside him, by the throat, a little
tender lamb doomed for the sacrifice.

A dancing woman with jewels in her ears, and half

E

naked to the waist, sounding the brazen cymbals above her head, drew a score of youths after her in Barabbas' train.

On one of the flat roof tops, reclining on purple and fine linen, looking down on the street below from the thick foliage of her citron boughs and her red Syrian roses, was an Egyptian wanton ; and leaning beside her, tossing golden apples in her bosom, was a young centurion of the Roman guard, languid and laughing, with his fair chest bare to the heat, and his armour flung in a pile beside him.

And thus, in like manner, every figure bore its parable ; and above all was the hard, hot, cruel, cloudless sky of blue, without one faintest mist to break its horrible serenity, whilst high in the azure ether and against the sun, an eagle and a vulture fought, locked close, and tearing at each other's breasts.

Six nights this conception occupied him. His days were not his own, he spent them in a rough mechanical labour which his strength executed while his mind was far away from it ; but the nights were all his, and at the end of the sixth night the thing arose, perfect as far as his hand could perfect it ; begotten by a chance and ignorant word as have been many of the greatest works the world has seen ;—oaks sprung from the acorn that a careless child has let fall.

When he had finished it his arm dropped to his side, he stood motionless ; the red glow of the dawn lighting the depths of his sleepless eyes.

IT was a level green silent country which was round her, with little loveliness and little colour ; but as

she went she laughed incessantly in the delirious gladness of her liberty.

She tossed her head back to watch the flight of a
single swallow; she caught a handful of green leaves
and buried her face in them. She listened in a very
agony of memory to the rippling moisture of a little
brook. She followed with her eyes the sweeping vapours
of the rain-clouds, and when a west wind rose and blew
a cluster of loose apple blossoms between her eyes—she
could no longer bear the passionate pain of all the long-
lost sweetness, but flinging herself downward, sobbed
with the ecstasy of an exile's memories.

The hell in which she had dwelt had denied them to
her for so long.

"Ah God!" she thought, "I know now—one cannot
be utterly wretched whilst one has still the air and the
light and the winds of the sky."

And she arose, calmer, and went on her way; wondering, even in that hour, why men and women trod the
daily measures of their lives with their eyes downward
and their ears choked with the dust; hearkening so little
to the sound of the breeze in the grasses, looking so little
to the passage of the clouds against the sun.

THE ground ascended as it stretched seaward, but on
it there were only wide dull fields of colza or of
grass lying, sickly and burning, under the fire of the
late afternoon sun.

The slope was too gradual to break their monotony.

Above them was the cloudless weary blue; below them
was the faint parched green; other colour there was none;

one little dusky panting bird flew by pursued by a kite;
that was the only change.

She asked him no questions; she walked mutely and
patiently by his side; she hated the dull heat, the colourless waste, the hard scorch of the air, the dreary change-
lessness of the scene. But she did not say so. He had
chosen to come to them.

A league onward the fields were merged into a heath,
uncultivated and covered with short prickly furze; on the
brown earth between the stunted bushes a few goats were
cropping the burnt-up grasses. Here the slope grew
sharper, and the earth seemed to rise up between the sky
and them, steep and barren as a house-roof.

Once he asked her—

"Are you tired?"

She shook her head.

Her feet ached, and her heart throbbed; her limbs
were heavy like lead in the heat and the toil. But she
did not tell him so. She would have dropped dead from
exhaustion rather than have confessed to him any weakness.

He took the denial as it was given, and pressed onward
up the ascent.

The sun was slanting towards the west; the skies
seemed like brass; the air was sharp, yet scorching; the
dull brown earth still rose up before them like a wall;
they climbed it slowly and painfully, their hands and their
teeth filled with its dust, which drifted in a cloud before
them. He bade her close her eyes, and she obeyed him.
He stretched his arm out and drew her after him up the
ascent, which was slippery from drought and prickly from
the stunted growth of furze.

On the summit he stood still and released her.

"Now look."

She opened her eyes with the startled, half-questioning

stare of one led out from utter darkness into a full and sudden light.

Then, with a great cry, she sank down on the rock, trembling, weeping, laughing, stretching out her arms to the new glory that met her sight, dumb with its grandeur, delirious with its delight.

For what she saw was the sea.

Before her dazzled sight all its beauty stretched, the blueness of the waters meeting the blueness of the skies; radiant with all the marvels of its countless hues; softly stirred by a low wind that sighed across it; bathed in a glow of gold that streamed on it from the westward; rolling from north to south in slow, sonorous measure, filling the silent air with the ceaseless melody of its wondrous voice.

The lustre of the sunset beamed upon it; the cool fresh smell of its waters shot like new life through all the scorch and stupor of the day; its white foam curled and broke on the brown curving rocks and wooded inlets of the shores; innumerable birds, that gleamed like silver, floated or flew above its surface; all was still, still as death, save only for the endless movement of those white swift wings and the murmur of the waves, in which all meaner and harsher sounds of earth seemed lost and hushed to slumber and to silence.

The sea alone reigned, as it reigned in the young years of the earth when men were not; as, may be, it will be its turn to reign again in the years to come, when men and all their works shall have passed away and be no more seen nor any more remembered.

Arslàn watched her in silence.

He was glad that it should awe and move her thus. The sea was the only thing for which he cared, or which had any power over him. In the northern winters of his youth he had known the ocean, in one wild night's work, undo all that men had done to check and rule it, and burst through all the barriers that they had raised against it, and throw down the stones of the altar and quench the fires of the hearth, and sweep through the fold and the byre, and flood the cradle of the child and the grave of the grandsire.

He had seen its storms wash away at one blow the corn harvests of years, and gather in the sheep from the hills, and take the life of the shepherd with the life of the flock. He had seen it claim lovers locked in each other's arms, and toss the fair curls of the first-born as it tossed the riband weeds of its deeps. And he had felt small pity; it had rather given him a certain sense of rejoicing and triumph to see the water laugh to scorn those who were so wise in their own conceit, and bind beneath its chains those who held themselves masters over all beasts of the field and birds of the air.

Other men dreaded the sea and cursed it; but he in his way loved it almost with passion, and could he have chosen the manner of his death would have desired that it should be by the sea and through the sea; a death cold and serene and dreamily voluptuous: a death on which no woman should look and in which no man should have share.

He watched her now for some time without speaking. When the first paroxysm of her emotion had exhausted itself, she stood motionless, her figure like a statue of bronze against the sun, her head sunk upon her breast, her arms outstretched as though beseeching that wondrous brightness which she saw to take her to itself and make her one with it. Her whole attitude expressed an unutterable worship. She was like one who for the first time hears of God.

"What is it you feel?" he asked her suddenly. He knew without asking; but he had made it his custom to dissect all her joys and sufferings with little heed whether he thus added to either.

At the sound of his voice she started, and a shiver shook her as she answered him slowly, without withdrawing her gaze from the waters.

"It has been there always—always—so near me?"

"Before the land, the sea was."

"And I never knew!"—

Her head drooped on her breast; great tears rolled silently down her cheeks; her arms fell to her sides; she shivered again and sighed. She knew all that she had lost—this is the greatest grief that life holds.

"You never knew," he made answer. "There was only a sand-hill between you and all this glory; but the sand-hill was enough. Many people never climb theirs all their lives long."

The words and their meaning escaped her.

She had for once no remembrance of him, nor any other sense save of this surpassing wonder that had thus burst on her—this miracle that had been near her for so long, yet of which she had never in all her visions dreamed.

She was quite silent; sunk there on her knees, motionless, and gazing straight, with eyes unblenching, at the light.

There was no sound near them, nor was there anything in sight except where above against the deepest azure of the sky two curlews were circling around each other, and in the distance a single ship was gliding, with sails silvered by the sun. All signs of human life lay far behind; severed from them by those steep scorched slopes swept only by the plovers and the bees. And all the while she looked slow tears gathered in her eyes and fell, and the loud hard beating of her heart was audible in the hushed stillness of the upper air.

He waited awhile: then he spoke to her.

"Since it pains you, come away."

A great sob shuddered through her.

"Give me that pain," she muttered, "sooner than any joy. Pain? pain?—it is life, heaven—liberty!"

For suddenly those words which she had heard spoken around her, and which had been to her like the mutterings of the deaf and the dumb, became real to her with thousand meanings.

The seagulls were lost in the heights of the air; the ship sailed on into the light till the last gleam of its canvas vanished; the sun sank westward lower and lower till it glowed in a globe of flame upon the edge of the water: she never moved; standing there on the summit of the cliff, with her head drooped upon her breast, her form thrown out dark and motionless against the gold of the western sky, on her face still that look of one who worships with intense honour and passionate faith an unknown God.

The sun sank entirely, leaving only a trail of flame across the heavens; the waters grew grey and purple in the shadows; one boat, black against the crimson reflections of the west, swept on swiftly with the in-rushing tide; the wind rose and blew long curls of seaweed on the rocks; the shores of the bay were dimmed in a heavy mist, through which the lights of the little hamlets dimly glowed, and the distant voices of fishermen calling to each other as they drew in their deep-sea nets came faint and weirdlike.

WHAT she wanted was to live. Live as the great moor bird did that she had seen float one day over these pale, pure, blue skies, with its mighty wings outstretched in the calm grey weather; which came none knew whence, and which went none knew whither; which poised silent and stirless against the clouds; then called with a sweet wild love-note to its mate, and waited for him as he sailed in from the misty shadows where the sea lay; and with him rose yet higher and higher in the air; and passed westward, cleaving the fields of light, and so vanished;—a queen of the wind, a daughter of the sun; a creature of freedom, of victory, of tireless movement, and of boundless space, a thing of heaven and of liberty.

I N the springtime of the year three gods watched by the river.

The golden flowers of the willows blew in the low winds; the waters came and went; the moon rose full and cold over a silvery stream; the reeds sighed in the silence.

Two winters had drifted by and one hot drowsy summer since their creator had forsaken them, and all the white still shapes upon the walls already had been slain by the cold breath of Time. The green weeds waved in the empty casements; the chance-sown seeds of thistles and of bell-flowers were taking leaf between the square stones of the paven places; on the deserted threshold lichens and brambles climbed together; the filmy ooze of a rank vegetation stole over the loveliness of Persephone and devoured one by one the divine offspring of Zeus; about the feet of the bound sun king in Pheræ and over the calm serene mockery of Hermes' smile the grey nets of the spiders' webs had been woven to and fro, across and across, with the lacing of a million threads, as Fate weaves round the limbs and covers the eyes of mortals as they stumble blindly from their birthplace to their grave. All things, the damp and the dust, the frost and the scorch, the newts and the rats, the fret of the flooded waters, and the stealing sure inroad of the mosses that everywhere grew from the dews and the fogs, had taken and eaten, in hunger or sport, or had touched, and thieved from, then left, gangrened and ruined.

The three gods alone remained; who being the sons of

eternal night, are unharmed, unaltered, by any passage of
the years of earth. The only gods who never bend beneath the yoke of years; but unblenchingly behold the
nations wither as uncounted leaves, and the lands and
the seas change their places, and the cities and the empires pass away as a tale that is told; and the deities that
are worshipped in the temples alter in name and attributes
and cultus, at the wanton will of the age which begot
them.

In the still, cold, moonlit air their shadows stood together. Hand in hand; looking outward through the
white night-mists. Other gods perished with the faith of
each age as it changed; other gods lived by the breath
of men's lips, the tears of prayer, the smoke of sacrifice.
But they,—their empire was the universe.

In every young soul that leaps into the light of life
rejoicing blindly, Oneiros has dominion; and he alone.
In every creature that breathes, from the conqueror resting on a field of blood to the nest bird cradled in its bed
of leaves, Hypnos holds a sovereignty which nothing
mortal can long resist and live. And Thanatos,—to him
belongs every created thing, past, present, and to come;
beneath his feet all generations lie; and in the hollow of
his hand he holds the worlds; though the earth be tenant-
less, and the heavens sunless, and the planets shrivel in
their courses, and the universe be shrouded in an endless
night, yet through the eternal desolation Thanatos still
will reign, and through the eternal darkness, through the
immeasurable solitudes, he alone will wander, and he still
behold his work.

Deathless as themselves their shadows stood; and the
worm and the lizard and the newt left them alone and
dared not wind about their calm clear brows, and dared
not steal to touch the roses at their lips, knowing that ere
the birth of the worlds these were, and when the worlds
shall have perished these still will reign on :—the slow,

sure, soundless, changeless ministers of an eternal rest, of an eternal oblivion.

A late light strayed in from the grey skies, pale as the primrose flowers that grew amongst the reeds upon the shore; and found its way to them, trembling; and shone in the far-seeing depths of their unfathomable eyes.

The eyes which spake and said:

"Sleep, dreams, and death:—we are the only gods that answer prayer."

NIGHT had come; a dark night of earliest spring. The wild day had sobbed itself to sleep after a restless life with fitful breath of storm and many sighs of shuddering breezes.

The sun had sunk, leaving long tracks of blood-red light across one-half the heavens.

There was a sharp crisp coldness as of lingering frost in the gloom and the dulness. Heavy clouds, as yet unbroken, hung over the cathedral and the clustering roofs around it in dark and starless splendour.

Over the great still plains which stretched eastward and southward, black with the furrows of the scarce-budded corn, the wind blew hard; blowing the river and the many streamlets spreading from it into foam; driving the wintry leaves which still strewed the earth thickly, hither and thither in legions; breaking boughs that had weathered the winter hurricanes, and scattering the tender blossoms of the snowdrops and the earliest crocuses in all the little moss-grown garden ways.

The smell of wet grass, of the wood-born violets, of trees whose new life was waking in their veins, of damp earths turned freshly upwards by the plough, were all blown together by the riotous breezes.

Now and then a light gleamed through the gloom where a little peasant boy lighted home with a torch some old priest on his mule, or a boat went down the waters with a lamp hung at its prow. For it grew dark early, and people used to the river read a threat of a flood on its face.

A dim glow from the west, which was still tinged with the fire of the sunset, fell through a great square window set in a stone building, and striking across the sicklier rays of an oil lamp reached the opposing wall within.

It was a wall of grey stone, dead and lustreless like the wall of a prison-house, over whose surface a spider as colourless as itself dragged slowly its crooked hairy limbs loaded with the moisture of the place, which was an old tower, of which the country folk told strange tales, where it stood among the rushes on the left bank of the stream.

A man watched the spider as it went.

It crept on its heavy way across the faint crimson reflection from the glow of the sunken sun.

It was fat, well-nourished, lazy, content ; its home of dusky silver hung on high, where its pleasure lay in weaving, clinging, hoarding, breeding.   It lived in the dark ; it had neither pity nor regret ; it troubled itself neither for the death it dealt to nourish itself, nor for the light without, into which it never wandered ; it spun and throve and multiplied.

It was an emblem of the man who is wise in his generation ; of the man whom Cato the elder deemed divine ; of the Majority and the Mediocrity who rule over the earth and enjoy its fruits.

This man knew that it was wise ; that those who were like to it were wise also : wise with the holy wisdom which is honoured of other men.

He had been unwise—always ; and therefore he stood watching the sun die, with hunger in his soul, with famine in his body.

For many months he had been half famished, as were the wolves in his own northern mountains in the winter solstice.   For seven days he had only been able to crush

a crust of hard black bread between his teeth. For twenty
hours he had not done even so much as this. The tren-
cher on his tressel was empty; and he had not where-
withal to re-fill it.

He might have found some to fill it for him no doubt.
He lived amidst the poor, and the poor to the poor are
good, though they are bad and bitter to the rich. But he
did not open either his lips or his hand. He consumed
his heart in silence; and his vitals preyed in anguish on
themselves without his yielding to their torments.

He was a madman; and Cato, who measured the godli-
ness of man by what they gained, would have held him
accursed;—the madness that starves and is silent for an
idea is an insanity, scouted by the world and the gods.
For it is an insanity unfruitful; except to the future.
And for the future who cares,—save these madmen themselves?

He watched the spider as it went.

It could not speak to him as its fellow once spoke in
the old Scottish story. To hear as that captive heard,
the hearer must have hope, and a kingdom,—if only in
dreams.

This man had no hope; he had a kingdom indeed, but
it was not of earth; and, in an hour of sheer cruel bodily
pain, earth alone has dominion and power and worth.

The spider crawled across the grey wall; across the
glow from the vanished sun; across a coil of a dead pas-
sion-vine, that strayed loose through the floor; across the
classic shapes of a great cartoon drawn in chalks upon
the dull rugged surface of stone.

Nothing arrested it; nothing retarded it, as nothing
hastened it. It moved slowly on; fat, lustreless, indolent,
hueless; reached at length its den, and there squatted
aloft, loving the darkness; its young swarming around,
its prey held in its forceps, its nets cast about.

Through the open casement there came on the rising

wind of the storm, in the light of the last lingering sunbeam, a beautiful night-moth, begotten by some cruel
hot-house heat in the bosom of some frail exiled tropical
flower.

It swam in on trembling pinions, and alighted on the
golden head of a gathered crocus that lay dying on the
stones—a moth that should have been born to no world
save that of the summer world of a Midsummer Night's
Dream.

A shape of Ariel and Oberon ; slender, silver, purple,
roseate, lustrous-eyed, and gossamer-winged.

A creature of woodland waters, and blossoming forests ;
of the yellow chalices of kingcups and the white breasts
of river lilies, of moonbeams that strayed through a summer world of shadows, and dew-drops that glistened in
the deep folded hearts of roses. A creature to brush the
dreaming eyes of a poet, to nestle on the bosom of a
young girl sleeping : to float earthwards on a falling star,
to slumber on a lotus leaf.

A creature that amidst the still soft hush of woods and
waters still tells, to those who listen, of the world when
the world was young.

The moth flew on, and poised on the fading crocus
leaves, which spread out their pale gold on the level of
the grey floor.

It was weary, and its delicate wings drooped ; it was
storm-tossed, wind-beaten, drenched with mist and frozen
with the cold ; it belonged to the moon, to the dew, to the
lilies, to the forget-me-nots, and to the night ; and it
found that the hard grip of winter had seized it whilst yet
it had thought that the stars and the summer were with
it. It lived before its time,—and it was like the human
soul, which being born in the darkness of the world dares
to dream of light, and, wandering in vain search of a sun
that will never rise, falls and perishes in wretchedness.

It was beautiful exceedingly, with the brilliant tropical

beauty of a life that is short-lived. It rested a moment
on the stem of the pale flower, then with its radiant eyes
fastened on the point of light which the lamp thrust upward, it flew on high ; and, spreading out its transparent
wings and floating to the flame, kissed it, quivered once,
and died.

There fell among the dust and cinder of the lamp a
little heap of shrunken, fire-scorched, blackened ashes.

The wind whirled them upward from their rest, and
drove them forth into the night to mingle with the storm-
scourged grasses, the pale dead violets, the withered snow-
flowers, with all things frost-touched and forgotten.

The spider sat aloft, sucking the juices from the fettered
flies, teaching its spawn to prey and feed ; content in
squalor and in plenitude ; in sensual sloth, and in the
increase of its body and its hoard.

He watched them both : the success of the spider, the
death of the moth ; trite as a fable ; ever repeated as the
tides of the sea ; the two symbols of humanity ; of the
life which fattens on greed and gain, and the life which
perishes of divine desire.

THERE were no rare birds, no birds of moor and
mountain, in that cultivated and populous district ;
but to her all the little home-bred things of pasture and
orchard were full of poetry and of character.

The robins, with that pretty air of boldness with which
they veil their real shyness and timidity ; the strong and
saucy sparrows, powerful by the strength of all mediocrities
and majorities ; all the dainty families of finches in their
gay apparellings ; the plain brown bird that filled the
night with music ; the gorgeous oriole ruffling in gold, the
gilded princeling of them all ; the little blue warblers, the
violets of the air ; the kingfishers who had hovered so

long over the forget-me-nots upon the rivers that they had caught the colours of the flowers on their wings; the bright blackcaps green as the leaves, with their yellow waistcoats and velvet hoods, the innocent freebooters of the woodland liberties: all these were her friends and lovers, various as any human crowds of court or city.

She loved them; they and the fourfooted beasts were the sole things that did not flee from her; and the woeful and mad slaughter of them by the peasants was to her a grief passionate in its despair. She did not reason on what she felt; but to her a bird slain was a trust betrayed, an innocence defiled, a creature of heaven struck to earth.

Suddenly on the silence of the garden there was a little shrill sound of pain; the birds flew high in air, screaming and startled; the leaves of a bough of ivy shook as with a struggle.

She rose and looked; a line of twine was trembling against the foliage; in its noosed end the throat of the mavis had been caught; it hung trembling and clutching at the air convulsively with its little drawn-up feet. It had flown into the trap as it had ended its joyous song and soared up to join its brethren.

There were a score of such traps set in the miller's garden.

She unloosed the cord from about its tiny neck, set it free, and laid it down upon the ivy. The succour came too late; the little gentle body was already without breath; the feet had ceased to beat the air; the small soft head had drooped feebly on one side; the lifeless eyes had started from their sockets; the throat was without song for evermore.

"The earth would be good but for men," she thought, as she stood with the little dead bird in her hand.

Its mate, which was poised on a rose bough, flew straight to it, and curled round and round about the small slain body, and piteously bewailed its fate, and mourned,

refusing to be comforted, agitating the air with trembling
wings, and giving out vain cries of grief.

Vain ; for the little joyous life was gone ; the life that
asked only of God and Man a home in the green leaves ;
a drop of dew from the cup of a rose ; a bough to swing
on in the sunlight ; a summer day to celebrate in song.

All the winter through, it had borne cold and hunger
and pain without lament ; it had saved the soil from de-
stroying larvæ, and purified the trees from all foul germs ;
it had built its little home unaided, and had fed its nestlings without alms ; it had given its sweet song lavishly
to the winds, to the blossoms, to the empty air, to the
deaf ears of men ; and now it lay dead in its innocence ;
trapped and slain because a human greed begrudged it a
berry worth the thousandth part of a copper coin.

Out from the porch of the mill-house Claudis Flamma
came, with a knife in his hand and a basket, to cut lilies
for one of the choristers of the cathedral, since the morrow
would be the religious feast of the Visitation of Mary.

He saw the dead thrush in her hand, and chuckled to
himself as he went by.

" The tenth bird trapped since sunrise," he said, thinking how shrewd and how sure in their make were these
traps of twine that he set in the grass and the leaves.

She said nothing ; but the darkness of disgust swept
over her face, as he came in sight in the distance.

She knelt down and scraped a hole in the earth ; and
laid moss in it, and put the mavis softly on its green and
fragrant bier, and covered it with handfuls of fallen rose
leaves, and with a sprig or two of thyme.

Around her head the widowed thrush flew ceaselessly,
uttering sad cries ;—who now should wander with him
through the sunlight ?—who now should rove with him
above the blossoming fields ?—who now should sit with
him beneath the boughs hearing the sweet rain fall between the leaves ?—who now should wake with him whilst

F

yet the world was dark, to feel the dawn break ere
the east were red, and sing a welcome to the unborn
day?

A ND, indeed, to those who are alive to the nameless,
universal, eternal soul which breathes in all the
grasses of the fields, and beams in the eyes of all creatures
of earth and air, and throbs in the living light of palpitating
stars, and thrills through the young sap of forest trees, and
stirs in the strange loves of wind-borne plants, and hums
in every song of the bee, and burns in every quiver of the
flame, and peoples with sentient myriads every drop of
dew that gathers on a harebell, every bead of water that
ripples in a brook—to these the mortal life of man can
seem but little, save at once the fiercest and the feeblest
thing that does exist ; at once the most cruel and the
most impotent ; tyrant of direst destruction and bonds-
man of lowest captivity.

Hence, pity entered very little into his thoughts at any
time ; the perpetual torture of life did indeed perplex him,
as it perplexes every thinking creature, with wonder at
the universal bitterness that taints all creation, at the
universal death whereby all forms of life are nurtured, at
the universal anguish of all existence which daily and
nightly assails the unknown God in piteous protest at the
inexorable laws of inexplicable miseries and mysteries.
But because such suffering was thus universal, therefore
he almost ceased to feel pity for it ; of the two he pitied
the beasts far more than the human kind :—the horse
staggering beneath the lash in all the feebleness of hunger,
lameness, and old age ; the ox bleeding from the goad on
the hard furrows, or stumbling through the hooting crowd,
blind, footsore, and shivering, to its last home in the
slaughter-house ; the dog, yielding up its noble life inch
by inch under the tortures of the knife, loyally licking

the hand of the vivisector while he drove his probe
through its quivering nerves; the unutterable hell in
which all these gentle, kindly, and long-suffering creatures
dwelt for the pleasure or the vanity, the avarice or the
brutality of men,—these he pitied perpetually, with a
tenderness for them that was the softest thing in all his
nature.

"THERE lived once in the East, a great king; he
dwelt far away, amongst the fragrant fields of
roses, and in the light of suns that never set.

"He was young, he was beloved, he was fair of face
and form; and the people, as they hewed stone, or brought
water, said amongst themselves, 'Verily, this man is as a
god; he goes where he lists, and he lies still or rises up
as he pleases; and all fruits of all lands are culled for
him; and his nights are nights of gladness, and his days,
when they dawn, are all his to sleep through or spend as
he wills.' But the people were wrong. For this king was
weary of his life.

"His buckler was sown with gems, but his heart beneath it was sore. For he had been long bitterly harassed
by foes who descended on him as wolves from the hills
in their hunger, and he had been long plagued with
heavy wars and with bad rice harvests, and with many
troubles to his nation that kept it very poor, and forbade
him to finish the building of new marble palaces, and
the making of fresh gardens of delight, on which his
heart was set. So he, being weary of a barren land and
of an empty treasury, with all his might prayed to the
gods that all he touched might turn to gold, even as he
had heard had happened to some magician long before
in other ages. And the gods gave him the thing he
craved; and his treasury overflowed. No king had ever
been so rich, as this king now became in the short space
of a single summer-day.

"But it was bought with a price.

"When he stretched out his hand to gather the rose that blossomed in his path, a golden flower scentless and stiff was all he grasped. When he called to him the carrier-dove that sped with a scroll of love words across the mountains, the bird sank on his breast a carven piece of metal. When he was athirst and shouted to his cup-bearer for drink, the red wine ran a stream of molten gold. When he would fain have eaten, the pulse and the pomegranate grew alike to gold between his teeth. And lo! at eventide, when he sought the silent chambers of his harem, saying, 'Here at least shall I find rest,' and bent his steps to the couch whereon his best-beloved slave was sleeping, a statue of gold was all he drew into his eager arms, and cold shut lips of sculptured gold were all that met his own.

"That night the great king slew himself, unable any more to bear this agony; since all around him was desolation, even though all around him was wealth.

"Now the world is too like that king, and in its greed of gold it will barter its life away.

"Look you,—this thing is certain—I say that the world will perish, even as that king perished, slain as he was slain, by the curse of its own fulfilled desire.

"The future of the world is written. For God has granted their prayer to men. He has made them rich, and their riches shall kill them.

"When all green places have been destroyed in the builder's lust of gain :—when all the lands are but mountains of brick, and piles of wood and iron :—when there is no moisture anywhere; and no rain ever falls :—when the sky is a vault of smoke; and all the rivers reek with poison :—when forest and stream, and moor and meadow, and all the old green wayside beauty are things vanished and forgotten :—when every gentle timid thing of brake and bush, of air and water, has been killed because it

robbed them of a berry or a fruit :—when the earth is
one vast city, whose young children behold neither the
green of the field nor the blue of the sky, and hear no
song but the hiss of the steam, and know no music but
the roar of the furnace :—when the old sweet silence of
the country-side, and the old sweet sounds of waking
birds, and the old sweet fall of summer showers, and the
grace of a hedgerow bough, and the glow of the purple
heather, and the note of the cuckoo and cushat, and the
freedom of waste and of woodland, are all things dead,
and remembered of no man :—then the world, like the
Eastern king, will perish miserably of famine and of
drought, with gold in its stiffened hands, and gold in its
withered lips, and gold everywhere :—gold that the people
can neither eat nor drink, gold that cares nothing for
them, but mocks them horribly :—gold for which their
fathers sold peace and health, and holiness and liberty :—
gold that is one vast grave."

THE earth is crowded full with clay gods and false
prophets, and fresh legions for ever arriving to carry
on the old strife for supremacy ; and if a man pass unknown all the time that his voice is audible, and his
hand visible, through the sound and smoke of the battle,
he will dream in vain of any remembrance when the gates
of the grave shall have closed on him and shut him for
ever from sight.

When the world was in its youth, it had leisure to
treasure its recollections ; even to pause and look back,
and to see what flower of a fair thought, what fruit of a
noble art it might have overlooked or left down-trodden.

But now it is so old, and is so tired ; it is purblind
and heavy of foot ; it does not notice what it destroys ;
it desires rest, and can find none ; nothing can matter

greatly to it; its dead are so many that it cannot count them; and being thus worn and dulled with age, and suffocated under the weight of its innumerable memories, it is very slow to be moved, and swift—terribly swift—to forget.

Why should it not be?

It has known the best, it has known the worst, that ever can befall it.

And the prayer that to the heart of a man seems so freshly born from his own desire, what is it on the weary ear of the world, save the same old old cry which it has heard through all the ages, empty as the sound of the wind, and for ever—for ever—unanswered?

THERE is no more terrible woe upon earth than the woe of the stricken brain, which remembers the days of its strength, the living light of its reason, the sunrise of its proud intelligence, and knows that these have passed away like a tale that is told; like a year that is spent; like an arrow that is shot to the stars, and flies aloft, and falls in a swamp; like a fruit that is too well loved of the sun, and so, over-soon ripe, is dropped from the tree and forgot on the grasses, dead to all joys of the dawn and the noon and the summer, but still alive to the sting of the wasp, to the fret of the aphis, to the burn of the drought, to the theft of the parasite.

She only dimly understood, and yet she was smitten with awe and reverence at that endless grief which had no taint of cowardice upon it, but was pure as the patriot's despair, impersonal as the prophet's agony.

For the first time the intellect in her consciously awoke. For the first time she heard a human mind find voice even in its stupor and its wretchedness to cry aloud, in reproach to its unknown Creator:

"I am *yours!* Shall I perish with the body? Why have you ever bade me desire the light and seek it, if for ever you must thrust me into the darkness of negation? Shall I be Nothing?—like the muscle that rots, like the bones that crumble, like the flesh that turns to ashes, and blows in a film on the winds? Shall I die so? I? —the mind of a man, the breath of a god?"

HE could not bear to die without leaving behind his life some work the world would cherish.

Call it folly, call it madness, it is both: the ivory Zeus that was to give its sculptor immortality, lives but in tradition; the bronze Athene, that was to guard the Piræus in eternal liberty, has long been levelled with the dust; yet with every age the artist still gives life for fame, still cries, " Let my body perish, but make my soul immortal!"

THE spider had drawn his dusty trail across them; the rat had squatted at their feet; the darkness of night had enshrouded and defaced them; yet with the morning they arose, stainless, noble, undefiled.

Amongst them there was one colossal form, on which the sun poured with its full radiance.

This was the form of a captive grinding at a mill-stone; the majestic, symmetrical, supple form of a man who was also a god.

In his naked limbs there was a supreme power; in his glance there was a divine command; his head was lifted as though no yoke could ever lie on that proud neck; his foot seemed to spurn the earth as though no mortal tie had ever bound him to the sod that human steps bestrode: yet at the corn-mill he laboured, grinding wheat like the patient blinded oxen that toiled beside him.

For it was the great Apollo in Pheræ.

The hand which awoke the music of the spheres had been blood-stained with murder; the beauty which had the light and lustre of the sun had been darkened with passion and with crime; the will which no other on earth or in heaven could withstand had been bent under the chastisement of Zeus.

He whose glance had made the black and barren slopes of Delos to laugh with fruitfulness and gladness—he whose prophetic sight beheld all things past, present, and to come, the fate of all unborn races, the doom of all unspent ages—he, the Far-Striking King, laboured here beneath the curse of crime, greatest of all the gods, and yet a slave.

In all the hills and vales of Greece his Io pæan sounded still.

Upon his holy mountains there still arose the smoke of fires of sacrifice.

With dance and song the Delian maidens still hailed the divinity of Lêtô's son.

The waves of the pure Ionian air still rang for ever with the name of Delphinios.

At Pytho and at Clarus, in Lycia and in Phokis, his oracles still breathed forth upon their fiat terror or hope into the lives of men; and still in all the virgin forests of the world the wild beasts honoured him wheresoever they wandered, and the lion and the boar came at his bidding from the deserts to bend their free necks and their wills of fire meekly to bear his yoke in Thessaly.

Yet he laboured here at the corn-mill of Admetus; and watching him at his bondage there stood the slender, slight, wing-footed Hermes, with a slow, mocking smile upon his knavish lips, and a jeering scorn in his keen eyes, even as though he cried:

"O brother, who would be greater than I! For what hast thou bartered to me the golden rod of thy wealth and thy dominion over the flocks and the herds? For seven chords strung on a shell—for a melody not even thine own! For a lyre outshone by my syrinx hast thou sold all thine empire to me. Will human ears give heed to thy song now thy sceptre has passed to my hands? Immortal music only is left thee, and the vision foreseeing the future. O god! O hero! O fool! what shall these profit thee now?"

Thus to the artist by whom they had been begotten the dim white shapes of the deities spoke. Thus he saw them, thus he heard, whilst the pale and watery sunlight lit up the form of the toiler in Pheræ.

For even as it was with the divinity of Delos, so is it likewise with the genius of a man, which, being born of a god, yet is bound as a slave to the grindstone. Since even as Hermes mocked the Lord of the Unerring Bow, so is genius mocked of the world, when it has bartered the herds, and the grain, and the rod that metes wealth, for the seven chords that no ear, dully mortal, can hear.

And as he looked upon this symbol of his life, the captivity and the calamity, the strength and the slavery of his existence overcame him; and for the first hour since he had been born of a woman Arslàn buried his face in his hands and wept.

He could bend great thoughts to take the shapes that he chose, as the chained god in Pheræ bound the strong kings of the desert and forest to carry his yoke; yet, like the god, he likewise stood fettered to the mill to grind for bread.

ONE evening, a little later, he met her in the fields on the same spot where Marcellin first had seen her as a child amongst the scarlet blaze of the poppies.

The lands were all yellow with saffron and emerald with the young corn ; she balanced on her head a great brass jar ; the red girdle glowed about her waist as she moved : the wind stirred the folds of her garments ; her feet were buried in the shining grass ; clouds tawny and purple were behind her ; she looked like some Moorish phantom seen in a dream under a sky of Spain.

He paused and gazed at her with eyes half content, half cold.

She was of a beauty so uncommon, so strange, and all that was his for his art :—a great artist, whether in words, in melody, or in colour, is always cruel, or at the least seems so, for all things that live under the sun are to him created only to minister to his one inexorable passion.

Art is so vast, and human life is so little. It is to him only supremely just that the insect of an hour should be sacrificed to the infinite and eternal truth which must endure until the heavens themselves shall wither as a scroll that is held in a flame. It might have seemed to Arslàn base to turn her ignorance, and submission to his will, for the gratification of his amorous passions ; but to make these serve the art to which he had himself abandoned every earthly good was in his sight justified, as the death agonies of the youth whom they decked with roses and slew in sacrifice to the sun, were in the sight of the Mexican nation.

The youth whom the Mexicans slew, on the high hill of the city, with his face to the west, was always the choicest and the noblest of all the opening flower of their manhood : for it was his fate to be called to enter into the realms of eternal light, and to dwell face to face with the unbearable brightness without whose rays the universe would have perished frozen in perpetual night. So the artist, who is true to his art, regards every human sacrifice that he renders up to it ; how can he feel pity for a thing which perishes to feed a flame that he deems the life of the world ?

The steel that he draws out from the severed heart of his victim he is ready to plunge into his own vitals : no other religion can vaunt as much of its priests.

" What are you thinking of to-night ?" he asked her where she came through the fields by the course of a little flower-sown brook, fringed with tall bulrushes and waving willow-stems.

She lifted her eyelids with a dreamy and wistful regard.

" I was thinking—I wonder what the reed felt that you told me of—the one reed that a god chose from all its millions by the waterside and cut down to make into a flute."

" Ah ?—you see there are no reeds that make music now-a-days ; the reeds are only good to be woven into kreels for the fruits and the fish of the market."

" That is not the fault of the reeds ?"

" Not that I know ; it is the fault of men, most likely, who find the chink of coin in barter sweeter music than the song of the syrinx. But what do you think the reed felt then ?—pain to be so sharply severed from its fellows ?"

" No—or the god would not have chosen it."

" What then ?"

A troubled sigh parted her lips ; these old fables were fairest truths to her, and gave a grace to every humblest thing that the sun shone on, or the waters begat from their foam, or the winds blew with their breath into the little life of a day.

" I was trying to think. But I cannot be sure. These reeds have forgotten. They have lost their soul. They

want nothing but to feed among the sand and the mud,
and grow in millions together, and shelter the toads and
the newts,—there is not a note of music in them all—
except when the wind rises and makes them sigh, and
then they remember that long, long-ago the breath of a
great god was in them."

Arslàn looked at her where she stood; her eyes resting on the reeds, and the brook at her feet; the crimson
heat of the evening all about her, on the brazen amphora,
on the red girdle on her loins, on the thoughtful parted
lips, on the proud bent brows above which a golden butterfly floated as above the brows of Psyche.

He smiled; the smile that was so cold to her.

"Look: away over the fields, there comes a peasant
with a sickle; he comes to mow down the reeds to make
a bed for his cattle. If he heard you, he would think
you mad."

"They have thought me many things worse. What
matter?"

"Nothing at all;—that I know. But you seem to
envy that reed—so long ago—that was chosen?"

"Who would not?"

"Are you so sure? The life of the reed was always
pleasant;—dancing there in the light, playing with the
shadows, blowing in the winds; with the cool waters all
about it all day long, and the yellow daffodils and the
blue bell-flowers for its brethren."

"Nay;—how do you know?"

Her voice was low, and thrilled with a curious eager
pain.

"How do you know?" she murmured. "Rather,—it
was born in the sands, amongst the stones, of the chance
winds, of the stray germs,—no one asking, no one heeding, brought by a sunbeam, spat out by a toad—no one
caring where it dropped. Rather,—it grew there by
the river, and such millions of reeds grew with it, that

neither waters nor winds could care for a thing so common and worthless, but the very snakes twisting in and out despised it, and thrust the arrows of their tongues through it in scorn. And then—I think I see!—the great god walked by the edge of the river, and he mused on a gift to give man, on a joy that should be a joy on the earth for ever; and he passed by the lily white as snow, by the thyme that fed the bees, by the gold heart in the arum flower, by the orange flame of the tall sand-rush, by all the great water-blossoms which the sun kissed, and the swallows loved, and he came to the one little reed pierced with the snakes' tongues, and all alone amidst millions. Then he took it up, and cut it to the root, and killed it;—killed it as a reed,—but breathed into it a song audible and beautiful to all the ears of men. Was that death to the reed?—or life? Would a thousand summers of life by the waterside have been worth that one thrill of song when a god first spoke through it?"

Her face lightened with a radiance to which the passion of her words was pale and poor; the vibrations of her voice grew sonorous and changing as the sounds of music itself; her eyes beamed through unshed tears as planets through the rain.

OF all the forms with which he had peopled its loneliness, these had the most profound influence on her in their fair, passionless, majestic beauty, in which it seemed to her that the man who had forgotten them had repeated his own likeness. For they were all alike, yet unlike; of the same form and feature, yet different even in their strong resemblance, like elder and younger brethren who hold a close companionship. For Hypnos was still but a boy with his blue-veined eyelids closed, and his mouth rosy and parted like that of a slumbering child, and above his golden head a star rose in the purple night. Oneiros standing next was a youth whose eyes smiled as though they beheld visions that were welcome to him ; in his hand, amongst the white roses, he held a black wand of sorcery, and around his bended head there hovered a dim silvery nimbus. Thanatos alone was a man fully grown ; and on his calm and colourless face there were blended an unutterable sadness, and an unspeakable peace ; his eyes were fathomless, far-reaching, heavy laden with thought, as though they had seen at once the heights of heaven and the depths of hell ; and he, having thus seen, and knowing all things, had learned that there was but one good possible in all the universe,—that one gift which his touch gave, and which men in their blindness shuddered from and cursed. And above him and around him there was a great darkness.

So the gods stood, and so they spoke, even to her ; they seemed to her as brethren, masters, friends—these three immortals who looked down on her in their mute majesty.

They are the gods of the poor, of the wretched, of the outcast, of the proscribed,—they are the gods who respect not persons nor palaces,—who stay with the exile and flee from the king,—who leave the tyrant of a world to writhe in torment, and call a smile beautiful as the morning on the face of a beggar child,—who turn from the purple beds where wealth and lust and brutal power lie, and fill with purest visions the darkest hours of the loneliest nights, for genius and youth,— they are the gods of consolation and of compensation,—the gods of the exile, of the orphan, of the outcast, of the poet, of the prophet, of all whose bodies ache with the infinite pangs of famine, and whose hearts ache with the infinite woes of the world, of all who hunger with the body or the soul.

IT became mid-April. It was market-day for all the
country lying round that wondrous cathedral-spire,
which shot into the air far-reaching and ethereal, like
some fountain whose column of water had been arrested
aloft and changed to ice.

The old quiet town was busy, with a rich sunshine
shed upon it, in which the first yellow butterflies of the
year had begun to dance.

It was high noon, and the highest tide of the market.

Flower-girls, fruit-girls, egg-sellers, poultry-hucksters,
crowds of women, old and young, had jolted in on their
docile asses, throned on their sheepskin saddles ; and
now, chattering and chaffering, drove fast their trade. On
the steps of the cathedral boys with birds'-nests, knife-
grinders making their little wheels fly, cobblers hammering, with boards across their knees, travelling pedlars
with knapsacks full of toys and mirrors, and holy images,
and strings of beads, sat side by side in amicable com-
petition.

Here and there a priest passed, with his black robe
and broad hat, like a dusky mushroom amongst a bed
of many-hued gillyflowers. Here and there a soldier,
all colour and glitter, showed like a gaudy red tulip in
bloom amidst tufts of thyme.

The old wrinkled leathern awnings of the market-stalls
glowed like copper in the brightness of noon. The red
tiles of the houses edging the great square were gilded
with yellow houseleeks. The little children ran hither
and thither with big bunches of primroses or sheaves of
blue wood-hyacinths, singing. The red and blue serges
of the young girls' bodices were like the gay hues of the
anemones in their baskets. The brown faces of the old
dames under the white roofing of their headgear were
like the russet faces of the home-kept apples which they
had garnered through all the winter.

Everywhere in the shade of the flapping leather, and

the darkness of the wooden porches, there were the tender blossoms of the field and forest, of the hedge and garden.   The azure of the hyacinths, the pale saffron of the primroses, the cool hues of the meadow daffodils, the ruby eyes of the cultured jonquils, gleamed amongst wet rushes, grey herbs, and freshly budded leafage. Plovers' eggs nestled in moss-lined baskets; sheaves of velvet-coated wallflowers poured fragrance on the air; great plumes of lilac nodded on the wind, and amber feathers of laburnum waved above the homelier masses of mint and marjoram, and sage and chervil.

IDALIA.

WHATEVER fate rose for them with the dawn, this night at least was theirs : there is no love like that which lives victorious even beneath the shadow of death : there is no joy like that which finds its paradise even amid the cruelty of pain, the fierce long struggle of despair.

Never is the voluptuous glory of the sun so deep, so rich, as when its last excess of light burns above the purple edge of the tempest-cloud that soars upward to cover and devour it.

" AND we reign still ! "

She turned, as she spoke, towards the western waters, where the sea-line of the Ægean lay, while in her eyes came the look of a royal pride and of a deathless love.

" Greece cannot die. No matter what the land be now, Greece—*our* Greece—must live for ever. Her language lives ; the children of Europe learn it, even if they halt it in imperfect numbers. The greater the scholar, the humbler he still bends to learn the words of wisdom from her school. The poet comes to her for all his fairest myths, his noblest mysteries, his greatest masters. The sculptor looks at the broken fragments of her statues,

G

and throws aside his calliope in despair before those
matchless wrecks. From her soldiers learn how to die,
and nations how to conquer and to keep their liberties.
No deed of heroism is done but, to crown it, it is named
parallel to hers. They write of love, and who forgets the
Lesbian? They dream of freedom, and to reach it they
remember Salamis. They talk of progress, and while
they talk they sigh for all that they have lost in Acade-
mus. They seek truth, and while they seek, wearily long,
as little children, to hear the golden speech of Socrates,
that slave, and fisherman, and sailor, and stonemason,
and date-seller were all once free to hear in her Agora.
But for the light that shone from Greece in the breaking
of the Renaissance, Europe would have perished in its
Gothic darkness. They call her dead: she can never
die while her life, her soul, her genius breathe fire into
the new nations, and give their youth all of greatness and
of grace that they can claim. Greece dead! She reigns
in every poem written, in every art pursued, in every
beauty treasured, in every liberty won, in every godlike
life and godlike death, in your fresh lands, which, but for
her, would be barbarian now."

Where she stood, with her eyes turned westward to the
far-off snows of Cithæron and Mount Ida, and the shores
which the bronze spear of Pallas Athene once guarded
through the night and day, the dark light in her eyes
deepened, and the flush of a superb pride was on her
brow—it seemed Aspasia who lived again, and who
remembered Pericles.

THE chant of the Imaum rang up from the shore,
deep and sonorous, calling on the Faithful to
prayer, an hour before midnight. She listened dreamily
to the echoes that seemed to linger among the dark
foliage.

"I like those national calls to prayer," she said, as she
leaned over the parapet, while the fire-flies glittered
among the mass of leaves as the diamond sprays glistened
in her hair. "The Ave Maria, the Vespers, the Imaum's
chant, the salutation of the dawn or of the night, the
hymn before sleep, or before the sun ;—you have none of
those in your chill islands? You have only weary rituals,
and stuccoed churches, where the 'Pharisees for a pretence make long prayers!' As if *that* was not the best
—the only—temple!"

She glanced upward at the star-studded sky, and on
her face was that graver and gentler look which had
come there when she sang.

"I have held it so many a time," he answered her,
lying awake at night among the long grass of the Andes,
or under the palms of the desert. It was a strange delusion to build shrines to the honour of God while there
are still his own—the forests and the mountains.

"IT was a fair heritage to lose through a feeble vanity—
that beautiful Constantinople!" she said musingly.
"The East and the West—what an empire! More than
Alexander ever grasped at—what might not have been
done with it? Asian faith and Oriental sublimity, with
Roman power and Gothic force ; if there had been a hand
strong enough to weld all these together, what a world
there might have been!"

"But to have done that would have been to attain the
Impossible," he answered her. "Oil and flame, old and
new, living and dying, tradition and scepticism, iconoclast
and idolater, you cannot unite and harmonise these antagonisms?"

She gave a sign of dissent.

"The prophet or the hero unites all antagonisms,

because he binds them all to his own genius. The Byzantine empire had none such; the nearest was Julian, but he believed less in himself than in the gods; the nearest after him was Belisarius—the fool of a courtesan, and he was but a good soldier; he was no teacher, no liberator, no leader for the nations. John Vatices came too late. A man must be his own convert before he can convert others. Zoroaster, Christ, Mahommed, Cromwell, Napoleon, believed intensely in their own missions; hence their influence on the peoples. How can we tell what Byzantium might have become under one mighty hand? It was torn in pieces among courtesans, and parasites, and Christian fanatics, and Houmousians and Houmoiousians! I have the blood of the Commneni in me. I think of it with shame when I remember what they might have been."

"You come from the Roman Emperors?"

"The Roman Emperors?" she repeated. "When the name was a travesty, an ignominy, a reproach! When Barbarians thronged the Forum, and the representative of Galilee fishermen claimed power in the Capitol? Yes; I descend, they say, from the Commneni; but I am far prouder that, on the other hand, I come from pure Athenians. I belong to two buried worlds. But the stone throne of the Areopagus was greater than the gold one of Manuel."

"THAT animal life is to be envied perhaps," she said. "Their pride is centred in a silver hairpin; their conscience is committed to a priest; their credulity is contented with tradition; their days are all the same, from the rising of one sun to another; they do not love, they do not hate; they are like the ass that they drive, follow one patient routine, and only take care for their food. Perhaps they are to be envied!"

"You would not lose 'those thoughts that wander through eternity,' to gain in exchange the peace from ignorance of the peasant or the dullard?"

She turned her face to him, with its most beautiful smile on her lips and in her eyes.

"No, I would not : you are right. Better to know the secrets of the gods, even though with pain, than to lead the dull, brute life, though painless. It is only in our dark hours that we would sell our souls for a dreamless ease."

"Dark hours ! *You* should not know them. Ah, if you would but trust me with some confidence ! if there were but some way in which I could serve you !"

Her eyes met his with gratitude, even while she gave him a gesture of silence. She thought how little could the bold, straight stroke of this man's frank chivalry cut through the innumerable and intricate chains that entangled her own life. The knightly Excalibur could do nothing to sever the filmy but insoluble meshes of secret intrigues.

"It is a saint's-day : I had forgotten it," she said to turn his words from herself, while the bell of the campanile still swung through the air. "I am a pagan, you see : I do not fancy that you care much for creeds yourself."

"Creeds? I wish there were no such word. It has only been a rallying-cry for war, an excuse for the bigot to burn his neighbour."

"No. Long ago, under the Andes, Nezahualcoytl held the same faith that Socrates had vainly taught in the Agora ; and Zengis Khan knew the truth of theism like Plato ; yet the world has never generally learnt it. It is the religion of nature—of reason. But the faith is too simple and too sublime for the multitude. The mass of minds needs a religion of mythics, legend, symbolism, and fear. What is impalpable escapes it ; and it must give an outward and visible shape to its belief, as it gives in its art a human form to its deity. Come, since we agree in our creed, I will take you to my temple—a temple not made by hands."

" I NEVER had a fair field !"—it may be sometimes a coward's apology; but it is many a time the epitome of a great, cramped, tortured, wasted life, which strove like a caged eagle to get free, and never could beat down the bars of the den that circumstances and prejudice had forged. The world sees the few who do reach freedom, and, watching their bold upright flight, says rashly, "will can work all things." But they who perish by the thousand, the fettered eagles who never see the sun ; who pant in darkness, and wear their breasts bare beating on the iron that will never yield ; who know their strength, yet cannot break their prison ; who feel their wings, yet never can soar up to meet the sweet wild western winds of liberty ; who lie at last beaten, and hopeless, and blind, with only strength enough to long for death to come and quench all sense and thought in its annihilation,—who thinks of them—who counts them ?

THE earliest dawn had broken eastward, where the mountains stretched—the dawn of a southern summer, that almost touches the sunset of the past night—but under the dense shadows of the old woods that had sheltered the mystic rites of Gnostics and echoed with the Latin hymns to Pan, no light wandered. There was only a dim silvery haze that seemed to float over the whiteness of the tall-stemmed arum lilies and the foam-bells of the water that here and there glimmered under the rank vegetation, where it had broken from its hidden

channels up to air and space. Not a sound disturbed
the intense stillness ; that the night waned and the world
wakened, brought no change to the solitudes that men
had forgotten, and only memories of dead-deserted gods
still haunted in the places of their lost temples, whose
columns were now the sea-pines' stems, and on whose
fallen altars and whose shattered sculptures the lizard
made her shelter and the wind-sown grasses seeded and
took root. Of the once graceful marble beauty and the
incense-steeped stones of sacrifice nothing remained but
moss-grown shapeless fragments, buried beneath a pall
of leaves by twice a thousand autumns. Yet the ancient
sanctity still rested on the nameless, pathless woods ;
the breath of an earlier time, of a younger season of the
earth, seemed to lie yet upon the untroubled forest ways ;
the whisper of the unseen waters had a dream-like, unreal
cadence ; in the deep shade, in the warm fragrance and
the heavy gloom, there was a voluptuous yet mournful
charm—the world seemed so far, the stars shone so
near ; there were the sweetness of rest and the oblivion
of passion.

DEATH is not ours to deal. And were it ours, should
we give him the nameless mystic mercy which
all men live to crave—give it as the chastisement of
crime ? Death ! It is rest to the aged, it is oblivion to
the atheist, it is immortality to the poet ! It is a vast,
dim, exhaustless pity to all the world. And would you
summon it as your hardest cruelty to sin ?

They were silent ; she stirred their souls—she had
not bound their passions.

"A traitor merits death," they muttered.

"Merits it ! Not so. The martyr, the liberator, the
seeker of truth, may deserve its peace ; how has the
traitor won them ? You deem yourselves just ; your

justice errs. If you would give him justice, make him
live. Live to know fear lest every wind among the
leaves may whisper of his secret; live to feel the look
of a young child's eyes a shame to him; live to envy
every peasant whose bread has not been bought with
tainted coin; live to hear ever in his path the stealing
step of haunting retribution; live to see his brethren
pass by him as a thing accurst; live to listen in his age
to white-haired men, who once had been his comrades,
tell to the youth about them the unforgotten story of his
shame. Make him live thus if you would have justice."

They answered nothing; a shudder ran through them
as they heard.

"And—if you have as I—a deliverance that forbids
you even so much harshness, still let him live, and bury
his transgression in your hearts. Say to him as I say,
' Your sin was great, go forth and sin no more.' "

"ONE is not an assassin !"
        "Since when have you discovered that ?"
The flush grew darker on Count Conrad's forehead;
he moved restlessly under the irony, and drank down a
draught of red fiery Roussillon without tasting it more
than if it had been water. Then he laughed; the same
careless musical laughter with which he had made the
requiem over a violet—a laugh which belonged at once to
the most careless and the most evil side of his character.

"Since sophism came in, which was with Monsieur
Cain, when he asked, 'Am I my brother's keeper?' It
was ingenious that reply; creditable to a beginner, without social advantages. 'An assassin !' Take the word
boldly by the beard, and look at it. What is there
objectionable ? "

"Nothing—except to the assassinated."

"It has had an apotheosis ever since the world began," pursued Phaulcon, unheeding, in his bright vivacity. "Who are celebrated in Scripture? Judith, Samuel, David, Moses, Joab. Who is a patriot? Brutus. Who is an immortal? Harmodius and Aristogiton. Who is a philosopher? Cicero, while he murmurs '*Vixerunt !*' after slaying Lentulus. Who is a hero? Marius, who nails the senators' heads to the rostræ. Who is a martyr? Charles, who murders Strafford. What is religion? Christianity, that has burnt and slain millions. Who is a priest? Calvin, who destroys Servetus; or Pole, who kills Latimer, which you like. Who is a saint? George of Cappadocia, who slaughters right and left. Who is a ruler? Sulla, who slays Ofella. Who is a queen? Christina, who stabs Monaldeschi; Catherine, who strangles Peter; Isabella, who slays Moors and Jews by the thousand. Murderers all! Assassination has always been deified; and before it is objected to, the world must change its creeds, its celebrities, and its chronicles. 'Monsieur, you are an assassin,' says an impolite world. 'Messieurs,' says the polite logician, 'I found my warrant in your Bible, and my precedent in your Brutus. What you deify in Aristogiton and Jael you mustn't damn in Ankarström and me.' Voilà! What could the world say?"

"That you would outwit Belial with words, and beguile Beelzebub out of his kingdom with sophistry."

A VILLAGE COMMUNE.

POWER is sweet, and when you are a little clerk you love its sweetness quite as much as if you were an emperor, and maybe you love it a good deal more.

HE saw no reason why he should not become a deputy, and even a minister before he died, and indeed there was no reason whatever. He was only a clerk at fifty pounds a year; but he had a soul above all scruples, and a heart as hard as a millstone.

HE was only a clerk indeed, at a slender salary, and ate his friends' tomatoes publicly in the little back room of the caffè; but he had the soul of a statesman. When a donkey kicks, beat it; when it dies, skin it; so only will it profit you; that was his opinion, and the public was the donkey of Messer Nellemane.

PIPPO and Viola feared everything, yet knew not what they feared ; it is a ghostly burden of dread, that which the honest poor carry with them all through their toiling hungry days, the vague oppressive dread of this law which is always acting the spy on them, always dogging their steps, always emptying their pockets. The poor can understand criminal law, and its justice and its necessity easily enough, and respect its severities ; but they cannot understand the petty tyrannies of civil law ; and it wears their lives out, and breaks their spirits. When it does not break their spirits it curdles their blood and they become socialists, nihilists, international-ists, anything that will promise them riddance of their spectre and give them vengeance. We in Italy are all of us afraid of socialism, we who have anything to lose ; and yet we let the syndics, and their secretaries, conciliators, and chancellors sow it broadcast in dragon's teeth of petty injustices and petty cruelties, that soon or late will spring up armed men, hydra-headed and torch in hand !

THE law should be a majesty, solemn, awful, unerring : just, as man hopes that God is just ; and from its throne it should stretch out a mighty hand to seize and grasp the guilty, and the guilty only. But when the law is only a petty, meddlesome, cruel, greedy spy, mingling in every household act and peering in at every window pane, then the poor who are guiltless would be justified if they spat in its face, and called it by its right name, a foul extortion.

THE Italian tongue chatters like a magpie's ; if they did not let the steam off thus they would be less easily ruled than they are ; but no great talker ever did any great thing yet, in this world.

A RETENTIVE memory is of great use to a man, no doubt; but the talent of oblivion is on the whole more useful.

SARTA ROSALIA is in a lovely pastoral country; the country that seems to thrill with Theocritus' singing, as it throbs with the little tamborine of the cicala; a country running over with beautiful greenery, and with climbing creepers hanging everywhere, from the vine on the maples to the china-rose hedges, and with the deep-blue shadows, and the sun-flushed whiteness of the distant mountains lending to it in the golden distance that solemnity and ethereal charm which, without mountains somewhere within sight, no country ever has. But since the advent of "freedom" it is scarred and wounded; great scar-patches stretch here and there where woods have been felled by the avarice illumined in the souls of landowners; hundreds and thousands of bare poles stand stark and stiff against the river light which have been glorious pyramids of leaf shedding welcome shadows on the river path; and many a bold round hill like the *ballons* of the Vosges, once rich of grass as they, now shorn of wood, and even of undergrowth, lift a bare stony front to the lovely sunlight, and never more will root of tree, or seed of flower or of fern, find bed there.

Such is Progress.

FOR the first time his *liberi pensieri* were distasteful to him and unsatisfactory; for atheism makes a curse a mere rattle of dry peas in a fool's bladder, as it makes a blessing a mere flutter of a breath. Messer Nellemane for the first time felt that the old religion has

its advantages over agnosticism ; it gave you a hell for
your rivals and your enemies !

H E had never heard of Virgil and of Theocritus—but
it hurt him to have these sylvan pictures spoiled ;
these pictures which are the same as those they saw and
sang ; the threshing barns with the piles of golden grain,
and the flails flying to merry voices ; the young horses
trampling the wheat loose from its husk with bounding
limbs and tossing manes ; the great arched doorways,
with the maidens sitting in a circle breaking the maize
from its withered leaves, and telling old-world stories,
and singing sweet *fiorellini* all the while ; the hanging
fields broken up in hill and vale with the dun-coloured
oxen pushing their patient way through labyrinths of vine
boughs, and clouds of silvery olive leaf : the bright
laborious day, with the sun-rays turning the sickle to a
semi-circlet of silver, as the mice ran, and the crickets
shouted, and the larks soared on high : the merry supper
when the day was done, with the thrill and thrum of the
mandolini, and the glisten of the unhoused fire-flies,
whose sanctuary had been broken when the bearded
barley and the amber corn fell prone : all these things
rose to his memory : they had made his youth and manhood glad and full of colour : they were here still for his
sons a little while, but when his sons should be all grown
men, then those things would have ceased to be, and even
their very memory would have perished, most likely, while
the smoke of the accursed engines would have sullied the
pure blue sky, and the stench of their foul vapours would
have poisoned the golden air.

He roused himself and said wearily to Pippo,

"There is a tale I have heard somewhere of a man
who sold his birthright for gold, and when the gold was

in his hands, then it changed to withered leaves and brown moss: I was thinking, eh? that the world is much like that man!"

WHEN all your politics and policies are summed up in the one intention to do well for yourself, great simplicity is given to your theories, if not to your practice.

THE ministerialists . . . made florid and beautiful speeches full of sesquipedalian phrases in which they spoke about the place of Italy among the great powers, the dangers of jealousy and invasion from other nations, the magnificence of the future, the blessings of education, the delights of liberty, the wickedness of the opposition, the sovereign rights of the people; and said it all so magnificently and so bewilderingly that the people never remembered till it was too late that they had said nothing about opposing the cow-tax—or indeed any taxes at all, but listened and gaped, and shouted, and clapped; and being told that they could sit at a European Congress to decide the fate of Epirus, were for the moment oblivious that they had bad bread, dear wine, scant meat, an army of conscripts, and a bureaucracy that devoured them as maggots a cheese. What is political eloquence for, if not to make the people forget such things as these?

TO sell your grapes to foreigners and have none at all at home is a spirited commerce, and fine free trade; that the poor souls around are all poisoned with cheap chemicals in the absence of wine, is only an evidence of all that science can do.

IT is the noblest natures that tyranny drives to frenzy.

THE bureaucratic mind, all the world over, believes the squeak of the official penny whistle to be as the trump of archangels and the voice of Sinai. That all the people do not fall down prostrate at the squeak is, to this order of mind, the one unmentionable sin.

IT is not true that no Italian ever tells the truth, as commentators on the country say, but it is sadly true that when one does he suffers for it.

A DAY in prison to a free-born son of the soil, used to work with the broad bright sky alone above his head, is more agony than a year of it is to a cramped city-worker used only to the twilight of a machine-room or a workshop, only to an air full of smuts and smoke, and the stench of acids, and the dust of filed steel or sifted coal. The sufferings of the two cannot be compared, and one among many of the injustices the law, all over the world, commits, is that it never takes into considera- tion what a man's past has been. There are those to whom a prison is as hell ; there are those to whom it is something better than the life they led.

SHE was an old woman, and had been bred up in the old faiths ; faiths that were not clear indeed to her nor ever reasoned on, but yet gave her consolation, and a great, if a vague hope. Now that we tell the poor there is no such hope, that when they have worked and starved long enough, then they will perish altogether, like bits of candle that have burnt themselves out, that they are mere machines made of carbon and hydrogen, which, when they have had due friction, will then crumble back into the dust ; now that we tell them all this, and call this the spread of education, will they be as patient?

TAKE hope from the heart of man, and you make him a beast of prey.

ONE of the cruellest sins of any state, in giving petty and tyrannous authority into petty and tyrannous hands, is that it thus brings into hatred and disgust the true and high authority of moral law.

IN these modern times of cowardice, when great ministers dare not say the thing they think, and high magistrates stoop to execute decrees they abhor, it is scarcely to be hoped for that moral courage will be a plant of very sturdy growth in the souls of carpenters, and coopers, and bakers, and plumbers, and day-labourers, who toil for scarce a shilling a day.

HE had been wronged, and a great wrong is to the nature as a cancer is to the body; there is no health.

A JUST chastisement may benefit a man, though it seldom does, but an unjust one changes all his blood to gall.

IN these days, Christian Europe decides that not only the poor man lying by the wayside, but also the Samaritan who helps him, are sinners against political economy, and its law forbids what its religion orders : people must settle the contradiction as they deem best ; they generally are content to settle it by buttoning up their pockets, and passing by, on the other side.

IN this lovely land that brims over with flowers like a cup over-filled, where the sun is as a magician for ever changing with a wand of gold all common things to paradise ; where every wind shakes out the fragrance of a world of fruit and flower commingled ; where, for so little, the lute sounds and the song arises ; here, misery looks more sad than it does in sadder climes, where it is like a home-born thing, and not an alien tyrant as it is here.

YOU cannot cage a field bird when it is old ; it dies for want of flight, of air, of change, of freedom. No use will be the stored grain of your cages ; better for the bird a berry here and there, and peace of gentle death at last amidst the golden gorse or blush of hawthorn buds.

"WHAT is England?"
   "It is a place where the poor souls have no wine of their own, I think ; and they make cannons and cheese.

1!

You see their people over here now and then. They carry red Bibles, and they go about with their mouths open to catch flies, and they run into all the little old dusty places; you must have seen them."

"And why do we want to have anything to do with them?"

"They will come in ships and fire at us, if we are not bigger and stronger than they. We must build iron houses that float, and go on the sea and meet them."

PUCK.

"ANIMALISM," forsooth!—a more unfair word don't exist. When we animals never drink only just enough to satisfy thirst, never eat except when we have genuine appetites, never indulge in any sort of debauch, and never strain excess till we sink into the slough of satiety, shall "animalism" be a word to designate all that men and women dare to do? "Animalism!" You ought to blush for such a libel on our innocent and reasonable lives when you regard your own! You men who scorch your throats with alcohols, and kill your lives with absinthe; and squander your gold in the Kursaal, and the Cecle, and the Arlington; and have thirty services at your dinner betwixt soup and the "chasse;" and cannot spend a summer afternoon in comfort unless you be drinking deep the intoxication of hazard in your debts and your bets on the Heath or the Downs, at Hurlingham or at Tattersalls' Rooms. You women, who sell your souls for bits of stones dug from the bowels of the earth; who stake your honour for a length of lace two centuries old; who replace the bloom your passions have banished with the red of poisoned pigments; who wreathe your aching heads with purchased tresses torn from prisons, and madhouses, and coffins; who spend your lives in one incessant struggle, first the rivalry of vanity and then the rivalry of ambition; who deck out greed, and selfish-

ness, and worship of station or gold, as "love," and then
wonder that your hapless dupes, seizing the idol that you
offer them as worthy of their worship, fling it from them
with a curse, finding it dumb, and deaf, and merciless, a
thing of wood and stone.

"Animalism," forsooth! God knows it would be well
for you, here and hereafter, men and women both, were
you only patient, continent, and singleminded, only
faithful, gentle, and longsuffering, as are the brutes that
you mock, and misuse, and vilify in the supreme blindness
of your egregious vanity!

I WAS horribly cold and hungry; and this is a combination which kills sentiment in bigger people than
myself. The emotions, like a hothouse flower or a sea-
dianthus, wither curiously when aired in an east wind, or
kept some hours waiting for dinner.

IN truth, too, despite all the fine chances that you certainly give your peasants to make thorough beasts of
themselves, they are your real aristocrats, and have the
only really good manners in your country. In an old
north-country dame, who lives on five shillings a week,
in a cottage like a dream of Teniers' or Van Tol's, I have
seen a fine courtesy, a simple desire to lay her best at
her guest's disposal, a perfect composure, and a freedom
from all effort, that were in their way the perfection of
breeding. I have seen these often in the peasantry, in
the poor. It is your middle classes, with their incessant
flutter, and bluster, and twitter, and twaddle; with their
perpetual strain after effect; with their deathless desire
to get one rung of the ladder higher than they ever can
get; with their preposterous affectations, their pedantic

unrealities, their morbid dread of remark, their everlasting imitations, their superficial education, their monotonous commonplaces, and their nervous deference to opinion ;— it is your middle classes that have utterly destroyed good manners, and have made the prevalent mode of the day a union of boorishness and servility, of effervescence and of apathy—a court suit, as it were, worn with muddy boots and a hempen shirt.

I THINK Fanfreluche spoke with reason. Coincidence is a god that greatly influences mortal affairs. He is not a cross-tempered deity either, always ; and when you beat your poor fetish for what seems to you an untoward accident, you may do wrong ; he may have benefited you far more than you wot.

NOW I believe that when a woman's own fair skin is called rouge, and her own old lace is called imitation, she must in some way or other have roused sharply the conscience or the envy of her sisters who sit in judgment.

I CANNA go to church. Look'ee,—they's allus a readin' o' cusses, and damnin', and hell fire, and the like ; and I canna stomach it. What for shall they go and say as all the poor old wimmin i' tha parish is gone to the deil 'cause they picks up a stick or tew i' hedge, or likes to mumble a charm or tew o'er their churnin'? Them old wimmin be rare an' good i' ither things. When I broke my ankle three years agone, old Dame Stuckley kem o'er, i' tha hail and the snaw, a matter of five mile and more, and she turned o' eighty ; and she nursed me, and tidied the place, and did all as was wanted to be done, 'cause Avice was away, working somewhere's ; and she'd never let me gie her aught for it. And I heard ta passon tell her as she were sold to hell, 'cause the old soul have a bit of belief like in witch-stones, and allus sets one aside her spinnin' jenny, so that the thrid shanna knot nor break. Ta passon he said, God cud mak tha thrid run smooth, or knot it, just as He chose, and 'twas wicked to think she could cross His will. And the old dame, she said, Weel, sir, I dinna b'lieve tha Almighty would ever spite a poor old crittur like me, don't 'ee think it ? But if we're no to help oursells i' this world, what for have He gied us the trouble o' tha thrid to spin ? and why no han't He made tha shirts, an' tha sheets, an' tha hose grow theersells ? And ta passon niver answered her that, he only said she was fractious and blas-*phe*-mous. Now she warn't, she spoke i' all innocence, and she mint what she said—she mint it. Passons niver can answer ye plain, right-down, nataral questions like this'n, and that's why I wunna ga ta tha church.

D INNA ye meddle, Tam ; it's niver no good a threshin' other folk's corn ; ye allays gits the flail agin i' yer own eye somehow.

T HE flowers hang in the sunshine, and blow in the breeze, free to the wasp as to the bee. The bee chooses to make his store of honey, that is sweet, and fragrant, and life-giving ; the wasp chooses to make his from the same blossoms, but of a matter hard, and bitter, and useless. Shall we pity the wasp because, of his selfish passions, he selects the portion that shall be luscious only to his own lips, and spends his hours only in the thrusting-in of his sting? Is not such pity—wasted upon the wasp—an insult to the bee who toils so wearily to gather in for others; and who, because he stings not man, is by man maltreated? Now it seems to me, if I read them aright, that vicious women, and women that are of honesty and honour, are much akin to the wasp and to the bee.

MY dear, a gentleman may forget his appointments, his love vows, and his political pledges; he may forget the nonsense he talked, the dances he engaged for, the women that worried him, the electors that bullied him, the wife that married him, and he may be a gentleman still; but there are two things he must never forget, for no gentleman ever does—and they are, to pay a debt that is a debt of honour, and to keep a promise to a creature that can't force him to keep it.

A GENIUS? You must mistake. I have always heard that a genius is something that they beat to death first with sticks and stones, and set up on a great rock to worship afterwards. Now they make her very happy whilst she is alive. She cannot possibly be a genius.

I LEARNED many wondrous things betwixt Epsom and Ascot. A brief space, indeed, yet one that to me seemed longer than the whole of my previous life, so crowded was it every hour with new and marvellous experiences. Worldly experiences, I mean. Intellectually, I am not sure that I acquired much.

Indeed, to a little brain teeming with memories of the Théâtres Beaumarchais, Voltaire, Molière, Feuillet, Sardou, Sandeau, &c., which I had heard read so continually at the Dower-House amongst the Fens, the views of dramatic literature held at the Coronet appeared of the most extraordinary character. They certainly had one merit—simplicity.

The verb "to steal" was the only one that a successful dramatic author appeared to be required to conjugate.

For your music steal from the music-halls; for your costumes steal from *Le Follet;* for your ideas steal from anybody that happens to carry such a thing about him; for your play, in its entirety, steal the plot, the characters, the romance, the speeches, and the wit, if it have any, of some attractive novel; and when you have made up your parcel of thefts, tie it together with some string of stage directions, herald it as entirely original, give a very good supper to your friends on the press, and bow from your box as the "Author."

You will certainly be successful: and if the novelist ever object, threaten him with an action for interference with *your* property.

These I found were the laws laid down by London dramatists; and they assuredly were so easy to follow and so productive to obey, that if any Ben Jonson or Beaumarchais, Sheridan or Marivaux, had arisen and attempted to infringe them, he would have infallibly been regarded as a very evil example, and been extinguished by means of journalistic slating and stall-siflage.

BY the way, permit me, in parenthesis, to say that one of the chief causes of that preference for the *demi-monde* which you daily and hourly discover more and more, is the indulgence it shows to idleness. Because your lives are so intense now, and always at high pressure —for that very reason are you more indolent also in little things. It bores you to dress; it bores you to talk; it bores you to be polite. Sir Charles Grandison might find ecstasy in elaborating a bow, a wig, or a speech; you like to give a little nod, cut your hair very short, and make "awfully" do duty for all your adjectives.

"*Autres temps, autres mœurs.*" You are a very odd mixture. You will go to the ends of the earth on the scent of big game; but you shirk all social exertion with a cynical laziness. You will come from Damascus at a stretch without sleeping, and think nothing of it; but you find it a wretched thing to have to exert yourself to be courteous in a drawing-room.

Therefore the *demi-monde* suits you with a curious fitness, and suits you more and more every year. I am afraid it is not very good for you. I don't mean for your morals; I don't care the least about them, I am a dog of the world; I mean for your manners. It makes you slangy, inert, rude, lazy. And yet what perfect gentlemen you can be still, and what grace there is in your careless, weary ease, when you choose to be courteous; and you always *do* choose, that I must say for you, when you find a woman who is really worth the trouble.

I NEVER knew quite whether I liked her—how can you with those women of the world? She was kind and insincere; she was gentle and she was cruel; she was generous and ungenerous; she was true as steel, and she was false as Judas—what would you?—she was a woman of the world, with several sweet natural impulses, and all a coquette's diplomacies.

She tended me with the greatest solicitude one day that autumn, when I had run a thorn into my foot: and the very next day, when I was well again, she laughed to see me worried on the lawn by a bull-terrier. If you have not met a woman like that, I wonder where you have lived.

YOU must be spider or fly, as somebody says. Now all my experience tells me that men are mostly the big, good-natured, careless blue-bottles, half-drunk with their honey of pleasure, and rushing blindly into any web that dazzles them a little in the sunshine; and women are the dainty, painted, patient spiders that just sit and weave, and weave, and weave, till—pong!—Bluebottle is in head foremost, and is killed, and sucked dry, and eaten up at leisure.

You men think women do not know much of life. Pooh! I, Puck, who have dwelt for many of my days on their boudoir cushions, and eaten of their dainty little dinners, and been smuggled under their robes even into operas, balls, and churches, tell you that is an utter fallacy. They do not choose you to know that they know it, very probably; but there is nothing that is hidden from them, I promise you.

DON'T you know that whilst broad, intellectual scepticism is masculine, narrow, social scepticism is feminine? To get hearty, reverent, genuine belief in the innocence of a slandered woman, go to a man: where the world has once doubted, women, the world-worshippers, will for ever after doubt also. You can never bring women to see that the pecked-at fruit is always the richest and sweetest; they always take the benison of the wooing bird to be the malison of the hidden worm!

NOT very long ago I was down away in the vale of Belvoir. I stayed with my friends at a great stately place, owned by as gallant a gentleman as ever swung

himself into saddle. His wife was a beautiful woman,
and he treated her with the courtliest tenderness : indeed,
I often heard their union cited as one of almost unequalled
felicity. "He never had a thought that he did not tell
me," I heard his wife once say to a friend. "Not a single
thought, I know, all these twelve years of our marriage."
It was a happy belief—many women have the like—but
it was an unutterably foolish one ; for the minds of the
best and truest amongst you are, in many things, as sealed
books to those whom you care for the most.

One bitter, black hunting-day, a day keen and cold,
with frost, as men feared, in the air, and with the ground
so hard that even the Duke's peerless "dandies," perfect
hounds though they are, scarcely could keep the scent,
there came terrible tidings to the Hall—he had met with
a crashing fall. His horse had refused at timber, and
had fallen upon him, kicking his head with the hind hoofs
repeatedly. They had taken him to the nearest farm-
house, insensible ; even dead already, they feared. His
wife and the elder amongst the beautiful children fled
like mad creatures across the brown fallows, and the
drear blackened meadows. The farm, happily, was not
far : I sped with them.

When they reached him he was not quite lifeless, but
he knew none of them ; his head had been beaten in by
the plates of the kicking hoofs ; and they waited for his
death with every moment, in the little old dusky room,
with its leaded lattices, and its odour of dried lavender,
and its bough of holly above the hearth. For this had
chanced upon Christmas Eve.

To his wife's agonies, to his children's moans, he was
silent : he knew nothing ; he lay with closed eyes and
crushed brain—deaf, blind, mute. Suddenly the eyes
opened, and stared at the red winter sun where it glowed
dimly through the squares of the lattice-panes. "Dolores!"

he cried aloud; "Dolores! Dolores!" It was the name of none there.

"My God! What woman is it he calls?" his wife asked in her torture. But none ever knew. Through half the night his faint pulse beat, his faint breath came and went; but consciousness never more returned, and for ever he muttered only that one name, that name which was not her own. And when they laid the dead body in its shroud, they found on the left arm above the elbow the word "Dolores" marked on the skin, as sailors stamp letters in their flesh. But whose it was, or what woe or passion it recorded, none ever knew—not even his wife, who had believed she shared his every thought. And to his grave his dead and secret love went with him.

This man was but a gay, frank, high-spirited gentleman, of no great knowledge, and of no great attainments, riding fearlessly, laughing joyously, living liberally; not a man, one would have said, to know any deep passions, to treasure any bitter memories—and yet he had loved one woman so well that he had never spoken of her, and never forgotten her; never—not even in his death-hour, when the poor, stunned, stifled brain had forgotten all other things of earth.

And so it seems to me that it is very often with you, and that you bear with you through your lifetime the brand of an unforgotten name, branded deep in, in days of passion, that none around you ever wot of, and that the wife who sleeps on your heart never knows.

It is dead—the old love—long dead. And yet, when your last hour shall come, and your senses shall be dizzy with death, the pale loves of the troth and the hearth will fade from you, and this love alone will abide.

" MODERN painters do not owe you much, sir," said a youngster to him once, writhing under the *Midas'* ruthless flagellation of his first Academy picture.

" On the contrary," said the great censor, taking his snuff; "they owe me much, or might have owed me much. If they had only listened to me, they would have saved every shilling that they have thrown away on canvas !"

IN your clubs and your camps, in your mischievous moods and your philosophic moods, always indeed theoretically, you consider all women immoral (except just, of course, your own mothers) ; but practically, when your good-feeling is awakened, or your honest faith honestly appealed to, you will believe in a woman's honour with a heartiness and strength for which she will look in vain in her own sex. According to your jests, the world is one vast harem, of which all the doors are open to every man, and whose fair inmates are all alike impressionable to the charm of intrigue or to the chink of gold. But, in simple earnest and reality, I have heard the wildest and most debonair amongst you—once convinced of the honour and innocence looking from a woman's eyes—stand up in defence of these when libelled in her absence, with a zeal and a stanchness that did my heart good.

HIS simple creed, "the good faith of a gentleman," forbade him to injure what lay defenceless at his mercy.

Ah ! revile that old faith as you will, it has lasted longer than any other cultus ; and whilst altars have reeled, and idols been shattered, and priests changed their teachings, and peoples altered their gods, the old faith has lasted through all ; and the simple instinct of the Greek eupatrid and of the Roman patrician still moves the heart of the English gentleman—the instinct of *Noblesse oblige.*

"THE exception proves the rule," runs your proverb ; but why, I wonder, is it that you always only believe in the rule, and are always utterly sceptical as to the existence of the exception?

THE sun shone in over the roofs ; the bird in its cage began a low tremulous song ; the murmur of all the crowded streets came up upon the silence ; and Nellie lay there dead ;—the light upon her curly hair, and on her mouth the smile that had come there at his touch.

"Ah, my dear !" said Fanfreluche, as she ceased her story, with a half-soft and half-sardonic sadness, "she was but a little, ignorant, common player, who made but three pounds a week, and who talked the slang of the streets, and who thought shrimps and tea a meal for the gods, and who made up her own dresses with her own hands, out of tinsel and tarlatanes and trumperies, and who knew no better than to follow the blind, dumb instincts of good that, self-sown and uncultured, lived in her—God knows how !—as the harebells, with the dew on them, will live amidst the rank, coarse grass of grave-yards. She was but a poor little player, who tried to be honest where all was corruption, who tried to walk straightly where all ways were crooked. So she died to-day in a garret, my dear."

IF all men in whose hearts lives a dull, abiding grief, whose throbs death and death only ever will still, deserted for desert or ocean your world of fame and of fashion, how strangely that world would look! How much eloquence would be dumb in your senatorial chambers; how many a smile would be missing from your ball-rooms and hunting-fields; how many a frank laugh would die off for ever from your ear; how many a well-known face would vanish from your clubs, from your park, from your dinner-tables, from your race-stands!

And how seldom would it be those that you had pitied who would go!—how often would the vacant place be that place where so many seasons through you had seen, and had envied, the gayest, the coldest, the most light-hearted, the most cynical amongst you!

Ah! let Society be thankful that men in their bitterness do not now fly, as of old, to monastery or to hermitage; for, did they do so, Society would send forth her gilded cards to the wilderness.

"*UNE vie manquée!*" says the world.
      Is there any threnody over a death half so unutterably sad as that one jest over a life?

"*Manquée!*"—the world has no mercy on a hand that has thrown the die and has lost; no tolerance for the player who, holding fine cards, will not play them by the rules of the game. "*Manquée!*" the world says, with a polite sneer, of the lives in which it beholds no blazoned achievement, no public success.

And yet, if it were keener of sight, it might see that those lives, not seldom, may seem to have missed of their mark, because their aim was high over the heads of the multitude; or because the arrow was sped by too eager a hand in too rash a youth, and the bow lies unstrung in that hand when matured. It might see that those lives which look so lost, so purposeless, so barren of attainment, so devoid of object or fruition, have sometimes nobler deeds in them and purer sacrifice than lies in the home-range of its own narrowed vision. "*Manquée!*" —do not cast that stone idly : how shall you tell, as you look on the course of a life that seems to you a failure, because you do not hear its "*Io triumphe*" on the lips of a crowd, what sweet dead dreams, what noble vain desires, what weariness of futile longing, what conscious waste of vanished years—nay, what silent acts of pure nobility, what secret treasures of unfathomed love—may lie within that which seems in your sight even as a waste land untilled, as a fire burnt out, as a harp without chords, as a bird without song ?

GENIUS is oftentimes but a poor fool, who, clinging to a thing that belongs to no age, Truth, does oftentimes live on a pittance and die in a hospital ; but whosoever has the gift to measure aright their generation is invincible—living, they shall enjoy all the vices undetected ; and dead, on their tombstones they shall possess all the virtues.

CANT, naked, is honoured throughout England. Cant, clothed in gold, is a king never in England resisted.

"BEN DARE, he be dead ?" he asked suddenly. "They told me so by Darron's side."*
Ambrose bent his head, silently.
"When wur't ?"
"Last simmar-time, i' th' aftermath."
"It were a ston' as killed him ?"
"Ay," said Ambrose, softly shading his eyes with his

---

* The river Derwent.

hand from the sun that streamed through the aisles of pine.

"How wur't?"

"They was a blastin'. He'd allus thoct as he'd dee that way, you know. They pit mair pooder i' quarry than common; and the ston' it split, and roared, and crackit, wi' a noise like tha crack o' doom. And one bit on 't, big as ox, were shot i' th' air, an' fell, unlookit for like, and dang him tew the groun', and crushit him,—a-lyin' richt athwart his brist."

"An' they couldna stir it?"

"They couldna. I heerd tha other min screech richt tew here, an' I knew what it wur, tha shrill screech comin' jist i' top o' tha blastin' roar; an' I ran, an' ran—na gaze-hound fleeter. An' we couldna raise it—me an' Tam, an' Job, an' Gideon o' the Mere, an' Moses Legh o' Wissen Edge, a' strong min and i' our prime. We couldna stir it, till Moses o' Wissen Edge he thoct o' pittin' fir-poles underneath—poles as was sharp an' slim i' thur ends, an' stout an' hard further down. Whin tha poles was weel thrust under we heaved, an' heaved, an' heaved, and got it slanted o' one side, and drawed him out; an' thin it were too late, too late! A' tha brist was crushit in—frushed flesh and bone together. He jist muttered i' his throat, 'Tha little lass, tha little lass!' and then he turned him on his side, and hid his face upo' the sod. When we raised him he wur dead."

The voice of Ambrose sank very low; and where he leaned over his smithy door the tears fell slowly down his sun-bronzed cheeks.

"Alack a day!" sighed Daffe, softly. "Sure a better un niver drew breath i' the varsal world!"

"An' that's trew," Ambrose made answer, his voice hushed and very tender.

"He was varra changed like," murmured Daffe, his hand wandering amongst the golden blossoms of the

I

stonecrop. "He niver were the same crittur arter the lass went awa'. He niver were the same—niver. Ta seemed tew mak an auld man o' him a' at once."

"It did," said Ambrose, brokenly. "He couldna bear tew look na tew spik to nane o' us. He were bent i' body, an' gray o' head, that awfu' night when he kem back fra' the waking. It were fearfu' tew see; and we couldna dew naught. Th' ony thing as he'd take tew were Trust."

"Be dog alive?"

"Na. Trust he'd never quit o' Ben's grave. He wouldna take bit na drop. He wouldna be touchit; not whin he was clem would he be tempted awa'. And he died—jist tha fifth day arter his master."

"An' the wench? Hev' 'ee e'er heerd on her?"

"Niver—niver. Mappen she's dead and gone tew. She broke Ben's heart for sure; long ere tha ston' crushit life out o't."

"And wheer may he lie?"

Ambrose clenched his brawny hand, his eyes darkened, his swarthy face flushed duskily.

"Wheer? What think 'ee, Daffe? When we took o' him up for the burial, ta tha church ower theer beyant tha wood, the passon he stoppit us, a' tha gate of tha buryin' field. The passon he med long words, and sed as how a unb'liever sud niver rest i' blessed groun', sin he willna iver enter into the sight o' tha Lord. He sed as how Ben were black o' heart and wicked o' mind, an' niver set fute i' church-door, and niver ate o' tha sacrament bread, and niver not thocht o' God nor o' Devil; an' he wouldna say tha rites o'er him an' 'twere iver so, an' he wouldna let him lie i' tha holy earth, nor i' tha pale o' tha graveyard. Well, we couldna gae agin him—we poor min, an' he a squire and passon tew. Sae we took him back, five weary mile; and we brocht him here, and we dug his grave under them pines, and we pit a cross o' tha bark to mark the place, and we laid old Trust, when he died, by his side. I were mad with grief like, thin; it were awfu' ta ha' him forbad Christian burial."

"Dew it matter?" asked the gentle Daffe, wistfully. He had never been within church-doors himself.

Ambrose gave a long troubled sigh.

"Aweel! at first it seemed awfu'—awfu'! And to think as Ben 'ud niver see the face o' his God was mair fearfu' still. But as time gees on and on—I can see his grave fra' here, tha cross we cut is tha glimmer o' white on that stem ayont,—it dew seem as 'tis fitter like fer him to lie i' tha fresh free woods, wi' tha birds a' chirmin' abuve him, an' a' tha forest things as he minded a flyin', an' nestin', an' runnin', an' rejoicin' arount him. 'Tis allus so still there, an' peacefu'. 'Tis blue and blue now, wi' tha hy'cinths; and there's one bonnie mavis as dew make her home wi' each spring abuve the gravestone. 'Bout not meetin' his God, I dunno—I darena saw nowt anent it—but, for sure, it dew seem to me that we canna meet Him no better, nor fairer, than wi' lips that ha ne'er lied to man nor to woman, and wi' hands as niver hae harmed the poor dumb beasts nor the prattlin' birds. It dew seem so. I canna tell."

As the words died off his lips the sun fell yet more brightly through the avenues of the straight, dark, odorous pines; sweet silent winds swept up the dewy scents of mosses, and of leaves, and of wild hyacinths; and on the stillness of that lonely place there came one tremulous, tender sound. It was the sound of the mavis singing.

"I canna tell; but for sure it is well with him?" said Ambrose; and he bared his head, and bowed it humbly, as though in the voice of the mavis he heard the answer of God:

"It is well."

Ah! I trust that it may be so for you; that the sweetness of your arrogant dreams of an unshared eternity be not wholly a delusion; that for you—although to us you do deny it—there may be found pity, atonement, compensation, in some great Hereafter.

"I HAVE heard a very great many men and women call the crows carrion birds, and the jackals carrion beasts, with an infinite deal of disgust and much fine horror at what they were pleased to term 'feasting on corpses;' but I never yet heard any of them admit their own appetite for the rotten 'corpse' of a pheasant, or the putrid haunch of a deer, to be anything except the choice taste of an epicure!"

"But they do cook the corpses!" I remonstrated; whereupon she grinned with more meaning than ever.

"Exactly what I am saying, my dear. Their love of synonyms has made them forget that they are *carnivori*, because they talk so sweetly of the *cuisine*. A poor, blundering, honest, ignorant lion only kills and eats when the famine of his body forces him to obey that law of slaughter which is imposed on all created things, from the oyster to the man, by what we are told is the beautiful and beneficent economy of Creation. Of course, the lion is a brutal and bloodthirsty beast of prey, to be hunted down off the face of the earth as fast as may be. Whereas man—what does he do? He devours the livers of a dozen geese in one *pâté;* he has lobsters boiled alive, that the scarlet tint may look tempting to his palate; he has fish cut up or fried in all its living agonies, lest he should lose one *nuance* of its flavour; he has the calf and the lamb killed in their tender age, that he may eat dainty sweetbreads; he has quails and plovers slaughtered in the nesting-season, that he may taste a slice of their breasts; he crushes oysters in his teeth whilst life is in them; he has scores of birds and animals slain for one dinner, that

he may have the numberless dishes which fashion exacts ;
and then—all the time talking softly of *rissôle* and *mayon-
naise*, of *consommé* and *entremet*, of *croquette* and *côtelette*
—the dear *gourmet* discourses on his charming science,
and thanks God that he is not as the parded beasts that
prey !"

"Well," said I, sulkily, for I am fond myself of a good
vol-au-vent,—"well, you have said that eating is a law in
the economies—or the waste—of creation. Is it not well
to clothe a distasteful and barbaric necessity in a refining
guise and under an elegant nomenclature ?"

"Sophist !" said Fanfreluche, with much scorn, though
she herself is as keen an epicure and as suave a sophist,
for that matter, as I know,—"I never denied that it was
well for men to cheat themselves, through the art of their
cooks, into believing that they are not brutes and beasts
of prey—it is well exceedingly—for their vanity. Life is
sustained only by the destruction of life. Cookery, the
divine, can turn this horrible fact into a poetic idealism ;
can twine the butcher's knife with lilies, and hide the
carcass under roses. But I do assuredly think that, when
they sit down every night with their *menu* of twenty services, they should not call the poor lion bad names for
eating an antelope once a fortnight."

And, with the true consistency of preachers, Fanfreluche helped herself to a Madeira stewed kidney which
stood amongst other delicacies on the deserted luncheon
table.

"IF this play should succeed it will be a triumph of true
art," said another critical writer to Dudley Moore.

That great personage tapped his Louis-Quinze snuff-
box with some impatience.

"Pardon me, but it is not possible to have art at all
on the stage. Art is a pure idealism. You can have it

in a statue, a melody, a poem ; but you cannot have it on the stage, which is at its highest but a graphic realism. The very finest acting is only fine in proportion as it is an exact reproduction of physical life. How, then, can it be art, which is only great in proportion as it escapes from the physical life into the spiritual?"

"But may not dramatic art escape thither also?" asked the critic, who was young, and deferred to him.

"Impossible, sir. It is shackled with all the forms of earth, and—worse still—with all its shams and common-places. When we read *Othello*, we only behold the tem-pest of the passions and the wreck of a great soul ; but when we see *Othello*, we are affronted by the colour of the Moor's skin, and are brought face to face with the vulgarities of the bolster !"

"Then there is no use in a stage at all?"

"I am not prepared to conclude that. It is agreeable to a vast number of people : as a Frith or an O'Neil is agreeable to a vast number of people to whom an Ary Scheffer or a Delaroche would be unintelligible. It is better, perhaps, that this vast number should look at Friths and O'Neils than that they should never look on any painting at all. Now the stage paints rudely, often tawdrily ; still it does paint. It is better than nothing. I take it that the excellence, as the end, of histrionic art is to portray, to the minds of the many, poetic conceptions which, without such realistic rendering, would remain unknown and impalpable to all save the few. Histrionic art is at its greatest only when it is the follower and the interpreter of literature ; the actor translates the poet's meanings into the common tongue that is understood of the people. But how many on the miserable stage of this country have ever had either humility to perceive, or capability to achieve this?"

The other critic smiled.

"I imagine not one, in our day. Their view of their

profession is similar to Mrs. Delamere's, when Max Mon-
crief wrote that sparkling comedy for her. 'My dear,'
she said to him, 'why did you trouble yourself to put all
that wit and sense into it? We didn't want *that*. I
shall wear all my diamonds, and I have ordered three
splendid new dresses !'"

ALL day long the fowls kept it alive with sound and
movement; for of all mercurial and fussy things
there is nothing on the face of the earth to equal cocks
and hens. They have such an utterly exaggerated sense,
too, of their own importance; they make such a clacking
and clucking over every egg, such a scratching and
trumpeting over every morsel of treasure-trove, and such
a striding and stamping over every bit of well-worn
ground. On the whole, I think poultry have more humanity in them than any other race, footed or feathered;
and cocks certainly must have been the first creatures
that ever hit on the great art of advertising. Myself I
always fancy that the souls of this feathered tribe pass
into the bodies of journalists; but this may be a mere
baseless association of kindred ideas in my mind.

SHE kissed the dog on the forehead; then pointed to
the kreel of shells and seaweed on the red, smooth
piece of rock.
"Take care of them, dear Bronze," she murmured;
"and wait till I come back. Wait here."
She did not mean to command; she only meant to
console him by the appointment of some service.
Bronze looked in her face with eyes of woe and longing;
but he made no moan or sound, but only stretched him-

self beside the kreel on guard. I am always glad to think that as she went she turned, and kissed him once again.

The boat flew fast over the water. When boats leave you, and drag your heart with them, they always go like that ; and when they come, and your heart darts out to meet them, then they are so slow !

The boat flew like a seagull, the sun bright upon her sail. Bronze, left upon the rock, lifted his head and gave one long, low wail. It echoed woefully and terribly over the wide, quiet waters. They gave back no answer—not even the poor answer that lies in echo.

It was very still there. Nothing was in sight except that single little sail shining against the light, and flying —flying—flying.

Now and then you could hear a clock striking in the distant village, the faint crow of a cock, the far-off voices of children calling to one another.

The little sea-mouse stole athwart a pool ; the grey sea-crabs passed like a little army ; the tiny sea creatures that dwelt in rosy shells thrust their delicate heads from their houses to peep and wonder at the sun. But all was noiseless. How dared they make a sound, when that great sea, that was at once their life and death, was present with its never-ceasing " Hush ! "

Bronze never moved, and his eyes never turned from the little boat that went and left him there—the little boat that fast became merely a flash and speck of white against the azure air, no bigger than the breadth of a sea-gull's wings.

An hour drifted by. The church-clock on the cliffs had struck four times ; a deep-toned, weary bell, that tolled for every quarter, and must often have been heard, at dead of night, by dying men, drowning unshriven and unhouselled.

Suddenly the sand about us, so fawn-hued, smooth,

and beautifully ribbed, grew moist, and glistened with a gleam of water, like eyes that fill with tears.

Bronze never saw : he only watched the boat. A little later the water gushed above the sand, and, gathering in a frail rippling edge of foam, rolled up and broke upon the rock.

And still he never saw ; for still he watched the boat.

Awhile, and the water grew in volume, and filled the mouse's pool till it brimmed over, and bathed the dull grasses till they glowed like flowers ; and drew the sea-crabs and the tiny dwellers of the shells back once more into its wondrous living light.

And all around the fresh tide rose, silently thus about the rocks and stones ; gliding and glancing in all the channels of the shore, until the sands were covered, and the grasses gathered in, and all the creeping, hueless things were lost within its space ; and in the stead of them, and of the bronzed palm-leaves of weed, and of the great brown boulders gleaming in the sun, there was but one vast lagoon of shadowless bright water everywhere.

And still he never saw ; for still he watched the boat.

By this time the tide, rolling swiftly in before a strong sou'-wester, had risen midway against the rock on which we had been left, and was breaking froth and foam upon the rock's worn side. For this rock alone withstood the passage of the sea : there was naught else but this to break the even width of water. All other things save this had been subdued and reapen.

It was all deep water around ; and the water glowed a strange emerald green, like the green in a lizard or snake. The shore, that had looked so near, now seemed so far, far off ; and the woods were hidden in mist, and the cottages were all blurred with the brown of the cliff, and there came no sound of any sort from the land—no distant bell, no farm-bird's call, no echo of children's voices.

There was only one sound at all; and that was the low, soft, ceaseless murmuring of the tide as it glided inward.

The waters rose till they touched the crest of the rock; but still he never moved. Stretched out upon the stone, guarding the things of her trust, and with his eyes fastened on the sail which rose against the light, he waited thus—for death.

I was light, and a strong swimmer. I had been tossed on those waves from my birth. Buffeted, fatigued, blind with the salt sea-spray, drenched with the weight of the water, I struggled across that calm dread width of glassy coldness, and breathless reached the land.

By signs and cries I made them wot that something needed them at sea. They began to get ready a little boat, bringing it down from its wooden rest on high dry ground beneath the cliff. Whilst they pushed and dragged through the deep-furrowed sand I gazed seaward. The shore was raised; I could see straight athwart the waters. They now were level with the rock; and yet he had never moved.

The little skiff had passed round the bend of a bluff, and was out of his sight and ours.

The boat was pushed into the surf; they threw me in. They could see nothing, and trusted to my guidance.

I had skill enough to make them discover whither it was I wanted them to go. Then, looking in their eagerness whither my eyes went, they saw him on the rock, and with a sudden exercise of passionate vigour, bent to their oars and sent the boat against the hard opposing force of the resisting tide. For they perceived that, from some cause, he was motionless there, and could not use his strength; and they knew that it would be shame to their manhood if, within sight of their land, the creature who had succoured their brethren in the snow, and saved the two-year child from the storm, should perish before their sight on a calm and unfretted sea and in a full noon sun.

It was but a furlong to that rock; it was but the breadth of the beach, that at low water stretched uncovered; and yet how slowly the boat sped, with the ruthless tide sweeping it back as fast as the oars bore it forward!

So near we seemed to him that one would have thought a stone flung from us through the air would have lit far beyond him; and yet the space was enough, more than enough, to bar us from him, filled as it was with the strong adverse pressure of those low, swift, in-rushing waves.

The waters leaped above the summit of the rock, and for a moment covered him. A great shout went up from the rowers beside me. They strained in every nerve to reach him; and the roll of a fresh swell of water lifted the boat farther than their uttermost effort could achieve, but lifted her backward, backward to the land.

When the waters touched him he arose slowly, and stood at bay like a stag upon a headland, when the hounds rage behind, and in front yawns the fathomless lake.

He stood so that he still guarded the things of his trust; and his eyes were still turned seaward, watching for the vanished sail.

Once again the men, with a loud cry to him of courage and help, strained at their oars, and drove themselves a yard's breadth farther out. And once again the tide, with a rush of surf and shingle, swept the boat back, and seemed to bear her to the land as lightly as though she were a leaf with which a wind was playing.

The waters covered the surface of the rock. It sank from sight. The foam was white about his feet, and still he stood there—upon guard. Everywhere there was the brilliancy of noontide sun; everywhere there was the beaming calmness of the sea, that spread out, far and wide, in one vast sheet of light; from the wooded line of the shore there echoed the distant gaiety of a woman's laugh. A breeze, softly stirring through the warm air, brought with it from the land the scent of myrtle thickets and wild flowers. How horrible they were—the light, the calm, the mirth, the summer fragrance!

For one moment he stood there erect; his dark form sculptured, lion-like, against the warm yellow light of noon; about his feet the foam.

Then, all noiselessly, a great, curled, compact wave surged over him, breaking upon him, sweeping him away. The water spread out quickly, smooth and gleaming like the rest. He rose, grasping in his teeth the kreel of weed and shells.

He had waited until the last. Driven from the post he would not of himself forsake, the love of life awoke in him; he struggled against death.

Three times he sank, three times he rose. The sea was now strong, and deep, and swift of pace, rushing madly in; and he was cumbered with that weight of osier and of weed, which yet he never yielded, because it had been her trust. With each yard that the tide bore him forward, by so much it bore us backward. There was but the length of a spar between us, and yet it was enough!

He rose for the fourth time, his head above the surf, the kreel uplifted still, the sun-rays full upon his brown weary eyes, with all their silent agony and mute appeal. Then the tide, fuller, wilder, deeper with each wave that rolled, and washing as it went all things of the shore from their places, flung against him, as it swept on, a great rough limb of driftwood. It struck him as he rose; struck him across the brow. The wave rushed on; the tide came in; the black wood floated to the shore; he never rose again.

And scarcely that span of the length of a spar had parted us from him when he sank!

All the day through they searched, and searched with all the skill of men sea-born and sea-bred. The fisher, whose little child he had saved in the winter night, would not leave him to the things of the deep. And at sunset they found him, floating westward, in the calm water where the rays of the sun made it golden and warm. He was quite dead ; but in his teeth there still was clenched the osier kreel, washed empty of its freight.

They buried him there ; on the shore underneath the cliff, where a great wild knot of myrtle grows, and the honeysuckle blooms all over the sand. And when Lord Beltran in that autumn came, and heard how he had died in the fulfilling of a trust, he had a stone shapen and carved ; and set it against the cliff, amongst the leafage and flowers, high up where the highest winter tide will not come. And by his will the name of Bronze was cut on it in deep letters that will not wear out, and on which the sun will strike with every evening that it shall pass westward above the sea ; and beneath the name he bade three lines be chiselled likewise, and they are these :

"HE CHOSE DEATH RATHER THAN UNFAITHFULNESS.
HE KNEW NO BETTER.
HE WAS A DOG."

"THEY are all words. Creatures that take out their grief in crape and mortuary tablets can't feel very much."

"'There are many lamentations, from Lycidas to Lesbia, which prove that whether for a hero or a sparrow—" I began timidly to suggest.

"That's only a commonplace," snapped my lady. "They chatter and scribble ; they don't feel. They write stanzas of 'gush' on Maternity ; and tear the little bleating calf from its mother to bleed to death in a long, slow agony. They maunder twaddle about Infancy over some ugly red lump of human flesh, in whose creation their vanity happens to be involved ; and then go out and send the springtide lamb to the slaughter, and shoot the parent birds as they fly to the nest where their fledglings are screaming in hunger ! Pooh ! Did you never find out the value of their words? Some one of them has said that speech was given them to conceal their thoughts. It is true that they use it for that end ; but it was given them for this reason. At the time of the creation, when all except man had been made, the Angel of Life, who had been bidden to summon the world out of chaos, moving over the fresh and yet innocent earth, thought to himself, ' I have created so much that is doomed to suffer for ever, and for ever be mute ; I will now create an animal that shall be compensated for all suffering by listening to the sound of its own voluble chatter.' Whereon the Angel called Man into being, and cut the *frænum* of his tongue, which has clacked incessantly ever since, all through the silence of the centuries."

 THERE was once a dog, my dear, that was hit by three men, one after another, as they went by him where he lay in the sun ; and in return he bit them—deep—and they let him alone then, and ever after sought to propitiate him. Well, the first he bit in the arm, where there was a brand for deserting ; and the second he bit in the throat, where there was a hideous mole ; and the third he bit in the shoulder, where there was the mark of a secret camorra. Now, not one of these three durst speak of the wounds in places they all wished to hide ; and whenever afterwards they passed the dog, they gave him fair words, and sweet bones, and a wide berth. It is the dogs, and the satirists, and the libellers, and the states-

men who know how to bite like that—in the weak part—
that get let alone, and respected, and fed on the fat of the
land.

FOR him by whom a thirsty ear is lent to the world's
homage, the tocsin of feebleness, if not of failure, has
already sounded.

The gladness of the man is come when the crowds lisp
his name, and the gold fills his hand, and the women's
honeyed adulations buzz like golden bees about his path;
but how often is the greatness of the artist gone, and gone
for ever!

Because when the world denies you it is easy to deny.
the world; because when the bread is bitter it is easy
not to linger at the meal; because when the oil is low it
is easy to rise with dawn; because when the body is
without surfeit or temptation it is easy to rise above earth
on the wings of the spirit. Poverty is very terrible to
you, and kills your soul in you sometimes; but it is like
the northern blast that lashes men into Vikings; it is not
the soft, luscious south wind that lulls them into lotos-
eaters.

I HAVE grave doubts of Mrs. Siddons. She was a
goddess of the age of fret and fume, of stalk and
strut, of trilled R's and of nodding plumes. If we had
Siddons now I fear we should hiss; I am quite sure we
should yawn. She must have been Melpomene always;
Nature never.

OH, how wise you are and how just!—if there be a
spectacle on earth to rejoice the angels, it is your
treatment of the animals that you say God has given
unto you!

It is not for me, a little dog, to touch on such awful mysteries; but—sometimes—I wonder, if ever He ask you how you have dealt with His gift, what will you answer then?

If all your slaughtered millions should instead answer for you—if all the countless and unpitied dead, all the goaded, maddened beasts from forest and desert who were torn asunder in the holidays of Rome; and all the innocent, playful, gentle lives of little homebred creatures that have been racked by the knives, and torn by the poisons, and convulsed by the torments, of your modern Science, should, instead, answer, with one mighty voice, of a woe no longer inarticulate, of an accusation no more disregarded, what then? Well! Then, if it be done unto you as you have done, you will seek for mercy and find none in all the width of the universe; you will writhe, and none shall release you; you will pray, and none shall hear.

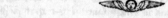

"THESE fine things don't make one's happiness," I murmured pensively to Fanfreluche.

"No, my dear, they don't," the little worldling admitted. "They do to women; they're so material, you see. They are angels—O yes, of course!—but they're uncommonly sharp angels where money and good living are concerned. Just watch them—watch the tail of their eye—when a cheque is being written or an *éprouvette* being brought to table. And after all, you know, minced chicken is a good deal nicer than dry bread. Of course we can easily be sentimental and above this sort of thing, when the chicken *is* in our mouths where we sit by the fire; but if we were gnawing wretched bones, out in the cold of the streets, I doubt if we should feel in such a sublime mood. All the praises of poverty are sung by the minstrel who has got a golden harp to chant them

on ; and all the encomiums on renunciation come from
your *bon viveur* who never denied himself aught in his
life !"

EMOTIONS are quite as detrimental to a dog's tail as
they are to a lady's complexion. Joseph Buona-
parte's American wife said to an American gentleman,
whom I heard quote her words, that she "never laughed
because it made wrinkles :" there is a good deal of wisdom
in that cachinatory abstinence. There is nothing in the
world that wears people (or dogs) so much as feeling of
any kind, tender, bitter, humoristic, or emotional.

How often you commend a fresh-coloured matron with
her daughters, and a rosy-cheeked hunting squire in his
saddle, who, with their half-century of years, yet look so
comely, so blooming, so clear-browed, and so smooth-
skinned. How often you distrust the weary delicate
creature, with the hectic flush of her rouge, in society;
and the worn, tired, colourless face of the man of the
world who takes her down to dinner. Well, to my fancy,
you may be utterly wrong. An easy egotism, a contented
sensualism, may have carried the first comfortably and
serenely through their bank-note-lined paradise of com-
mon-place existence. How shall you know what heart-
sickness in their youth, what aching desires for joys
never found, what sorrowful power of sympathy, what
fatal keenness of vision, have blanched the faded cheek,
and lined the weary mouth, of the other twain?

"SHEEP and men are very much alike," said Trust,
who thought both very poor creatures. "Very
much alike indeed. They go in flocks, and can't give
a reason why. They leave their fleece on any bramble
that is strong enough to insist on fleecing them. They

K

bleat loud at imagined evils, while they tumble straight into real dangers. And for going off the line, there's nothing like them. There may be pits, thorns, quagmires, spring-guns, what not, the other side of the hedge, but go off the straight track they will—and no dog can stop them. It's just the sheer love of straying. You may bark at them right and left; go they will, though they break their legs down a limekiln. Oh, men and sheep are wonderfully similar; take them all in all."

AH! you people never guess the infinite woe we dogs suffer in new homes, under strange tyrannies; you never heed how we shrink from unfamiliar hands, and shudder at unfamiliar voices, how lonely we feel in unknown places, how acutely we dread harshness, novelty, and scornful treatment. Dogs die oftentimes of severance from their masters; there is Greyfriars' Bobby now in Edinboro' town who never has been persuaded to leave his dead owner's grave all these many years through. You see such things, but you are indifferent to them. "It is only a dog," you say; "what matter if the brute fret to death?"

You don't understand it of course; you who so soon forget all your own dead—the mother that bore you, the mistress that loved you, the friend that fought with you shoulder to shoulder; and of course, also, you care nothing for the measureless blind pains, the mute helpless sorrows, the vague lonely terrors, that ache in our little dumb hearts.

LUCRETIUS has said how charming it is to stand under a shelter in a storm, and see another hurrying through its rain and wind; but a woman would

refine that sort of cruelty, and would not be quite content unless she had an umbrella beside her that she
refused to lend.

"OH, pooh, my dear!" cried Fanfreluche. "He has
robbed his host at cards, and abused his host
behind his back; to fulfil the whole duty of a nineteenth
century guest it only remains for him to betray his host
in love!"

"You think very ill of men?" I muttered; I was, indeed, slightly weary of her sceptical supercilious treatment of all things; your pseudo-philosopher, who will
always think he has plumbed the ocean with his silver-
topped cane, is a great bore sometimes.

"I think very well of men," returned Fanfreluche.
"You are mistaken, my dear. There are only two things
that they never are honest about—and that is their sport
and their women. When they get talking of their rock-
eters, or their runs, their pigeon-score, or their *bonnes
fortunes*, they always lie—quite unconsciously. And if
they miss their bird or their woman, isn't it always because the sun was in their eyes as they fired, or because
she wasn't half good-looking enough to try after?—bless
your heart, I know them!"

"If you do, you are not complimentary to them," I
grumbled.

"Can't help that, my dear," returned Fanfreluche.
"Gracious! whatever is there that stands the test of
knowing it well? I have heard Beltran say, that you find
out what an awful humbug the Staubbach is when you
go up to the top and see you can straddle across it. Well,
the Staubbach is just like everything in this life. Keep
your distance, and how well the creature looks!—all
veiled in its spray, and all bright with its prismatic
colours, so deep, and so vast, and so very impressive.

But just go up to the top, scale the crags of its character, and measure the height of its aspirations, and fathom the torrent of its passions, and sift how much is the foam of speech, and how little is the well-spring of thought. Well, my dear, it is a very uncommon creature if it don't turn out just like the Staubbach."

I THINK if you knew what you did, even the most thoughtless amongst you would not sanction with your praise, and encourage with your coin, the brutality that trains dancing-dogs.

Have human mimes if you will; it is natural to humanity to caper and grimace and act a part : but for pity's sake do not countenance the torture with which Avarice mercilessly trains us "dumb beasts" for the trade of tricks.

"The Clown-dog draws throngs to laugh and applaud," says some advertisement : yes, and I knew a very clever clown-dog once. His feet were blistered with the hot irons on which he had been taught to dance ; his teeth had been drawn lest he should use his natural weapons against his cowardly tyrants ; his skin beneath his short white hair was black with bruises ; though originally of magnificent courage, his spirit had been so broken by torture that he trembled if a leaf blew against him ; and his eyes—well, if the crowds that applauded him had once looked at those patient, wistful, quiet eyes, with their unutterable despair, those crowds would have laughed no more, unless they had indeed been devils.

Who has delivered us unto you to be thus tortured, and martyred? Who?—Oh, that awful eternal mystery that ye yourselves cannot explain !

BELIEVE me, it is the light or the darkness of our own fate that either gives "greenness to the grass and glory to the flower," or leaves both sickly, wan, and colourless. A little breadth of sunny lawn, the spreading shadow of a single beech, the gentle click of a little garden-gate, the scent of some simple summer roses—how fair these are in your memory because of a voice which then was on your ear, because of eyes that then gazed in your own. And the grandeur of Nile, and the lustre of the after-glow, and the solemn desolation of Carnac, and the wondrous beauty of the flushed sea of tossing reeds, are all cold, and dead, and valueless, because in those eyes no love now lies for you; because that voice, for you, is now for ever silent.

FOR, write as you will of the glory of poverty, and of the ennui of pleasure, there is no life like this life, wherein to the sight and the sense all things minister; wherefrom harsh discord and all unloveliness are banished: where the rare beauty of high-born women is common; where the passions at their wildest still sheathe themselves in courtesy's silver scabbard; where the daily habits of existence are made graceful and artistic; where grief, and woe, and feud, and futile longing for lost loves, can easiest be forgot in delicate laughter and in endless change. Artificial? Ah, well, it may be so! But since nevermore will you return to the life of the savage, to the wigwam of the squaw, it is best, methinks, that the Art of Living—the great *Savoir Vivre*—should be brought, as you seek to bring all other arts, up to uttermost perfection.

MEN are very much in society as women will them to be. Let a woman's society be composed of men gently born and bred, and if she find them either coarse or stupid, make answer to her—"You must have been coarse or stupid yourself."

And if she demur to the *tu quoque* as to a base and illogical form of argument, which we will grant that it usually is, remind her that the cream of a pasturage may be pure and rich, but if it pass into the hands of a clumsy farm serving-maid, then shall the cheese made thereof be neither Roquefort nor Stilton, but rough and flavourless and uneatable, "like a Banbury cheese, nothing but paring." Now, the influence of a woman's intelligence on the male intellects about her is as the churn to the cream : it can either enrich and utilise it, or impoverish and waste it. It is not too much to say that it almost invariably, in the present decadence of the salon and parrot-jabbering of the suffrage, has the latter effect alone.

HUMILIATION is a guest that only comes to those who have made ready his resting-place, and will give him a fair welcome. My father used to say to me, "Child, when you grow to womanhood, whether you be rich or poor, gentle or simple, as the balance of your life may turn for or against you, remember always this one thing—that no one can disgrace you save yourself. Dishonour is like the Aaron's Beard in the hedgerows, it can only poison if it be plucked." They call the bella-donna Aaron's Beard in the country, you know ; and it is true that the cattle, simple as they are, are never harmed by it ; just because, though it is always in their path, they never stop and taste it. I think it may just be so with us ; with any sort of evil.

"EVERY pleasure has its penalty. If a woman be celebrated, the world always thinks she must be wicked. If she's wise, she laughs. It is the bitter that you must take with the sweet, as you get the sorrel flavour with the softness of the cream, in your soup à la Bonne Femme. But the cream would clog without it, and the combination is piquant."

"Only to jaded palates," I retorted; for I have often tasted the Bonne Femme, and detest it.

By the way, what exquisite irony lies in some of your kitchen nomenclature!

ONCE at a great house in the west I saw a gathering on the young lord's coming of age. There were half the highest people in England there; and a little while before the tenantry went to their banquet in the marquees, the boy-peer and his guests were all out on the terraces and the lawns. With him was a very noble deer-hound, whom he had owned for four years.

Suddenly the hound, Red Comyn, left his titled master, and plunged head-foremost through the patrician crowd, and threw himself in wild raptures on to a poor, miserable, tattered, travelling cobbler, who had dared to creep in through the open gates and the happy crowds, hoping for a broken crust. Red Comyn pounced on him, and caressed him, and laid massive paws upon his shoulders, and gave him maddest welcome—this poor hungry man, in the midst of that aristocratic festival.

The cobbler could scarcely speak awhile; but when he got his breath, his arms were round the hound, and his eyes were wet with tears.

"Please pardon him, my lord," he said, all in a quiver and a tremble. "He was mine once from the time he was pupped for a whole two year; and he loved me, poor soul, and he ha'n't forgot. He don't know no better, my lord—he's only a dog."

No; he didn't know any better than to remember, and be faithful, and to recognise a friend, no matter in what woe or want. Ah, indeed, dogs are far behind you!

For the credit of "the order," it may be added that Red Comyn and the cobbler have parted no more, but dwell together still upon that young lord's lands.

APPEARANCES are so and so, hence facts must be so and so likewise, is Society's formula. This sounds mathematical and accurate; but as facts, nine times out of ten, belie appearances, the logic is very false. There is something, indeed, comically stupid in your satisfied belief in the surface of any parliamentary or public facts that may be presented to you, varnished out of all likeness to the truth by the suave periods of writer or speaker. But there is something tragically stupid about your dogged acceptation of any social construction of a private life, damned out of all possibility of redemption by the flippant deductions of chatter-box or of slanderer.

Now and then you poor humanities, who are always so dimly conscious that you are all lies to one another, get a glimpse of various truths from some cynical dead man's diary, or some statesman's secret papers. But you never are warned: you placidly continue greedily to gobble up, unexamined, the falsehoods of public men; and impudently to adjudicate on the unrevealed secrets of private lives.

YOU are given, very continually, to denouncing or lamenting the gradual encroachment of mob-rule. But, alas! whose fault, pray, is it that bill-discounters dwell as lords in ancient castles; that money-lenders

reign over old, time-honoured lands ; that low-born hire-
lings dare to address their master with a grin and sneer,
strong in the knowledge of his shameful secrets ; and
that the vile daughters of the populace are throned in
public places, made gorgeous with the jewels which, from
the heirlooms of a great patriciate, have fallen to be the
gew-gaws of a fashionable infamy ?

Ah, believe me, an aristocracy is a feudal fortress which,
though it has merciless beleaguers in the Jacquerie of
plebeian Envy, has yet no foe so deadly as its own in-
ternal traitor of Lost Dignity !

"BUT ye dunna get good wage ?" said the miner, with
practical wisdom.

"We doan't," confessed the East Anglian, "we doan't.
And that theer botherin' machinery as do the threshin',
and the reapin', and the sawin', and the mowin', hev a
ruined us. See !—in old time, when ground was frost-bit
or water-soaked, the min threshed in-doors, in barns, and
kep in work so. But now the machine, he dew all theer
is to dew, and dew it up so quick. Theer's a many more
min than theer be things to dew. In winter-time measter
he doan't want half o' us ; and we're just out o' labour ;
and we fall sick, cos o' naethin' to eat ; and goes tew
parish—able-bodied min strong as steers."

"Machine's o' use i' mill-work," suggested one of the
northerners.

"O' use ! ay, o' coorse 'tis o' use—tew tha measters,"
growled the East Anglian. "But if ye warn't needed at
yer mill cos the iron beast was a weavin' and a reelin'
and a dewin' of it all, how'd yer feel? Wi' six children,
mebbe, biggest ony seven or eight, a crazin' ye for bread.
And ye mayn't send 'em out, cos o' labour-laws, to pick
up a halfpenny for theerselves ; and tha passon be all

agin yer, cos ye warn't thrifty and didn't gev a penny for the forrin blacks out o' the six shillin' a week? Would yer think iron beast wor o' use thin? or would yer damn him hard?"

THE poetic faculty—as you call the insight and the sympathy which feels a divinity in all created things and a joy unutterable in the natural beauty of the earth —is lacking in the generality of women, notwithstanding their claims to the monopoly of emotion. If it be not, how comes it that women have given you no great poet since the days of Sappho?

It is women's deficiency in intellect, you will observe. Not a whit : it is women's deficiency in sympathy.

The greatness of a poet lies in the universality of his sympathies. And women are not sympathetic, because they are intensely self-centred.

ALL living things seemed to draw closer together in the perils and privations of the winter, as you men do in the frost of your frights or your sorrows. In summer —as in prosperity—every one is for himself, and is heedless of others because he needs nothing of them.

IT was covered, from the lowest of its stones to the top of its peaked roof, with a gigantic rose-thorn.

"Sure the noblest shrub as ever God have made," would Ben say, looking at its massive, cactus-like branches, with their red, waxen, tender-coloured berries. The cottage was very old, and the rose-thorn was the growth of centuries. Men's hands had never touched it. It had stretched where it would, ungoverned, unhampered, unarrested. It had a beautiful dusky glow about it always, from its peculiar thickness and its blended hues ; and in the chilly weather the little robin red-breasts would come and flutter into it, and screen themselves in its shelter from the cold, and make it rosier yet with the brightness of their little ruddy throats.

"Tha Christ-birds do allus seem safest like i' tha Christ-bush," Ben would say softly, breaking off the larger half of his portion of oaten cake, to crumble for the robins with the dawn. I never knew what he meant, though I saw he had some soft, grave, old-world story in his thoughts, that made the rose-thorn and the red-breasts both sacred to him.

" A H, my dear, you little dream the ecstatic delight that exists in Waste, for the vulgarity of a mind that has never enjoyed Possession, till it comes to riot at one blow in Spoliation !"

"I do wish you would answer me plainly," I said, sulkily, " without—without——"

"Epigrams !" she added, sharply ; "I daresay you do, my dear. Epigrams are the salts of life ; but they wither up the grasses of foolishness, and naturally the grasses hate to be sprinkled therewith."

W E are ill appreciated, we cynics ; on my honour if cynicism be not the highest homage to Virtue there is, I should like to know what Virtue wants. We sigh over her absence, and we glorify her perfections. But Virtue is always a trifle stuck-up, you know, and she is very difficult to please.

She is always looking uneasily out of the "tail of her eye" at her opposition-leader Sin, and wondering why Sin dresses so well, and drinks such very good wine. We

"cynics" tell her that under Sin's fine clothes there is a
breast cancer-eaten, and at the bottom of the wine there
is a bitter dreg called satiety; but Virtue does not much
heed that; like the woman she is, she only notes that
Sin drives a pair of ponies in the sunshine, while she herself is often left to plod wearily through the everlasting
falling rain. So she dubs us "cynics" and leaves us—
who can wonder if we won't follow her through the rain?
Sin smiles so merrily if she makes us pay toll at the end;
whereas Virtue—ah me, Virtue *will* find such virtue in
frowning!

WOMEN always put me in mind of that bird of yours,
the cuckoo.

Your poetry and your platitudes have all combined to
attach a most sentimental value to cuckoos and women.
All sorts of pretty phantasies surround them both; the
spring-tide of the year, the breath of early flowers, the
verse of old dead poets, the scent of sweet summer rains,
the light of bright dewy dawns—all these things you have
mingled with the thought of the cuckoo, till its first call
through the woods in April brings all these memories with
it. Just so in like manner have you entangled your poetic
ideals, your dreams of peace and purity, all divinities of
patience and of pity, all sweet saintly sacrifice and sorrow,
with your ideas of women.

Well—cuckoos and women, believe me, are very much
like each other, and not at all like your phantasy:—to
get a well-feathered nest without the trouble of making
it, and to keep easily in it themselves, no matter who may
turn out in the cold, is both cuckoo and woman all over;
and, while you quote Herrick and Wordsworth about
them as you walk in the dewy greenwood, they are busy
slaying the poor lonely fledglings, that their own young
may lie snug and warm.

"THEN everybody is a hypocrite?"

"Not a bit, child. We always like what we haven't got ; and people are quite honest very often in their professions, though they give the lie direct to them in their practice. People can talk themselves into believing that they believe anything. When the preacher discourses on the excellence of holiness, he may have been a thorough-going scamp all his life ; but it don't follow he's dishonest, because he's so accustomed to talk goody-goody talk that it runs off his lips as the thread off a reel——"

"But he must know he's a scamp?"

"Good gracious me, why should he? I have met a thousand scamps ; but I never met one who considered himself so. Self-knowledge isn't so common. Bless you, my dear, a man no more sees himself, as others see him, in a moral looking-glass, than he does in a mirror out of his dressing-box. I know a man who has forged bills, run off with his neighbour's wife, and left sixty thousand pounds odd in debts behind him ; but he only thinks himself 'a victim of circumstances'—honestly thinks it too. A man never is so honest as when he speaks well of himself. Men are always optimists when they look inwards, and pessimists when they look round them."

I yawned a little ; nothing is so pleasant, as I have known later, as to display your worldly wisdom in epigram and dissertation, but it is a trifle tedious to hear another person display theirs.

When you talk yourself, you think how witty, how original, how acute you are ; but when another does so, you are very apt to think only—What a crib from Rochefoucauld!

TWO LITTLE WOODEN SHOES.

BRUSSELS has stones that are sermons, or rather that are quaint, touching, illuminated legends of the middle ages, which those who run may read.

Brussels is a gay little city that lies as bright within its girdle of woodland as any butterfly that rests upon moss.

The city has its ways and wiles of Paris. It decks itself with white and gold. It has music under its trees and soldiers in its streets, and troops marching and counter-marching along its sunny avenues. It has blue and pink, and yellow and green, on its awnings and on its house-fronts. It has a merry open-air life on its pavements at little marble tables before little gay-coloured cafés. It has gilded balconies and tossing flags and comic operas, and leisurely pleasure-seekers, and tries always to believe and make the world believe that it is Paris in very truth.

But this is only the Brussels of the noblesse and the foreigners.

There is a Brussels that is better than this—a Brussels that belongs to the old burgher-life, to the artists and the craftsmen, to the master masons of Moyen-age, to the same spirit and soul that once filled the free men of Ghent and the citizens of Bruges and the besieged of Leyden, and the blood of Egmont and of Horne.

Down there by the water-side, where the old quaint walls lean over the yellow sluggish stream, and the green barrels of the Antwerp barges swing against the dusky piles of the crumbling bridges :

In the grey square desolate courts of the old palaces, where in cobwebbed galleries and silent chambers the Flemish tapestries drop to pieces :

In the great populous square, where, above the clamorous and rushing crowds, the majestic front of the Maison du Roi frowns against the sun, and the spires and pinnacles of the Burgomaster's gathering-halls tower into the sky in all the fantastic luxuriance of Gothic fancy :

Under the vast shadowy wings of angels in the stillness of the cathedral, across whose sunny aisles some little child goes slowly all alone, laden with lilies for the Feast of the Assumption, till their white glory hides its curly head :

In all strange quaint old-world niches withdrawn from men in silent grass-grown corners, where a twelfth-century corbel holds a pot of roses, or a Gothic arch yawns beneath a wool-warehouse, or a water-spout with a grinning faun's head laughs in the grim humour of the Moyenage above the bent head of a young lace-worker ;—

In all these, Brussels, although more worldly than her sisters of Ghent and Bruges, and far more worldly yet than her Teuton cousins of Freiburg and Nürnberg, Brussels is in her own way still like some monkish story, mixed up with the Romaunt of the Rose, or rather like some light French vaudeville, all jests and smiles, illustrated in motley contrast with helm and hauberk, cope and cowl, praying knights and fighting priests, winged griffins and nimbused saints, flame-breathing dragons and enamoured princes, all mingled together in the illuminated colours and the heroical grotesque romance of the Middle Ages.

And it was this side of the city that Bébée knew, and she loved it well and would not leave it for the market of the Madeleine.

IT was a warm grey evening, the streets were full; there were blossoms in all the balconies, and gay colours in all the dresses. The old tinker put his tools together and whispered to her—

"Bébée, as it is your feast-day, come and stroll in St. Hubert's gallery, and I will buy you a horn of sugar-plums or a ribbon, and we can see the puppet-show afterwards, eh?"

But the children were waiting at home: she would not spend the evening in the city; she only thought she would just kneel a moment in the cathedral and say a little prayer or two for a minute—the saints were so good in giving her so many friends.

There is something very touching in the Netherlander's relation with his Deity. It is all very vague to him; a jumble of veneration and familiarity, of sanctity and profanity, without any thought of being familiar, or any idea of being profane.

There is a homely poetry, an innocent affectionateness, in it characteristic of the people.

He talks to his good angel Michel, and to his friend that dear little Jesus, much as he would talk to the shoemaker over the way, or the cooper's child in the doorway.

It is a very unreasonable, foolish, clumsy sort of religion, this theology in wooden shoes; it is half grotesque, half pathetic; the grandmothers pass it on to the grandchildren, as they pass the bowl of potatoes round the stove in the long winter nights; it is as silly as possible, but it comforts them as they carry faggots over the frozen canals or wear their eyes blind over the squares of lace; and it has in it the supreme pathos of a perfect confidence, of an utter childlike and undoubting trust.

This had been taught to Bébée, and she went to sleep every night in the firm belief that the sixteen little angels of the Flemish prayer kept watch and ward over her bed.

SHE said her prayer, and thanked the saints for all their gifts and goodness, her clasped hands against her silver shield; her basket on the pavement by her; abovehead the sunset rays streaming purple and crimson and golden through the painted windows that are the wonder of the world.

When her prayer was done she still kneeled there; her head thrown back to watch the light; her hands clasped still; and on her upturned face the look that made the people say, "What does she see?—the angels or the dead?"

She forgot everything. She forgot the cherries at home, and the children even. She was looking upward at the stories of the painted panes; she was listening to the message of the dying sunrays; she was feeling vaguely, wistfully, unutterably the tender beauty of the sacred place and the awful wonder of the world in which she with her sixteen years was all alone, like a little blue cornflower amongst the wheat that goes for grist, and the barley that makes men drunk.

For she was alone, though she had so many friends. Quite alone sometimes, for God had been cruel to her, and had made her a lark without song.

HE went leisurely, travelling up the bright Meuse river, and across the monotony of the plains, then green with wheat a foot high, and musical with the many bells of the Easter kermesses in the quaint old-world villages.

There was something so novel, so sleepy, so harmless, so mediæval, in the Flemish life, that it soothed him. He had been swimming all his life in salt, sea-fed rapids; this sluggish, dull canal-water, mirroring between its rushes a life that had scarcely changed for centuries, had a charm for him.

L

He stayed awhile in Antwerpen. The town is ugly and beautiful; it is like a dull, quaint, grès de Flandre jug, that has precious stones set inside its rim. It is a burgher ledger of bales and barrels, of sale and barter, of loss and gain; but in the heart of it there are illuminated leaves of missal vellum, all gold and colour, and monkish story and heroic ballad, that could only have been executed in the days when Art was a religion.

"OH—to-morrow perhaps, or next year—or when Fate fancies.

"Or rather—when I choose," he thought to himself, and let his eyes rest with a certain pleasure on the little feet that went beside him in the grass, and the pretty neck that showed ever and again, as the frills of her linen bodice were blown back by the wind, and her own quick motion.

Bébée looked also up at him; he was very handsome, or seemed so to her, after the broad, blunt, characterless faces of the Brabantois around her. He walked with an easy grace, he was clad in picture-like velvets, he had a beautiful poetic head, and eyes like deep-brown waters, and a face like one of Jordaens' or Rembrandt's cavaliers in the galleries where she used to steal in of a Sunday, and look up at the paintings, and dream of what that world could be in which those people had lived.

"*You* are of the people of Rubes' country, are you not?" she asked him.

"Of what country, my dear?"

"Of the people that live in the gold frames," said Bébée, quite seriously. "In the galleries, you know. I know a charwoman that scrubs the floors of the Arenenberg, and she lets me in sometimes to look—and you are just like those great gentlemen in the gold frames, only you have not a hawk and a sword, and they always have.

I used to wonder where they came from, for they are not like any of us one bit, and the charwoman—she is Lisa Dredel, and lives in the street of the Pot d'Etain—always said, 'Dear heart, they all belong to Rubes' land—we never see their like now-a-days.' But *you* must come out of Rubes' land—at least, I think so ; do you not?"

He caught her meaning; he knew that Rubes was the homely abbreviation of Rubens, that all the Netherlanders used, and he guessed the idea that was reality to this little, lonely, fanciful mind.

"Perhaps I do," he answered her with a smile, for it was not worth his while to disabuse her thoughts of any imagination that glorified him to her. "Do you not want to see Rubes' world, little one? To see the gold and the grandeur, and the glitter of it all?—never to toil or get tired?—always to move in a pageant?—always to live like the hawks in the paintings you talk of, with silver bells hung round you, and a hood all sewn with pearls?"

"No," said Bébée, simply. "I should like to see it— just to see it, as one looks through a grating into the king's grapehouses here. But I should not like to live in it. I love my hut, and the starling, and the chickens— and what would the garden do without me?—and the children, and the old Annémie? I could not anyhow, anywhere be any happier than I am. There is only one thing I wish."

"And what is that?"

"To know something. Not to be so ignorant. Just look—I can read a little, it is true ; my hours, and the letters, and when Krebs brings in a newspaper I can read a little of it—not much. I know French well, because Antoine was French himself, and never did talk Flemish to me ; and they, being Flemish, cannot, of course, read the newspapers at all, and so think it very wonderful indeed in me. But what I want is to know things, to know all about what *was* before ever I was living. Ste.

Gudule now—they say it was built hundreds of years before; and Rubes again—they say he was a painter-king in Antwerpen before the oldest woman like Annémie ever began to count time. I am sure books tell you all those things, because I see the students coming and going with them; and when I saw once the millions of books in the Rue de la Musée, I asked the keeper what use they were for, and he said, 'to make men wise, my dear.' But Bac the cobbler, who was with me,—it was a fête day—Bac, *he* said, 'Do you not believe that, Bébée? they only muddle folk's brains; for one book tells them one thing, and another book another, and so on, till they are dazed with all the contrary lying; and if you see a bookish man, be sure you see a very poor creature who could not hoe a patch, or kill a pig, or stitch an upper-leather, were it ever so.' But I do not believe that Bac said right. Did he?"

"I am not sure. On the whole, I think it is the truest remark on literature I have ever heard, and one that shows great judgment in Bac. Well?"

"Well—sometimes, you know," said Bébée, not under-standing his answer, but pursuing her thoughts confiden-tially; "sometimes I talk like this to the neighbours, and they laugh at me. Because Mère Krebs says that when one knows how to spin, and sweep, and make bread, and say one's prayers, and milk a goat or a cow, it is all a woman wants to know this side of heaven. But for me, I cannot help it—when I look at those windows in the cathedral, or at those beautiful twisted little spires that are all over our Hôtel de Ville, I want to know who the men were that made them—what they did and thought—how they looked and spoke—how they learned to shape stone into leaves and grasses like that—how they could imagine all those angel faces on the glass. When I go alone in the quite early morning or at night when it is still—sometimes in winter I have to stay till it is dark over the lace—I hear their feet come after me, and they whisper to me close, 'Look what beautiful things we have done, Bébée, and you all forget us quite. We did what never will die, but our names are as dead as the stones.' And then I am so sorry for them and ashamed. And I want to know more. Can you tell me?"

He looked at her earnestly; her eyes were shining, her cheeks were warm, her little mouth was tremulous with eagerness.

"Did any one ever speak to you in that way?" he asked her.

"No," she answered him. "It comes into my head of itself. Sometimes I think the cathedral angels put it there. For the angels must be tired, you know; always pointing to God and always seeing men turn away. I used to tell Antoine sometimes. But he used to shake his head and say that it was no use thinking; most likely Ste. Gudule and St. Michael had set the church down in the night all ready made—why not? God made the trees, and they were more wonderful, he thought, for his part. And so perhaps they are, but that is no answer. And I do *want* to know. I want some one who will tell me,— and if you come out of Rubes' country as I think, no doubt you know everything, or remember it?"

He smiled.

THE Sun came and touched the lichens of the roof into gold.

Bébée smiled at it gaily as it rose above the tops of the trees, and shone on all the little villages scattered over the plains.

"Ah, dear Sun!" she cried to it. "I am going to be wise. I am going into great Rubes' country. I am going to hear of the Past and the Future. I am going to listen

to what the Poets say. The swallows never would tell
me anything; but now I shall know as much as they
know. Are you not glad for me, O Sun?"

The Sun came over the trees, and heard and said
nothing. If he had answered at all he must have said :—

"The only time when a human soul is either wise or
happy, is in that one single moment when the hour of
my own shining or of the moon's beaming seems to that
single soul to be past and present and future, to be at
once the creation and the end of all things. Faust knew
that; so will you."

But the Sun shone on and held his peace. He sees all
things ripen and fall. He can wait. He knows the end.
It is always the same.

He brings the fruit out of the peach-flower, and rounds
it and touches it into ruddiest rose and softest gold; but
the sun knows well that the peach must drop—whether
into the basket to be eaten by kings, or on to the turf to
be eaten by ants. What matter which very much after
all?

The Sun is not a cynic; he is only wise because he is
Life and He is death, the creator and the corrupter of all
things.

"AND where are you going so fast, as if those wooden
shoes of yours were sandals of mercury?"

"Mercury—is that a shoemaker?"

"No, my dear. He did a terrible bit of cobbling once,
when he made Woman. But he did not shoe her feet
with swiftness that I know of; she only runs away to be
run after, and if you do not pursue her, she comes back
—always."

Bébée did not understand at all.

"I thought God made women?" she said, a little awe-
stricken.

THERE is a dignity of peasants as well as of kings—
the dignity that comes from all absence of effort,
all freedom from pretence. Bébée had this, and she
had more still than this : she had the absolute simplicity of childhood with her still.

Some women have it still when they are fourscore.

PROSPER BAR, who is a Calvinist, always says,
"Do not mix up prayer and play ; you would not
cut a gherkin in your honey ;" but I do not know why
he called prayer a gherkin, because it is sweet enough—
sweeter than anything, I think.

THERE is not much change in the great Soignies
woods. They are aisles on aisles of beautiful green
trees, crossing and recrossing ; tunnels of dark foliage
that look endless ; long avenues of beech, of oak, of elm,
or of fir, with the bracken and the brushwood growing
dense between ; a delicious forest growth everywhere,
shady even at noon, and, by a little past midday, dusky
as evening ; with the forest fragrance, sweet and dewy,
all about, and under the fern the stirring of wild game,
and the white gleam of little rabbits, and the sound of
the wings of birds.

Soignies is not legend-haunted like the Black Forest,
nor king-haunted like Fontainebleau, nor sovereign of
two historic streams like the brave woods of Heidel-
berg ; nor wild and romantic, and broken with black
rocks, and poetised by the shade of Jaques, and swept
through by a perfect river, like its neighbours of Ar-
dennes ; nor throned aloft on mighty mountains like the
majestic oak glades of the Swabian hills of the ivory-
carvers.

Soignies is only a Flemish forest in a plain, throwing its shadow over corn-fields and cattle-pastures, with no panorama beyond it and no wonders in its depth. But it is a fresh, bold, beautiful forest for all that.

It has only green leaves to give—green leaves always, league after league; but there is about it that vague mystery which all forests have, and this universe of leaves seems boundless, and Pan might dwell in it, and St. Hubert, and John Keats.

"I AM going to learn to be very wise, dear," she told them; "I shall not have time to dance or to play."

"But people are not merry when they are wise, Bébée," said Franz, the biggest boy.

"Perhaps not," said Bébée; "but one cannot be everything, you know, Franz."

"But surely you would rather be merry than anything else?"

"I think there is something better, Franz. I am not sure; I want to find out; I will tell you when I know."

"Who has put that into your head, Bébée?"

"The angels in the Cathedral," she told them, and the children were awed and left her, and went away to play blindman's buff by themselves on the grass by the swan's water.

"But for all that the angels have said it," said Franz to his sisters, "I cannot see what good it will be to her to be wise, if she will not care any longer afterwards for almond gingerbread and currant cake."

TO vice, innocence must always seem only a superior kind of chicanery.

" AY, dear; when the frost kills your brave rosebush,
root and bud, do you think of the thorns that
pricked you, or only of the fair sweet-smelling things
that flowered all your summer?"

FLOWERS belong to fairyland; the flowers and the
birds, and the butterflies are all that the world has
kept of its golden age; the only perfectly beautiful things
on earth, joyous, innocent, half divine, useless, say they
who are wiser than God.

WHEN the day was done, Bébée gave a quick sigh
as she looked across the square. She had so
wanted to tell him that she was not ungrateful, and she
had a little moss-rose ready, with a sprig of sweetbriar,
and a tiny spray of maiden-hair fern that grew under
the willows, which she had kept covered up with a leaf
of sycamore all the day long.

No one would have it now.

The child went out of the place sadly, as the carillon
rang. There was only the moss-rose in her basket, and
the red and white currants that had been given her for
her dinner.

She went along the twisting, many-coloured, quaintly-
fashioned streets, till she came to the water-side.

It is very ancient, there still; there are all manner of
old buildings, black and brown and grey, peaked roofs,
gabled windows, arched doors, crumbling bridges, twisted
galleries leaning to touch the dark surface of the canal,
dusky wharves crowded with barrels, and bales, and
cattle, and timber, and all the various freightage that
the good ships come and go with all the year round, to
and from the Zuyder Zee, and the Baltic water, and the

wild Northumbrian shores, and the iron-bound Scottish headlands, and the pretty grey Norman seaports, and the white sandy dunes of Holland, with the toy towns and the straight poplar-trees.

Bébée was fond of watching the brigs and barges, that looked so big to her, with their national flags flying, and their tall masts standing thick as grass, and their tawny sails flapping in the wind, and about them the sweet, strong smell of that strange, unknown thing, the sea.

Sometimes the sailors would talk with her; sometimes some old salt, sitting astride of a cask, would tell her a mariner's tale of far-away lands and mysteries of the deep; sometimes some curly-headed cabin-boy would give her a shell or a plume of seaweed, and try and make her understand what the wonderful wild water was like, which was not quiet and sluggish and dusky as this canal was, but was for ever changing and moving, and curling and leaping, and making itself now blue as her eyes, now black as that thunder-cloud, now white as the snow that the winter wind tossed, now pearl-hued and opaline as the convolvulus that blew in her own garden.

And Bébée would listen, with the shell in her lap, and try to understand, and gaze at the ships and then at the sky beyond them, and try to figure to herself those strange countries, to which these ships were always going, and saw in fancy all the blossoming orchard province of green France, and all the fir-clothed hills and rushing rivers of the snow-locked Swedish shore, and saw too, doubtless, many lands that had no place at all except in dream-land, and were more beautiful even than the beauty of the earth, as poets' countries are, to their own sorrow, oftentimes.

But this dull day Bébée did not go down upon the wharf; she did not want the sailor's tales; she saw the masts and the bits of bunting that streamed from them,

and they made her restless, which they had never done
before. Instead she went in at a dark old door and
climbed up a steep staircase that went up and up and
up, as though she were mounting Ste. Gudule's belfry
towers ; and at the top of it entered a little chamber in
the roof, where one square unglazed hole that served for
light looked out upon the canal, with all its crowded
craft, from the dainty schooner yacht, fresh as gilding
and holystone could make her, that was running for
pleasure to the Scheldt, to the rude, clumsy coal-barge,
black as night, that bore the rough diamonds of Belgium
to the snow-buried roofs of Christiania and Stromsöon.

In the little dark attic there was a very old woman in
a red petticoat and a high cap, who sat against the
window, and pricked out lace patterns with a pin on
thick paper. She was eighty-five years old, and could
hardly keep body and soul together.

Bébée, running to her, kissed her.

"O mother Annémie, look here! Beautiful red and
white currants, and a roll ; I saved them for you. They
are the first currants we have seen this year. Me? oh,
for me, I have eaten more than are good ! You know I
pick fruit like a sparrow, always. Dear mother Annémie,
are you better? Are you quite sure you are better to-
day ? "

The little old withered woman, brown as a walnut and
meagre as a rush, took the currants, and smiled with a
childish glee, and began to eat them, blessing the child
with each crumb she broke off the bread.

"Why had you not a grandmother of your own, my
little one?" she mumbled. "How good you would have
been to her, Bébée?"

"Yes," said Bébée seriously, but her mind could not
grasp the idea. It was easier for her to believe the
fanciful lily-parentage of Antoine's stories. "How much
work have you done, Annémie? Oh, all that? all that?

But there is enough for a week. You work too early and too late, you dear Annémie."

"Nay, Bébée, when one has to get one's bread, that cannot be. But I am afraid my eyes are failing. That rose now, is it well done?"

"Beautifully done. Would the Baës take them if they were not? You know he is one that cuts every centime in four pieces."

"Ah! sharp enough, sharp enough—that is true. But I am always afraid of my eyes. I do not see the flags out there so well as I used to do."

"Because the sun is so bright, Annémie; that is all. I myself, when I have been sitting all day in the Place in the light, the flowers look pale to me. And you know it is not age with *me*, Annémie?"

The old woman and the young girl laughed together at that droll idea.

"You have a merry heart, dear little one," said old Annémie. "The saints keep it to you always."

"May I tidy the room a little?"

"To be sure, dear, and thank you too. I have not much time, you see; and somehow my back aches badly when I stoop."

"And it is so damp here for you, over all that water!" said Bébée, as she swept and dusted and set to rights the tiny place, and put in a little broken pot a few sprays of honeysuckle and rosemary that she had brought with her. "It is so damp here. You should have come and lived in my hut with me, Annémie, and sat out under the vine all day, and looked after the chickens for me when I was in the town. They are such mischievous little souls; as soon as my back is turned one or other is sure to push through the roof, and get out amongst the flower-beds. Will you never change your mind, and live with me, Annémie? I am sure you would be happy, and the starling says your name quite plain, and he is such a

funny bird to talk to ; you never would tire of him. Will
you never come ? It is so bright there, and green and
sweet-smelling, and to think you never even have seen
it !—and the swans and all,—it is a shame."

"No, dear," said old Annémie, eating her last bunch
of currants. "You have said so so often, and you are
good and mean it, that I know. But I could not leave
the water. It would kill me.

"Out of this window you know I saw my Jeannot's
brig go away—away—away—till the masts were lost in
the mists. Going with iron to Norway ; the Fleur
d'Epine of this town, a good ship, and a sure, and he
her mate ; and as proud as might be, and with a little
blest Mary in lead round his throat.

"She was to be back in port in eight months bringing
timber. Eight months—that brought Easter time.

"But she never came. Never, never, never, you know.

"I sat here watching them come and go, and my
child sickened and died, and the summer passed, and
the autumn, and all the while I looked—looked—looked ;
for the brigs are all much alike ; only his I always saw as
soon as she hove in sight because he tied a hank of flax
to her mizzen mast ; and when he was home safe and
sound I spun the hank into hose for him ; that was a
fancy of his, and for eleven voyages, one on another, he
had never missed to tie the flax nor I to spin the hose.

"But the hank of flax I never saw this time ; nor the
brave brig ; nor my good man with his sunny blue eyes.

"Only one day in winter, when the great blocks of ice
were smashing hither and thither, a coaster came in and
brought tidings of how off in the Danish waters they had
come on a waterlogged brig, and had boarded her, and
had found her empty, and her hull riven in two, and her
crew all drowned and dead beyond any manner of doubt.
And on her stern there was her name painted white, the
Fleur d'Epine, of Brussels, as plain as name could be ;

and that was all we ever knew—what evil had struck her, or how they had perished, nobody ever told.

"Only the coaster brought that bit of beam away, with the Fleur d'Epine writ clear upon it.

"But you see I never *know* my man is dead.

"Any day—who can say?—any of those ships may bring him aboard of her, and he may leap out on the wharf there, and come running up the stairs as he used to do, and cry, in his merry voice, 'Annémie, Annémie, here is more flax to spin, here is more hose to weave!' For that was always his homeward word; no matter whether he had had fair weather or foul, he always knotted the flax to his mast-head.

"So you see, dear, I could not leave here. For what if he came and found me away? He would say it was an odd fashion of mourning for him.

"And I could not do without the window, you know. I can watch all the brigs come in ; and I can smell the shipping smell that I have loved all the days of my life ; and I can see the lads heaving, and climbing, and furling, and mending their bits of canvas, and hauling their flags up and down.

"And then who can say?—the sea never took him, I think—I think I shall hear his voice before I die.

"For they do say that God is good."

Bébée sweeping very noiselessly, listened, and her eyes grew wistful and wondering. She had heard the story a thousand times ; always in different words, but always the same little tale, and she knew how old Annémie was deaf to all the bells that tolled the time, and blind to all the whiteness of her hair, and all the wrinkles of her face, and only thought of her sea-slain lover as he had been in the days of her youth.

WHEN we suffer very much ourselves, anything that smiles in the sun seems cruel—a child, a bird, a dragonfly—nay, even a fluttering ribbon, or a spear-grass that waves in the wind.

BÉBÉE, whose religion was the sweetest and vaguest mingling of Pagan and Christian myths, and whose faith in fairies and in saints was exactly equal in strength and in ignorance—Bébée filled the delf pot anew carefully, then knelt down on the turf in that little green corner, and prayed in devout hopeful childish good faith to the awful unknown Powers who were to her only as gentle guides and kindly playmates.

Was she too familiar with the Holy Mother?

She was almost fearful that she was; but then the Holy Mother loved flowers so well, Bébée could not feel aloof from her, nor be afraid.

"When one cuts the best blossoms for her, and tries to be good, and never tells a lie," thought Bébée, "I am quite sure, as she loves the lilies, that she will never altogether forget me."

THE loveliest love is that which dreams high above all storms, unsoiled by all burdens; but, perhaps, the strongest love is that which, whilst it adores, drags its feet through mire, and burns its brow in heat for the thing beloved.

IT is, perhaps, the most beautiful square in all Northern Europe, with its black timbers and gilded carvings, and blazoned windows, and majestic scutcheons, and fantastic pinnacles. This Bébée did not know, but she loved it, and she sat resolutely in front of the Broodhuis, selling her flowers, smiling, chatting, helping the old woman, counting her little gains, eating her bit of bread at noonday like any other market girl; but, at times, glancing up to the stately towers and the blue sky, with a look on her face that made the old tinker and cobbler whisper together—"What does she see there?—the dead people or the angels?"

The truth was that even Bébée herself did not know very surely what she saw—something that was still nearer to her than even this kindly crowd that loved her. That was all she could have said had anybody asked her.

But none did.

No one wanted to hear what the dead said; and for the angels, the tinker and the cobbler were of opinion that one had only too much of them sculptured about everywhere, and shining on all the casements—in reverence be it spoken of course.

FAME.

"THERE is no soul in them," he muttered, and he set
down his lamp and frowned; a sullen mechanical
art made him angered like an insult to heaven; and these
were soulless; their drawing was fine, their anatomy faultless, their proportions and perspective excellent; but there
all merit ended. They were worse than faulty—they were
commonplace. There is no sin in Art so deadly as that.

HE had been only a poor lad, a coppersmith's son,
here in Munich; one among many, and beaten
and cursed at home very often for mooning over folly
when others were hard at work. But he had minded
neither curse nor blow. He had always said to himself,
"I am a painter." Whilst camps were soaked with blood
and echoing only the trumpets of war, he had only seen
the sweet divine smile of Art. He had gone barefoot to
Italy for love of it, and had studied, and laboured, and
worshipped, and been full of the fever of great effort and
content with the sublime peace of conscious power. He
had believed in himself: it is much. But it is not all.
As years had slid away and the world of men would not
believe in him, this noble faith in himself grew a weary
and bitter thing. One shadow climbed the hills of the

M

long years with him and was always by his side : this
constant companion was Failure.

Fame is very capricious, but Failure is seldom incon-
stant. Where it once clings, there it tarries.

IT was a brilliant and gay day in Munich. It was the
beginning of a Bavarian summer, with the great
plain like a sea of grass with flowers for its foam, and
the distant Alps of Tyrol and Vorarlberg clearly seen in
warm, transparent, buoyant weather.

Down by the winding ways of the river there were
birch and beechen thickets in glory of leaf ; big water-
lilies spread their white beauty against the old black
timbers of the water-mills ; and in the quaint, ancient
places of the old streets, under the gables and beams,
pots of basil, and strings of green pease, and baskets
of sweet-smelling gillyflowers and other fragrant old-
fashioned things, blossomed wherever there was a
breadth of blue sky over them or a maiden's hand
within ; whilst above the towers and steeples, above the
clanging bells of the Domkirche and the melon-shaped
crest of the Frauenkirche, and all the cupolas and spires
and minarets in which the city abounds, the pigeons
went whirling and wheeling from five at sunrise to seven
of sunset, flocks of grey and blue and black and white,
happy as only birds can be, and as only birds can be
when they are doves of Venice or of Munich, with all
the city's hearths and homes for their granaries, and
with the sun and the clouds for their royal estate.

In the wide, dull new town it was dusty and hot ; the
big squares were empty and garish-looking ; the blistering
frescoes on the buildings were gaudy and out of place ;
the porticoes and friezes were naked and staring, and
wanted all that belongs to them in Italy. All the deep,
intense shadows, the sultry air, the sense of immeasurable

space and of unending light, the half-naked figures graceful as a plume of maize, the vast projecting roofs, the
spouts of tossing water, the brown bare-foot straw-plaiter
passing in a broad path of sunshine, the old bronze lamp
above the painted shrine, the gateway framing the ethereal
landscape of amethystine horizons and silvery olive ways
—they want all these, do these classic porticoes and pedi-
ments of Italy, and they seem to stare, conscious of a
discordance and a lack of harmony in the German air.
But in the old town there is beauty still ; in the timbered
house-fronts, in the barred and sculptured casements, in
the mighty gables, in the gilded and pictured signs, in
the sunburnt walls, in the grey churches, in the furriers'
stalls, in the toysellers' workshops, in the beetling fortresses, in the picturesque waysides, here is the old
Munich of the Minnesingers and master masons, of the
burghers and the *burschen,* of the Schefflertanz, and of
the merry Christchild Fair. And old Munich keeps all
to itself, whether with winter snow on its eaves, or
summer leaves in its lattices ; and here the maidens still
wear coloured kerchiefs on their heads and clattering
shoes on their feet ; and here the students still look
like etchings for old ballads, with long hair on their
shoulders and grey cloaks worn jauntily ; and here
something of the odour and aspect of the Middle Ages
lingers as about an illuminated roll of vellum that has
lain long put away and forgotten in a desk, with faded
rose-leaves and a miniature that has no name.

The Munich of builder-king Ludwig is grand, no doubt,
and tedious and utterly out of place, with mountains of
marble and granite, and acres of canvas more or less
divine, and vast straight streets that make one weep
from weariness, and frescoed walls with nude women
that seem to shiver in the bitter Alpine winds ; it is
great, no doubt, but ponderously unlovely, like the bronze
Bavaria that looks over the plain, who can hold six men

in her head, but can never get fire in her eyes nor meaning
in her mouth—clumsy Athenæ-Artemis that she is.

New Munich, striving to be Athens or Rome, is monotonous and tiresome, but old Munich is quaint and humble,
and historical and romancical, with its wooden pavements
under foot, and its clouds of doves above head; indeed,
has so much beauty of its own, like any old painted
Missal or golden goblet of the *moyen âge*, that it seems
incredible to think that any man could ever have had
the heart to send the hammers of masons against it, and
set up bald walls of plaster in its stead. Wandering in
old Munich—there is not much of it left, alas!—is like
reading a black-letter ballad about Henry the Lion or
Kaiser Max; it has sombre nooks and corners, bright
gleams of stained casements, bold oriels, and sculptured
shields, arcades and arches, towers and turrets, light and
shade, harmony and irregularity, all, in a word, that old
cities have, and old Teutonic cities beyond all others;
and when the Metzgersprung is in full riot round the
Marienplatz, or on Corpus Christi day, when the King
and the Court and the Church, the guilds and the senate
and the magistracy, all go humbly through the flower-
strewn streets, it is easy to forget the present and to
think that one is still in the old days with the monks,
who gave their name to it, tranquil in their work-rooms
and the sound of battle all over the lands around them.

It was the Corpus Christi day in Munich now, and the
whole city, the new and the old, had hung itself with garlands and draperies, with pictures and evergreens, with
flags and tapestries, and the grand procession had passed
to and from the church, and the archbishop had blessed
the people, and the king had bared his handsome head
to the sun and the Holy Ghost, and it was all over for
the year, and the people were all happy and satisfied and
sure that God was with them and their town; especially
the people of the old quarters, who most loved and

clung to these ceremonials and feasts ; good God-fearing
families, labouring hard, living honestly and wholesomely,
gay also in a quiet, mirthful, innocent fashion—much such
people as their forefathers were before them, in days when
Gustavus Adolphus called their city the golden saddle on
the lean horse.

The lean horse, by which he meant the sterile plains,
which yield little except hay, looks rich with verdure in
the mellow afternoon light, when midsummer is come,
and the whole populace, men, women, and children, on
Sundays and feast-days pour out of the city gates eagerly
to their own little festivities under the cherry-trees of the
little blue and white coffee-houses along the course of
the river, when the beanflowers are in bloom. For out
of the old city you go easily beyond the walls to the
grey glacier water of " Isar rolling rapidly," not red with
blood now as after Hohenlinden, but brilliant and bois-
terous always, with washerwomen leaning over it with
bare arms, and dogs wading where rushes and dams
break the current, and the hay blowing breast-high
along the banks, and the students chasing the girls
through it, and every now and then upon the wind the
music of a guitar, light and dancing, or sad and slow,
according as goes the heart of the player that tunes it.
At this season Bavaria grows green, and all is fresh and
radiant. Outside the town all the country is a sheet of
cherry-blossom and of clover. Night and day, carts full
of merrymakers rattle out under the alders to the dancing
places amongst the pastures, or to the *Sommerfrischen*
of their country friends. Whoever has a kreuzer to spend
will have a draft of beer and a whiff of the lilac-scented
air, and the old will sit down and smoke their painted
pipes under the eaves of their favourite *Gasthof*, and the
young will roam with their best-loved maidens through
the shadows of the Anlagen, or still farther on under the
high beech-trees of Grosshesslohe.

MOTHS.

THE ear has its ecstasy as have other senses.

AS there is love without dominion, so there is dominion without love.

WHEN Fame stands by us all alone, she is an angel clad in light and strength; but when Love touches her she drops her sword, and fades away, ghostlike and ashamed.

SOCIETY only thought her—unamiable. True, she never said an unkind thing, or did one; she never hurt man or woman; she was generous to a fault; and to aid even people she despised would give herself trouble unending. But these are serious, simple qualities which do not show much, and are soon forgotten by those who benefit from them. Had she laughed more, danced more taken more kindly to the fools and their follies, she might have been acid of tongue and niggard of sympathy; the world would have thought her much more amiable.

" I F she would only listen to me !" thought her mother,
in the superior wisdom of her popular little life.
"If she would only kiss a few women in the morning,
and flirt with a few men in the evening, it would set
her all right with them in a month. It is no use doing
good to anybody ; they only hate you for it. You have
seen them in their straits ; it is like seeing them without
their wig or their teeth ; they never forgive it. But to be
pleasant, always to be pleasant, that is the thing. And
after all it costs nothing."

M ARRIAGE, as our world sees it, is simply a conve-
nience ; a somewhat clumsy contrivance to tide
over a social difficulty.

A SIN ! did the world know of such a thing? Hardly.
Now and then, for sake of its traditions, the world
took some hapless boy, or some still yet unhappier woman,
and pilloried one of them, and drove them out under a
shower of stones, selecting them by caprice, persecuting
them without justice, slaying them because they were
friendless. But that was all. For the most part sin was
an obsolete thing, archaic and unheard of.

M USIC is not a science, any more than poetry is. It
is a sublime instinct, like genius of all kinds.

C HARITY in various guises is an intruder the poor
see often ; but courtesy and delicacy are visitors
with which they are seldom honoured.

THERE is no shame more bitter to endure than to despise oneself. It is harder to keep true to high laws and pure instincts in modern society than it was in the days of martyrdom.

ONE weeps for the death of children, but perhaps the change of them into callous men and women is a sadder change to see after all.

HONOUR is an old-world thing, but it smells sweet to those in whose hand it is strong.

YOUNG lives are tossed upon the stream of life like rose-leaves on a fast-running river, and the rose-leaves are blamed if the river be too strong and too swift for them and they perish. It is the fault of the rose-leaves.

EVERY pretty woman should be a flirt, every clever woman a politician; the aim, the animus, the intrigue, the rivalry which accompany each of these pursuits make the salt without which the great dinner were tasteless.

IN these old Austrian towns the churches are always very reverent places; dark and tranquil; overladen, indeed, with ornament and image, but too full of shadow for these to much offend; there is the scent of centuries of incense; the walls are yellow with the damp of ages. Mountain suzerains and bold reiters, whose deeds are still sung of in twilight to the zither, deep beneath the moss-grown pavement; their shields and crowns are worn flat to the stone they were embossed on by the passing feet of generations of worshippers. High above in the darkness there is always some colossal carved Christs. Through the half-opened iron-studded door there is always the smell of pinewood, the gleam of water, the greenness of Alpine grass; often, too, there is the silvery falling of rain, and the fresh smell of it comes through the church by whose black benches and dim lamps there will be sure to be some old bent woman praying.

THE moths will eat all that fine delicate feeling away, little by little; the moths of the world will eat the unselfishness first, and then the innocence, and then the honesty, and then the decency; no one will see them eating, no one will see the havoc being wrought, but little by little the fine fabric will go, and in its place will be dust. Ah, the pity of it! The pity of it! The webs come out of the great weaver's loom lovely enough, but the moths of the world eat them all.

SHE had five hundred dear friends, but this one she was really fond of; that is to say, she never said anything bad of her, and only laughed at her good-naturedly when she had left a room; and this abstinence is as strong a mark of sincerity now-a-days as dying for another used to be in the old days of strong feeling and the foolish expression of them.

GRATITUDE is such an unpleasant quality, you know; there is always a grudge behind it!

THE richest soil always bears the rankest mushrooms: France is always bearing mushrooms.

POSITION, she thought, was the only thing that, like old wine or oak furniture, improved with years.

POSITION is a pillory: sometimes they pelt one with rose-leaves, and sometimes with rotten eggs, but one is for ever in the pillory!

WE are too afraid of death: that fear is the shame of Christianity.

HE never could prevail on his vanity to break with her, lest men should think she had broken with him.

SHE would go grandly to the guillotine, but she will never understand her own times. She has dignity; we have not a scrap; we have forgotten what it was like; we go into a passion at the amount of our bills; we play and never pay; we smoke and we wrangle; we laugh loud, much too loud; we inspire nothing unless, now and then, a bad war or a disastrous speculation; we live showily, noisily, meanly, gaudily.

BIG brains do not easily hold trifles . . . little packets of starch that this world thinks are the staff of life.

PEHL, like a young girl, is prettiest in the morning.
Pehl is calm and sedate, and simple and decorous.
Pehl is like some tender, fair, wholesome yet patrician
beauty, like the pretty aristocratic Charlotte in Kaul-
bach's picture, who cuts the bread-and-butter, yet looks
a patrician. Pehl has nothing of the *belle petite,* like
her sister of Baden ; nothing of the titled *cocadetta,* like
her cousin of Monaco ; Pehl does not gamble or riot or
conduct herself madly in any way ; she is a little old-
fashioned still in a courtly way ; she has a little rusticity
still in her elegant manners ; she is like the noble dames
of the past ages, who were so high of rank and so proud
of habit, yet were not above the distilling-room and the
spinning-wheel ; who were quiet, serious, sweet, and smelt
of the rose-leaves with which they filled their big jars.

THE pity of modern Society is that all its habits make
as effectual a disguise morally as our domino in
carnival does physically. Everybody looks just like
everybody else. Perhaps, as under the domino, so under
the appearance, there may be great nobility or great
deformity ; but all look alike. Were Socrates amongst
us, he would only look like a club bore ; and were there
Messalina, she would only look—well—look much like
our Duchesse Jeunne !

SHE did not know that from these swamps of flattery,
intrigue, envy, rivalry, and emulation there rises a
miasma which scarcely the healthiest lungs can withstand. She did not know that though many may be
indifferent to the tempting of men, few indeed are impenetrable to the smile and the sneer of women ; that
to live your own life in the midst of the world is a harder

thing than it was of old to withdraw to the Thebaid; that to risk "looking strange" requires a courage perhaps cooler and higher than the soldier's or the saint's; and that to stand away from the contact and custom of your "set" is a harder and sterner work than it was of old to go into the sanctuary of La Trappe or Port Royal.

THE world has grown apathetic and purblind. Critics rage and quarrel before a canvas, but the nations do not care; quarries of marble are hewn into various shapes, and the throngs gape before them and are indifferent; writers are so many that their writings blend in the public mind in a confused phantasmagoria, where the colours run into one another, and the lines are all waved and indistinct; the singer alone still keeps the old magic power, "The beauty that was Athens, once the glory that was Rome's," still holds the divine Cadmus, still sways the vast thronged auditorium, till the myriads hold their breath like little children in delight and awe. The great singer alone has the magic sway of fame; and if he close his lips, "The gaiety of nations is eclipsed," and the world seems empty and silent, like a wood in which the birds are all dead.

IN A WINTER CITY.

THE Duc found no topic that suited her. It was the
Corso di Gala that afternoon, would she not go?

No : her horses hated masks, and she hated noise.

The Veglione on Sunday—would she not go to that?

No : those things were well enough in the days of
Philippe d'Orléans, who invented them, but they were
only now as stupid as they were vulgar; anybody was
let in for five francs.

Did she like the new weekly journal that was electrify-
ing Paris?

No : she could see nothing in it : there was no wit
now-a-days—only personalities, which grew more gross
every year.

The Duc urged that personalities were as old as Cra-
tinus and Archilochus, and that five hundred years before
Christ the satires of Hipponax drove Bupalus to hang
himself.

She answered that a bad thing was not the better for
being old.

People were talking of a clever English novel trans-
lated everywhere, called "In a Hothouse," the hothouse
being society—had she seen it?

No : what was the use of reading novels of society
by people who never had been in it? The last English
"society" novel she had read had described a cabinet

minister in London as going to a Drawing-room in the crowd, with everybody else, instead of by the *petite entrée;* they were always full of such blunders.

Had she read the new French story "Le Bal de Mademoiselle Bibi?"

No: she had heard too much of it; it made you almost wish for a Censorship of the Press.

The Duc agreed that literature was terribly but truly described as "un tas d'ordures soigneusement enveloppé.'

She said that the "tas d'ordures" without the envelope was sufficient for popularity, but that the literature of any age was not to be blamed—it was only a natural growth, like a mushroom; if the soil were noxious, the fungus was bad.

The Duc wondered what a censorship would let pass if there were one.

She said that when there was one it had let pass Crebillon, the Chevalier Le Clos, and the "Bijoux Indiscrets;" it had proscribed Marmontel, Helvetius, and Lanjuinais. She did not know how one man could be expected to be wiser than all his generation.

The Duc admired some majolica she had purchased.

She said she began to think that majolica was a false taste; the metallic lustre was fine, but how clumsy the forms! one might be led astray by too great love of old work.

The Duc praised a magnificent Sèvres panel, just painted by Riocreux and Goupil, and given to her by Princess Olga on the New Year.

She said it was well done, but what charm was there in it? All their modern iron and zinc colours, and hydrate of aluminum, and oxide of chromium, and purple of Cassius, and all the rest of it, never gave one-tenth the charm of those old painters who had only green greys and dull blues and tawny yellows, and never could get any kind of red whatever; Olga had meant to please

her, but she, for her part, would much sooner have had a
little panel of Abruzzi, with all the holes and defects in
the pottery, and a brown contadina for a Madonna;
there was some interest in that,—there was no interest
in that gorgeous landscape and those brilliant hunting
figures.

The Duc bore all the contradictions with imperturbable
serenity and urbanity, smiled to himself, and bowed himself out in perfect good-humour.

"Tout va bien," he thought to himself; "Miladi must
be very much in love to be so cross."

The Duc's personal experience amongst ladies had
made him of opinion that love did not improve the
temper.

"IN love!" she echoed, with less languor and more of
impetuosity than she had ever displayed, "are you
ever in love, any of you, ever? You have senses and vanity
and an inordinate fear of not being in the fashion—and
so you take your lovers as you drink your stimulants and
wear your wigs and tie your skirts back—because everybody else does it, and not to do it is to be odd, or prudish,
or something you would hate to be called. Love! it is
an unknown thing to you all. You have a sort of miserable hectic passion, perhaps, that is a drug you take as
you take chlorodyne—just to excite you and make your
jaded nerves a little alive again, and yet you are such
cowards that you have not even the courage of passion,
but label your drug Friendship, and beg Society to
observe that you only keep it for family uses like arnica
or like glycerine. You want notoriety; you want to
indulge your fancies, and yet keep your place in the
world. You like to drag a young man about by a chain,
as if he were the dancing monkey that you depended
upon for subsistence. You like other women to see that

you are not too *passée* to be every whit as improper as if
you were twenty. You like to advertise your successes
as it were with drum and trumpet, because if you did not,
people might begin to doubt that you had any. You
like all that, and you like to feel there is nothing you do
not know and no length you have not gone, and so you
ring all the changes on all the varieties of intrigue and
sensuality, and go over the gamut of sickly sentiment and
nauseous license as an orchestra tunes its strings up
every night! That is what all you people call love; I
am content enough to have no knowledge of it."

" I WOULD rather have the crudest original thing than
the mere galvanism of the corpse of a dead genius.
I would give a thousand paintings by Froment, Damousse,
or any of the finest living artists of Sèvres, for one piece
by old Van der Meer of Delft; but I would prefer a
painting on Sèvres done yesterday by Froment or Damousse, or even any much less famous worker, provided
only it had originality in it, to the best reproduction of a
Van der Meer that modern manufacturers could produce."

"I think you are right; but I fear our old pottery-
painters were not very original. They copied from the
pictures and engravings of Mantegna, Raffaelle, Mar-
cantonio, Marco di Ravenna, Beatricius, and a score of
others."

"The application was original, and the sentiment they
brought to it. Those old artists put so much heart into
their work."

"Because when they painted a *stemma* on the glaze
they had still feudal faith in nobility, and when they
painted a Madonna or Ecce Homo they had still child-
like belief in divinity. What does the pottery-painter of
to-day care for the coat of arms or the religious subject
he may be commissioned to execute for a dinner service

or a chapel? It may be admirable painting—if you give a very high price—but it will still be only manufacture."

"Then what pleasant lives those pottery painters of the early days must have led! They were never long stationary. They wandered about decorating at their fancy, now here and now there; now a vase for a pharmacy, and now a stove for a king. You find German names on Italian ware, and Italian names on Flemish grès; the Nuremberger would work in Venice, the Dutchman would work in Rouen. Sometimes, however, they were accused of sorcery; the great potter, Hans Kraut, you remember, was feared by his townsmen as possessed by the devil, and was buried ignominiously outside the gates, in his nook of the Black Forest. But on the whole they were happy, no doubt; men of simple habits and of worthy lives."

"You care for art yourself, M. Della Rocca?"

There came a gleam of interest in her handsome, languid, hazel eyes, as she turned them upon him.

"Every Italian does," he answered her. "I do not think we are ever, or I think, if ever, very seldom connoisseurs in the way that your Englishman or Frenchman is so. We are never very learned as to styles and dates; we cannot boast the huckster's eye of the northern bric-à-brac hunter; it is quite another thing with us; we love art as children their nurses' tales and cradle-songs. It is a familiar affection with us, and affection is never very analytical. The Robbia over the chapel-door, the apostle-pot that the men in the stables drink out of; the Sodoma or the Beato Angelico that hangs before our eyes daily as we dine; the old bronze *secchia* that we wash our hands in as boys in the Loggia—these are all so homely and dear to us that we grow up with a love for them all as natural as our love for our mothers. You will say the children of all rich people see beautiful and ancient things from their birth: so they do, but not *as*

N

we see them. Here they are too often degraded to the basest household uses, and made no more account of than the dust which gathers on them; but that very neglect of them makes them the more kindred to us. Art elsewhere is the guest of the salon—with us she is the playmate of the infant and the serving-maid of the peasant: the mules may drink from an Etruscan sarcophagus, and the pigeons be fed from a *patina* of the twelfth century."

TASTE, mon cher Della Rocca, is the only sure guarantee in these matters. Women, believe me, never have any principle. Principle is a backbone, and no woman—except bodily—ever possesses any backbone. Their priests and their teachers and their mothers fill them with doctrines and conventionalities—all things of mere word and wind. No woman has any settled principles; if she have any vague ones, it is the uttermost she ever reaches, and those can always be overturned by any man who has any influence over her. But Taste is another matter altogether. A woman whose taste is excellent is preserved from all eccentricities and most follies. You never see a woman of good sense *afficher* her improprieties or advertise her liaisons as women of vulgarity do. Nay, if her taste be perfect, though she have weaknesses, I doubt if she will ever have vices. Vice will seem to her like a gaudy colour, or too much gold braid, or very large plaits, or buttons as big as saucers, or anything else such as vulgar women like. Fastidiousness, at any rate, is very good *postiche* for modesty: it is always decent, it can never be coarse. Good taste, inherent and ingrained, natural and cultivated, cannot alter. Principles—ouf !—they go on and off like a slipper; but good taste is indestructible; it is a compass that never errs. If your wife have it—well, it is

possible she may be false to you ; she is human, she is
feminine; but she will never make you ridiculous, she
will never compromise you, and she will not romp in a
cotillon till the morning sun shows the paint on her face
washed away in the rain of her perspiration. Virtue is,
after all, as Mme. de Montespan said, "une chose tout
purement géographique." It varies with the hemisphere
like the human skin and the human hair ; what is vile in
one latitude is harmless in another. No philosophic
person can put any trust in a thing which merely depends
upon climate ; but, Good Taste——

GOSSIP is like the poor devil in the legend of Fugger's
Teufelspalast at Trent ; it toils till cock-crow picking
up the widely-scattered grains of corn by millions till the
bushel measure is piled high ; and lo !—the five grains
that are *the* grains always escape its sight and roll away
and hide themselves. The poor devil, being a primitive
creature, shrieked and flew away in despair at his failure.
Gossip hugs its false measure and says loftily that the five
real grains are of no consequence whatever.

THE Lady Hilda sighed. This dreadful age, which
has produced communists, pétroleuses, and liberal
thinkers, had communicated its vague restlessness even
to her; although she belonged to that higher region
where nobody ever thinks at all, and everybody is more
or less devout in seeming at any rate, because disbelief
is vulgar, and religion is an "affaire des mœurs," like
decency, still the subtle philosophies and sad negations
which have always been afloat in the air since Voltaire
set them flying, had affected her slightly.

She was a true believer, just as she was a well-dressed woman, and had her creeds just as she had her bath in the morning, as a matter of course.

Still, when she did come to think of it, she was not so very sure. There was another world, and saints and angels and eternity ; yes, of course—but how on earth would all those baccarat people ever fit into it? Who could, by any stretch of imagination, conceive Madame Mila and Maurice des Gommeux in a spiritual existence around the throne of Deity?

And as for punishment and torment and all that other side of futurity, who could even think of the mildest purgatory as suitable to those poor flipperty-gibbet inanities who broke the seventh commandment as gaily as a child breaks his indiarubber ball, and were as incapable of passion and crime as they were incapable of heroism and virtue?

There might be paradise for virtue and hell for crime, but what in the name of the universe was to be done with creatures that were only all Folly? Perhaps they would be always flying about like the souls Virgil speaks of, "suspensæ ad ventos," to purify themselves ; as the sails of a ship spread out to dry. The Huron Indians pray to the souls of the fish they catch ; well, why should they not? a fish has a soul if Modern Society has one ; one could conceive a fish going softly through shining waters for ever and for ever in the ecstasy of motion ; but who could conceive Modern Society in the spheres?

"ONE grows tired of everything," she answered with a little sigh.

"Everything that is artificial, you mean. People think Horace's love of the rural life an affectation. I believe it to be most sincere. After the strain of the conventionality and the adulation of the Augustan court, the natural existence of the country must have been welcome to him. I know it is the fashion to say that a love of Nature belongs only to the Moderns, but I do not think so. Into Pindar, Theocritus, Meleager, the passion for Nature must have entered very strongly; what *is* modern is the more subjective, the more fanciful feeling which makes Nature a sounding-board to echo all the cries of man."

"But that is always a northern feeling?"

"Inevitably. With us Nature is too *riante* for us to grow morbid about it. The sunshine that laughs around us nine months of every year, the fruits that grow almost without culture, the flowers that we throw to the oxen to eat, the very stones that are sweet with myrtle, the very sea sand that is musical with bees in the rosemary, everything we grow up amongst from infancy, makes our love of Nature only a kind of unconscious joy in it; but here even the peasant has that, and the songs of the men that cannot read or write are full of it. If a field labourer sing to his love he will sing of the narcissus and the crocus, as Meleager sang to Heliodora twenty centuries ago."

THAT is an Italian amorous fancy. Romeo and Othello are the typical Italian lovers. I never can tell how a northerner like Shakespeare could draw either. You are often very unfaithful; but *while* you are faithful you are ardent, and you are absorbed in the woman. That is one of the reasons why an Italian succeeds in love as no other man does. " L'art de brûler silencieuse ment le cœur d'un femme" is a supreme art with you. Compared with you, all other men are children. You have been the supreme masters of the great passion since the days of Ovid.

BOREDOM is the ill-natured pebble that always *will* get in the golden slipper of the pilgrim of pleasure.

"THEY say," the great assassin who slays as many thousands as ever did plague or cholera, drink or warfare ; "they say," the thief of reputation, who steals, with stealthy step and coward's mask, to filch good names away in the dead dark of irresponsible calumny ; "they say," a giant murderer, iron-gloved to slay you, a fleet, elusive, vaporous will-o'-the-wisp, when you would seize and choke it ; "they say," mighty Thug though it be which strangles from behind the purest victim, had not been ever known to touch the Lady Hilda.

ALL her old philosophies seemed falling about her like shed leaves, and her old self seemed to her but a purposeless frivolous chilly creature. The real reason she would not face, and indeed as yet was not conscious of; the reason that love had entered into her, and that love, if it be worth the name, has always two handmaidens : swift sympathy, and sad humility, keeping step together.

THE Femme Galante has passed through many various changes, in many countries. The dames of the Decamerone were unlike the fair athlete-seekers of the days of Horace; and the powdered coquettes of the years of Molière, were sisters only by the kinship of a common vice to the frivolous and fragile faggot of impulses, that is called Frou-frou.

The Femme Galante has always been a feature in every age ; poets, from Juvenal to Musset, have railed at her; artists, from Titian to Winterhalter, have painted her; dramatists, from Aristophanes to Congreve and Dumas Fils, have pointed their arrows at her; satirists, from Archilochus and Simonides to Hogarth and Gavarni, have poured out their aqua-fortis for her. But the real Femme Galante of to-day has been missed hitherto.

Frou-frou, who stands for her, is not in the least the true type. Frou-frou is a creature that can love, can suffer, can repent, can die. She is false in sentiment and in art, but she is tender after all; poor, feverish, wistful, changeful morsel of humanity. A slender, helpless, breathless, and frail thing who, under one sad, short sin, sinks down to death.

But Frou-frou is in no sense the true Femme Galante of her day. Frou-frou is much more a fancy than a fact. It is not Frou-frou that Molière would have handed down to other generations in enduring ridicule, had he been living now. To her he would have doffed his hat with dim eyes; what he would have fastened for all time in his pillory would have been a very different, and far more conspicuous offender.

The Femme Galante, who has neither the scruples nor the follies of poor Frou-frou, who neither forfeits her place nor leaves her lord; who has studied adultery as one of the fine arts and made it one of the domestic virtues; who takes her wearied lover to her friends' houses as she takes her muff or her dog, and teaches her sons and daughters to call him by familiar names; who writes to the victim of her passions with the same pen that calls her boy home from school; and who smooths her child's curls with the same fingers that stray over her lover's lips; who challenges the world to find a flaw in her, and who smiles serene at her husband's table on a society she is careful to conciliate; who has woven the most sacred ties and most unholy pleasures into so deft a braid, that none can say where one commences or the other ends; who uses the sanctity of her maternity to cover the lawlessness of her license; and who, incapable alike of the self-abandonment of love or of the self-sacrifice of duty, has not even such poor, cheap honour as, in the creatures of the streets, may make guilt loyal to its dupe and partner.

This is the Femme Galante of the passing century, who, with her hand on her husband's arm, babbles of her virtue in complacent boast; and ignoring such a vulgar word as Sin, talks with a smile of Friendship. Beside her Frou-frou were innocence itself, Marion de l'Orme were honesty, Manon Lescaut were purity, Cleopatra were chaste, and Faustine were faithful.

She is the female Tartuffe of seduction, the Précieuse Ridicule of passion, the parody of Love, the standing gibe of Womanhood.

SHE was always in debt, though she admitted that her husband allowed her liberally. She had eighty thousand francs a year by her settlements to spend on herself, and he gave her another fifty thousand to do as she pleased with : on the whole about one half what he allowed to Blanche Souris, of the Château Gaillard theatre.

She had had six children, three were living and three were dead; she thought herself a good mother, because she gave her wet-nurses ever so many silk gowns, and when she wanted the children for a fancy ball or a drive, always saw that they were faultlessly dressed, and besides she always took them to Trouville.

She had never had any grief in her life, except the loss of the Second Empire, and even that she got over when she found that flying the Red Cross flag had saved her hotel, without so much as a teacup being broken in

it, that MM. Worth and Offenbach were safe from all
bullets, and that society, under the Septennate, promised to be every bit as *leste* as under the Empire.

In a word, Madame Mila was a type of the women
of her time.

The women who go semi-nude in an age which has
begun to discover that the nude in sculpture is very
immoral; who discuss "Tue-la" in a generation which
decrees Molière to be coarse, and Beaumont and Fletcher
indecent; who have the Journal pour Rire on their
tables in a day when no one who respects himself would
name the Harlot's Progress; who read Beaudelaire and
patronise Térésa and Schneider in an era which finds
"Don Juan" gross, and Shakespeare far too plain; who
strain all their energies to rival Mlles. Rose Thé and
La Petite Boulotte in everything; who go shrimping or
oyster-hunting on fashionable sea-shores, with their legs
bare to the knee; who go to the mountains with con-
fections, high heels, and gold-tipped canes, shriek over
their gambling as the dawn reddens over the Alps, and
know no more of the glories of earth and sky, of sunrise and sunset, than do the porcelain pots that hold
their paint, or the silver dressing-box that carries their
hair-dye.

Women who are in convulsions one day, and on the
top of a drag the next; who are in hysterics for their
lovers at noon, and in ecstasies over baccarat at midnight; who laugh in little nooks together over each
other's immoralities, and have a moral code so elastic
that it will pardon anything except innocence; who
gossip over each other's dresses, and each other's passions, in the self-same, self-satisfied chirp of content-
ment, and who never resent anything on earth, except
any eccentric suggestion that life could be anything
except a perpetual fête à la Watteau in a perpetual blaze
of lime-light.

Pain?—Are there not chloral and a flattering doctor?
Sorrow?—Are there not a course at the Baths, play at
Monte Carlo, and new cases from Worth? Shame?
—Is it not a famine fever which never comes near a
well-laden table? Old Age?—Is there not white and
red paint, and heads of dead hair, and even false
bosoms? Death? Well, no doubt there is death, but
they do not realise it; they hardly believe in it, they
think about it so little.

There is something unknown somewhere to fall on
them some day that they dread vaguely, for they are
terrible cowards. But they worry as little about it as
possible. They give the millionth part of what they
possess away in its name to whatever church they belong
to, and they think they have arranged quite comfortably
for all possible contingencies hereafter.

If it make things safe, they will head bazaars for the
poor, or wear black in holy week, turn lottery-wheels for
charity, or put on fancy dresses in the name of bene-
volence, or do any little amiable trifle of that sort. But
as for changing their lives,—*pas si bête!*

A bird in the hand they hold worth two in the bush;
and though your birds may be winged on strong desire,
and your bush the burning portent of Moses, they will
have none of them.

These women are not all bad; oh, no! they are like
sheep, that is all. If it were fashionable to be virtuous,
very likely they would be so. If it were *chic* to be
devout, no doubt they would pass their life on their
knees. But, as it is, they know that a flavour of vice
is as necessary to their reputation as great ladies, as
sorrel-leaves to soup à la bonne femme. They affect a
license if they take it not.

They are like the barber, who said, with much pride,
to Voltaire, "Je ne suis qu'un pauvre diable de perru-
quier, mais je ne crois pas en Dieu plus que les autres."

They may be worth very little, but they are desperately
afraid that you should make such a mistake as to think
them worth anything at all. You are not likely, if you
know them. Still, they are apprehensive.

Though one were to arise from the dead to preach to
them, they would only make of him a nine days' wonder,
and then laugh a little, and yawn a little, and go on in
their own paths.

Out of the eater came forth meat, and from evil there
may be begotten good; but out of nullity there can only
come nullity. They have wadded their ears, and though
Jeremiah wailed of desolation, or Isaiah thundered the
wrath of heaven, they would not hear,—they would go
on looking at each other's dresses.

What could Paul himself say that would change them?

You cannot make sawdust into marble; you cannot
make sea-sand into gold. "Let us alone," is all they
ask; and it is all that you could do, though the force
and flame of Horeb were in you.

IT is very curious, but loss of taste in the nobles has
always been followed by a revolution of the mob.
The *décadence* always ushers in the democracy.

PLEASURE alone cannot content any one whose
character has any force, or mind any high intelligence. Society is, as you say, a book we soon
read through, and know by heart till it loses all interest.
Art alone cannot fill more than a certain part of our
emotions; and culture, however perfect, leaves us un-
satisfied. There is only one thing that can give to life
what your poet called the light that never was on sea
or land—and that is human love.

"YES, it is a curious thing that we do not succeed in fresco. The grace is gone out of it ; modern painters have not the lightness of touch necessary ; they are used to masses of colour, and they use the palette knife as a mason the trowel. The art, too, like the literature of our time, is all detail ; the grand suggestive vagueness of the Greek drama and of the Umbrian frescoes are lost to us under a crowd of elaborated trivialities ; perhaps it is because art has ceased to be spiritual or tragic, and is merely domestic or melodramatic ; the Greeks knew neither domesticity nor melodrama, and the early Italian painters were imbued with a faith which, if not so virile as the worship of the Phidian Zeus, yet absorbed them and elevated them in a degree impossible in the tawdry Sadduceeism of our own day. By the way, when the weather is milder you must go to Orvieto ; you have never been there, I think ; it is the Prosodion of Signorelli. What a fine Pagan he was at heart ! He admired masculine beauty like a Greek ; he must have been a singularly happy man— few more happy——"

A LEAF IN THE STORM.

THE Berceau de Dieu was a little village in the valley of the Seine.

As a lark drops its nest amongst the grasses, so a few peasant people had dropped their little farms and cottages amidst the great green woods on the winding river. It was a pretty place, with one steep, stony street, shady with poplars and with elms; quaint houses, about whose thatch a cloud of white and grey pigeons fluttered all day long; a little aged chapel with a conical red roof; and great barns covered with ivy and thick creepers, red and purple, and lichens that were yellow in the sun.

All around it there were the broad, flowering meadows, with the sleek cattle of Normandy fattening in them, and the sweet dim forests where the young men and maidens went on every holy-day and feast-day in the summer-time to seek for wood-anemones, and lilies of the pools, and the wild campanula, and the fresh dog-rose, and all the boughs and grasses that made their house-doors like garden-bowers, and seemed to take the cushat's note and the linnet's song into their little temple of God.

The Berceau de Dieu was very old indeed.

Men said that the hamlet had been there in the day of the Virgin of Orléans; and a stone cross of the twelfth century still stood by the great pond of water at the bottom of the street, under the chestnut-tree, where the villagers gathered to gossip at sunset when their work was done.

It had no city near it, and no town nearer than four leagues. It was in the green core of a pastoral district, thickly wooded and intersected with orchards. Its produce of wheat, and oats, and cheese, and fruit, and eggs, was more than sufficient for its simple prosperity. Its people were hardy, kindly, laborious, happy; living round the little grey chapel in amity and good-fellowship.

Nothing troubled it. War and rumours of war, revolutions and counter-revolutions, empires and insurrections, military and political questions,—these all were for it things unknown and unheard of—mighty winds that arose and blew and swept the lands around it, but never came near enough to harm it, lying there, as it did, in its loneliness like any lark's nest.

" I AM old : yes, I am very old," she would say, looking up from her spinning-wheel in her house-door, and shading her eyes from the sun, "very old—ninety-two last summer. But when one has a roof over one's head, and a pot of soup always, and a grandson like mine, and when one has lived all one's life in the Berceau de Dieu, then it is well to be so old. Ah, yes, my little ones—yes, though you doubt it, you little birds that have just tried your wings—it is well to be so old. One has time to think, and thank the good God, which one never seemed to have a minute to do in that work, work, work, when one was young."

THE end soon came.

From hill to hill the Berceau de Dieu broke into flames. The village was a lake of fire, into which the statue of the Christ, burning and reeling, fell. Some few peasants, with their wives and children, fled to the woods, and there escaped one torture to perish more slowly of cold and famine. All other things perished. The rapid stream of the flame licked up all there was in its path. The bare trees raised their leafless branches on fire at a thousand points. The stores of corn and fruit were lapped by millions of crimson tongues. The pigeons flew screaming from their roosts and sank into the smoke. The dogs were suffocated on the thresholds they had guarded all their lives. The calf was stifled in the byre. The sheep ran bleating with the wool burning on their living bodies. The little caged birds fluttered helpless, and then dropped, scorched to cinders. The aged and the sick were stifled in their beds. All things perished.

The Berceau de Dieu was as one vast furnace, in which every living creature was caught and consumed and changed to ashes.

The tide of war has rolled on and left it a blackened waste, a smoking ruin, wherein not so much as a mouse may creep or a bird may nestle. It is gone, and its place can know it never more.

Never more.

But who is there to care?

It was but as a leaf which the great storm withered as it passed.

"LOOK you," she had said to him oftentimes, "in my babyhood there was the old white flag upon the château. Well, they pulled that down and put up a red one. That toppled and fell, and there was one of three colours. Then somebody with a knot of white lilies in his hand came one day and set up the old white one afresh; and before the day was done that was down again, and the tricolour again up where it is still. Now some I know fretted themselves greatly because of all these changes of the flags, but as for me, I could not see that any one of them mattered : bread was just as dear, and sleep was just as sweet, whichever of the three was uppermost."

A DOG OF FLANDERS.

IN the spring and summer especially were they glad.
Flanders is not a lovely land, and around the burgh
of Rubens it is perhaps least lovely of all.

Corn and colza, pasture and plough, succeed each
other on the characterless plain in wearying repetition,
and save by some gaunt grey tower, with its peal of
pathetic bells, or some figure coming athwart the fields,
made picturesque by a gleaner's bundle or a woodman's
faggot, there is no change, no variety, no beauty anywhere; and he who has dwelt upon the mountains or
amidst the forests feels oppressed as by imprisonment
with the tedium and the endlessness of that vast and
dreary level.

But it is green and very fertile, and it has wide
horizons that have a certain charm of their own even
in their dulness and monotony; and amongst the rushes
by the water-side the flowers grow, and the trees rise
tall and fresh where the barges glide with their great
hulks black against the sun, and their little green
barrels and vari-coloured flags gay against the leaves.

Anyway, there is a greenery and breadth of space
enough to be as good as beauty to a child and a
dog; and these two asked no better, when their work
was done, than to lie buried in the lush grasses on
the side of the canal, and watch the cumbrous vessels

O

drifting by, and bringing the crisp salt smell of the sea amongst the blossoming scents of the country summer.

ANTWERP, as all the world knows, is full at every turn of old piles of stones, dark and ancient and majestic, standing in crooked courts, jammed against gateways and taverns, rising by the water's edge, with bells ringing above them in the air, and ever and again out of their arched doors a swell of music pealing.

There they remain, the grand old sanctuaries of the past, shut in amidst the squalor, the hurry, the crowds, the unloveliness and the commerce of the modern world; and all day long the clouds drift and the birds circle, and the winds sigh around them, and beneath the earth at their feet there sleeps—RUBENS.

And the greatness of the mighty Master still rests upon Antwerp; wherever we turn in its narrow streets his glory lies therein, so that all mean things are thereby transfigured; and as we pace slowly through the winding ways, and by the edge of the stagnant water, and through the noisome courts, his spirit abides with us, and the heroic beauty of his visions is about us, and the stones that once felt his footsteps and bore his shadow seem to arise and speak of him with living voices. For the city which is the tomb of Rubens still lives to us through him, and him alone.

Without Rubens, what were Antwerp? A dirty, dusky, bustling mart, which no man would ever care to look upon save the traders who do business on its wharves. With Rubens, to the whole world of men it is a sacred name, a sacred soil, a Bethlehem where a god of Art saw light, a Golgotha where a god of Art lies dead.

It is so quiet there by that great white sepulchre— so quiet, save only when the organ peals, and the choir

cries aloud the Salve Regina or the Kyrie Eleison.
Sure no artist ever had a greater gravestone than that
pure marble sanctuary gives to him in the heart of his
birthplace in the chancel of St. Jacques?

O nations! closely should you treasure your great
men, for by them alone will the future know of you.
Flanders in her generations has been wise. In his
life she glorified this greatest of her sons, and in his
death she magnifies his name. But her wisdom is
very rare.

THE night was very wild. The lamps under the
wayside crosses were blown out: the roads were
sheets of ice; the impenetrable darkness hid every trace
of habitations; there was no living thing abroad. All
the cattle were housed, and in all the huts and home-
steads men and women rejoiced and feasted. There
was only the dog out in the cruel cold—old and famished
and full of pain, but with the strength and the patience
of a great love to sustain him in his search.

The trail of Nello's steps, faint and obscure as it was
under the new snow, went straightly along the accustomed tracks into Antwerp. It was past midnight when
Patrasche traced it over the boundaries of the town and
into the narrow, tortuous, gloomy streets. It was all
quite dark in the town. Now and then some light
gleamed ruddily through the crevices of house-shutters,
or some group went homeward with lanterns chanting
drinking-songs. The streets were all white with ice:
the high walls and roofs loomed black against them.
There was scarce a sound save the riot of the winds
down the passages as they tossed the creaking signs and
shook the tall lamp-irons.

So many passers-by had trodden through and through
the snow, so many diverse paths had crossed and re-

crossed each other, that the dog had a hard task to retain any hold on the track he followed. But he kept on his way, though the cold pierced him to the bone, and the jagged ice cut his feet, and the hunger in his body gnawed like a rat's teeth. But he kept on his way—a poor, gaunt, shivering, drooping thing in the frozen darkness, that no one pitied as he went—and by long patience traced the steps he loved into the very heart of the burgh and up to the steps of the great cathedral.

"He is gone to the things that he loved," thought Patrasche; he could not understand, but he was full of sorrow and of pity for the art-passion that to him was so incomprehensible and yet so sacred.

The portals of the cathedral were unclosed after the midnight mass. Some heedlessness in the custodians, too eager to go home and feast or sleep, or too drowsy to know whether they turned the keys aright, had left one of the doors unlocked. By that accident the footfalls Patrasche sought had passed through into the building, leaving the white marks of snow upon the dark stone floor. By that slender white thread, frozen as it fell, he was guided through the intense silence, through the immensity of the vaulted space—guided straight to the gates of the chancel, and stretched there upon the stones he found Nello. He crept up noiselessly, and touched the face of the boy. "Didst thou dream that I should be faithless and forsake thee? I—a dog?" said that mute caress.

The lad raised himself with a low cry and clasped him close.

"Let us lie down and die together," he murmured. "Men have no need of us, and we are all alone."

In answer, Patrasche crept closer yet, and laid his head upon the young boy's breast. The great tears stood in his brown sad eyes : not for himself—for himself he was happy.

They lay close together in the piercing cold. The
blasts that blew over the Flemish dykes from the northern seas were like waves of ice, which froze every living
thing they touched. The interior of the immense vault
of stone in which they were was even more bitterly chill
than the snow-covered plains without. Now and then
a bat moved in the shadows; now and then a gleam of
light came to the ranks of carven figures. Under the
Rubens they lay together, quite still, and soothed almost
into a dreaming slumber by the numbing narcotic of the
cold. Together they dreamed of the old glad days
when they had chased each other through the flowering
grasses of the summer meadows, or sat hidden in the
tall bulrushes by the water's side, watching the boats
go seaward in the sun.

No anger had ever separated them; no cloud had
ever come between them; no roughness on the one
side, no faithlessness on the other, had ever obscured
their perfect love and trust. All through their short
lives they had done their duty as it had come to them,
and had been happy in the mere sense of living, and
had begrudged nothing to any man or beast, and had
been quite content because quite innocent. And in the
faintness of famine and of the frozen blood that stole
dully and slowly through their veins, it was of the days
they had spent together that they dreamed, lying there
in the long watches of the night of the Noël.

Suddenly through the darkness a great white radiance
streamed through the vastness of the aisles; the moon,
that was at her height, had broken through the clouds;
the snow had ceased to fall; the light reflected from the
snow without was clear as the light of dawn. It fell
through the arches full upon the two pictures above,
from which the boy on his entrance had flung back the
veil: the Elevation and the Descent of the Cross were
for one instant visible as by day.

Nello rose to his feet and stretched his arms to them : the tears of a passionate ecstasy glistened on the paleness of his face.

"I have seen them at last !" he cried aloud. "O God, it is enough !"

His limbs failed under him, and he sank upon his knees, still gazing upward at the majesty that he adored. For a few brief moments the light illumined the divine visions that had been denied to him so long—light, clear and sweet and strong as though it streamed from the throne of Heaven.

Then suddenly it passed away : once more a great darkness covered the face of Christ.

The arms of the boy drew close again the body of the dog.

"We shall see His face—*there*," he murmured ; "and He will not part us, I think ; He will have mercy."

On the morrow, by the chancel of the cathedral, the people of Antwerp found them both. They were both dead : the cold of the night had frozen into stillness alike the young life and the old. When the Christmas morning broke and the priests came to the temple, they saw them lying thus on the stones together. Above, the veils were drawn back from the great visions of Rubens, and the fresh rays of the sunrise touched the thorn-crowned head of the God.

As the day grew on there came an old, hard-featured man, who wept as women weep.

"I was cruel to the lad," he muttered, "and now I would have made amends—yea, to the half of my substance—and he should have been to me as a son."

There came also, as the day grew apace, a painter who had fame in the world, and who was liberal of hand and of spirit.

"I seek one who should have had the prize yesterday had worth won," he said to the people,—"a boy of rare promise and genius. An old woodcutter on a fallen tree at eventide—that was all his theme. But there was greatness for the future in it. I would fain find him, and take him with me and teach him art."

. . . . .

Death had been more pitiful to them than longer life would have been. It had taken the one in the loyalty of love, and the other in the innocence of faith, from a world which for love has no recompense, and for faith no fulfilment.

All their lives they had been together, and in their deaths they were not divided ; for when they were found the arms of the boy were folded too closely around the dog to be severed without violence, and the people of their little village, contrite and ashamed, implored a special grace for them, and, making them one grave, laid them to rest there side by side—for ever.

A·BRANCH OF LILAC.

AND indeed I loved France: still, in the misery of my
life, I loved her for all that I had had from her.

I loved her for her sunny roads, for her cheery laughter,
for her vine-hung hamlets, for her contented poverty, for
her gay, sweet mirth, for her pleasant days, for her starry
nights, for her little bright groups at the village fountain,
for her old, brown, humble peasants at her wayside crosses,
for her wide, wind-swept plains all red with her radiant
sunsets. She had given me beautiful hours; she is the
mother of the poor, who sings to them so that they forget
their hunger and their nakedness; she had made me
happy in my youth. I was not ungrateful.

It was in the heats of September that I reached my
country. It was just after the day of Sedan. I heard
all along the roads, as I went, sad, sullen murmurs of our
bitter disasters. It was not the truth exactly that was
ever told at the poor wine-shops and about the harvest-
fields, but it was near enough to the truth to be horrible.

The blood-thirst which had been upon me ever since
that night when I found her chair empty seemed to burn
and seethe, till I saw nothing but blood—in the air, in the
sun, in the water.

I REMEMBER in that ghastly time seeing a woman
put the match to a piece whose gunner had just
dropped dead. She fired with sure aim: her shot swept

straight into a knot of horsemen on the Neuilly road,
and emptied more than one saddle.

"You have a good sight," I said to her.

She smiled.

"This winter," she said slowly, "my children have all
died for want of food—one by one, the youngest first.
Ever since then I want to hurt something—always. Do
you understand?"

I did understand: I do not know if you do. It is just
these things that make revolutions.

WHEN I sit in the gloom here I see all the scenes of
that pleasant life pass like pictures before me.

No doubt I was often hot, often cold, often footsore,
often ahungered and athirst : no doubt ; but all that has
faded now. I only see the old, lost, unforgotten brightness ; the sunny roads, with the wild poppies blowing in
the wayside grass ; the quaint little red roofs and peaked
towers that were thrust upward out of the rolling woods ;
the clear blue skies, with the larks singing against the
sun ; the quiet, cool, moss-grown towns, with old dreamy
bells ringing sleepily above them ; the dull casements
opening here and there to show a rose like a girl's cheek,
and a girl's face like the rose ; the little wineshops
buried in their climbing vines and their tall, many-
coloured hollyhocks, from which sometimes a cheery
voice would cry, "Come, stay for a stoup of wine, and
pay us with a song."

Then, the nights when the people flocked to us, and
the little tent was lighted, and the women's and the
children's mirth rang out in peals of music ; and the men
vied with each other as to which should bear each of us
off to have bed and board under the cottage roof, or in
the old mill-house, or in the weaver's garret ; the nights
when the homely supper-board was brightened and thought

honoured by our presence; when we told the black-eyed daughter's fortunes, and kept the children round-eyed and flushing red with wonder at strange tales, and smoked within the leaf-hung window with the father and his sons; and then went out, quietly, alone in the moonlight, and saw the old cathedral white and black in the shadows and the light; and strayed a little into its dim aisles, and watched the thorn-crowned God upon the cross, and in the cool fruit-scented air, in the sweet, silent dusk, moved softly with noiseless footfall and bent head, as though the dead were there.

Ah, well! they are all gone, those days and nights. Begrudge me not their memory. I am ugly, and very poor, and of no account; and I die at sunrise, so they say. Let me remember whilst I can: it is all oblivion *there*. So they say.

WHETHER I suffered or enjoyed, loved or hated, is of no consequence to any one. The dancing-dog suffers intensely beneath the scourge of the stick, and is capable of intense attachment to any one who is merciful enough not to beat him; but the dancing-dog and his woe and his love are nothing to the world: I was as little.

There is nothing more terrible, nothing more cruel, than the waste of emotion, the profuse expenditure of fruitless pain, which every hour, every moment, as it passes, causes to millions of living creatures. If it were of any use who would mind? But it is all waste, frightful waste, to no end, to no end.

AH, well! it is our moments of blindness and of folly that are the sole ones of happiness for all of us on earth. We only see clearly, I think, when we have reached the depths of woe.

FRANCE was a great sea in storm, on which the lives of all men were as frail boats tossing to their graves. Some were blown east, some west : they passed each other in the endless night, and never knew, the tempest blew so strong.

WINTER tries hardly all the wandering races : if the year were all summer, all the world would be Bohemians.

WE poured out blood like water, and much of it was the proud blue blood of the old nobility. We should have saved France, I am sure, if there had been any one who had known how to consolidate and lead us. No one did ; so it was all of no use.

Guerillas like us can do much, very much, but to do so much that it is victory we must have a genius amidst us. And we had none. If the First Bonaparte had been alive and with us, we should have chased the foe as Marius the Cimbri.

I think other nations will say so in the future : at the present they are all dazzled, they do not see clearly—they are all worshipping the rising sun. It is blood-red, and it blinds them.

IT is so strange ! We see a million faces, we hear a million voices, we meet a million women with flowers in their breasts and light in their fair eyes, and they do not touch us. Then we see one, and she holds for us life or death, and plays with them idly so often—as idly as a child with toys. She is not nobler, better, or more beautiful than were all those we passed, and yet the world is empty to us without her.

SIGNA.

IN the garden of these children all the flora of Italy was gathered and was growing.

The delights of an Italian garden are countless. It is not like any other garden in the world. It is at once more formal and more wild, at once greener with more abundant youth and venerable with more antique age. It has all Boccaccio between its walls, all Petrarca in its leaves, all Raffaelle in its skies. And then the sunshine that beggars words and laughs at painters!—the boundless, intense, delicious, heavenly light! What do other gardens know of that, save in orange-groves of Granada and rose thickets of Damascus?

The old broken marble statues, whence the water dripped and fed the water-lily; the great lemon-trees in pots big enough to drown a boy, the golden globes among their emerald leaves; the magnolias, like trees cast in bronze, with all the spice of India in their cups; the spires of ivory bells that the yuccas put forth, like belfries for fairies; the oleanders taller than a man, red and white and blush colour; the broad velvet leaves of the flowering rush; the dark majestic ilex oaks, that made the noon like twilight; the countless graces of the vast family of acacias; the high box hedges, sweet and pungent in the sun; the stone ponds, where the gold-fish slept through the sultry day; the wilderness

of carnations; the huge roses, yellow, crimson, snow-
white, and the small noisette and the banksia with its
million of pink stars; myrtles in dense thickets, and
camellias like a wood of evergreens; cacti in all quaint
shapes, like fossils astonished to find themselves again
alive; high walls, vine-hung and topped by pines and
cypresses; low walls with crowds of geraniums on their
parapets, and the mountains and the fields beyond them;
marble basins hidden in creepers where the frogs dozed
all day long; sounds of convent bells and of chapel
chimes; green lizards basking on the flags; great sheds
and granaries beautiful with the clematis and the wisteria
and the rosy trumpets of the bignonia; great wooden
places cool and shady, with vast arched entrances, and
scent of hay, and empty casks, and red earthen amphoræ,
and little mice scudding on the floors, and a sun-dial
painted on the wall, and a crucifix set above the weather-
cock, and through the huge unglazed windows sight of
the green vines with the bullocks in the harvest-carts
beneath them, or of some hilly sunlit road with a mule-
team coming down it, or of a blue high hill with its pine-
trees black against the sky, and on its slopes the yellow
corn and misty olive. This was their garden; it is ten
thousand other gardens in the land.

The old painters had these gardens, and walked in
them, and thought nothing better could be needed for
any scene of Annunciation or Adoration, and so put
them in beyond the windows of Bethlehem or behind
the Throne of the Lamb—and who can wonder?

IN these little ancient burghs and hillside villages, scattered up and down between mountain and sea, there
is often some boy or girl, with a more wonderful voice,
or a more beautiful face, or a sweeter knack of song, or
a more vivid trick of improvisation than the others; and

this boy or girl strays away some day with a little bundle of clothes, and a coin or two, or is fetched away by some far-sighted pedlar in such human wares, who buys them as bird-fanciers buy the finches from the nets ; and then, years and years afterwards, the town or hamlet hears indistinctly of some great prima donna, or of some lark-throated tenor, that the big world is making happy as kings, and rich as kings' treasurers, and the people carding the flax or shelling the chestnuts say to one another, "That was little black Lià, or that was our old Momo ;" but Momo or Lià the village or the vine-field never sees again.

THE heart of silver falls ever into the hands of brass. The sensitive herb is eaten as grass by the swine.

FATE will have it so. Fate is so old, and weary of her task ; she must have some diversion. It is Fate who blinded Love for sport, and on the shoulders of Possession hung the wallet full of stones and sand— Satiety.

AS passion yet unknown thrills in the adolescent, as maternity yet undreamed of stirs in the maiden ; so the love of art comes to the artist before he can give a voice to his thought or any name to his desire.

Signa heard "beautiful things" as he sat in the rising moonlight, with the bells of the little bindweed white about his feet.

That was all he could have said.

Whether the angels sent them on the breeze, or the birds brought them, or the dead men came and sang them to him, he could not tell. Indeed, who can tell?

Where did Guido see the golden hair of St. Michael gleam upon the wind? Where did Mozart hear the awful cries of the risen dead come to judgment? What voice was in the fountain of Vaucluse? Under what nodding oxlip did Shakespeare find Titania asleep? When did the Mother of Love come down, chaster in her unclothed loveliness than vestal in her veil, and with such vision of her make obscure Cleomenes immortal?

Who can tell?

Signa sat dreaming, with his chin upon his hands, and his eyes wandering over all the silent place, from the closed flowers at his feet to the moon in her circles of mist.

Who walks in these paths now may go back four hundred years. They are changed in nothing. Through their high hedges of rhododendron and of jessamine that grow like woodland trees it would still seem but natural to see Raffaelle with his court-train of students, or Signorelli splendid in those apparellings which were the comment of his age; and on these broad stone terraces with the lizards basking on their steps and the trees opening to show a vine-covered hill with the white oxen creeping down it and the blue mountains farther still behind, it would be but fitting to see a dark figure sitting and painting lilies upon a golden ground, or cherubs' heads upon a panel of cypress wood, and to hear that this painter was the monk Angelico.

The deepest charm of these old gardens, as of their country, is, after all, that in them it is possible to forget the present age.

In the full, drowsy, voluptuous noon, when they are a gorgeous blaze of colour and a very intoxication of fragrance, as in the ethereal white moonlight of midnight, when, with the silver beams and the white blossoms and the pale marbles, they are like a world of snow, their charm is one of rest, silence, leisure, dreams, and passion all in one; they belong to the days when art was a living power, when love was a thing of heaven or of hell, and when men had the faith of children and the force of gods.

Those days are dead, but in these old gardens you can believe still that you live in them.

"PIPPA!" echoed Istriel. His memories were wakened by the name, and went back to the days of his youth, when he had gone through the fields at evening, when the purple beanflower was in bloom.

"What is your name then?" he asked, with a changed sound in his voice, and with his fair cheek paler.

"I am Bruno Marcillo; I come from the hills above the Lastra a Signa."

Istriel rose, and looked at him; he had not remembered dead Pippa for many a year. All in a moment he did remember: the long light days, the little grey-walled town, the meetings in the vine-hung paths, when sunset burned the skies; the girl with the pearls on her round brown throat, the moonlit nights, with the strings of the guitar throbbing, and the hearts of the lovers leaping; the sweet, eager, thoughtless passion that swayed them one to another, as two flowers are blown together in the mild soft winds of summer; he remembered it all now.

And he had forgotten so long; forgotten so utterly; save now and then, when in some great man's house he had chanced to see some painting done in his youth, and sold then for a few gold coins, of a tender tempestuous face, half smiling and half sobbing, full of storm and sunshine, both in one; and then at such times had thought, "Poor little fool! she loved me too well;—it is the worst fault a woman has."

Some regret he had felt, and some remorse when he had found the garret empty, and had lost Pippa from

sight in the great sea of chance; but she had wearied
him, importuned him, clung to him; she had had the
worst fault, she had loved him too much. He had been
young and poor, and very ambitious; he had been soon
reconciled; he had soon learned to think that it was a
burden best fallen from his shoulders. No doubt she
had suffered; but there was no help for that—some one
always suffered when these ties were broken—so he had
said to himself. And then there had come success and
fame, and the pleasures of the world and the triumphs
of art, and Pippa had dropped from his thoughts as dead
blossoms from a bough; and he had loved so many other
women, that he could not have counted them; and the
memory of that boy-and-girl romance in the green hill
country of the old Etruscan land had died away from
him like a song long mute.

Now, all at once, Pippa's hand seemed to touch him—
Pippa's voice seemed to rouse him—Pippa's eyes seemed
to look at him.

I T was very early in the morning.

There had been heavy rains at night, and there was,
when the sun rose, everywhere, that white fog of the Valdarno country which is like a silvery cloud hanging over
all the earth. It spreads everywhere and blends together
land and sky; but it has breaks of exquisite transparen-
cies, through which the gold of the sunbeam shines, and
the rose of the dawn blushes, and the summits of the
hills gleam here and there, with a white monastery, or a
mountain belfry, or a cluster of cypresses seen through
it, hung in the air as it were, and framed like pictures in
the silvery mist.

It is no noxious steam rising from the rivers and the
rains: no grey and oppressive obliteration of the face of

P

the world like the fogs of the north ; no weight on the
lungs and blindness to the eyes ; no burden of leaden
damp lying heavy on the soil and on the spirit ; no wall
built up between the sun and men ; but a fog that is as
beautiful as the full moonlight is—nay, more beautiful,
for it has beams of warmth, glories of colour, glimpses of
landscape such as the moon would coldly kill ; and the
bells ring, and the sheep bleat, and the birds sing underneath its shadow ; and the sun-rays come through it,
darted like angels' spears : and it has in it all the promise
of the morning, and all the sounds of the waking day.

A GREAT darkness was over all his mind like the
plague of that unending night which brooded over
Egypt.

All the ferocity of his nature was scourged into its
greatest strength ; he was sensible of nothing except the
sense that he was beaten in the one aim and purpose of
his life.

Only—if by any chance he could still save the boy.

That one thought—companion with him, sleeping and
waking, through so many joyless nights—stayed with him
still.

It seemed to him that he would have strength to scale
the very heights of heaven, and shake the very throne of
God until He heard—to save the boy.

The night was far gone ; the red of the day-dawn began
to glow, and the stars paled.

He did not know how time went ; but he knew the
look of the daybreak. When the skies looked so through
his grated windows at home, he rose and said a prayer,
and went down and unbarred his doors, and led out his
white beasts to the plough, or between the golden lines
of the reaped corn ; all that was over now.

The birds were waking on the old green hills and the crocus flowers unclosing; but he——

"I shall never see it again," he thought, and his heart yearned to it, and the great, hot, slow tears of a man's woe stole into his aching eyes and burned them. But he had no pity on himself.

He had freedom and health and strength and manhood, and he was still not old, and still might win the favour of women, and see his children laugh—if he went back to the old homestead, and the old safe ways of his fathers. And the very smell of the earth there was sweet to him as a virgin's breath, and the mere toil of the ground had been dear to him by reason of the faithful love that he bore to his birthplace. But he had no pity on himself.

"My soul for his," he had said; and he cleaved to his word and kept it.

In his day he had been savage to others. He was no less so to himself.

He had done all that he knew how to do. He had crushed out the natural evil of him and denied the desires of the flesh, and changed his very nature to do good by Pippa's son: and it had all been of no use; it had all been spent in vain, as drowning seamen's cries for help are spent on angry winds and yawning waters. He had tried to follow God's will and to drive the tempter from him, for the boy's sake; and it had all been of no avail. Through the long score of years his vain sacrifices echoed dully by him as a dropt stone through the dark shaft of a well.

Perhaps it was not enough.

Perhaps it was needful that he should redeem the boy's soul by the utter surrender and eternal ruin of his own— perhaps. After all it was a poor love which balanced cost; a meek, mean love which would not dare to take guilt upon it for the thing it cherished.

To him crime was crime in naked utter blackness;

without aught of those palliatives with which the cultured and philosophic temper can streak it smooth and paint its soft excuse, and trace it back to influence or insanity. To him sin was a mighty, hideous, hell-born thing, which being embraced dragged him who kissed it on the mouth, downward and downward into bottomless pits of endless night and ceaseless torment. To him the depths of hell and heights of heaven were real as he had seen them in the visions of Orgagna.

Yet he was willing to say, "Evil, be thou my good!" if by such evil he could break the bonds of passion from the life of Pippa's son.

He had in him the mighty fanaticism which has made at once the tyrants and the martyrs of the world.

"Leave him to me," he had said, and then the strength and weakness, and ruthless heat, and utter self-deliverance of his nature leaped to their height, and nerved him with deadly passion.

"There is but one way," he said to himself;—there was but one way to cut the cords of this hideous, tangled knot of destiny and let free the boy to the old ways of innocence.

"He will curse me," he thought; "I shall die—never looking on his face—never hearing his voice. But he will be freed—so. He will suffer—for a day—a year. But he will be spared the truth. And he is so young—he will be glad again before the summer comes."

For a moment his courage failed him.

He could face the thought of an eternity of pain, and not turn pale, nor pause. But to die with the boy's curse on him—that was harder.

"It is selfishness to pause," he told himself. "He will loathe me always; but what matter?—he will be saved; he will be innocent once more; he will hear his 'beautiful things' again; he will never know the truth; he will be at peace with himself, and forget before the summer

comes. He never has loved me—not much. What does
it matter?—so that he is saved. When he sees his mother
in heaven some day, then she will say to him—'It was
done for your sake.' And I shall know that he sees then,
as God sees. That will be enough."

THE boy looked out through the iron bars of his open
lattice into the cold, still night, full of the smell of
fallen leaves and fir cones. The tears fell down his cheeks;
his heart was oppressed with a vague yearning, such as
made Mozart weep, when he heard his own Lacrimosa
chanted.

It is not fear of death, it is not desire of life.

It is that unutterable want, that nameless longing,
which stirs in the soul that is a little purer than its fellow,
and which, burdened with that prophetic pain which men
call genius, blindly feels its way after some great light,
that knows must be shining somewhere upon other worlds,
though all the earth is dark.

When Mozart wept, it was for the world he could never
reach—not for the world he left.

HE had been brought up upon this wooded spur,
looking down on the Signa country; all his loves
and hatreds, joys and pains, had been known here; from
the time he had plucked the maple leaves in autumn for
the cattle with little brown five-year-old hands he had
laboured here, never seeing the sun set elsewhere except
on that one night at the sea. He was close rooted to the
earth as the stonepines were and the oaks. It had always
seemed to him that a man should die where he took life

first, amongst his kindred and under the sods that his
feet had run over in babyhood. He had never thought
much about it, but unconsciously the fibres of his heart
had twisted themselves round all the smallest and the
biggest things of his home as the tendrils of a strong ivy
bush fasten round a great tower and the little stones
alike.

The wooden settle where his mother had sat ; the shrine
in the house wall ; the copper vessels that had glowed in
the wood-fuel light when a large family had gathered
there about the hearth ; the stone well under the walnut-
tree where dead Dina had often stayed to smile on him ;
the cypress-wood presses where Pippa had kept her feast-
day finery and her pearls ; the old vast sweet-smelling
sheds and stables where he had threshed and hewn and
yoked his oxen thirty years if one : all these things, and
a hundred like them, were dear to him with all the
memories of his entire life ; and away from them he could
know no peace.

He was going away into a great darkness. He had
nothing to guide him. The iron of a wasted love, of a
useless sacrifice, was in his heart. His instinct drove
him where there was peril for Pippa's son—that was
all.

If this woman took the lad away from him, where was
there any mercy or justice, earthly or divine? That was
all he asked himself, blindly and stupidly ; as the oxen
seem to ask it with their mild, sad eyes as they strain
under the yoke and goad, suffering and not knowing why
they suffer.

Nothing was clear to Bruno.

Only life had taught him that Love is the brother of
Death.

One thing and another had come between him and the
lad he cherished. The dreams of the child, the desires
of the youth, the powers of art, the passion of genius, one

by one had come in between him and loosened his hold,
and made him stand aloof as a stranger. But Love he
had dreaded most of all; Love which slays with one
glance dreams and art and genius, and lays them dead as
rootless weeds that rot in burning suns.

Now Love had come.

He worked all day, holding the sickness of fear off him
as best he could, for he was a brave man ;—only he had
wrestled with fate so long, and it seemed always to beat
him, and almost he grew tired.

He cut a week's fodder for the beasts, and left all things
in their places, and then, as the day darkened, prepared
to go.

Tinello and Pastore lowed at him, thrusting their
broad white foreheads and soft noses over their stable
door.

He turned and stroked them in farewell.

"Poor beasts !" he muttered; "shall I never muzzle
and yoke you ever again ?"

His throat grew dry, his eyes grew dim. He was like
a man who sails for a voyage on unknown seas, and
neither he nor any other can tell whether he will ever
return.

He might come back in a day ; he might come back
never.

Multitudes, well used to wander, would have laughed
at him. But to him it was as though he set forth on the
journey which men call death.

In the grey lowering evening he kissed the beasts on
their white brows. There was no one there to see his
weakness, and year on year he had decked them with
their garlands of hedge flowers and led them up on God's
day to have their strength blessed by the priest—their
strength that laboured with his own from dawn to dark
over the bare brown fields.

Then he turned his back on his old home, and went

down the green sides of the hill, and lost sight of his birthplace as the night fell.

All through the night he was borne away by the edge of the sea, along the wild windy shores, through the stagnant marshes and the black pools where the buffalo and the wild boar herded, past the deserted cities of the coast, and beyond the forsaken harbours of Æneas and of Nero.

The west wind blew strong; the clouds were heavy; now and then the moon shone on a sullen sea; now and then the darkness broke over rank maremma vapours; at times he heard the distant bellowing of the herds, at times he heard the moaning of the water; mighty cities, lost armies, slaughtered hosts, foundered fleets, were underneath that soil and sea; whole nations had their sepulchres on that low, wind-blown shore. But of these he knew nothing.

It only seemed to him, that day would never come.

Once or twice he fell asleep for a few moments, and waking in that confused noise of the stormy night and the wild water and the frightened herds, thought that he was dead, and that this sound was the passing of the feet of all the living multitude going for ever to and fro, unthinking, over the depths of the dark earth where he lay.

TO behold the dominion of evil; the victory of the liar; the empire of that which is base; to be powerless to resist, impotent to strip it bare; to watch it suck under a beloved life as the whirlpool the gold-freighted vessel; to know that the soul for which we would give our own to everlasting ruin is daily, hourly, momentarily subjugated, emasculated, possessed, devoured by those alien powers of violence and fraud which have fastened upon it as their prey; to stand by fettered and mute, and cry out to heaven that in this conflict the angels themselves should descend to wrestle for us, and yet know that all the while the very stars in their courses shall sooner stand still than this reign of sin be ended :—this is the greatest woe that the world holds.

Beaten, we shake in vain the adamant gates of a brazen iniquity ; we may bruise our breasts there till we die ; there is no entrance possible. For that which is vile is stronger than all love, all faith, all pure desire, all passionate pain ; that which is vile has all the forces that men have called the powers of hell.

TO him the world was like the dark fathomless waste of waters shelving away to nameless shapeless perils such as the old Greek mariners drew upon their charts as compassing the shores they knew.

He had no light of knowledge by which to pursue in hope or fancy the younger life that would be launched into the untried realms. To him such separation was as death.

He could not write ; he could not even read what was written. He could only trust to others that all was well with the boy.

He could have none of that mental solace which supports the scholar ; none of that sense of natural loveliness which consoles the poet ; his mind could not travel beyond the narrow circlet of its own pain ; his eyes could not see beauty everywhere from the green fly at his foot to the sapphire mountains above his head ; he only noticed the sunset to tell the weather ; he only looked across the plain to see if the rain-fall would cross the river. When the autumn crocus sank under his share, to him it was only a weed best withered ; in hell he believed, and for heaven he hoped, but only dully, as things certain that the priests knew; but all consolations of the mind or the fancy were denied to him. Superstitions, indeed, he had, but these were all;—sad-coloured fungi in the stead of flowers.

The Italian has not strong imagination.

His grace is an instinct; his love is a frenzy; his gaiety is rather joy than jest; his melancholy is from temperament, not meditation; nature is little to him; and his religion and his passions alike must have physical indulgence and perpetual nearness, or they are nothing.

He lived in almost absolute solitude. Sometimes it grew dreary, and the weeks seemed long.

Two years went by—slowly.

Signa did not come home. The travel to and fro took too much money, and he was engrossed in his studies, and it was best so; so Luigi Dini said, and Bruno let it be. The boy did not ask to return. His letters were very brief and not very coherent, and he forget to send messages to old Teresina or to Palma. But there was no fear for him.

The sacristan's friends under whose roof he was wrote once in a quarter, and spoke well of him always, and said that the professors did the same, and that a gentler lad or one more wedded to his work they never knew. And so Bruno kept his soul in patience, and said, " Do not trouble him; when he wishes he will come—or if he want anything. Let him be."

To those who have traversed far seas and many lands, and who can bridge untravelled countries by the aid of experience and of understanding, such partings have pain, but a pain lessened by the certain knowledge of their span and purpose. By the light of remembrance or of imagination they can follow that which leaves them.

But Bruno had no such solace.

To him all that was indefinite was evil; all that was unfamiliar was horrible. It is the error of ignorance at all times.

HE played for himself, for the air, for the clouds, for the trees, for the sheep, for the kids, for the waters, for the stones; played as Pan did, and Orpheus and Apollo.

His music came from heaven and went back to it. What did it matter who heard it on earth?

A lily would listen to him as never a man could do; and a daffodil would dance with delight as never woman could;—or he thought so at least, which was the same thing. And he could keep the sheep all round him, charmed and still, high above on the hillside, with the sad pines sighing.

What did he want with people to hear? He would play for them; but he did not care. If they felt it wrongly, or felt it not at all, he would stop, and run away.

"If they are deaf I will be dumb," he said. "The dogs and the sheep and the birds are never deaf—nor the hills—nor the flowers. It is only people that are deaf. I suppose they are always hearing their own steps and voices and wheels and windlasses and the cries of the children and the hiss of the frying-pans. I suppose that is why. Well, let them be deaf. Rusignuola and I do not want them."

So he said to Palma under the south wall, watching a butterfly, that folded was like an illuminated shield of black and gold, and with its wings spread was like a scarlet pomegranate blossom flying. Palma had asked him why he had run away from the bridal supper of

Griffeo, the coppersmith's son,—just in the midst of his music; run away home, he and his violin.

"They were not deaf," resumed Palma. "But your music was so sad—and they were merry."

"I played what came to me," said Signa.

"But you are merry sometimes."

"Not in a little room with oilwicks burning, and a stench of wine, and people round me. People always make me sad."

"Why that?"

"Because—I do not know:—when a number of faces are round me I seem stupid; it is as if I were in a cage; I feel as if God went away, farther, farther, farther!"

"But God made men and women."

"Yes. But I wonder if the trapped birds, and the beaten dogs, and the smarting mules, and the bleeding sheep think so."

"Oh, Signa!"

"I think they must doubt it," said Signa.

"But the beasts are not Christians, the priests say so," said Palma, who was a very true believer.

"I know. But I think they are. For they forgive. We never do."

"Some of us do."

"Not as the beasts do. Agnoto's house-lamb, the other day, licked his hand as he cut its throat. He told me so."

"That was because it loved him," said Palma.

"And how can it love if it have not a soul?" said Signa.

Palma munched her crust. This sort of meditation, which Signa was very prone to wander in, utterly confused her.

She could talk at need, as others could, of the young cauliflowers, and the spring lettuces, and the chances of the ripening corn, and the look of the budding grapes,

and the promise of the weather, and the likelihood of
drought, and the Parocco's last sermon, and the gossips'
last history of the neighbours, and the varying prices of
fine and of coarse plaiting; but anything else—Palma
was more at ease with the heavy pole pulling against her,
and the heavy bucket coming up sullenly from the water-
hole.

She felt, when he spoke in this way, much as Bruno
did—only far more intensely—as if Signa went away
from her—right away into the sky somewhere—as the
swallows went when they spread their wings to the east,
or the blue wood-smoke when it vanished.

"You love your music better than you do Bruno, or
me, or anything, Signa," she said, with a little sorrow
that was very humble, and not in the least reproach-
ful.

"Yes," said Signa, with the unconscious cruelty of one
in whom Art is born predominant. "Do you know,
Palma," he said suddenly, after a pause—"Do you know
—I think I could make something beautiful, something
men would be glad of, if only I could be where they
would care for it."

"We do care," said the girl gently.

"Oh, in a way. That is not what I mean," said the
boy, with a little impatience which daily grew on him
more, for the associates of his life. "You all care; you
all sing; it is as the finches do in the fields, without
knowing at all what it is that you do. You are all like
birds. You pipe—pipe—pipe, as you eat, as you work,
as you play. But what music do we ever have in the
churches? Who amongst you really likes all that music
when I play it off the old scores that Gigi says were
written by such great men, any better than you like the
tinkling of the mandolines when you dance in the threshing barns? I am sure you all like the mandolines best.
I know nothing here. I do not even know whether what

I do is worth much or nothing. I think if I could hear great music once—if I could go to Florence——"

"To Florence?" echoed Palma.

THE contadino not seldom goes through all his life without seeing one league beyond the fields of his labour, and the village that he is registered at, married at, and buried at, and which is the very apex of the earth to him. Women will spin and plait and hoe and glean within half a dozen miles of some great city whose name is an art glory in the mouths of scholars, and never will have seen it, never once perhaps, from their birth down to their grave. A few miles of vine-bordered roads, a breadth of corn-land, a rounded hill, a little red roof under a mulberry tree, a church tower with a saint upon the roof, and a bell that sounds over the walnut-trees—these are their world : they know and want to know no other.

A narrow life, no doubt, yet not without much to be said for it. Without unrest, without curiosity, without envy ; clinging like a plant to the soil ; and no more willing to wander than the vinestakes which they thrust into the earth.

To those who have put a girdle round the earth with their footsteps, the whole world seems much smaller than does the hamlet or farm of his affections to the peasant :—and how much poorer ! The vague, dreamful wonder of an untravelled distance—of an untracked horizon—has after all more romance in it than lies in the whole globe run over in a year.

Who can ever look at the old maps in Herodotus or Xenophon without a wish that the charm of those unknown limits and those untraversed seas was ours ?— without an irresistible sense that to have sailed away, in

vaguest hazard, into the endless mystery of the utterly
unknown, must have had a sweetness and a greatness in
it that is never to be extracted from "the tour of the
world in ninety days."

" SHE takes a whim for him ; a fancy of a month ; he
thinks it heaven and eternity. She has ruined
him. His genius is burned up ; his youth is dead ; he
will do nothing more of any worth. Women like her
are like the Indian drugs, that sleep and kill. How is
that any fault of mine? He could see the thing she
was. If he will fling his soul away upon a creature
lighter than thistle-down, viler than a rattlesnake's
poison, poorer and quicker to pass than the breath of
a gnat—whose blame is that except his own? There
was a sculptor once, you know, that fell to lascivious
worship of the marble image he had made ; well,—poets
are not even so far wise as that. They make an image
out of the gossamer rainbow stuff of their own dreams,
and then curse heaven and earth because it dissolves to
empty air in their fond arms—whose blame is that? The
fools are made so—— "

NOT only the fly on the spoke takes praise to itself
for the speed of the wheel, but the stone that
would fain have hindered it, says, when the wheel un-
hindered has passed it, "Lo! see how much I helped!"

THE woman makes or mars the man : the man the woman. Mythology had no need of the Fates.

There is only one; the winged blind god that came by night to Psyche.

ALL in a moment his art perished.

When a human love wakes it crushes fame like a dead leaf, and all the spirits and ministers of the mind shrink away before it, and can no more allure, no more console, but, sighing, pass into silence and are dumb.

LIFE, without a central purpose around which it can revolve, is like a star that has fallen out of its orbit. With a great affection or a great aim gone, the practical life may go on loosely, indifferently, mechanically, but it takes no grip on outer things, it has no vital interest, it gravitates to nothing.

MEN who dwell in solitude are superstitious. There is no "chance" for them.

The common things of earth and air to them grow portents : and it is easier for them to believe that the universe revolves to serve the earth, than to believe that men are to the universe as the gnats in the sunbeam to the sun; they can sooner credit that the constellations are charged with their destiny, than that they can suffer and die without arousing a sigh for them anywhere in all creation. It is not vanity, as the mocker too hastily thinks. It is the helpless, pathetic cry of the mortal to the immortal nature from which he springs :

"Leave me not alone: confound me not with the matter that perishes : I am full of pain—have pity !"

To be the mere sport of hazard as a dead moth is on

the wind—the heart of man refuses to believe it can be
so with him. To be created only to be abandoned—he
will not think that the forces of existence are so cruel
and so unrelenting and so fruitless. In the world he
may learn to say that he thinks so, and is resigned to
it; but in loneliness the penumbra of his own existence
lies on all creation, and the winds and the stars and the
daylight and night and the vast unknown mute forces of
life—all seem to him that they must of necessity be either
his ministers or his destroyers.

OF all the innocent things that die, the impossible
dreams of the poet are the things that die with
most pain, and, perhaps, with most loss to humanity.
Those who are happy die before their dreams. This
is what the old Greek saying meant.

The world had not yet driven the sweet, fair follies
from Signa's head, nor had it yet made him selfish. If
he had lived in the age when Timander could arrest by
his melodies the tide of revolution, or when the harp of
the Persian could save Bagdad from the sword and flame
of Murad, all might have been well with him. But the
time is gone by when music or any other art was a king.
All genius now is, at its best, but a servitor—well or ill fed.

SILENTLY he put his hand out and grasped Signa's,
and led him into the Spanish Chapel, and sank on
his knees.

The glory of the morning streamed in from the cloister;
all the dead gold and the faded hues were transfigured
by it; the sunbeams shone on the face of Laura, the
deep sweet colours of Bronzino's Cœna glowed upward
in the vault amidst the shadows; the company of the

Q

blessed, whom the old painters had gathered there, cast off the faded robes that the Ages had wrapped them in, and stood forth like the tender spirits that they were, and seemed to say, " Nay, we, and they who made us, we are not dead, but only waiting."

It is all so simple and so foolish there ; the war-horses of Taddeo that bear their lords to eternity as to a joust of arms ; the heretic dogs of Memmi, with their tight wooden collars ; the beauteous Fiammetta and her lover, thronging amongst the saints ; the little house, where the Holy Ghost is sitting, with the purified saints listening at the door, with strings tied to their heads to lift them into paradise ; it is all so quaint, so childlike, so pathetic, so grotesque,—like a set of wooden figures from its Noah's Ark that a dying child has set out on its little bed, and that are so stiff and ludicrous, and yet which no one well can look at and be unmoved, by reason of the little cold hand that has found beauty in them.

As the dying child to the wooden figures, so the dead faith gives to the old frescoes here something that lies too deep for tears ; we smile, and yet all the while we say ;—if only we could believe like this ; if only for us the dead could be but sleeping !

IT was past midnight, and the moon had vanished behind her mountain, withdrawing her little delicate curled golden horn, as if to blow with it the trumpet-call of morning.

SUCH pretty, neat, ready lying as this would stand him in better stead than all the high spirit in the world ; which, after all, only serves to get a man into hot water in this life and eternal fire in the next.

IN the country of Virgil, life remains pastoral still. The field labourer of northern countries may be but a hapless hind, hedging and ditching dolefully, or at best serving a steam-beast with oil and fire; but in the land of the Georgics there is the poetry of agriculture still.

Materially it may be an evil and a loss—political economists will say so; but spiritually it is a gain. A certain peace and light lie on the people at their toil. The reaper with his hook, the plougher with his oxen, the girl who gleans amongst the trailing vines, the child that sees the flowers tossing with the corn, the men that sing to get a blessing on the grapes—they have all a certain grace and dignity of the old classic ways left with them. They till the earth still with the simplicity of old, looking straight to the gods for recompense. Great Apollo might still come down amidst them and play to them in their threshing-barns, and guide his milk-white beasts over their furrows,—and there would be nothing in the toil to shame or burden him. It will not last. The famine of a world too full will lay it waste; but it is here a little while longer still.

FOR Discontent already creeps into each of these happy households, and under her fox-skin hood says, "Let me in—I am Progress."

IN most men and women, Love waking wakes, with itself, the soul.

In poets Love waking kills it.

WHEN God gives genius, I think He makes the brain of some strange, glorious stuff, that takes all strength out of the character, and all sight out of the

eyes. Those artists—they are like the birds we blind:
they sing, and make people weep for very joy to hear
them; but they cannot see their way to peck the worms,
and are for ever wounding their breasts against the wires.
No doubt it is a great thing to have genius; but it is a
sort of sickness after all; and when love comes——

L IPPO knew that wise men do not do harm to whatever they may hate.

They drive it on to slay itself.

So without blood-guiltiness they get their end, yet
stainless go to God.

H E was a little shell off the seashore that Hermes had
taken out of millions like it that the waves washed
up, and had breathed into, and had strung with fine
chords, and had made into a syrinx sweet for every human
ear.

Why not break the simple shell for sport? She did
not care for music. Did the gods care—they could make
another.

S TART a lie and a truth together, like hare and hound;
the lie will run fast and smooth, and no man will
ever turn it aside; but at the truth most hands will fling
a stone, and so hinder it for sport's sake, if they can.

H E heard the notes of a violin, quite faint and distant,
but sweet as the piping of a blackbird amongst the
white anemones of earliest spring.

"NATURE makes some folks false as it makes lizards wriggle," said he. "Lippo is a lizard. No dog ever caught him napping, though he looks so lazy in the sun."

HE did not waver. He did not repine. He made no reproach, even in his own thoughts. He had only lost all the hope out of his life and all the pride of it.

But men lose these and live on ; women also.

He had built up his little kingdom out of atoms, little by little ; atoms of time, of patience, of self-denial, of hoarded coins, of snatched moments ;—built it up little by little, at cost of bodily labour and of bodily pain, as the pyramids were built brick by brick by the toil and the torment of unnoticed lives.

It was only a poor little nook of land, but it had been like an empire won to him.

With his foot on its soil he had felt rich.

And now it was gone—gone like a handful of thistle-down lost on the winds, like a spider's web broken in a shower of rain. Gone : never to be his own again. Never.

He sat and watched the brook run on, the pied birds come to drink, the throstle stir on the olive, the cloud shadows steal over the brown, bare fields.

The red flush of sunrise faded. Smoke rose from the distant roofs. Men came out on the lands to work. Bells rang. The day began.

He got up slowly and went away ; looking backwards, looking backwards, always.

Great leaders who behold their armed hosts melt like snow, and great monarchs who are driven out discrowned from the palaces of their fathers, are statelier figures and have more tragic grace than he had ;—only a peasant leaving a shred of land, no bigger than a rich man's dwelling-house will cover;—but vanquished leader or exiled monarch never was more desolate than Bruno, when the full sun rose and he looked his last look upon the three poor fields, where for ever the hands of other men would labour, and for ever the feet of other men would wander.

H E only heard the toads cry to one another, feeling rain coming, "Crake! crake! crake! We love a wet world as men an evil way. The skies are going to weep; let us be merry. Crock! crock! crock!"

And they waddled out—slow, quaint, black things, with arms akimbo, and stared at him with their shrewd, hard eyes. They would lie snug a thousand years with a stone and be quite happy.

Why were not men like that?

Toads are kindly in their way, and will get friendly. Only men seem to them such fools.

The toad is a fakeer, and thinks the beatitude of life lies in contemplation. Men fret and fuss and fume, and are for ever in haste; the toad eyes them with contempt.

I WOULD die this hour, oh, so gladly, if I could be quite sure that my music would be loved, and be remembered. I do not know: there can be nothing like it, I think:—a thing you create, that is all your own, that is the very breath of your mouth, and the very voice of your soul; which is all that is best in you, the very gift of God; and then to know that all this may be lost eternally, killed, stifled, buried, just for want of men's faith and a little gold! I do not think there can be any loss like it, nor any suffering like it, anywhere else in the world. Oh, if only it would do any good, I would fling my body into the grave to-morrow, happy, quite happy;

if only afterwards, they would sing my songs, all over the earth, and just say, "God spoke to him; and he has told men what He said."

NO one can make much music with the mandoline, but there is no other music, perhaps, which sounds so fittingly to time and place, as do its simple sonorous tender chords when heard through the thickets of rose-laurel or the festoons of the vines, vibrating on the stillness of the night under the Tuscan moon. It would suit the serenade of Romeo; Desdemona should sing the willow song to it, and not to the harp; Paolo pleaded by it, be sure, many a time to Francesca; and Stradella sang to it the passion whose end was death; it is of all music the most Italian, and it fills the pauses of the love-songs softly, like a sigh or like a kiss.

Its very charm is, that it says so little. Love wants so little said.

And the mandoline, though so mournful and full of languor as Love is, yet can be gay with that caressing joy born of beautiful nothings, which makes the laughter of lovers the lightest-hearted laughter that ever gives silver wings to time.

IT was a quaint, vivid, pretty procession, full of grace and of movement—classic and homely, pagan and mediæval, both at once—bright in hue, rustic in garb, poetic in feeling.

Teniers might have painted the brown girls and boys leaping and singing on the turf, with their brandishing boughs, their flaring torches, their bare feet, their tossing arms; but Leonardo or Guercino would have been wanted for the face of the young singer whom they carried, with the crown of the leaves and of the roses on

his drooped head, like the lotus flowers on the young
Antinous.

Piero di Cosimo, perhaps, in one of his greatest moments of brilliant caprice, might best have painted the
whole, with the background of the dusky hill-side; and
he would have set it round with strange arabesques in
gold, and illumined amongst them in emblem the pipe of
the shepherd, and the harp of the muse, and the river-
rush that the gods would cut down and fill with their
breath and the music of heaven.

Bruno stood by, and let the innocent pageant pass,
with its gold of autumn foliage and its purples of crocus-
like colchicum.

He heard their voices crying in the court: "We have
got him—we have brought him. Our Signa, who is
going to be great!"

A LL life had been to him as the divining-rod of Aaron,
blooming ever afresh with magic flowers. Now
that the flame of pain and passion burned it up, and left
a bare sear brittle bough, he could not understand.

Love is cruel as the grave.

The poet has embraced the universe in his visions,
and heard harmony in every sound, from deep calling
through the darkest storm to deep, as from the lightest
leaf-dancing in the summer wind; he has found joy in
the simplest things, in the nest of a bird, in the wayside
grass, in the yellow sand, in the rods of the willow; the
lowliest creeping life has held its homily and solace, and
in the hush of night he has lifted his face to the stars,
and thought that he communed with their Creator and
his own. Then—all in a moment—Love claims him,
and there is no melody anywhere save in one single
human voice, there is no heaven for him save on one
human breast; when one face is turned from him there

is darkness on all the earth; when one life is lost—let the
stars reel from their courses and the world whirl and
burn and perish like the moon; nothing matters; when
Love is dead there is no God.

BRUNO lay down that night, but for an hour only.
He could not sleep.

He rose before the sun was up, in the grey wintry break
of day, while the fog from the river rose like a white wall
built up across the plain.

It is the season when the peasant has the least to do.
Ploughing, and sowing, and oil-pressing, all are past;
there is little labour for man or beast; there is only
garden work for the vegetable market, and the care of
the sheep and cattle, where there are any. In large
households, where many brothers and sisters get round
the oil lamp and munch roast chestnuts and thrum a
guitar, or tell ghost stories, these short empty days are
very well; sometimes there is a stranger lost coming over
the pinewoods, sometimes there is a snow-storm, and the
sheep want seeing to; sometimes there is the old roister-
ing way of keeping Twelfth-night, even on these lonely
wind-torn heights; where the house is full and merry,
the short winter passes not so very dully; but in the
solitary places, where men brood alone, as Bruno did,
they are heavy enough; all the rest of the world might
be dead and buried, the stillness is so unbroken, the
loneliness so great.

He got up and saw after his few sheep above amongst
the pines; one or two of them were near lambing; then
he laboured on his garden mould amongst the potato
plants and cauliflowers, the raw mist in his lungs and the
sea-wind blowing. It had become very mild; the red
rose on his house-wall was in bud, and the violets were

beginning to push from underneath the moss; but the mornings were always very cold and damp.

An old man came across from Carmignano to beg a pumpkin-gourd or two; he got a scanty living by rubbing them up and selling them to the fishermen down on the Arno. Bruno gave them. He had known the old creature all his life.

"You are dull here," said the old man, timidly; because every one was more or less afraid of Bruno.

Bruno shrugged his shoulders and took up his spade again.

"Your boy does grand things, they say," said the old man; "but it would be cheerfuller for you if he had taken to the soil."

Bruno went on digging.

"It is like a man I know," said the pumpkin-seller, thinking the sound of his own voice must be a charity. "A man that helped to cast church-bells. He cast bells all his life; he never did anything else at all. 'It is brave work,' said he to me once, 'sweating in the furnace there and making the metal into tuneful things to chime the praise of all the saints and angels; but when you sweat and sweat and sweat, and every bell you make just goes away and is swung up where you never see or hear it ever again—that seems sad; my bells are all ringing in the clouds, saving the people's souls, greeting Our Lady; but they are all gone ever so far away from me. I only hear them ringing in my dreams.' Now, I think the boy is like the bells—to you."

Bruno dug in the earth.

"The man was a fool," said he. "Who cared for his sweat or sorrow? It was his work to melt the metal. That was all."

"Ay," said the pumpkin-seller, and shouldered the big, yellow, wrinkled things that he had begged; "but never to hear the bells—that is sad work."

Bruno smiled grimly.

"Sad ! He could hear some of them as other people did, no doubt, ringing far away against the skies while he was in the mud. That was all he wanted ; if he were wise, he did not even want so much as that. Good-day."

It was against his wont to speak so many words on any other thing than the cattle or the olive harvest or the prices of seeds and grain in the market in the town. He set his heel upon his spade and pitched the earth-begrimed potatoes in the skip he filled.

The old man nodded and went—to wend his way to Carmignano.

Suddenly he turned back : he was a tender-hearted, fanciful soul, and had had a long, lonely life himself.

"I tell you what," he said, a little timidly ; "perhaps the bells, praising God always, ringing the sun in and out, and honouring Our Lady ; perhaps they went for something in the lives of the men that made them ? I think they must. It would be hard if the bells got everything, the makers nothing."

Over Bruno's face a slight change went. His imperious eyes softened. He knew the old man spoke in kindness.

"Take these home with you. Nay ; no thanks," he said, and lifted on the other's back the kreel full of potatoes dug for the market.

The old man blessed him, overjoyed ; he was sickly and very poor ; and hobbled on his way along the side of the mountains.

Bruno went to other work.

If the bells ring true and clear, and always to the honour of the saints, a man may be content to have sweated for it in the furnace and to be forgot ; but—if it be cracked in a fire and the pure ore of it melt away shapeless?

.   .   .   .   .   .

"Toccò" was sounding from all the city clocks. He met another man he knew, a farmer from Montelupo.

"Brave doings!" said the Montelupo man. "A gala night to-night for the foreign prince, and your boy summoned, so they say. No doubt you are come in to see it all?"

Bruno shook himself free quickly, and went on; for a moment it occurred to him that it might be best to wait and see Signa in the town; but then he could not do that well. Nothing was done at home, and the lambs could not be left alone to the shepherd lad's inexperience; only a day old, one or two of them, and the ground so wet, and the ewes weakly. To leave his farm would have seemed to Bruno as to leave his sinking ship does to a sailor. Besides, he had nothing to do with all the grandeur; the king did not want *him.*

All this stir and tumult and wonder and homage in the city was for Signa; princes seemed almost like his servants, the king like his henchman! Bruno was proud, under his stern, calm, lofty bearing, which would not change, and would not let him smile, or seem so womanish-weak as to be glad for all the gossiping.

The boy wanted no king or prince.

He said so to them with erect disdain.

Yet he was proud.

"After all, one does hear the bells ringing," he thought; his mind drifting away to the old Carmignano beggar's words. He was proud, and glad.

He stopped his mule by Strozzi palace, and pushed his way into the almost empty market to the place called the Spit or Fila, where all day long and every day before the roaring fires the public cooks roast flesh and fowl to fill the public paunch of Florence.

Here there was a large crowd, pushing to buy the frothing, savoury hot meats. He thrust the others aside, and bought half a kid smoking, and a fine capon, and

thrust them in his cart. Then he went to a shop near,
and bought some delicate white bread, and some foreign
chocolate, and some snowy sugar.

"No doubt," he thought, "the boy had learned to like
daintier fare than theirs in his new life;" theirs, which
was black crusts and oil and garlic all the year round,
with meat and beans, perhaps, on feast nights, now and
then, by way of a change. Then as he was going to get
into his seat he saw among the other plants and flowers
standing for sale upon the ledge outside the palace a
damask rose-tree—a little thing, but covered with buds
and blossoms blushing crimson against the stately old
iron torch-rings of the smith Caprera. Bruno looked at
it—he who never thought of flowers from one year's end
on to another, and cut them down with his scythe for his
oxen to munch as he cut grass. Then he bought it.

The boy liked all beautiful innocent things, and had
been always so foolish about the lowliest herb. It would
make the dark old house upon the hill look bright to
him. Ashamed of the weaknesses that he yielded to,
Bruno sent the mule on at its fastest pace; the little red
rose-tree nodding in the cart.

He had spent more in a day than he was accustomed
to spend in three months' time.

But then the house looked so cheerless.

As swiftly as he could make the mule fly, he drove
home across the plain.

The boy was there, no doubt; and would be cold and
hungry, and alone.

Bruno did not pause a moment on his way, though
more than one called to him as he drove, to know if it
were true indeed that this night there was to be a gala
for the Lamia and the princes.

He nodded, and flew through the chill grey afternoon,
splashing the deep mud on either side of him.

The figure of St. Giusto on his high tower; the leafless

vines and the leafless poplars; the farriers' and coopers' workshops on the road; grim Castel Pucci, that once flung its glove at Florence; the green low dark hills of Castagnolo; villa and monastery, watch-tower and bastion, homestead and convent, all flew by him, fleeting and unseen; all he thought of was that the boy would be waiting, and want food.

He was reckless and furious in his driving always, but his mule had never been beaten and breathless as it was that day when he tore up the ascent to his own farm as the clocks in the plain tolled four.

He was surprised to see his dog lie quiet on the steps.

"Is he there?" he cried instinctively to the creature, which rose and came to greet him.

There was no sound anywhere.

Bruno pushed his door open.

The house was empty.

He went out again and shouted to the air.

The echo from the mountain above was all his answer. When that died away the old silence of the hills was unbroken.

He returned and took the food and the little rose-tree out of his cart.

He had bought them with eagerness, and with that tenderness which was in him, and for which dead Dina had loved him to her hurt. He had now no pleasure in them. A bitter disappointment flung its chill upon him.

Disappointment is man's most frequent visitor—the uninvited guest most sure to come; he ought to be well used to it; yet he can never get familiar.

Bruno ought to have learned never to hope.

But his temper was courageous and sanguine: such madmen hope on to the very end.

He put the things down on the settle, and went to put up the mule. The little rose-tree had been too roughly blown in the windy afternoon; its flowers were falling, and some soon strewed the floor.

Bruno looked at it when he entered.

It hurt him; as the star Argol had done.

He covered the food with a cloth, and set the flower out of the draught. Then he went to see his sheep.

There was no train by the seaway from Rome until night. Signa would not come that way now, since he had to be in the town for the evening.

"He will come after the theatre," Bruno said to himself, and tried to get the hours away by work. He did not think of going into the city again himself. He was too proud to go and see a thing he had never been summoned to; too proud to stand outside the doors and stare with the crowd while Pippa's son was honoured within.

Besides, he could not have left the lambs all a long winter's night; and the house all unguarded; and nobody there to give counsel to the poor mute simpleton whom he had now to tend his beasts.

"He will come after the theatre," he said.

The evening seemed very long.

The late night came. Bruno set his door open, cold though it was; so that he should catch the earliest sound of footsteps. The boy, no doubt, he thought, would drive to the foot of the hill, and walk the rest.

It was a clear night after the rain of many days.

He could see the lights of the city in the plain fourteen miles or so away.

What was doing down there?

It seemed strange;—Signa being welcomed there, and he himself knowing nothing—only hearing a stray word or two by chance.

Once or twice in his younger days he had seen the city in gala over some great artist it delighted to honour; he could imagine the scene and fashion of it all well enough; he did not want to be noticed in it, only he would have

liked to have been told, and to have gone down and
seen it, quietly wrapped in his cloak, amongst the
throng.

That was how he would have gone, had he been told.

He set the supper out as well as he could, and put wine
ready, and the rose-tree in the midst. In the lamplight
the little feast did not look so badly.

He wove wicker-work round some uncovered flasks by
way of doing something. The bitter wind blew in; he
did not mind that; his ear was strained to listen. Midnight passed. The wind had blown his lamp out. He
lighted two great lanthorns, and hung them up against
the doorposts; it was so dark upon the hills.

One hour went; another; then another. There was
no sound. When yet another passed, and it was four
of the clock, he said:

"He will not come to-night. No doubt they kept him
late, and he was too tired. He will be here by sunrise."

He threw himself on his bed for a little time, and closed
the door. But he left the lanthorns hanging outside; on
the chance.

He slept little; he was up while it was still dark, and
the robins were beginning their first twittering notes.

"He will be here to breakfast," he said to himself, and
he left the table untouched, only opening the shutters so
that when day came it should touch the rose at once and
wake it up; it looked so drooping, as though it felt the
cold.

Then he went and saw to his beasts and to his work.

The sun leapt up in the cold, broad, white skies. Signa
did not come with it.

The light brightened. The day grew. Noon brought
its hour of rest.

The table still stood unused. The rose-leaves had
fallen in a little crimson pool upon it. Bruno sat down
on the bench by the door, not having broken his fast.

"They are keeping him in the town," he thought. "He will come later."

He sat still a few moments, but he did not eat.

In a little while he heard a step on the dead winter leaves and tufts of rosemary. He sprang erect; his eyes brightened; his face changed. He went forward eagerly :

"Signa !—my dear !—at last !"

He only saw under the leafless maples and brown vine tendrils a young man that he had never seen, who stopped before him breathing quickly from the steepness of the ascent.

"I was to bring this to you," he said, holding out a long gun in its case. "And to tell you that he, the youth they all talk of—Signa—went back to Rome this morning; had no time to come, but sends you this, with his dear love and greeting, and will write from Rome to-night. Ah, Lord ! There was such fuss with him in the city. He was taken to the foreign princes, and then the people !—if you had heard them !—all the street rang with the cheering. This morning he could hardly get away for all the crowd there was. I am only a messenger. I should be glad of wine. Your hill is steep."

Bruno took the gun from him, and put out a flask of his own wine on the threshold ; then shut close the door.

It was such a weapon as he had coveted all his life long, seeing such in gunsmiths' windows and the halls of noblemen : a breech-loader, of foreign make, beautifully mounted and inlaid with silver.

He sat still a little while, the gun lying on his knees ; there was a great darkness on his face. Then he gripped it in both hands, the butt in one, the barrel in the other, and dashed the centre of it down across the round of his great grindstone.

The blow was so violent, the wood of the weapon snapped with it across the middle, the shining metal

R

loosened from its hold. He struck it again, and again, and again; until all the polished walnut was flying in splinters, and the plates of silver, bent and twisted, falling at his feet; the finely tempered steel of the long barrel alone was whole.

He went into his woodshed, and brought out branches of acacia brambles, and dry boughs of pine, and logs of oak; dragging them forth with fury. He piled them in the empty yawning space of the black hearth, and built them one on another in a pile; and struck a match and fired them, tossing pine-cones in to catch the flames.

In a few minutes a great fire roared alight, the turpentine in the pine-apples and fir-boughs blazing like pitch. Then he fetched the barrel of the gun, and the oaken stock, and the silver plates and mountings, and threw them into the heat.

The flaming wood swallowed them up; he stood and watched it.

After a while a knock came at his house-door.

"Who is there?" he called.

"It is I," said a peasant's voice. "There is so much smoke, I thought you were on fire. I was on the lower hill, so I ran up—is all right with you?"

"All is right with me."

"But what is the smoke?"

"I bake my bread."

"It will be burnt to cinders."

I make it, and I eat it. Whose matter is it?"

The peasant went away muttering, with slow unwilling feet.

Bruno watched the fire.

After a brief time its frenzy spent itself; the flames died down; the reddened wood grew pale, and began to change to ash; the oaken stock was all consumed, the silver was melted and fused into shapeless lumps, the steel tube alone kept shape unchanged, but it was

blackened and choked up with ashes, and without
beauty or use.

Bruno watched the fire die down into a great mound
of dull grey and brown charred wood.

Then he went out, and drew the door behind him, and
locked it.

The last red rose dropped, withered by the heat.

THERE is always song somewhere. As the wine
waggon creaks down the hill, the waggoner will
chant to the corn that grows upon either side of him.
As the miller's mules cross the bridge, the lad as he cracks
his whip will hum to the blowing alders. In the red
clover, the labourers will whet their scythes to a trick of
melody. In the quiet evenings a Kyrie Eleison will rise
from the thick leaves that hide a village chapel. On the
hills the goatherd, high in air amongst the arbutus
branches, will scatter on the lonely mountain-side stanzas
of purest rhythm. By the sea-shore, where Shelley died,
the fisherman, rough and salt and weather-worn, will string
notes of sweetest measure under the tamarisk-tree on his
mandoline. But the poetry and the music float on the
air like the leaves of roses that blossom in a solitude, and
drift away to die upon the breeze; there is no one to
notice the fragrance, there is no one to gather the leaves.

BUT then life does not count by years. Some suffer a
lifetime in a day, and so grow old between the rising
and the setting of a sun.

BUT he was not obstinate. He only stretched towards
the light he saw, as the plant in the cellar will stretch
through the bars.

Tens of millions of little peasants come to the birth, and grow up and become men, and do the daily bidding of the world, and work and die, and have no more of soul or Godhead in them than the grains of sand. But here and there, with no lot different from his fellows, one is born to dream and muse and struggle to the sun of higher desires, and the world calls such a one Burns, or Haydn, or Giotto, or Shakespeare, or whatever name the fierce light of fame may burn upon and make irridescent.

THE mighty lives have passed away into silence, leaving no likeness to them on earth ; but if you would still hold communion with them, even better than to go to written score or printed book or painted panel or chiselled marble or cloistered gloom is it to stray into one of these old quiet gardens, where for hundreds of years the stone naiad has leaned over the fountain, and the golden lizard hidden under the fallen caryatide, and sit quite still, and let the stones tell you what they remember, and the leaves say what the sun once saw ; and then the shades of the great dead will come to you. Only you must love them truly, else you will see them never.

"HOW he loves that thing already—as he never will love me," thought Bruno, looking down at him in the starlight, with that dull sense of hopeless rivalry and alien inferiority which the self-absorption of genius inflicts innocently and unconsciously on the human affections that cling to it, and which later on love avenges upon it in the same manner.

WHO can look at the old maps in Herodotus or Xenophon, without a wish that the charm of those unknown limits and those untraversed seas was ours?—without an irresistible sense that to have sailed away, in vaguest hazard, into the endless mystery of the utterly unknown, must have had a sweetness and a greatness in it that is never to be extracted from the "tour of the world in ninety days."

FAIR faiths are the blossoms of life. When the faith drops, spring is over.

IN the country of Virgil, life remains pastoral still. The field-labourer of northern counties may be but a hapless hind, hedging and ditching dolefully, or at least serving a steam-beast with oil and fire, but in the land of the Georgics there is the poetry of agriculture still.

THE fatal desire of fame, which is to art the corroding element, as the desire of the senses is to love—bearing with it the seeds of satiety and mortality—had entered into him without his knowing what it was that ailed him.

GENIUS lives in isolation, and suffers from it. But perhaps it creates it. The breath of its lips is like ether; purer than the air around it, it changes the air for others into ice.

CONSCIENCE and genius—the instinct of the heart, and the desire of the mind—the voice that warns and the voice that ordains : when these are in conflict, it is bitter for life in which they are at war; most bitter of all when that life is in its opening youth, and sure of everything, and yet sure of nothing.

BETWEEN them there was that bottomless chasm of mental difference, across which mutual affection can throw a rope-chain of habit and forbearance for the summer days, but which no power on earth can ever bridge over with that iron of sympathy which stands throughout all storms.

WHEN the heart is fullest of pain, and the mouth purest with truth, there is a cruel destiny in things, which often makes the words worst chosen and surest to defeat the end they seek.

THERE is a chord in every human heart that has a sigh in it if touched aright. When the artist finds the key-note which that chord will answer to—in the dullest as in the highest—then he is great.

LIFE without a central purpose around which it can revolve, is like a star that has fallen out of its orbit. With a great affection or a great aim gone, the practical life may go on loosely, indifferently, mechanically, but it takes no grip on outer things, it has no vital interest, it gravitates to nothing.

FAME has only the span of a day, they say. But to live in the hearts of the people—that is worth something.

KEEP young. Keep innocent. Innocence does not come back : and repentance is a poor thing beside it.

THE chimes of the monastery were ringing out for the first mass ; deep bells of sweet tone, that came down the river like a benediction on the day. Signa kneeled down on the grass.

"Did you pray for the holy men?" Bruno asked him when they rose, and they went on under the tall green quivering trees.

"No," said Signa under his breath. "I prayed for the devil."

"FOR him?" echoed Bruno aghast; "what are you about, child? Are you possessed? Do you know what the good priests would say?"

"I prayed for him," said Signa. "It is he who wants it. To be wicked *there* where God is, and the sun, and the bells"——

"But he is the foe of God. It is horrible to pray for him."

"No," said Signa, sturdily. "God says we are to forgive our enemies, and help them. I only asked Him to begin with His."

Bruno was silent.

TRICOTRIN.

AT every point where her eyes glanced there was a
picture of exquisite colour, and light, and variety.

But the scene in its loveliness was so old to her, so
familiar, that it was scarcely lovely, only monotonous.
With all a child's usual ignorant impatience of the joys
of the present—joys so little valued at the time, so futilely
regretted in the after-years—she was heedless of the
hour's pleasure, she was longing for what had not come.

ON the whole, the Waif fared better, having fallen to
the hands of a vagabond philosopher, than if she
had drifted to those of a respected philanthropist. The
latter would have had her glistening hair shorn short,
as a crown with which that immortal and inconsistent
socialist Nature had no justification in crowning a
foundling, and, in his desire to make her fully expiate
the lawless crime of entering the world without purse or
passport, would have left her no choice, as she grew into
womanhood, save that between sinning and starving.
The former bade the long fair tresses float on the air,
sunny rebels against bondage, and saw no reason why
the childhood of the castaway should not have its share
of childish joyousness as well as the childhood prince-
begotten and palace-cradled ; holding that the fresh life

just budded on earth was as free from all soil, no matter
whence it came, as is the brook of pure rivulet water, no
matter whether it spring from classic lake or from darksome cavern.

THE desire to be "great" possessed her. When that
insatiate passion enters a living soul, be it the soul
of a woman-child dreaming of a coquette's conquests, or
a crowned hero craving for a new world, it becomes
blind to all else. Moral death falls on it ; and any sin
looks sweet that takes it nearer to its goal. It is a passion that generates at once all the loftiest and all the
vilest things, which between them ennoble and corrupt
the world—even as heat generates at once the harvest
and the maggot, the purpling vine and the lice that
devour it. It is a passion without which the world
would decay in darkness, as it would do without heat,
yet to which, as to heat, all its filthiest corruption is due.

A WOMAN'S fair repute is like a blue harebell—a
touch can wither it.

VIVA had gained the "great world ;" and because
she had gained it all the old things of her lost post
grew unalterably sweet to her now that they no longer
could be called hers. The brown, kind, homely, tender
face of grand'mère ; the gambols of white and frolicsome
Bébé ; the woods where, with every spring, she had filled
her arms with sheaves of delicate primroses ; the quaint
little room with its strings of melons and sweet herbs, its
glittering brass and pewter, its wood-fire with the soup-
pot simmering above the flame ; the glad free days in

the vineyard and on the river, with the winds blowing
fragrance from over the clover and flax, and the acacias
and lindens ; nay, even the old, quiet, sleepy hours within
the convent-walls, lying on the lush unshaven grass,
while the drowsy bells rang to vespers or compline,—all
became suddenly precious and dear to her when once
she knew that they had drifted away from her for evermore.

THEN he bent his head, letting her desire be his law;
and that music, which had given its hymn for the
vintage-feast of the Loire, and which had brought back
the steps of the suicide from the river-brink in the darkness of the Paris night, which sovereigns could not command and which held peasants entranced by its spell,
thrilled through the stillness of the chamber.

Human in its sadness, more than human in its eloquence,
now melancholy as the Miserere that sighs through the
gloom of a cathedral at midnight, now rich as the glory
of the afterglow in Egypt, a poem beyond words, a prayer
grand as that which seems to breathe from the hush of
mountain solitudes when the eternal snows are lighted
by the rising of the sun—the melody of the violin filled
the silence of the closing day.

The melancholy, ever latent in the vivid natures of
men of genius, is betrayed and finds voice in their Art.
Goethe laughs with the riotous revellers, and rejoices
with the summer of the vines, and loves the glad abandonment of woman's soft embraces, and with his last words
prays for Light. But the profound sadness of the great
and many-sided master-mind thrills through and breaks
out in the intense humanity, the passionate despair of
Faust; the melancholy and the yearning of the soul are
there.

With Tricotrin they were uttered in his music.

" LET me be but amused! Let me only laugh if I die!"
cries the world in every age. It has so much of
grief and tragedy in its own realities, it has so many
bitter tears to shed in its solitude, it has such weariness
of labour without end, it has such infinitude of woe to
regard in its prisons, in its homes, in its battlefields, in
its harlotries, in its avarices, in its famines; it is so
heart-sick of them all, that it would fain be lulled to for-
getfulness of its own terrors; it asks only to laugh for
awhile, even if it laugh but at shadows.

"The world is vain, frivolous, reckless of that which is
earnest; it is a courtesan who thinks only of pleasure, of
adornment, of gewgaws, of the toys of the hour!" is the
reproach which its satirists in every age hoot at it.

Alas! it is a courtesan who, having sold herself to evil,
strives to forget her vile bargain; who, having washed
her cheeks white with saltest tears, strives to believe that
the paint calls the true colour back; who, having been
face to face for so long with blackest guilt, keenest hunger,
dreadest woe, strives to lose their ghosts, that incessantly
follow her, in the tumult of her own thoughtless laughter.

"Let me be but amused!"—the cry is the aching cry
of a world that is overborne with pain, and with longing
for the golden years of its youth; that cry is never louder
than when the world is most conscious of its own infamy.

In the Roman Empire, in the Byzantine Empire, in
the Second Empire of Napoleonic France, the world,
reeking with corruption, staggering under the burden of
tyrannies, and delivered over to the dominion of lust, has
shrieked loudest in its blindness of suffering, "Let me
only laugh if I die!"

NOT as others! Why, my Waif? Is your foot less
swift, your limb less strong, your face less fair than
theirs? Does the sun shine less often, have the flowers

less fragrance, does sleep come less sweetly to you than
to them? Nature has been very good, very generous to
you, Viva. Be content with her gifts. What you lack is
only a thing of man's invention—a quibble, a bauble, a
Pharisee's phylactery. Look at the river-lilies that drift
yonder—how white they are, how their leaves enclose
and caress them, how the water buoys them up and plays
with them! Well, are they not better off than the poor
rare flowers that live painfully in hothouse air, and are
labelled, and matted, and given long names by men's
petty precise laws? You are like the river-lilies. O child,
do not pine for the glass house that would ennoble you,
only to force you and kill you?

WRONG to be proud, you ask? No. But then the
pride must be of a right fashion. It must be the
pride which says, " Let me not envy, for that were mean-
ness. Let me not covet, for that were akin to theft. Let
me not repine, for that were weakness." It must be the
pride which says, " I can be sufficient for myself. My
life makes my nobility ; and I need no accident of rank,
because I have a stainless honour." It must be pride too
proud to let an aged woman work where youthful limbs
can help her ; too proud to trample basely on what lies
low already ; too proud to be a coward, and shrink from
following conscience in the confession of known error ;
too proud to despise the withered toil-worn hands of the
poor and old, and be vilely forgetful that those hands
succoured you in your utmost need of helpless infancy !

PHILOSOPHY, Viva, is the pomegranate of life, ever
cool and most fragrant, and the deeper you cut in it
the richer only will the core grow. Power is the Dead-

Sea apple, golden and fair to sight while the hand strives to reach it, dry grey ashes between dry fevered lips when once it is grasped and eaten!

PLEASURE is but labour to those who do not know also that labour in its turn is pleasure.

HAPPY! As a mollusc is happy so long as the sea sweeps prey into its jaws; what does the mollusc care how many lives have been shipwrecked so long as the tide wafts it worms? She has killed her conscience, Viva; there is no murder more awful. It is to slay what touch of God we have in us!

HAVE I been cruel, my child? Your fever of discontent needed a sharp cure. Life lies before you, Viva, and you alone can mould it for yourself. Sin and anguish fill nine-tenths of the world: to one soul that basks in light, a thousand perish in darkness; I dare not let you go on longer in your dangerous belief that the world is one wide paradise, and that the highroad of its joys is the path of reckless selfishness. Can you not think that there are lots worse than that of a guiltless child who is well loved and well guarded, and has all her future still before her?

IT rests with you to live your life nobly or vilely. We have not our choice to be rich or poor, to be happy or unhappy, to be in health or in sickness; but we have our choice to be worthy or worthless. No antagonist can kill our soul in us ; that can perish only from its own suicide. Ever remember that.

BUT they are hollow inside, you still urge ? fie, for shame ! What a plea that is ! Have you the face to make it ? If you have, let me bargain with you.

When all the love that is fair and false goes begging for believers, and all the passion that is a sham fails to find one fool to buy it ; when all the priests and politicians clap in vain together the brazen cymbals of their tongues, because their listeners will not hearken to brass clangour, nor accept it for the music of the spheres ; when all the creeds, that feast and fatten upon the cowardice and selfishness of men, are driven out of hearth and home, and mart and temple, as impostors that put on the white beard of reverence and righteousness to pass current a cheater's coin ; when all the kings that promise peace while they swell their armouries and armies ; when all the statesmen that chatter of the people's weal as they steal up to the locked casket where coronets are kept ; when all the men who talk of " glory," and prate of an " idea " that they may stretch their nation's boundary, and filch their neighbour's province—when all these are no longer in the land, and no more looked on with favour, then I will believe your cry that you hate the toys which are hollow.

CAN an ignorant or an untrained brain follow the theory of light, or the metamorphosis of plants ? Yet it may rejoice in the rays of a summer sun, in the scent of a nest of wild-flowers. So may it do in my music. Shall I ask higher payment than the God of the sun and the violets asks for Himself ?

ONCE there were three handmaidens of Krishna's; invisible, of course, to the world of men. They begged of Krishna, one day, to test their wisdom, and Krishna gave them three drops of dew. It was in the season of drought,—and he bade them go and bestow them where each deemed best in the world.

Now one flew earthward, and saw a king's fountain leaping and shining in the sun; the people died of thirst, and the fields and the plains were cracked with heat, but the king's fountain was still fed and played on. So she thought, "Surely, my dew will best fall where such glorious water dances?" and she shook the drop into the torrent.

The second hovered over the sea, and saw the Indian oysters lying under the waves, among the sea-weed and the coral. Then she thought, "A rain-drop that falls in an oyster's shell becomes a pearl; it may bring riches untold to man, and shine in the diadem of a monarch. Surely it is best bestowed where it will change to a jewel?" —and she shook the dew into the open mouth of a shell.

The third had scarcely hovered a moment over the parched white lands, ere she beheld a little, helpless brown bird dying of thirst upon the sand, its bright eyes glazed, its life going out in torture. Then she thought, "Surely my gift will be best given in succour to the first and lowliest thing I see in pain?"—and she shook the dew-drop down into the silent throat of the bird, that fluttered, and arose, and was strengthened.

Then Krishna said that she alone had bestowed her power wisely; and he bade her take the tidings of rain to the aching earth, and the earth rejoiced exceedingly. Genius is the morning dew that keeps the world from perishing in drought. Can you read my parable?

TO die when life can be lived no longer with honour is greatness indeed ; but to die because life galls and wearies and is hard to pursue—there is no greatness in that? It is the suicide's plea for his own self-pity. You live under tyranny, corruption, dynastic lies hard to bear, despotic enemies hard to bear, I know. But you forget —what all followers of your creed ever forget—that without corruption, untruth, weakness, ignorance in a nation itself, such things could not be in its rulers. Men can bridle the ass and can drive the sheep ; but who can drive the eagle or bridle the lion? A people that was strong and pure no despot could yoke to his vices.

NO matter ! He must have *race* in him. Heraldry may lie ; but voices do not. Low people make money, drive in state, throng to palaces, receive kings at their tables by the force of gold ; but their antecedents always croak out in their voices. They either screech or purr ; they have no clear modulations ; besides, their women always stumble over their train, and their men bow worse than their servants.

ERE long he drew near a street which in the late night was still partially filled with vehicles and with foot-passengers, hurrying through the now fast-falling snow, and over the slippery icy pavements. In one spot a crowd had gathered—of artisans, women, soldiers, and idlers, under the light of a gas-lamp. In the midst of the throng some gendarmes had seized a young girl, accused by one of the bystanders of having stolen a broad silver piece from his pocket.

She offered no resistance ; she stood like a stricken

thing, speechless and motionless, as the men roughly
laid hands on her.

Tricotrin crossed over the road, and with difficulty
made his way into the throng of blouses and looked at
her. Degraded she was, but scarcely above a child's
years; and her features had a look as if innocence were
in some sort still there, and sin still loathed in her soul.
As he drew near he heard her mutter,

"Mother, mother! She will die of hunger!—it was for
her, only for her!"

He stooped in the snow, and letting fall, unperceived,
a five-franc piece, picked it up again.

"Here is some silver," he said, turning to the infuriated
owner, a lemonade-seller, who could ill afford to lose it now
that it was winter, and people were too cold for lemonade,
and who seized it with rapturous delight.

"That is it, monsieur, that is it. Holy Jesus! how can
I thank you? Ah, if I had convicted the poor creature—
and all in error!—I should never have forgiven myself!
Messieurs les gendarmes, let her go! It was my mistake.
My silver piece was in the snow!"

The gendarmes reluctantly let quit their prey: they
muttered, they hesitated, they gripped her arms tighter,
and murmured of the prison-cell.

"Let her go," said Tricotrin quietly: and in a little
while they did so,—the girl stood bareheaded and motionless in the snow like a frost-bound creature.

Soon the crowd dispersed: nothing can be still long in
Paris, and since there had been no theft there was no
interest! they were soon left almost alone, none were
within hearing.

Then he stooped to her: she had never taken off him
the wild, senseless, incredulous gaze of her great eyes.

"Were you guilty?" he asked her.

She caught his hands, she tried to bless him and to
thank him, and broke down in hysterical sobs.

S

"I took it—yes! What would you have? I took it
for my mother. She is old, and blind, and without food.
It is for her that I came on the streets; but she does not
know it, it would kill her to know; she thinks my money
honest; and she is so proud and glad with it! That was
the first thing I *stole!* O God! are you an angel? If they
had put me in prison my mother would have starved!"

He looked on her gently, and with a pity that fell upon
her heart like balm.

"I saw it was your first theft. Hardened robbers do
not wear your stricken face," he said softly, as he slipped
two coins into her hand. "Ah, child! let your mother
die rather than allow her to eat the bread of your dishonour: which choice between the twain do you not think
a mother would make? And know your trade she must,
soon or late. Sin no more, were it only for that love you
bear her."

THEIR lives had drifted asunder, as two boats drift
north and south on a river, the distance betwixt
them growing longer and longer with each beat of the oars
and each sigh of the tide. And for the lives that part
thus, there is no reunion. One floats out to the open
and sunlit sea; and one passes away to the grave of the
stream. Meet again on the river they cannot.

"THEY shudder when they read of the Huns and the
Ostrogoths pouring down into Rome," he mused,
as he passed toward the pandemonium. "They keep a
horde as savage, imprisoned in their midst, buried in the
very core of their capitals, side by side with their churches
and palaces, and never remember the earthquake that
would whelm them if once the pent volcano burst, if once
the black mass covered below took flame and broke to

the surface! Statesmen multiply their prisons, and
strengthen their laws against the crime that is done—
and they never take the canker out of the bud, they never
save the young child from pollution. Their political
economy never studies prevention; it never cleanses the
sewers, it only curses the fever-stricken!"

"WHAT avail?" he thought. "What avail to strive
to bring men nearer to the right? They love
their darkness best—why not leave them to it? Age after
age the few cast away their lives striving to raise and to
ransom the many. What use? Juvenal scourged Rome,
and the same vices that his stripes lashed then, laugh
triumphant in Paris to-day! The satirist, and the poet,
and the prophet strain their voices in vain as the crowds
rush on; they are drowned in the chorus of mad sins and
sweet falsehoods! O God! the waste of hope, the waste
of travail, the waste of pure desire, the waste of high
ambitions!—nothing endures but the wellspring of lies
that ever rises afresh, and the bay-tree of sin that is green,
and stately, and deathless!"

HE himself went onward through the valley, through
the deep belt of the woods, through the avenues of
the park. The whole front of the antique building was
lighted, and the painted oriels gleamed ruby, and amber,
and soft brown, in the dusky evening, through the green
screen of foliage.

The fragrance of the orange alleys, and of the acres of
flowers, was heavy on the air; there was the sound of
music borne down the low southerly wind; here and there
through the boughs was the dainty glisten of gliding

silks :—it was such a scene as once belonged to the terraces and gardens of Versailles.

From beyond the myrtle fence and gilded railings which severed the park from the pleasaunce, enough could be seen, enough heard, of the brilliant revelry within to tell of its extravagance, and its elegance, in the radiance that streamed from all the illumined avenues.

He stood and looked long; hearing the faint echo of the music, seeing the effulgence of the light through the dark myrtle barrier.

A very old crippled peasant, searching in the grass for truffles, with a little dog, stole timidly up and looked too.

"How can it feel, to live like *that?*" he asked, in a wistful, tremulous voice.

Tricotrin did not hear : his hand was grasped on one of the gilded rails with a nervous force as from bodily pain.

The old truffle-gatherer, with his little white dog panting at his feet, crossed himself as he peered through the myrtle screen.

"God!" he muttered; "how strange it seems that people are there who never once knew what it was to want bread, and to find it nowhere, though the lands all teemed with harvest! They never feel hungry, or cold, or hot, or tired, or thirsty : they never feel their bones ache, and their throat parch, and their entrails gnaw! These people ought not to get to heaven—they have it on earth !"

Tricotrin heard at last : he turned his head and looked down on the old man's careworn, hollow face.

"'Verily they have their reward,' you mean? Nay, that is a cruel religion, which would excruciate hereafter those who enjoy now. Judge them not; in their laurel crowns there is full often twisted a serpent. The hunger of the body is bad indeed, but the hunger of the mind is worse perhaps; and from that they suffer, because from every fulfilled desire springs the pain of a fresh satiety."

The truffle-hunter, wise in his peasant-fashion, gazed
wistfully up at the face above him, half comprehending
the answer.

"It may be so," he murmured; "but then—they *have*
enjoyed! Ah, Christ! that is what I envy them. Now
we—we die, starved amidst abundance; we see the years
go, and the sun never shines once in them; and all we
have is a hope—a hope that may be cheated at last; for
none have come back from the grave to tell us whether
that fools us as well."

"I INCLINE to think you live twenty centuries too late,
or—twenty centuries too early."

Viva turned on him a swift and eager glance.

"Of course!" she said, with a certain emotion, whose
meaning he could not analyse. "Was there ever yet a
man of genius who was not either the relic of some great
dead age, or the precursor of some noble future one, in
which he alone has faith?"

"Chut!" said Tricotrin, rapidly; he could not trust
himself to hear her speak in his own defence. "Fine
genius mine! To fiddle to a few villagers, and dash
colour on an alehouse shutter! I have the genius of indolence, if you like. As to my belonging to a bygone age,
—well! I am not sure that I have not got the soul in me
of some barefooted friar of Moyen Age, who went about
where he listed, praying here, laughing there, painting a
missal with a Pagan love-god, and saying a verse of
Horace instead of a chant of the Church. Or, maybe, I
am more like some Greek gossiper, who loitered away his
days in the sun, and ate his dates in the market-place,
and listened here and there to a philosopher, and—just
by taking no thought—hit on a truer philosophy than

ever came out of Porch or Garden. Ah, my Lord of
Estmere! you have two hundred servants over there at
Villiers, I have been told; do you not think I am better
served here by one little, brown-eyed, brown-cheeked
maiden, who sings her Béranger like a lark, while she
brings me her dish of wild strawberries? There is fame
too for you—his—the King of the Chansons! When a
girl washes her linen in the brook—when a herdsman
drives his flock through the lanes—when a boy throws
his line in a fishing-stream—when a grisette sits and
works at her attic lattice—when a student dreams under
the linden leaves—he is on their lips, in their hearts, in
their fancies and joys. What a power! What a dominion! Wider than any that emperors boast!"

"And," added Estmere, with a smile, "if you were not
Tricotrin you would be Béranger?"

"AYE! Hymns forbad at noonday are ever so sung
at night; and oftentimes, what at noon would
have been a lark's chant of liberty, grows at night to a
vampire's screech for blood!" he murmured. "They are
gay at your château up yonder."

BE not a coward who leaves the near duty that is as
cruel to grasp as a nettle, and flies to gather the far-
off duty that will flaunt in men's sight like a sun-flower.

"A GREAT Character!" says Society, when it means
—"a great Scamp!"

ESTMERE laid the panel down as he heard.
"Whoever painted it must have genius."

"Genius!" interrupted Tricotrin. "Pooh! What is genius? Only the power to see a little deeper and a little clearer than most other people. That is all."

"The power of vision? Of course. But that renders it none the less rare."

"Oh yes, it is rare—rare like kingfishers, and sandpipers, and herons, and black eagles. And so men always shoot it down, as they do the birds, and stick up the dead body in glass cases, and label it, and stare at it, and bemoan it as 'so singular,' having done their best to insure its extinction!"

Estmere looked keenly at him.

"Surely genius that secretes itself as your friend's must do," he said, touching the panel afresh, "commits suicide, and desires its own extinction."

"Pshaw!" said Tricotrin, impatiently, and with none of his habitual courtesy. "You think the kingfisher and the black eagle have no better thing to live for than to become the decorations of a great personage's glass cabinets. You think genius can find no higher end than to furnish frescoes and panellings for a nobleman's halls and ante-chambers. You mistake very much ; the mistake is a general one in your order. But believe me, the kingfisher enjoys his brown moorland stream, and his tufts of green rushes, and his water-swept bough of hawthorn ; the eagle enjoys his wild rocks, and his sweep through the air, and his steady gaze at the sun that blinds all human eyes ;—and neither ever imagine that the great men below pity them because they are not stuffed, and labelled, and praised by rule in their palaces! And genius is much of the birds' fashion of thinking. It lives its own life ; and is not, as your connoisseurs are given to fancy, wretched unless you see fit in your graciousness to deem it worth the glass-case of your criticism, and the straw-stuffing of your gold. For it knows, as kingfisher and eagle know also, that stuffed birds nevermore use their wings, and are evermore subject to be bought and be sold."

A GAINST the foreign foes of your country die in your youth if she need it. But against her internecine enemies live out your life in continual warfare. When I tell you this, do you dream that I spare you? Children! —you have yet to learn what life is! Who could think it hard to die in the glory of strife, drunk with the sound of the combat, and feeling no pain in the swoon of a triumph? Few men whose blood was hot and young would ask a greater ending. But to keep your souls in patience; to strive unceasingly with evil; to live in self-negation, in ceaseless sacrifices of desire; to give strength to the weak, and sight to the blind, and light where there is darkness, and hope where there is bondage; to do all these through many years unrecognised of men, content only that they are done with such force as lies within you, —this is harder than to seek the cannons' mouths, this is more bitter than to rush, with drawn steel, on your tyrants.

Your women cry out against you because you leave them to starve and to weep while you give your hearts to revolution and your bodies to the sword. Their cry is the cry of selfishness, of weakness, of narrowness, the cry of the sex that sees no sun save the flame on its hearth: yet there is truth in it—a truth you forget. The truth—that, forsaking the gold-mine of duty which lies at your feet, you grasp at the rainbow of glory; that, neglectful of your own secret sins, you fly at public woes and at national crimes. Can you not see that if every man took heed of the guilt of his own thoughts and acts, the world would be free and at peace? It is easier to rise with the knife unsheathed than to keep watch and ward over your own passions; but do not cheat yourself into believing that it is nobler, and higher, and harder. What reproach is cast against all revolutionists ?—that the men who have nothing to lose, the men who are reckless and outlawed, alone raise the flag of revolt. It is a satire ; but in every satire there lies the germ of a terrible fact.

You—you who are children still, you whose manhood is still a gold scarcely touched in your hands, a gold you can spend in all great ways, or squander for all base uses ;—you can give the lie to that public reproach, if only you will live in such wise that your hands shall be clean, and your paths straight, and your honour unsullied through all temptations. Wait, and live so that the right to judge, to rebuke, to avenge, to purify, become yours through your earning of them. Live nobly first ; and then teach others how to live.

" SO you have brought Fame to Lélis, my English lord?" said Tricotrin, without ceremony. " That was a good work of yours. She is a comet that has a strange fancy only to come forth like a corpse-candle, and dance over men's graves. It is her way. When men will have her out in the noon of their youth, she kills them ; and the painter's bier is set under his Transfiguration, and the soldier's body is chained to the St. Helena rock, and the poet's grave is made at Missolonghi. It is always so."

Estmere bowed his head in assent ; he was endeavouring to remember where he had once met this stranger who thus addressed him—where he had once heard these mellow, ringing, harmonious accents.

" Was it because you were afraid of dying in your prime that you would never woo Fame then yourself?" asked Lélis, with a smile.

" Oh-hè !" answered Tricotrin, seating himself on a

deal box that served as a table, and whereat he and the artist had eaten many a meal of roast chestnuts and black coffee; "I never wanted her; she is a weather vane, never still two moments; she is a spaniel that quits the Plantagenet the moment the battle goes against him, and fawns on Bolingbroke; she is an alchemist's crucible, that has every fair and rich thing thrown into it, but will only yield in return the calcined stones of chagrin and disappointment; she is a harlot, whose kisses are to be bought, and who runs after those who brawl the loudest and swagger the finest in the world's market-places. No! I want nothing of her. My lord here condemned her as I came in; he said she was the offspring of echoing parrots, of imitative sheep, of fawning hounds. Who can want the creature of such progenitors?"

"THERE are many kinds of appreciation. The man of science appreciates when he marvels before the exquisite structure of the sea-shell, the perfect organism of the flower; but the young girl appreciates, too, when she holds the shell to her ear for its music, when she kisses the flower for its fragrance. Appreciation! It is an affair of the reason, indeed; but it is an affair of the emotions also."

"And you prefer what is born of the latter?"

"Not always; but for my music I do. It speaks in an unknown tongue. Science may have its alphabet, but it is feeling that translates its poems. Delaroche, who leaves off his work to listen; Descamps, in whose eyes I see tears; Ingres, who dreams idyls while I play; a young poet whose face reflects my thoughts, an old man whose youth I bring back, an hour of pain that I soothe, an hour of laughter that I give ; these are my recompense. Think you I would exchange them for the gold showers and the diamond boxes of a Farinelli ?"

" Surely not. All I meant was that you might gain a world-wide celebrity did you choose——"

" Gain a honey-coating that every fly may eat me and every gnat may sting ? I thank you. I have a taste to be at peace, and not to become food to sate the public famine for a thing to tear."

Estmere smiled ; he did not understand the man who thus addressed him, but he was attracted despite all his strongest prejudices.

" You are right ! Under the coat of honey is a shirt of turpentine. Still—to see so great a gift as yours wasted——"

" Wasted? Because the multitudes have it, such as it is, instead of the units? Droll arithmetic ! I am with you in thinking that minorities should have a good share of power, for all that is wisest and purest is ever in a minority, as we know ; but I do not see, as you see, that minorities should command a monopoly—of sweet sounds or of anything else."

" I speak to the musician, not to the politician," said Estmere, with the calm, chill contempt of his colder manner : the cold side of his character was touched, and his sympathies were alienated at once.

Tricotrin, indifferent to the hint as to the rebuff, looked at him amusedly.

" Oh, I know you well, Lord Estmere ; I told you so not long ago, to your great disgust. You and your Order think no man should ever presume to touch politics unless his coat be velvet and his rent-roll large, like yours. But, you see, we of the *école buissonnière* generally do as we like ; and we get pecking at public questions for the same reason as our brother birds peck at the hips and the haws—because we have no granaries as you have.

You do not like Socialism? Ah! and yet affect to follow it."

"I!" Estmere looked at this wayside wit, this wine-house philosopher, with a regard that asked plainly, "Are you fool or knave?"

"To be sure," answered Tricotrin. "You have chapel and chaplain yonder at your château, I believe? The Book of the Christians is the very manual of Socialism: '*You* read the Gospel, Marat?' they cried. 'To be sure,' said Marat. 'It is the most republican book in the world, and sends all the rich people to hell.' If you do not like my politics, *beau sire*, do not listen to the Revolutionist of Galilee."

NOT rare on this earth is the love that cleaves to the thing it has cherished through guilt, and through wrong, and through misery. But rare, indeed, is the love that still lives while its portion is oblivion, and the thing which it has followed passes away out to a joy that it cannot share, to a light that it cannot behold.

For this is as the love of a god, which forsakes not, though its creatures revile, and blaspheme, and deride it.

EVER and anon the old, dark, eager, noble face was lifted from its pillow, and the withered lips murmured three words:

"Is she come?"

For Tricotrin had bent over her bed, and had murmured, "I go to seek her, she is near;" and grand'mère had believed and been comforted, for she knew that no lie passed his lips. And she was very still · and only the nervous working of the hard, brown, aged hand showed the longing of her soul.

Life was going out rapidly, as the flame sinks fast in a lamp whose oil is spent. The strong and vigorous frame, the keen and cheery will, had warded off death so long and bravely ; and now they bent under, all suddenly, as those hardy trees will bend after a century of wind and storm—bend but once, and only to break for ever.

The red sun in the west was in its evening glory ; and through the open lattice there were seen in the deep blue of the sky, the bough of a snow-blossomed pear-tree, the network of the ivy, and the bees humming among the jasmine flowers. From the distance there came faintly the musical cries of the boatmen down the river, the voices of the vine-tenders in the fields, the singing of a throstle on a wild-grape tendril.

Only, in the little darkened chamber the old peasant lay quite still—listening, through all the sweet and busy sounds of summer, for a step that never came.

And little by little all those sounds grew fainter on her ear : the dulness of death was stealing over all her senses ; and all she heard was the song of the thrush where the bird swayed on the vine, half in, half out, of the lattice.

But the lips moved still, though no voice came, with the same words : " Is she come ? " and when the lips no more could move, the dark and straining wistfulness of the eyes asked the question more earnestly, more terribly, more ceaselessly.

The thrush sang on, and on, and on ; but to the prayer of the dying eyes no answer came.

The red sun sank into the purple mists of cloud ; the song of the bird was ended ; the voice of the watching girl murmured, " They will come too late ! "

For, as the sun faded off from the vine in the lattice, and the singing of the bird grew silent, grand'mère raised herself with her arms outstretched, and the strength of her youth returned in the hour of dissolution.

"They never come back!" she cried. "They never come back! nor will she! One dead in Africa—and one crushed beneath the stone—and one shot on the barricade. The three went forth together; but not one returned. We breed them, we nurse them, we foster them; and the world slays them body and soul, and eats the limbs that lay in our bosoms, and burns up the souls that we knew so pure. And she went where they went: she is dead like them."

Her head fell back; her mouth was grey and parched, her eyes had no longer sight; a shiver ran through the hardy frame that winter storms and summer droughts had bruised and scorched so long; and a passionless and immeasurable grief came on the brown, weary, age-worn face.

"All dead!" she murmured in the stillness of the chamber, where the song of the bird had ceased, and the darkness of night had come.

Then through her lips the last breath quivered in a deep-drawn sigh, and the brave, patient, unrewarded life passed out for ever.

"YOU surely find no debtor such an ingrate, no master such a tyrant, as the People?"

"Perhaps. But, rather I find it a dog that bullies and tears where it is feared, but may be made faithful by genuine courage and strict justice shown to it."

"The experience of the musician, then, must be much more fortunate than the experience of the statesman."

"Why, yes. It is ungrateful to great men, I grant; but it has the irritation of its own vague sense that it is but their tool, their ladder, their grappling-iron, to excuse

it. Still—I know well what you mean; the man who
works for mankind works for a taskmaster who makes
bitter every hour of his life only to forget him with the
instant of his death; he is ever rolling the stone of human
nature upward toward purer heights, to see it recoil and
rush down into darkness and bloodshed. I know——"

A PROVENCE ROSE.

FLOWERS are like your poets : they give ungrudgingly, and, like all lavish givers, are seldom recompensed in kind.

We cast all our world of blossom, all our treasure or fragrance, at the feet of the one we love ; and then, having spent ourselves in that too abundant sacrifice, you cry, "A yellow, faded thing ! to the dust-hole with it !" and root us up violently, and fling us to rot with the refuse and offal ; not remembering the days when our burden of beauty made sunlight in your darkest places, and brought the odours of a lost paradise to breathe over your bed of fever.

Well, there is one consolation. Just so likewise do you deal with your human wonder-flower of genius.

I SIGHED at my square open pane in the hot, sulphurous mists of the street, and tried to see the stars and could not. For, between me and the one small breadth of sky which alone the innumerable roofs left visible, a vintner had hung out a huge gilded imperial crown as a sign on his roof-tree ; and the crown, with its sham gold turning black in the shadow, hung between me and the planets.

I knew that there must be many human souls in a like

plight with myself, with the light of heaven blocked from
them by a gilded tyranny, and yet I sighed, and sighed,
and sighed, thinking of the white pure stars of Provence
throbbing in the violet skies.

A rose is hardly wiser than a poet, you see : neither
rose nor poet will be comforted, and be content to dwell
in darkness because a crown of tinsel swings on high.

A H ! In the lives of you who have wealth and leisure
we, the flowers, are but one thing among many : we
have a thousand rivals in your porcelains, your jewels,
your luxuries, your intaglios, your mosaics, all your treasures of art, all your baubles of fancy. But in the lives
of the poor we are alone : we are all the art, all the treasure, all the grace, all the beauty of outline, all the purity
of hue that they possess : often we are all their innocence
and all their religion too.

Why do you not set yourselves to make us more abundant in those joyless homes, in those sunless windows?

F OR the life of a painter is beautiful when he is still
young, and loves truly, and has a genius in him
stronger than calamity, and hears a voice in which he
believes say always in his ear, " Fear nothing. Men
must believe as I do in thee, one day. And meanwhile—
we can wait ! "

And a painter in Paris, even though he starve on a few
sous a day, can have so much that is lovely and full of
picturesque charm in his daily pursuits : the long, wondrous galleries full of the arts he adores ; the *réalité de
l'idéal* around him in that perfect world ; the slow, sweet,
studious hours in the calm wherein all that is great in

humanity alone survives; the trance — half adoration,
half aspiration, at once desire and despair—before the
face of the Mona Lisa; then, without, the streets so glad
and so gay in the sweet, living sunshine; the quiver of
green leaves among gilded balconies; the groups at every
turn about the doors; the glow of colour in market-place
and peopled square; the quaint grey piles in old historic
ways; the stones, from every one of which some voice
from the imperishable Past cries out; the green and silent
woods, the little leafy villages, the winding waters garden-
girt; the forest heights, with the city gleaming and golden
in the plain; all these are his.

With these—and youth—who shall dare say the painter
is not rich—ay, though his board be empty, and his cup
be dry?

I had not loved Paris—I, a little imprisoned rose,
caged in a clay pot, and seeing nothing but the sky-line
of the roofs. But I grew to love it, hearing from René
and from Lili of all the poetry and gladness that Paris
made possible in their young and burdened lives, and
which could have been thus possible in no other city of
the earth.

City of Pleasure you have called her, and with truth;
but why not also City of the Poor? For what city, like
herself, has remembered the poor in her pleasure, and
given to them, no less than to the richest, the treasure of
her laughing sunlight, of her melodious music, of her gracious hues, of her million flowers, of her shady leaves, of
her divine ideals?

PIPISTRELLO.

IT was a strange, gaunt wilderness of stone, this old villa of the Marchioni. It would have held hundreds of serving-men. It had as many chambers as one of the palaces down in Rome; but life is homely and frugal here, and has few graces. The ways of everyday Italian life in these grand old places are like nettles and thistles set in an old majolica vase that has had knights and angels painted on it. You know what I mean, you who know Italy. Do you remember those pictures of Vittario Carpacio and of Gentile? They say that is the life our Italy saw once in her cities and her villas;—that is the life she wants. Sometimes when you are all alone in these vast deserted places the ghosts of all that pageantry pass by you, and they seem fitter than the living people for these courts and halls.

I HAD been no saint. I had always been ready for jest or dance or intrigue with a pretty woman, and sometimes women far above me had cast their eyes down on the arena as in Spain ladies do in the bull-ring to pick a lover out thence for his strength: but I had never cared. I had loved, laughed, and wandered away with the stroller's happy liberty; but I had never cared. Now all at once the whole world seemed dead; dead, heaven and earth; and only one woman's two eyes left living in the universe; living, and looking into my soul and burning it to ashes. Do you know what I mean? No?—ay, then you know not love.

SOMETIMES I think love is the darkest mystery of life: mere desire will not explain it, nor will the passions or the affections. You pass years amidst crowds, and know naught of it; then all at once you meet a stranger's eyes, and never are you free. That is love. Who shall say whence it comes? It is a bolt from the gods that descends from heaven and strikes us down into hell. We can do nothing.

IN Italy one wants so little; the air and the light, and a little red wine, and the warmth of the wind, and a handful of maize or of grapes, and an old guitar, and a niche to sleep in near a fountain that murmurs and sings to the mosses and marbles—these are enough in Italy.

PETTY laws breed great crimes. Few rulers, little or big, remember that.

L'ESPRIT du clocher is derided nowadays. But it may well be doubted whether the age which derides it will give the world anything one-half as tender and true in its stead. It is peace because it is content; and it is a peace which has in it the germ of heroism: menaced, it produces patriotism—the patriotism whose symbol is Tell.

THE tyrannies of petty law hurt the authority of the State more with the populace than all the severity of a Draconian code against great offences. Petty laws may annoy but can never harm the rich, for they can always evade them or purchase immunity; but petty laws for the poor are as the horse-fly on the neck and on the eyelids of the horse.

IT was in the month of April; outside the walls and on the banks of Tiber, still swollen by the floods of winter, one could see the gold of a million daffodils and the bright crimson and yellow of tulips in the green corn. The scent of flowers and herbs came into the town and filled its dusky and narrow ways; the boatmen had green branches fastened to their masts; in the stillness of evening one heard the song of crickets, and even a mosquito would come and blow his shrill little trumpet, and one was willing to say to him "Welcome!" because on his little horn he blew the glad news, "Summer is here!"

HELD IN BONDAGE.

"A YOUNG man married is a man that's marred."
That's a golden rule, Arthur; take it to heart.
Anne Hathaway, I have not a doubt, suggested it; experience is the sole asbestos, only unluckily one seldom gets
it before one's hands are burnt irrevocably. Shakespeare
took to wife the ignorant, rosy-cheeked Warwickshire
peasant girl at *eighteen!* Poor fellow! I picture him,
with all his untried powers, struggling like new-born
Hercules for strength and utterance, and the great germ
of poetry within him, tingeing all the common realities of
life with its rose hue; genius giving him power to see
with god-like vision the "fairies nestling in the cowslip
chalices," and the golden gleam of Cleopatra's sails; to
feel the "spiced Indian air" by night, and the wild working
of kings' ambitious lust; to know by intuition, alike the
voices of nature unheard by common ears, and the fierce
schemes and passions of a world from which social position shut him out! I picture him in his hot, imaginative
youth, finding his first love in the yeoman's daughter at
Shottery, strolling with her by the Avon, making her an
"odorous chaplet of sweet summer buds," and dressing
her up in the fond array of a boy's poetic imaginings!
Then—when he had married her, he, with the passionate
ideals of Juliets and Violas, Ophelias and Hermiones in

his brain and heart, must have awakened to find that the
voices so sweet to him were dumb to her. The "cinque
spotted cowslip bells" brought only thoughts of wine to
her. When he was watching "certain stars shoot madly
from their spheres," she most likely was grumbling at him
for mooning there after curfew bell. When he was learning Nature's lore in "the fresh cup of the crimson rose,"
she was dinning in his ear that Hammet and Judith
wanted worsted socks. When he was listening in fancy
to the "sea-maid's song," and weaving thoughts to which
a world still stands reverentially to listen, she was buzzing
behind him, and bidding him go card the wool, and
weeping that, in her girlhood, she had not chosen some
rich glover or ale-taster, instead of idle, useless, wayward
Willie Shakespeare. Poor fellow! He did not write, I
would swear, without fellow-feeling, and yearning over
souls similarly shipwrecked, that wise saw, "A young man
married is a man that's marred."

PASCARÈL.

WHEN a man's eyes meet yours, and his faith trusts
you, and his heart upon a vague impulse is laid
bare to you, it always has seemed to me the basest treach-
ery the world can hold to pass the gold of confidence
which he pours out to you from hand to hand as common
coin for common circulation.

CIRCUMSTANCE is so odd and so cruel a thing.
It is wholly apart from talent.

Genius will do so little for a man if he do not know
how to seize or seduce opportunity. No doubt, in his
youth, Ambrogiò had been shy, silent, out of his art timid,
and in his person ungraceful, and unlovely. So the world
had passed by him turning a deaf ear to his melodies, and
he had let it pass, because he had not that splendid audacity to grasp it perforce, and hold it until it blessed him,
without which no genius will ever gain the benediction of
the Angel of Fame.

Which is a fallen Angel, no doubt; but still, perhaps,
the spirit most worth wrestling with after all; since
wrestle we must in this world, if we do not care to
lie down and form a pavement for other men's cars of
triumph, as the Assyrians of old stretched themselves
on their faces before the coming of the chariot of their
kings.

ONE of the saddest things perhaps in all the sadness
of this world is the frightful loss at which so much
of the best and strongest work of a man's life has to be
thrown away at the onset. If you desire a name amongst
men, you must buy the crown of it at such a costly price!

True, the price will in the end be paid back to you, no
doubt, when you are worn out, and what you do is as
worthless as the rustling canes that blow together in
autumn by dull river sides : then you scrawl your signa-
ture across your soulless work, and it fetches thrice its
weight in gold.

But though you thus have your turn, and can laugh at
your will at the world that you fool, what can that com-
pensate you for all those dear dead darlings?—those bright
first-fruits, those precious earliest nestlings of your genius,
which had to be sold into bondage for a broken crust,
which drifted away from you never to be found again,
which you know well were a million fold better, fresher,
stronger, higher, better than anything you have begotten
since then ; and yet in which none could be found to
believe, only because you had not won that magic spell
which lies in—being known?

WHEN I think of the sweet sigh of the violin melodies through the white winter silence of Raffae-
lino's eager, dreamy eyes, misty with the student's unutterable sadness and delight ; of old Ambrogiò, with his
semicircle of children round him, lifting their fresh voices
at his word ; of the little robin that came every day upon
the waterpipe, and listened, and thrilled in harmony, and
ate joyfully the crumbs which the old maestro daily spared
to it from his scanty meal—when I think of those hours,
it seems to me that they must have been happiness too.

" Could we but know when we are happy !" sighs some

poet. As well might he write, "Could we but set the dewdrop with our diamonds! could we but stay the rainbow in our skies!"

EVERY old Italian city has this awe about it—holds close the past and moves the living to a curious sense that they are dead and in their graves are dreaming; for the old cities themselves have beheld so much perish around them, and yet have kept so firm a hold upon tradition and upon the supreme beauty of great arts, that those who wander there grow, as it were, bewildered, and know not which is life and which is death amongst them.

THE sun was setting.
  Over the whole Valdarno there was everywhere a faint ethereal golden mist that rose from the water and the woods.

The town floated on it as upon a lake; her spires, and domes, and towers, and palaces bathed at their base in its amber waves, and rising upward into the rose-hued radiance of the upper air. The mountains that encircled her took all the varying hues of the sunset on their pale heights until they flushed to scarlet, glowered to violet, wavered with flame, and paled to whiteness, as the opal burns and fades. Warmth, fragrance, silence, loveliness encompassed her; and in the great stillness the bell of the basilica tolled slowly the evening call to prayer.

Thus Florence rose before me.

A strange tremor of exceeding joy thrilled through me as I beheld the reddened shadows of those close-lying roofs, and those marble heights of towers and of temples. At last my eyes gazed on her! the daughter of flowers,

the mistress of art, the nursing mother of liberty and of
aspiration.

I fell on my knees and thanked God. I pity those
who, in such a moment, have not done likewise.

THERE is nothing upon earth, I think, like the smile
of Italy as she awakes when the winter has dozed
itself away in the odours of its oakwood fires.

The whole land seems to laugh.

The springtide of the north is green and beautiful, but
it has nothing of the radiance, the dreamfulness, the
ecstasy of spring in the southern countries. The springtide of the north is pale with the gentle colourless sweetness of its world of primroses ; the springtide of Italy is
rainbow-hued, like the profusion of anemones that laugh
with it in every hue of glory under every ancient wall and
beside every hill-fed stream.

Spring in the north is a child that wakes from dreams
of death ; spring in the south is a child that wakes from
dreams of love. One is rescued and welcomed from the
grave ; but the other comes smiling on a sunbeam from
heaven.

THE landscape that has the olive is spiritual as no
landscape can ever be from which the olive is
absent ; for where is there spirituality without some hue
of sadness ?

But this spiritual loveliness is one for which the human
creature that is set amidst it needs a certain education as
for the power of Euripides, for the dreams of Phædrus,
for the strength of Michaelangelo, for the symphonies of
Mozart or Beethoven.

The mind must itself be in a measure spiritualised ere
aright it can receive it.

It is too pure, too impalpable, too nearly divine, to be grasped by those for whom all beauty centres in strong heats of colour and great breadths of effect ; it floats over the senses like a string of perfect cadences in music ; it has a breath of heaven in it ; though on the earth it is not of the earth ; when the world was young, ere men had sinned on it, and gods forsaken it, it must have had the smile of this light that lingers here.

BAD? Good? Pshaw! Those are phrases. No one uses them but fools. You have seen the monkeys' cage in the beast-garden here. That is the world. It is not strength, or merit, or talent, or reason that is of any use there ; it is just which monkey has the skill to squeeze to the front and jabber through the bars, and make his teeth meet in his neighbours' tails till they shriek and leave him free passage—it is that monkey which gets all the cakes and the nuts of the folk on a feast-day. The monkey is not bad ; it is only a little quicker and more cunning than the rest ; that is all.

IT is a kind of blindness—poverty. We can only grope through life when we are poor, hitting and maiming ourselves against every angle.

COUNT art by gold, and it fetters the feet it once winged.

" IS that all you know?" he cried, while his voice rang like a trumpet-call. " Listen here, then, little lady, and learn better. What is it to be a player? It is this.

A thing despised and rejected on all sides ; a thing that
was a century since denied what they call Christian burial ;
a thing that is still deemed for a woman disgraceful, and
for a man degrading and emasculate ; a thing that is mute
as a dunce save when, parrot-like, it repeats by rote with
a mirthless grin or a tearless sob ; a wooden doll, as you
say, applauded as a brave puppet in its prime, hissed at
in its first hour of failure or decay ; a thing made up of
tinsel and paint, and patchwork, of the tailor's shreds and
the barber's curls of tow—a ridiculous thing to be sure.
That is a player. And yet again,—a thing without which
laughter and jest were dead in the sad lives of the populace ; a thing that breathes the poet's words of fire so that
the humblest heart is set aflame ; a thing that has a magic
on its lips to waken smiles or weeping at its will ; a thing
which holds a people silent, breathless, intoxicated with
mirth or with awe, as it chooses ; a thing whose grace
kings envy, and whose wit great men will steal ; a thing
by whose utterance alone the poor can know the fair follies of a thoughtless hour, and escape for a little space
from the dull prisons of their colourless lives into the
sunlit paradise where genius dwells—*that* is a player, too!"

THE instrument on which we histrions play is that
strange thing, the human heart. It looks a little
matter to strike its chords of laughter or of sorrow ; but,
indeed, to do that aright and rouse a melody which shall
leave all who hear it the better and the braver for the hearing, that may well take a man's lifetime, and, perhaps, may
well repay it.

OH, cara mia, when one has run about in one's time
with a tinker's tools, and seen the lives of the poor,
and the woe of them, and the wretchedness of it all, and

the utter uselessness of everything, and the horrible, intolerable, unending pain of all the things that breathe,
one comes to think that in this meaningless mystery
which men call life a little laughter and a little love are
the only things which save us all from madness—the
madness that would curse God and die.

IT always seems as if that well-spring of poetry and
art which arose in Italy, to feed and fertilise the
world when it was half dead and wholly barren under the
tyrannies of the Church and the lusts of Feudalism; it
would always seem, I say, as though that water of life
had so saturated the Italian soil, that the lowliest hut
upon its hills and plains will ever nourish and put forth
some flower of fancy.

The people cannot read, but they can rhyme. They
cannot reason, but they can keep perfect rhythm. They
cannot write their own names, but written on their hearts
are the names of those who made their country's greatness. They believe in the virtues of a red rag tied to a
stick amidst their fields, but they treasure tenderly the
heroes and the prophets of an unforgotten time. They
are ignorant of all laws of science or of sound, but when
they go home by moonlight through the maize yonder
alight with lùcciole, they will never falsify a note, or over-
load a harmony, in their love-songs.

The poetry, the art, in them is sheer instinct; it is not
the genius of isolated accident, but the genius of inalien-
able heritage.

DO you ever think of those artist-monks who have
strewed Italy with altar-pieces and missal miniatures
till there is not any little lonely dusky town of hers that
is not rich by art? Do you often think of them? I do.

There must have been a beauty in their lives—a great beauty—though they missed of much, of more than they ever knew or dreamed of, let us hope. In visions of the Madonna they grew blind to the meaning of a woman's smile, and illuminating the golden olive wreath above the heads of saints they lost the laughter of the children under the homely olive-trees without.

But they did a noble work in their day ; and leisure for meditation is no mean treasure, though the modern world does not number it amongst its joys.

One can understand how men born with nervous frames and spiritual fancies into the world when it was one vast battle-ground, where its thrones were won by steel and poison, and its religion enforced by torch and faggot, grew so weary of the never-ending turmoil, and of the riotous life which was always either a pageant or a slaughter-house, that it seemed beautiful to them to withdraw themselves into some peaceful place like this Badià and spend their years in study and in recommendation of their souls to God, with the green and fruitful fields before their cloister windows, and no intruders on the summer stillness as they painted their dreams of a worthier and fairer world except the blue butterflies that strayed in on a sunbeam, or the gold porsellini that hummed at the lilies in the Virgin's chalice.

FLORENCE, where she sits throned amidst her meadows white with Lenten lilies, Florence is never terrible, Florence is never old. In her infancy they fed her on the manna of freedom, and that fairest food gave her eternal youth. In her early years she worshipped ignorantly indeed, but truly always the day-star of liberty ; and it has been with her always so that the light shed upon her is still as the light of morning.

Does this sound a fanciful folly? Nay, there is a real truth in it.

The past is so close to you in Florence. You touch it at every step. It is not the dead past that men bury and then forget. It is an unquenchable thing; beautiful, and full of lustre, even in the tomb, like the gold from the sepulchres of the Ætruscan kings that shines on the breast of some fair living woman, undimmed by the dust and the length of the ages.

The music of the old greatness thrills through all the commonest things of life like the grilli's chant through the wooden cages on Ascension Day; and, like the song of the grilli, its poetry stays in the warmth of the common hearth for the ears of the little children, and loses nothing of its melody.

The beauty of the past in Florence is like the beauty of the great Duomo.

About the Duomo there is stir and strife at all times; crowds come and go; men buy and sell; lads laugh and fight; piles of fruit blaze gold and crimson; metal pails clash down on the stones with shrillest clangour; on the steps boys play at dominoes, and women give their children food, and merry maskers grin in carnival fooleries; but there in their midst is the Duomo all unharmed and undegraded, a poem and a prayer in one, its marbles shining in the upper air, a thing so majestic in its strength, and yet so human in its tenderness, that nothing can assail, and nothing equal it.

Other, though not many, cities have histories as noble, treasuries as vast; but no other city has them living and ever present in her midst, familiar as household words, and touched by every baby's hand and peasant's step, as Florence has.

Every line, every rood, every gable, every tower, has some story of the past present in it. Every tocsin that sounds is a chronicle; every bridge that unites the two banks of the river unites also the crowds of the living with the heroism of the dead.

In the winding dusky irregular streets, with the outlines of their logge and arcades, and the glow of colour that fills their niches and galleries, the men who " have gone before" walk with you; not as elsewhere mere gliding shades clad in the pallor of a misty memory, but present, as in their daily lives, shading their dreamful eyes against the noonday sun or setting their brave brows against the mountain wind, laughing and jesting in their manful mirth and speaking as brother to brother of great gifts to give the world. All this while, though the past is thus close about you the present is beautiful also, and does not shock you by discord and unseemliness as it will ever do elsewhere. The throngs that pass you are the same in likeness as those that brushed against Dante or Calvacanti ; the populace that you move amidst is the same bold, vivid, fearless, eager people with eyes full of dreams, and lips braced close for war, which welcomed Vinci and Cimabue and fought from Montaperto to Solferino.

And as you go through the streets you will surely see at every step some colour of a fresco on a wall, some quaint curve of a bas-relief on a lintel, some vista of Romanesque arches in a palace court, some dusky interior of a smith's forge or a wood-seller's shop, some Renaissance seal-ring glimmering on a trader's stall, some lovely hues of fruits and herbs tossed down together in a Tre Cento window, some gigantic mass of blossoms being borne aloft on men's shoulders for a church festivity of roses, something at every step that has some beauty or some charm in it, some graciousness of the ancient time, or some poetry of the present hour.

The beauty of the past goes with you at every step in Florence. Buy eggs in the market, and you buy them where Donatello bought those which fell down in a broken heap before the wonder of the crucifix. Pause in a narrow

U

bye-street in a crowd and it shall be that Borgo Allegri,
which the people so baptized for love of the old painter
and the new-born art. Stray into a great dark church at
evening time, where peasants tell their beads in the vast
marble silence, and you are where the whole city flocked,
weeping, at midnight to look their last upon the face of
their Michael Angelo. Pace up the steps of the palace of
the Signorìa and you tread the stone that felt the feet of
him to whom so bitterly was known "*com' è duro calle,
lo scendere è'l salir per l'altrùi scale.*" Buy a knot of
March anemoni or April arum lilies, and you may bear
them with you through the same city ward in which the
child Ghirlandajo once played amidst the gold and silver
garlands that his father fashioned for the young heads of
the Renaissance. Ask for a shoemaker and you shall
find the cobbler sitting with his board in the same old
twisting, shadowy street way, where the old man Toscan-
elli drew his charts that served a fair-haired sailor of
Genoa, called Columbus. Toil to fetch a tinker through
the squalor of San Niccolò, and there shall fall on you
the shadow of the bell-tower where the old sacristan
saved to the world the genius of the Night and Day.
Glance up to see the hour of the evening time, and there,
sombre and tragical, will loom above you the walls of the
communal palace on which the traitors were painted by
the brush of Sarto, and the tower of Giotto, fair and fresh
in its perfect grace as though angels had builded it in the
night just past, "*ond' ella toglie ancora e terza e nona,*"
as in the noble and simple days before she brake the
"*cerchia antìca.*"

Everywhere there are flowers, and breaks of songs, and
rills of laughter, and wonderful eyes that look as if they
too, like their Poets, had gazed into the heights of heaven
and the depths of hell.

And then you will pass out at the gates beyond the
city walls, and all around you there will be a radiance

and serenity of light that seems to throb in its intensity
and yet is divinely restful, like the passion and the peace
of love when it has all to adore and nothing to desire.

The water will be broad and gold, and darkened here
and there into shadows of porphyrine amber. Amidst
the grey and green of the olive and acacia foliage there
will arise the low pale roofs and flat-topped towers of
innumerable villages.

Everywhere there will be a wonderful width of amethystine hills and mystical depths of seven-chorded light.
Above, masses of rosy cloud will drift, like rose-leaves
leaning on a summer wind. And, like a magic girdle
which has shut her out from all the curse of age and
death and man's oblivion, and given her a youth and
loveliness which will endure so long as the earth itself
endures, there will be the circle of the mountains, purple
and white and golden, lying around Florence.

A MIDST all her commerce, her wars, her hard work,
her money-making, Florence was always domin-
ated and spiritualised, at her noisiest and worst, by a
poetic and picturesque imagination.

Florentine life had always an ideal side to it; and
an idealism, pure and lofty, runs through her darkest
histories and busiest times like a thread of gold through
a coat of armour and a vest of frieze.

The Florentine was a citizen, a banker, a workman,
a carder of wool, a weaver of silk, indeed; but he was
also always a lover, and always a soldier; that is, always
half a poet. He had his Caròccio and his Ginevra as
well as his tools and his sacks of florins. He had his
sword as well as his shuttle. His scarlet giglio was the
flower of love no less than the blazonry of battle on his
standard, and the mint stamp of the commonwealth on
his coinage.

Herein lay the secret of the influence of Florence : the secret which rendered the little city, stretched by her river's side, amongst her quiet meadows white with arums, a sacred name to all generations of men for all she dared and all she did.

"She amassed wealth," they say : no doubt she did— and why ?

To pour it with both hands to melt in the foundries of Ghiberti—to bring it in floods to cement the mortar that joined the marbles of Brunelleschi ! She always spent to great ends, and to mighty uses.

When she called a shepherd from his flocks in the green valley to build for her a bell-tower so that she might hear, night and morning, the call to the altar, the shepherd built for her in such fashion that the belfry has been the Pharos of Art for five centuries.

Here is the secret of Florence—supreme aspiration.

The aspiration which gave her citizens force to live in poverty, and clothe themselves in simplicity, so as to be able to give up their millions of florins to bequeath miracles in stone and metal and colour to the Future. The aspiration which so purified her soil, red with carnage, black with smoke of war, trodden continuously by hurrying feet of labourers, rioters, mercenaries, and murderers, that from that soil there could spring, in all its purity and perfection, the paradise-blossom of the Vita Nuova.

Venice perished for her pride and carnal lust ; Rome perished for her tyrannies and her blood-thirst ; but Florence—though many a time nearly strangled under the heel of the Empire and the hand of the Church— Florence was never slain utterly either in body or soul ; Florence still crowned herself with flowers even in her throes of agony, because she kept always within her that love—impersonal, consecrate, void of greed—which is the purification of the individual life and the regeneration of the body politic. "We labour for the ideal," said

the Florentines of old, lifting to heaven their red flower
de luce—and to this day Europe bows before what they
did and cannot equal it.

"But she had so many great men, so many mighty
masters !" I would urge, whereon Pascarèl would glance
on me with his lightest and yet utmost scorn.

"O wise female thing, who always traces the root to
the branch and deduces the cause from the effect ! Did
her great men spring up full-armed like Athene, or was
it the pure, elastic atmosphere of her that made her
mere mortals strong as immortals ? The supreme
success of modern government is to flatten down all men
into one uniform likeness, so that it is only by most
frightful, and often destructive, effort that any originality
can contrive to get loose in its own shape for a moment's
breathing space ; but in the Commonwealth of Florence
a man, being born with any genius in him, drew in
strength to do and dare greatly with the very air he
breathed."

Moreover, it was not only the great men that made
her what she was.

It was, above all, the men who knew they were not
great, but yet had the patience and unselfishness to do
their appointed work for her zealously, and with every
possible perfection in the doing of it.

It was not only Orcagna planning the Loggia, but
every workman who chiselled out a piece of its stone,
that put all his head and heart into the doing thereof.
It was not only Michaelangelo in his studio, but every
poor painter who taught the mere a, b, c, d of the craft
to a crowd of pupils out of the streets, who did whatsoever came before them to do mightily and with reverence.

In those days all the servants as well as the sovereigns of art were penetrated with the sense of her
holiness.

It was the mass of patient, intelligent, poetic, and sincere servitors of art, who, instead of wildly consuming their souls in envy and desire, cultured their one talent to the uttermost, so that the mediocrity of that age would have been the excellence of any other.

Not alone from the great workshops of the great masters did the light shine on the people. From every scaffold where a palace ceiling was being decorated with its fresco, from every bottega where the children of the poor learned to grind and to mingle the colours, from every cell where some solitary monk studied to produce an offering to the glory of his God, from every nook and corner where the youths gathered in the streets to see some Nunziata or Ecce Homo lifted to its niche in the city wall, from every smallest and most hidden home of art—from the nest under the eaves as well as from the cloud-reaching temples,—there went out amidst the multitudes an ever-flowing, ever-pellucid stream of light, from that Aspiration which is in itself Inspiration.

So that even to this day the people of Italy have not forgotten the supreme excellence of all beauty, but are, by the sheer instinct of inherited faith, incapable of infidelity to those traditions ; so that the commonest craftsman of them all will sweep his curves and shade his hues upon a plaster cornice with a perfection that is the despair of the maestri of other nations.

THE broad plains that have been the battleground of so many races and so many ages were green and peaceful under the primitive husbandry of the contadini.

Everywhere under the long lines of the yet unbudded vines the seed was springing, and the trenches of the earth were brimful with brown bubbling water left from the floods of winter, when Reno and Adda had broken loose from their beds.

Here and there was some old fortress grey amongst
the silver of the olive orchards; some village with white
bleak house-walls and flat roofs pale and bare against
the level fields; or some little long-forgotten city once
a stronghold of war and a palace for princes, now a
little hushed and lonely place, with weed-grown ramparts and gates rusted on their hinges, and tapestry
weavers throwing the shuttle in its deserted and dis-
mantled ways.

But chiefly it was always the green, fruitful, weary,
endless plain trodden by the bullocks and the goats,
and silent, strangely silent, as though fearful still of its
tremendous past.

THE long bright day draws to a close. The west is
in a blaze of gold, against which the ilex and the
acacia are black as funeral plumes. The innumerable
scents of fruits and flowers and spices, and tropical seeds,
and sweet essences, that fill the streets at every step
from shops and stalls, and monks' pharmacies, are fanned
out in a thousand delicious odours on the cooling air.
The wind has risen, blowing softly from mountain and
from sea across the plains through the pines of Pisa,
across to the oak-forests of green Casentlno.

Whilst the sun still glows in the intense amber of his
own dying glory, away in the tender violet hues of the
east the young moon rises.

Rosy clouds drift against the azure of the zenith, and
are reflected as in a mirror in the shallow river waters.

A little white cloud of doves flies homeward against
the sky.

All the bells chime for the Ave Maria.

The evening falls.

Wonderful hues, creamy, and golden, and purple, and
soft as the colours of a dove's throat, spread themselves

slowly over the sky; the bell tower rises like a shaft of porcelain clear against the intense azure; amongst the tall canes by the river the fire-flies sparkle; the shores are mirrored in the stream with every line and curve, and roof and cupola, drawn in sharp deep shadow; every lamp glows again thrice its size in the glass of the current, and the arches of the bridges meet their own image there; the boats glide down the water that is now white under the moon, now amber under the lights, now black under the walls, for ever changing; night draws on, then closes quite.

But it is night as radiant as day, and ethereal as day can never be; on the hills the cypresses still stand out against the faint gold that lingers in the west; there is the odour of carnations and of acacias everywhere.

Noiseless footsteps come and go.

People pass softly in shadow, like a dream.

YOU know how St. Michael made the Italian? he is saying to them, and the clear crystal ring of the sonorous Tuscan reaches to the farthest corner of the square. Nay?—oh, for shame! Well, then, it was in this fashion; long, long ago, when the world was but just called from chaos, the Dominiddio was tired, as you all know, and took his rest on the seventh day; and four of the saints, George and Denis and Jago and Michael, stood round him with their wings folded and their swords idle.

So to them the good Lord said: "Look at those odds and ends, that are all lying about after the earth is set rolling. Gather them up, and make them into four living nations to people the globe." The saints obeyed and set to the work.

St. George got a piece of pure gold and a huge lump

of lead, and buried the gold in the lead, so that none ever would guess it was there, and so sent it rolling and bumping to earth, and called it the English people.

St. Jago got a bladder filled with wind, and put in it the heart of a fox, and the fang of a wolf, and whilst it puffed and swelled like the frog that called itself a bull, it was despatched to the world as the Spaniard.

St. Denis did better than that; he caught a sunbeam flying, and he tied it with a bright knot of ribbons, and he flashed it on earth as the people of France; only, alas! he made two mistakes, he gave it no ballast, and he dyed the ribbons bloodred.

Now St. Michael, marking their errors, caught a sunbeam likewise, and many other things too; a mask of velvet, a poniard of steel, the chords of a lute, the heart of a child, the sigh of a poet, the kiss of a lover, a rose out of paradise, and a silver string from an angel's lyre.

Then with these in his hand he went and knelt down at the throne of the Father. "Dear and great Lord," he prayed, "to make my work perfect, give me one thing; give me a smile of God." And God smiled.

Then St. Michael sent his creation to earth, and called it the Italian.

But—most unhappily, as chance would have it— Satanas watching at the gates of hell, thought to himself, "If I spoil not his work, earth will be Eden in Italy." So he drew his bow in envy, and sped a poisoned arrow; and the arrow cleft the rose of paradise, and broke the silver string of the angel.

And to this day the Italian keeps the smile that God gave in his eyes; but in his heart the devil's arrow rankles still.

Some call this barbed shaft Cruelty; some Superstition; some Ignorance; some Priestcraft; maybe its poison is drawn from all four; be it how it may, it is the duty of all Italians to pluck hard at the arrow of hell, so that the smile of God alone shall remain with their children's children.

Yonder in the plains we have done much; the rest will lie with you, the Freed Nation.

THERE is an old legend, he made answer to me, an old monkish tale, which tells how, in the days of King Clovis, a woman, old and miserable, forsaken of all, and at the point of death, strayed into the Merovingian woods, and lingering there, and hearkening to the birds, and loving them, and so learning from them of God, regained, by no effort of her own, her youth; and lived, always young and always beautiful, a hundred years; through all which time she never failed to seek the forests when the sun rose, and hear the first song of the creatures to whom she owed her joy. Whoever to the human soul can be, in ever so faint a sense, that which the birds were to the woman in the Merovingian woods, he, I think, has a true greatness. But I am but an outcast, you know; and my wisdom is not of the world.

Yet it seemed the true wisdom, there, at least, with the rose light shining across half the heavens, and the bells ringing far away in the plains below over the white waves of the sea of olives.

ONLY for the people! Altro! did not Sperone and all the critics at his heels pronounce Ariosto only fit for the vulgar multitude? and was not Dante himself called the laureate of the cobblers and the bakers?

And does not Sacchetti record that the great man

took the trouble to quarrel with an ass-driver and a blacksmith because they recited his verses badly?

If he had not written "only for the people," we might never have got beyond the purisms of Virgilio, and the Ciceronian imitations of Bembo.

Dante now-a-days may have become the poet of the scholars and the sages, but in his own times he seemed to the sciolists a most terribly low fellow for using his mother tongue; and he was most essentially the poet of the vulgar—of the *vulgare eloquio,* of the *vulgare illustre;* and pray what does the " Commedia" mean if not a *canto villereccio,* a song for the rustics? Will you tell me that?

Only for the people! Ah, that is the error. Only! how like a woman that is! Any trash will do for the people; that is the modern notion; vile roulades in music, tawdry crudities in painting, cheap balderdash in print—all that will do for the people. So they say now-a-days.

Was the bell tower yonder set in a ducal garden or in a public place? Was Cimabue's masterpiece veiled in a palace or borne aloft through the throngs of the streets?

A MAN, be he bramble or vine, likes to grow in the open air in his own fashion; but a woman, be she flower or weed, always thinks she would be better under glass. When she gets the glass she breaks it—generally; but till she gets it she pines.

WHEN they grew up in Italy, all that joyous band,— Arlecchino in Bergamo, Stenterello in Florence, Pulcinello in Naples, Pantaleone in Venice, Dulcamara in Bologna, Beltramo in Milan, Brighella in Brescia—masked their mirthful visages and ran together and jumped on that travelling stage before the world, what a force they were for the world, those impudent mimes !

"Only Pantomimi?" When they joined hands with one another and rolled their wandering house before St. Mark's they were only players indeed ; but their laughter blew out the fires of the Inquisition, their fools' caps made the papal tiara look but paper toy, their wooden swords struck to earth the steel of the nobles, their arrows of epigram, feathered from goose and from falcon, slew, flying, the many-winged dragon of Superstition.

They were old as the old Latin land, indeed.

They had mouldered for ages in Etruscan cities, with the dust of uncounted centuries upon them, and been only led out in Carnival times, pale, voiceless, frail ghosts of dead powers, whose very meaning the people had long forgotten. But the trumpet-call of the Renaissance woke them from their Rip Van Winkle sleep.

They got up, young again, and keen for every frolic—Barbarossas of sock and buskin, whose helmets were caps and bells, breaking the magic spell of their slumber to burst upon men afresh ; buoyant incarnations of the new-born scorn for tradition, of the nascent revolts of democracy, with which the air was rife.

"Only Pantomimi?" Oh, altro !

The world when it reckons its saviours should rate high all it owed to the Pantomimi,—the privileged Pantomimi—who first dared take license to say in their quips and cranks, in their capers and jests, what had sent all speakers before them to the rack and the faggots.

Who think of that when they hear the shrill squeak of Pulcinello in the dark bye-streets of northern towns, or see lean Pantaleone slip and tumble through the transformation-scene of some gorgeous theatre?

Not one in a million.

Yet it is true for all that. Free speech was first due to the Pantomimi. A proud boast that. They hymn Tell and chant Savonarola and glorify the Gracchi, but I doubt if any of the gods in the world's Pantheon or the other world's Valhalla did so much for freedom as those merry mimes that the children scamper after upon every holiday.

WE are straws on the wind of the hour, too frail and too brittle to float into the future. Our little day of greatness is a mere child's puff-ball, inflated by men's laughter, floated by women's tears ; what breeze so changeful as the one, what waters so shallow as the other?—the bladder dances a little while ; then sinks, and who remembers?

DO you know the delicate delights of a summer morning in Italy? morning I mean between four and five of the clock, and not the full hot mid-day that means morning to the languid associations of this weary century.

The nights, perfect as they are, have scarcely more loveliness than the birth of light, the first rippling laughter of the early day.

The air is cool, almost cold, and clear as glass. There is an endless murmur from birds' throats and wings, and from far away there will ring from village or city the chimes of the first mass. The deep broad shadows lie so fresh, so grave, so calm, that by them the very dust is stilled and spiritualised.

Softly the sun comes, striking first the loftier trees and then the blossoming magnolias, and lastly the green lowliness of the gentle vines ; until all above is in a glow of new-born radiance, whilst all beneath the leaves still is dreamily dusk and cool.

The sky is of a soft sea-blue; great vapours will float here and there, iris-coloured and snow-white. The stone parapets of bridge and tower shine against the purple of the mountains, which are low in tone, and look like hovering storm-clouds. Across the fields dun oxen pass to their labour; through the shadows peasants go their way to mass; down the river a raft drifts slowly, with the pearly water swaying against the canes; all is clear, tranquil, fresh as roses washed with rain.

TO the art of the stage, as to every other art, there are two sides: the truth of it, which comes by inspiration—that is, by instincts subtler, deeper, and stronger than those of most minds; and the artifice of it, in which it must clothe itself to get understood by the people.

It is this latter which must be learnt; it is the leathern harness in which the horses of the sun must run when they come down to race upon earth.

FOR in Italy life is all contrast, and there is no laugh and love-song without a sigh beside them; there is no velvet mask of mirth and passion without the marble mask of art and death near to it. For everywhere the wild tulip burns red upon a ruined altar, and everywhere the blue borage rolls its azure waves through the silent temples of forgotten gods.

TO enter Bologna at midnight is to plunge into the depths of the middle ages.

Those desolate sombre streets, those immense dark
arches, dark as Tartarus, those endless arcades where
scarce a footfall breaks the stillness, that labyrinth of
marble, of stone, of antiquity ; the past alone broods over
them all.

As you go it seems to you that you see the gleam of a
snowy plume and the shine of a straight rapier striking
home through cuirass and doublet, whilst on the stones
the dead body falls, and high above over the lamp-iron,
where the torch is flaring, a casement uncloses, and a
woman's voice murmurs, with a cruel little laugh, "Cosa
fatta capo ha !"

There is nothing to break the spell of that old-world
enchantment.

Nothing to recall to you that the ages of Bentivoglio
and of Visconti have fled for ever.

The mighty Academy of Luvena Juris is so old, so old,
so old!—the folly and frippery of modern life cannot
dwell in it a moment ; it is as that enchanted throne
which turned into stone like itself whosoever dared to
seat himself upon its majestic heights.

For fifteen centuries Bologna has grimly watched and
seen the mad life of the world go by ; it sits amidst the
plains as the Sphynx amidst her deserts.

IT is women's way. They always love colour better
than form, rhetoric better than logic, priestcraft
better than philosophy, and flourishes better than fugues.
It has been said scores of times before I said it.

Nay, he pursued, thinking he had pained me, you
have a bright wit enough, and a beautiful voice, though
you sing without knowing very well what you do sing.
But genius you have not, look you ; say your thanksgiving
to the Madonna at the next shrine we come to ; genius
you have not.

What is it?

Well, it is hard to tell; but this is certain, that it puts peas unboiled into the shoes of every pilgrim who really gets up to its Olivet.

Genius has all manner of dead dreams and sorrowful lost loves for its scallop-shells; and the palm that it carries is the bundle of rods wherewith fools have beaten it for calling them blind.

Genius has eyes so clear that it sees straight down into the hearts of others through all their veils of sophistry and simulation; but its own heart is pierced often to the quick for shame of what it reads there.

It has such long and faithful remembrance of other worlds and other lives which most minds have forgotten, that beside the beauty of those memories all things of earth seem poor and valueless.

Men call this imagination or idealism; the name does not matter much; whether it be desire or remembrance, it comes to the same issue; so that genius, going ever beyond the thing it sees in infinite longing for some higher greatness which it has either lost or otherwise cannot reach, finds the art, and the humanity, and the creations, and the affections which seem to others so exquisite most imperfect and scarcely to be endured.

The heaven of Phædrus is the world which haunts Genius—where there shall not be women but Woman, not friends but Friendship, not poems but Poetry; everything in its uttermost wholeness and perfection; so that there shall be no possibility of regret nor any place for desire.

For in this present world there is only one thing which can content it, and that thing is music; because music has nothing to do with earth, but sighs always for the lands beyond the sun.

And yet all this while genius, though sick at heart, and alone, and finding little in man or in woman, in human art or in human nature, that can equal what it remembers —or, as men choose to say, it imagines—is half a child

too, always : for something of the eternal light which
streams from the throne of God is always shed about it,
though sadly dimmed and broken by the clouds and
vapours that men call their atmosphere.

Half a child always, taking a delight in the frolic of
the kids, the dancing of the daffodils, the playtime of the
children, the romp of the winds with the waters, the loves
of the birds in the blossoms. Half a child always, but
always with tears lying close to its laughter, and always
with desires that are death in its dreams.

No ; you have not genius, cara mia. Say your grazie
at the next shrine we pass.

THEREFORE, in those days men, giving themselves
leave to be glad for a little space, were glad with
the same sinewy force and manful singleness of purpose
as made them in other times laborious, self-denying,
patient, and fruitful of high thoughts and deeds.

Because they laboured for their fellows, therefore they
could laugh with them ; and because they served God,
therefore they dared be glad.

In those grave, dauntless, austere lives the Carnival's
jocund revelry was as one golden bead in a pilgrim's
rosary of thorn-berries.

They had aimed highly and highly achieved ; therefore
they could go forth amidst their children and rejoice.

But we—in whom all art is the mere empty Shibboleth
of a ruined religion whose priests are all dead ; we—
whose whole year-long course is one Dance of Death
over the putridity of our pleasures ; we—whose solitary
purpose it is to fly faster and faster from desire to satiety,
from satiety to desire, in an endless eddy of fruitless effort;
we—whose greatest genius can only raise for us some
inarticulate protest of despair against some unknown
God ;—we have strangled King Carnival and killed him,

X

and buried him in the ashes of our own unutterable
weariness and woe.

OH, I believe it was all true enough.
There were mighty Pascarèlli in the olden days.
But I am very glad that I was not of them; except,
indeed, that I should have liked to strike a blow or two
for Guido Calvacanti and have hindered the merry-
making of those precious rascals who sent him out to
die of the marsh fever.

Great?

No; certainly I would not be great. To be a
great man is endlessly to crave something that you
have not; to kiss the hands of monarchs and lick the
feet of peoples. To be great? Who was ever more
great than Dante, and what was his experience?—the
bitterness of begged bread, and the steepness of palace
stairs.

Besides, given the genius to deserve it, the up-shot
of a life spent for greatness is absolutely uncertain.
Look at Machiavelli.

After having laid down infallible rules for social and
public success with such unapproachable astuteness
that his name has become a synonym for unerring
policy, Machiavelli passed his existence in obedience
and submission to Rome, to Florence, to Charles, to
Cosmo, to Leo, to Clement.

He was born into a time favourable beyond every
other to sudden changes of fortune; a time in which
any fearless audacity might easily become the stepping-
stone to a supreme authority; and yet Machiavelli,
whom the world still holds as its ablest statesman—in
principle—never in practice rose above the level of
a servant of civil and papal tyrannies, and, when his
end came, died in obscurity and almost in penury.

Theoretically, Machiavelli could rule the universe ;
but practically he never attained to anything finer than
a more or less advantageous change of masters. To
reign doctrinally may be all very well, but when it only
results in serving actually, it seems very much better to
be obscure and content without any trouble.

"Fumo di gloria non vale fumo di pipa."

I, for one, at any rate, am thoroughly convinced
of that truth of truths.

I hearkened to him sorrowful ; for to my ignorant
eyes the witch candle of fame seemed a pure and perfect planet ; and I felt that the planet might have ruled
his horoscope had he chosen.

Is there no glory at all worth having, then? I murmured.

He stretched himself where he rested amongst the
arum-whitened grass, and took his cigaretto from his
mouth :

Well, there is one, perhaps. But it is to be had
about once in five centuries.

You know Or San Michele? It would have been
a world's wonder had it stood alone, and not been
companioned with such wondrous rivals that its own
exceeding beauty scarce ever receives full justice.

Where the jasper of Giotto and the marble of
Brunelleschi, where the bronze of Ghiberti and the
granite of Arnolfo rise everywhere in the sunlit air to
challenge vision and adoration, or San Michele fails
of its full meed from men. Yet, perchance, in all the
width of Florence there is not a nobler thing.

It is like some massive casket of silver oxydised
by time ; such a casket as might have been made to
hold the Tables of the Law by men to whose faith
Sinai was the holy and imperishable truth.

I know nothing of the rule or phrase of Architecture, but it seems to me surely that that square-set strength, as of a fortress, towering against the clouds, and catching the last light always on its fretted parapet, and everywhere embossed and enriched with foliage, and tracery, and the figures of saints, and the shadows of vast arches, and the light of niches gold-starred and filled with divine forms, is a gift so perfect to the whole world, that, passing it, one should need say a prayer for great Taddeo's soul.

Surely, nowhere is the rugged, changeless, mountain force of hewn stone piled against the sky, and the luxuriant, dreamlike, poetic delicacy of stone carven and shaped into leafage and loveliness more perfectly blended and made one than where Or San Michele rises out of the dim, many-coloured, twisting streets, in its mass of ebon darkness and of silvery light.

Well, the other day, under the walls of it I stood, and looked at its Saint George where he leans upon his shield, so calm, so young, with his bared head and his quiet eyes.

"That is our Donatello's," said a Florentine beside me—a man of the people, who drove a horse for hire in the public ways, and who paused, cracking his whip, to tell this tale to me. "Donatello did that, and it killed him. Do you not know? When he had done that Saint George, he showed it to his master. And the master said, 'It wants one thing only.' Now this saying our Donatello took gravely to heart, chiefly of all because his master would never explain where the fault lay; and so much did it hurt him, that he fell ill of it, and came nigh to death. Then he called his master to him. 'Dear and great one, do tell me before I die,' he said, 'what is the one thing my statue lacks.' The master smiled, and said, 'Only—speech.' 'Then I die happy,' said our Donatello. And he died —indeed, that hour."

"Now, I cannot say that the pretty story is true; it is not in the least true; Donato died when he was eighty-three, in the Street of the Melon; and it was he himself who cried, 'Speak then—speak!' to his statue, as it was carried through the city. But whether true or false the tale, this fact is surely true, that it is well—nobly and purely well—with a people when the men amongst it who ply for hire on its public ways think caressingly of a sculptor dead five hundred years ago, and tell such a tale standing idly in the noon-day sun, feeling the beauty and the pathos of it all.

"'Our Donatello' still to the people of Florence. 'Our own little Donato' still, our pet and pride, even as though he were living and working in their midst to-day, here in the shadows of the Stocking-maker's Street, where his Saint George keeps watch and ward.

"'Our little Donato' still, though dead so many hundred years ago.

"That is glory, if you will. And something more beautiful than any glory—Love."

He was silent a long while, gathering lazily with his left hand the arum lilies to bind them together for me.

Perhaps the wish for the moment passed over him that he had chosen to set his life up in stone, like to Donato's, in the face of Florence, rather than to weave its light and tangled skein out from the breaths of the wandering winds and the sands of the shifting shore.

COME out here in the young months of summer, and leave, as we left, the highways that grim walls fence in, and stray, as we strayed, through the field-paths and the bridle-roads in the steps of the contadini, and you will find this green world about your feet touched with the May-day suns to tenderest and most lavish wealth of nature.

The green corn uncurling underneath the blossoming vines. The vine foliage that tosses and climbs and coils in league on league of verdure. The breast-high grasses full of gold and red and purple from the countless flowers growing with it.

The millet filled with crimson gladioli and great scarlet poppies. The hill-sides that look a sheet of rose-colour where the lupinelli are in bloom. The tall plumes of the canes, new-born, by the side of every stream and rivulet.

The sheaves of arum leaves that thrust themselves out from every joint of masonry or spout of broken fountain. The flame of roses that burns on every handbreadth of untilled ground and springs like a rainbow above the cloud of every darkling roof or wall. The ocean spray of arbutus and acacia shedding its snow against the cypress darkness. The sea-green of the young ilex leaves scattered like light over the bronze and purple of the older growth. The dreamy blue of the iris lilies rising underneath the olives and along the edges of the fields.

ALL greatest gifts that have enriched the modern world have come from Italy. Take those gifts from the world, and it would lie in darkness, a dumb, barbaric, joyless thing.

Leave Rome alone, or question as you will whether she were the mightiest mother, or the blackest curse that ever came on earth. I do not speak of Rome, imperial or republican, I speak of Italy.

Of Italy, after the greatness of Rome dropped as the Labarum was raised on high, and the Fisher of Galilee came to fill the desolate place of the Cæsars.

Of Italy, when she was no more a vast dominion, ruling over half the races of the globe, from the Persian to the Pict, but a narrow slip bounded by Adriatic and Mediterranean, divided into hostile sections, racked by foreign foes, and torn by internecine feud.

Of Italy, ravaged by the Longobardo, plundered by the French, scourged by the Popes, tortured by the Kaisers; of Italy, with her cities at war with each other, her dukedoms against her free towns, her tyrants in conflict with her municipalities; of Italy, in a word, as she has been from the days of Theodoric and Theodolinda to the days of Napoleon and Francis Joseph. It is this Italy—our Italy—which through all the centuries of bloodshed and of suffering never ceased to bear aloft and unharmed its divining-rod of inspiration as S. Christopher bore the young Christ above the swell of the torrent and the rage of the tempest.

All over Italy from north to south men arose in the darkness of those ages who became the guides and the torchbearers of a humanity that had gone astray in the carnage and gloom.

The faith of Columbus of Genoa gave to mankind a new world. The insight of Galileo of Pisa revealed to it the truth of its laws of being. Guido Monacco of Arezzo bestowed on it the most spiritual of all earthly joys by finding a visible record for the fugitive creations of harmony ere then impalpable and evanescent as the passing glories of the clouds. Dante Alighieri taught to it the might of that vulgar tongue in which the child babbles at its mother's knee, and the orator leads a breathless multitude at his will to death or triumph. Teofilo of Empoli discovered for it the mysteries of colour that lie in the mere earths of the rocks and the shores, and the mere oils of the roots and the poppies. Arnoldo of Breccia lit for it the first flame of free opinion, and Amatus of Breccia perfected for it the most delicate and exquisite of all instruments of sound, which men of Cremona, or of Bologna, had first created. Maestro Giorgio, and scores of earnest workers whose names are lost in Pesaro and in Gubbio, bestowed on it those homelier treasures of the graver's and the potter's labours which have carried the alphabet of art into the lowliest home. Brunelleschi of Florence left it in legacy the secret of lifting a mound of marble to the upper air as easily as a child can blow a bubble; and Giordano Bruno of Nola found for it those elements of philosophic thought, which have been perfected into the clear and prismatic crystals of the metaphysics of the Teuton and the Scot.

From south and north, from east and west, they rose, the ministers and teachers of mankind.

From mountain and from valley, from fortress smoking under battle, and from hamlet laughing under vines; from her great wasted cities, from her small fierce walled towns, from her lone sea-shores ravaged by the galleys of the Turks, from her villages on hill and plain that struggled into life through the invaders' fires, and pushed their vineshoots over the tombs of kings, everywhere all over her peaceful soil, such men arose.

Not men alone who were great in a known art, thought or science, of these the name was legion; but men in whose brains, art, thought, or science took new forms, was born into new life, spoke with new voice, and sprang full armed a new Athene.

Leave Rome aside, I say, and think of Italy; measure her gifts, which with the lavish waste of genius she has flung broadcast in grand and heedless sacrifice, and tell me if the face of earth would not be dark and drear as any Scythian desert without these?

She was the rose of the world, aye—so they bruised and trampled her, and yet the breath of heaven was ever in her.

She was the world's nightingale, aye — so they burned her eyes out and sheared her wings, and yet she sang.

But she was yet more than these : she was the light of the world : a light set on a hill, a light unquenchable. A light which through the darkness of the darkest night has been a Pharos to the drowning faiths and dying hopes of man.

"IT must have been such a good life—a painter's—in those days; those early days of art. Fancy the gladness of it then—modern painters can know nothing of it.

"When all the delicate delights of distance were only half perceived; when the treatment of light and shadow was barely dreamed of; when aerial perspective was just breaking on the mind in all its wonder and power; when it was still regarded as a marvellous boldness to draw from the natural form in a natural fashion ;—in those early days only fancy the delights of a painter !

"Something fresh to be won at each step; something new to be penetrated at each moment; something beautiful and rash to be ventured on with each touch of colour,—the painter in those days had all the breathless pleasure of an explorer; without leaving his birthplace he knew the joys of Columbus.

"And then the reverence that waited on him.

"He was a man who glorified God amongst a people that believed in God.

"What he did was a reality to himself and those around him. Spinello fainted before the Satanas he portrayed, and Angelico deemed it blasphemy to alter a feature of the angels who visited him that they might live visibly for men in his colours in the cloister.

" Of all men the artist was nearest to heaven, therefore of all men was he held most blessed.

" When Francis Valois stooped for the brush he only represented the spirit of the age he lived in. It is what all wise kings do. It is their only form of genius.

" Now-a-days what can men do in the Arts ! Nothing.

" All has been painted—all sung—all said.

" All is twice told—in verse, in stone, in colour. There is no untraversed ocean to tempt the Columbus of any Art.

" It is dreary—very dreary—that. All had been said and done so much better than we can ever say or do it again. One envies those men who gathered all the paradise flowers half opened, and could watch them bloom.

" Art can only live by Faith : and what faith have we ?

" Instead of Art we have indeed Science ; but Science is very sad, for she doubts all things and would prove all things, and doubt is endless, and proof is a quagmire that looks like solid earth, and is but shifting waters."

His voice was sad as it fell on the stillness of Arezzo—Arezzo who had seen the dead gods come and go, and the old faiths rise and fall, there where the mule trod its patient way and the cicala sang its summer song above the place where the temple of the Bona Dea and the Church of Christ had alike passed away, so that no man could tell their place.

It was all quiet around.

" I would rather have been Spinello than Petrarca," he pursued, after a while. " Yes; though the sonnets will live as long as men love : and the old man's work has almost every line of it crumbled away.

" But one can fancy nothing better than a life such as Spinello led for nigh a century up on the hill here, painting, because he loved it, till death took him. Of all lives, perhaps, that this world has ever seen, the lives of painters, I say, in those days were the most perfect.

" Not only the magnificent pageants of Leonardo's, of
Raffaelle's, of Giorgone's : but the lowlier lives — the
lives of men such as Santi, and Ridolfi, and Benozzo,
and Francia, and Timoteo, and many lesser men than
they, painters in fresco and grisaille, painters of miniatures, painters of majolica and montelupo, painters who
were never great, but who attained infinite peacefulness
and beauty in their native towns and cities all over the
face of Italy.

"In quiet places, such as Arezzo and Volterra, and
Modena and Urbino, and Cortona and Perugia, there
would grow up a gentle lad who from infancy most loved
to stand and gaze at the missal paintings in his mother's
house, and the cœna in the monk's refectory, and when
he had fulfilled some twelve or fifteen years, his people
would give in to his wish and send him to some bottega
to learn the management of colours.

"Then he would grow to be a man ; and his town
would be proud of him, and find him the choicest of all
work in its churches and its convents, so that all his days
were filled without his ever wandering out of reach of his
native vesper bells.

" He would make his dwelling in the heart of his birthplace, close under its cathedral, with the tender sadness
of the olive hills stretching above and around; in the
basiliche or the monasteries his labour would daily lie ;
he would have a docile band of hopeful boyish pupils
with innocent eyes of wonder for all he did or said ; he
would paint his wife's face for the Madonna's, and his
little son's for the child Angel's; he would go out into
the fields and gather the olive bough, and the feathery
corn, and the golden fruits, and paint them tenderly on
ground of gold or blue, in symbol of those heavenly
things of which the bells were for ever telling all those
who chose to hear; he would sit in the lustrous nights
in the shade of his own vines and pity those who were

not as he was; now and then horsemen would come spurring in across the hills and bring news with them of battles fought, of cities lost and won; and he would listen with the rest in the market-place, and go home through the moonlight thinking that it was well to create the holy things before which the fiercest reiter and the rudest free-lance would drop the point of the sword and make the sign of the cross.

"It must have been a good life—good to its close in the cathedral crypt—and so common too; there were scores such lived out in these little towns of Italy, half monastery and half fortress, that were scattered over hill and plain, by sea and river, on marsh and mountain, from the daydawn of Cimabue to the afterglow of the Carracci.

"And their work lives after them; the little towns are all grey and still and half peopled now; the iris grows on the ramparts, the canes wave in the moats, the shadows sleep in the silent market-place, the great convents shelter half-a-dozen monks, the dim majestic churches are damp and desolate, and have the scent of the sepulchre.

"But there, above the altars, the wife lives in the Madonna and the child smiles in the Angel, and the olive and the wheat are fadeless on their ground of gold and blue; and by the tomb in the crypt the sacristan will shade his lantern and murmur with a sacred tenderness:—

"'Here he sleeps.'

"'He,' even now, so long, long after, to the people of his birthplace. Who can want more of life—or death?"

So he talked on in that dreamy, wistful manner that was as natural with him in some moments as his buoyant and ironical gaiety at others.

Then he rose as the shadows grew longer and pulled down a knot of pomegranate blossom for me, and we went together under the old walls, across the maize fields, down the slope of the hills to the olive orchard, where a peasant, digging deep his trenches against the autumn rains, had struck his mattock on the sepulchre of the Etruscan king.

There was only a little heap of fine dust when we reach the spot.

"THERE was so much more colour in those days," he had said, rolling a big green papone before him with his foot. "If, indeed, it were laid on sometimes too roughly. And then there was so much more play for character. Now-a-days, if a man dare go out of the common ways to seek a manner of life suited to him, and unlike others, he is voted a vagabond, or, at least, a lunatic, supposing he is rich enough to get the sentence so softened. In those days the impossible was possible—a paradox? oh, of course. The perfection of those days was, that they were full of paradoxes. No democracy will ever compass the immensity of Hope, the vastness of Possibility, with which the Church of those ages filled the lives of the poorest poor. Not hope spiritual only, but hope terrestrial, hope material and substantial. A swineherd, glad to gnaw the husks that his pigs left, might become the Viceregent of Christ, and spurn emperors prostrate before his throne. The most famished student who girt his lean loins to pass the gates of Pavia or Ravenna, knew that if he bowed his head for the tonsure he might live to lift it in a pontiff's arrogance in the mighty reality and the yet mightier metaphor of a Canosa. The abuses of the mediæval Church have been gibbeted in every language; but I doubt if the wonderful absolute *equality* which that Church actually contained and caused has ever been sufficiently remembered. Then only think how great it was to *be* great in those years, when men were fresh enough of heart to feel emotion and not ashamed to show it. Think of Petrarca's entry into Rome; think of the superb life

of Raffael ; think of the crowds that hung on the lips of
the Improvisatori : think of the influence of S. Bruno, of
S. Bernard, of S. Francis ; think of the enormous power
on his generation of Fra Girolamo! And if one were
not great at all, but only a sort of brute with stronger
sinews than most men, what a fearless and happy brute
one might be, riding with Hawkwood's Lances, or fighting
with the Black Bands ! Whilst, if one were a peaceable,
gentle soul, with a turn for art and grace, what a calm,
tender life one might lead in little, old, quiet cities,
painting praying saints on their tiptoes, or moulding
marriage-plates in majolica ! It must have been such a
great thing to live when the world was still all open-eyed
with wonder at itself, like a child on its sixth birthday.
Now-a-days, science makes a great discovery ; the tired
world yawns, feels its pockets, and only asks, "Will it
pay?" Galileo ran the risk of the stake, and Giordano
Bruno suffered at it ; but I think that chance of the
faggots must have been better to bear than the languid
apathy and the absorbed avarice of the present age, which
is chiefly tolerant because it has no interest except in new
invented ways for getting money and for spending it."

IN MAREMMA.

HE remembered two years before, when he had passed
through Italy on his way eastward, pausing in Fer-
rara, and Brescia, and Mantua, and staying longer in the
latter city on account of a trial then in course of hearing
in the court of justice, which had interested him by its
passionate and romantic history ; it had been the trial of
the young Count d'Este, accused of the assassination of
his mistress. Sanctis had gone with the rest of the town
to the hearing of the long and tedious examination of
the witnesses and of accused. It had been a warm day in
early autumn, three months after the night of the murder ;
Mantua had looked beautiful in her golden mantle of
sunshine and silver veil of mist ; there was a white, light
fog on the water meadows and the lakes, and under it
the willows waved and the tall reeds rustled ; whilst the
dark towers, the forked battlements, the vast Lombard
walls, seemed to float on it like sombre vessels on a foamy
sea.

He remembered the country people flocking in over
the bridge, the bells ringing, the red sails drifting by, the
townsfolk gathering together in the covered arcades and
talking with angry rancour against the dead woman's
lord. He remembered sitting in the hush and gloom of
the judgment-hall and furtively sketching the head of the
prisoner because of its extreme and typical beauty. He
remembered how at the time he had thought this accused
lover guiltless, and wondered that the tribunal did not

sooner suspect the miserly, malicious, and subtle meaning
of the husband's face. He remembered listening to the
tragic tale that seemed so well to suit those sombre,
feudal streets, those melancholy waters, seeing the three-
edged dagger passed from hand to hand, hearing how the
woman had been found dead in her beauty on her old
golden and crimson bed with the lilies on her breast, and
looking at the attitude of the prisoner—in which the
judges saw remorse and guilt, and he could only see the
unutterable horror of a bereaved lover to whom the
world was stripped and naked.

He had stayed but two days in Mantua, but those two
days had left an impression on him like that left by the
reading at the fall of night of some ghastly poem of the
middle ages. He had thought that they had condemned
an innocent man, as the judge gave his sentence of the
galleys for life: and the scene had often come back to
his thoughts.

The vaulted audience chamber ; the strong light pouring in through high grated windows ; the pillars of many-
coloured marbles, the frescoed roof ; the country people
massed together in the public place, with faces that were
like paintings of Mantegna or Masaccio ; the slender
supple form of the accused drooping like a bruised lily
between the upright figures of two carabineers ; the judge
leaning down over his high desk in black robes and
black square cap, like some Venetian lawgiver of Veronese
or of Titian ; and beyond, through an open casement, the
silvery, watery, sun-swept landscape that was still the
same as when Romeo came, banished, to Mantua. All
these had remained impressed upon his mind by the
tragedy which there came to its close as a lover, passionate as Romeo and yet more unfortunate, was condemned
to the galleys for his life. "They have ill judged a guiltless man," he had said to himself as he had left the court
with a sense of pain before injustice done, and went with

heart saddened by a stranger's fate into the misty air,
along the shining water where the Mills of the Twelve
Apostles were churning the great dam into froth, as they
had done through seven centuries, since first, with reverent care, the builder had set the sacred statues there
that they might bless the grinding of the corn.

Sitting now in the silence of the tomb, Sanctis recalled
that day, when, towards the setting of the sun, he had
strolled there by the water-wheels of the twelve disciples,
and allowed the fate of an unknown man, declared a
criminal by impartial judges, to cloud over for him the
radiance of evening on the willowy Serraglio and chase
away his peaceful thoughts of Virgil. He remembered
how the country people had come out by the bridge and
glided away in their boats, and talked of the murder of
Donna Aloysia ; and how they had, one and all of them,
said, going back over the lake water or along the reed-
fringed roads, to their farmhouses, that there could be
no manner of doubt about it—the lover had been moon-
struck and mad with jealousy, and his dagger had found
its way to her breast. They had not blamed him much,
but they had never doubted his guilt ; and the foreigner
alone, standing by the mill gateway, and seeing the golden
sun go down beyond the furthermost fields of reeds that
grew blood-red as the waters grew, had thought to himself
and said half aloud :

"Poor Romeo ! he is guiltless, even though the dagger
were his"——

And a prior, black-robed, with broad looped-up black
hat, who was also watching the sunset, breviary in hand,
had smiled and said, "Nay, Romeo, banished to us, had
no blood on his hand ; but this Romeo, native of our
city, has. Mantua will be not ill rid of Luitbrand d'Este."

Then he again, in obstinacy and against all the priest's
better knowledge as a Mantuan, had insisted and said,
"The man is innocent."

Y

And the sun had gone down as he had spoken, and the priest had smiled—a smile cold as a dagger's blade—perhaps recalling sins confessed to him of love that had changed to hate, of fierce delight ending in as fierce a death-blow. Mantua in her day had seen so much alike of love and hate.

"The man is innocent," he had said insisting, whilst the carmine light had glowed on the lagoons and bridges, and on the Lombard walls, and Gothic gables, and high bell-towers, and ducal palaces, and feudal fortresses of the city in whose street Crichton fell to the hired steel of bravoes.

SHE had the heaven-born faculty of observation of the poets, and she had that instinct of delight in natural beauty which made Linnæus fall on his knees before the English gorse and thank God for having made so beautiful a thing.

Her sympathies and her imaginings spent themselves in solitary song as she made the old strings of the lute throb in low cadence when she sat solitary by her hearth on the rock floor of the grave; and out of doors her eyes filled and her lips laughed when she wandered through the leafy land and found the warbler's nest hung upon the reeds, or the first branching asphodel in flower. She could not have told why these made her happy, why she could watch for half a day untired the little wren building where the gladwyn blossomed on the water's edge. It was only human life that hurt her, embittered her, and filled her with hatred of it.

As she walked one golden noon by the Sasso Scritto, clothed with its myrtle and thyme and its quaint cacti that later would bear their purple heads of fruit; the shining sea beside her, and above her the bold arbutus-covered heights, with the little bells of the sheep sounding on

their sides, she saw a large fish, radiant as a gem, with
eyes like rubies. Some men had it ; a hook was in its
golden gills, and they had tied its tail to the hook so
that it could not stir, and they had put it in a pail of
water that it might not die too quickly, die ere they could
sell it. A little further on she saw a large green and gold
snake, one of the most harmless of all earth's creatures,
that only asked to creep into the sunshine, to sleep in
its hole in the rock, to live out its short, innocent life
under the honey smile of the rosemary ; the same men
stoned it to death, heaping the pebbles and broken
sandstone on it, and it perished slowly in long agony,
being large and tenacious of life. Yet a little further
on, again, she saw a big square trap of netting, with a
blinded chaffinch as decoy. The trap was full of birds,
some fifty or sixty of them, all kinds of birds, from the
plain brown minstrel, beloved of the poets, to the merry
and amber-winged oriole, from the dark grey or russet-
bodied fly-catcher and whinchat to the glossy and handsome jay, cheated and caught as he was going back to
the north ; they had been trapped, and would be strung
on a string and sold for a copper coin the dozen ; and
of many of them the wings or the legs were broken and
the eyes were already dim. The men who had taken
them were seated on the thymy turf grinning like apes,
with pipes in their mouths, and a flask of wine between
their knees.

She passed on, helpless.

She thought of words that Joconda had once quoted
to her, words which said that men were made in God's
likeness !

WHILE it is winter the porphyrion sails down the
willowy streams beside the sultan-hen that is
to be his love, and sees her not, and stays not her

passage upon the water or through the air; she does
not live as yet to him. But when the breath of the
spring brings the catkins from the willows, and the
violets amidst the wood-moss on the banks, then he
awakes and beholds her; and then the stream reflects
but her shape for him, and the rushes are full of the
melody of his love-call. It was still winter with Este—
a bitter winter of discontent; and he had no eyes for
this water-bird that swam with him through the icy
current of his adversity.

To break the frozen flood that imprisoned him was
his only thought.

A IR is the king of physicians; he who stands often
with nothing between him and the open heavens
will gain from them health both moral and physical.

"YES; you have a right to know. After all, it was
ruin to me, but it is not much of a story; a tale-
teller with his guitar on a vintage night would soon
make a better one. I loved a woman. She lived in
Mantua. So did I, too. For her sake I lost three
whole years—three years of the best of my life. And
yet, what is gain except love, and what better than joy
can we have? A pomegranate is ripe but once. And
I—my pomegranate is rotten for evermore! We lived
in Mantua. It is a strange sad place. It was great
and gay enough once. Grander pomp than Mantua's
there was never known in Italy. Felix Mantua!—
and now it is all decaying, mouldering, sinking, fading;
it is silent as death; the mists, the waters, the empty
palaces, the walls that the marshes are eating little by
little every day, the grass and the moss and the wild
birds' nests on the roofs, on the temples, on the bridges,

all are desolate in Mantua now. Yet is it beautiful in
its loneliness, when the sunrise comes over the seas of
reeds, and the towers and the arches are reflected in
the pools and streams; and yet again at night, when
the moon is high and the lagoons are as sheets of silver,
and the shadows come and go over the bulrushes and
St. Andrea lifts itself against the stars. Yes; then it is
still Mantova la Gloriosa."

His voice dropped; the tears came into his closing
eyes as though he looked on the dead face of a familiar
friend.

He felt the home sickness of the exile, of the wanderer
who knows not where to lay his head.

The glory was gone from the city.

Its greatness was but as a ghost that glided through
its deserted streets calling in vain on dead men to
arise.

The rough red sail of the fishing-boat was alone on
the waters once crowded with the silken sails of gilded
galleys; the toad croaked and the stork made her nest
where the Lords of Gonzaga had gone forth to meet
their brides of Este or of Medici; Virgil, Alboin, great
Karl, Otho, Petrarca, Ariosto, had passed by here over
this world of waters and become no more than dreams;
and the vapours and the dust together had stolen the
smile from Giulio's Psyche, and the light from Mantegna's arabesques. On the vast walls the grass grew,
and in the palaces of princes the winds wandered and
the beggars slept. All was still, disarmed, lonely, forgotten; left to a silence like the silence of the endless
night of death. Yet it was dear to him; this sad and
stately city, waiting for the slow death of an unpitied and
lingering decay.

It was dear to him from habit, from birth, from
memory, from affinity, as the reeds of its stagnant
waters were dear to the sedge-warbler that hung its

slender nest on the stem of a rush. A price was set
on his head; and never more, he thought, would he
see the sunshine in ripples of gold come over the grey
lagoons.

NO one cared; the terrible, barren, acrid truth, that
science trumpets abroad as though it were some
new-found joy, touched her ignorance with its desolat-
ing despair. No one cared. Life was only sustained
by death. The harmless and lovely children of the air
and of the moor were given over, year after year,
century after century, to the bestial play and the ferocious appetites of men. The wondrous beauty of the
earth renewed itself only to be the scene of endless
suffering, of interminable torture. The human tyrant,
without pity, greedy as a child, more brutal than the
tiger in his cruelty, had all his way upon the innocent
races to which he begrudged a tuft of reeds, a palm's
breadth of moss or sand. The slaughter, the misery,
the injustice, renewed themselves as the greenness of
the world did. No one cared. There was no voice
upon the blood-stained waters. There was no rebuke
from the offended heavens. To all prayer or pain there
was eternal silence as the sole reply.

THE uneducated are perhaps unjustly judged sometimes. To the ignorant both right and wrong
are only instincts; when one remembers their piteous
and innocent confusion of ideas, the twilight of dim
comprehension in which they dwell, one feels that oftentimes the laws of cultured men are too hard on them,
and that, in a better sense than that of injustice and
reproach, there ought indeed to be two laws for rich
and poor.

IT needs a great nature to bear the weight of a great gratitude.

To a great nature it gives wings that bear it up to heaven; a lower nature feels it always as a clog that impatiently is dragged only so long as force compels.

WHEN the thoughts of youth return, fresh as the scent of new-gathered blossoms, to the tired old age which has so long forgot them, the coming of Death is seldom very distant.

THE boat went through the waters swiftly, as the wind blew more strongly; the sandy shore with its scrub of low-growing rock-rose and prickly Christ's thorn did not change its landscape, but what she looked at always was the sea; the sea that in the light had the smiling azure of a young child's eyes, and when the clouds cast shadows on it, had the intense impenetrable brilliancy of a jewel.

In the distance were puffs of white and grey, like smoke or mist; those mists were Corsica and Caprajà.

Elba towered close at hand.

Gorgona lay far beyond, with all the other little isles that seem made to shelter Miranda and Ariel, but of Gorgona she knew nothing; she was steering straight towards it, but it was many a league distant on the northerly water.

When she at last stopped her boat in its course she was at the Sasso Scritto : a favourite resting-place with her, where, on feast-days, when Joconda let her have liberty from housework and rush-plaiting and spinning of flax, she always came.

Northward, there was a long smooth level beach of sand, and beyond that a lagoon where all the water-

birds that love both the sea and the marsh came in
large flocks, and spread their wings over the broad
spaces in which the salt water and the fresh were
mingled. Beyond this there were cliffs of the humid
red tufa, and the myrtle and the holy thorn grew down
their sides, and met in summer the fragrant hesperis of
the shore.

These cliffs were fine bold bluffs, and one of them
had been called from time immemorial the Sasso Scritto,
—why, no one knew; the only writing on it was done
by the hand of Nature. It was steep and lofty; on its
summit were the ruins of an old fortress of the middle
ages; its sides were clothed with myrtle, aloe, and
rosemary, and at its feet were boulders of marble, rose
and white in the sun; rock pools, with exquisite network of sunbeams crossing their rippling surface, and
filled with green ribbon-grasses and red sea-foliage, and
shining gleams of broken porphyry, and pieces of agate
and cornelian.

The yellow sands hereabouts were bright just now
with the sea-daffodil, and the sea-stocks, which would
blossom later, were pricking upward to the Lenten light;
great clusters of southern-wood waved in the wind, and
the pungent sea-rush grew in long lines along the shore,
where the sand-piper was dropping her eggs, and the
blue-rock was carrying dry twigs and grass to his home
in the ruins above or the caverns beneath, and the
stock-doves in large companies were winging their way
over sea towards the Maritime or the Pennine Alps.

This was a place that Musa loved, and she would
come here and sit for hours, and watch the roseate
cloud of the returning flamingoes winging their way
from Sardinia, and the martins busy at their masonry
in the cliffs, and the Arctic longipennes going away
northward as the weather opened, and the stream-
swallows hunting early gnats and frogs on the water,

and the kingfisher digging his tortuous underground
home in the sand. Here she would lie for hours amongst
the rosemary, and make silent friendships with the popu-
lations of the air, while the sweet blue sky was above
her head, and the sea, as blue, stretched away till it
was lost in light.

Once up above, on these cliffs, the eye could sweep
over the sea north and south, and the soil was more
than ever scented with that fragrant and humble blue-
flowered shrub of which the English madrigals and
glees of the Stuart and Hanoverian poets so often speak,
and seem to smell. Behind the cliffs stretched moorland, marshes, woodland, intermingled, crossed by many
streams, holding many pools, blue-fringed in May with
iris, and osier beds, and vast fields of reeds, and breadths
of forest with dense thorny underwood, where all wild
birds came in their season, and where all was quiet save
for a bittern's cry, a boar's snort, a snipe's scream, on
the lands once crowded with the multitudes that gave
the eagle of Persia and the brazen trumpets of Lydia to
the legions of Rome.

Under their thickets of the prickly sloe-tree and the
sweet-smelling bay lay the winding ways of buried cities ;
their runlets of water rippled where kings and warriors
slept beneath the soil, and the yellow marsh lily, and
the purple and the rose of the wind-flower and the
pasque-flower, and the bright red of the Easter tulips, and
the white and the gold of the asphodels, and the colours
of a thousand other rarer and less homelike blossoms,
spread their innocent glory in their turn to the sky and
the breeze, above the sunken stones of courts and gates
and palaces and prisons.

These moors were almost as solitary as the deserts are.

Now and then against the blue of the sky and the
brown of the wood, there rose the shapes of shepherds
and their flocks ; now and then herds of young horses

went by, fleet and unconscious of their doom ; now and then the sound of a rifle cracked the silence of the windless air ; but these came but seldom.

Maremma is wide, and its people are scattered.

In autumn and in winter, hunters, shepherds, swineherds, sportsmen, birdcatchers, might spoil the solemn peace of these moors, but in spring and summer no human soul was seen upon them. The boar and the buffalo, the flamingo and the roebuck, the great plover and the woodcock, reigned alone.

" THEY say he sang too well, and that was why they burnt him," said Andreino to her to-day, after telling her for the hundredth time of what he had seen once on the Ligurian shore, far away yonder northward, when he, who knew nothing of Adonais or Prometheus, had been called, a stout seafaring man in that time, amongst other peasants of the country-side, to help bring in the wood for a funeral pyre by the sea.

He had known nought of the songs or the singer, but he loved to tell the tale he had heard then ; and say how he had seen, he himself, with his own eyes, the drowned poet burn, far away yonder where the pines stood by the sea, and how the flames had curled around the heart that men had done their best to break, and how it had remained unburnt in the midst, whilst all the rest drifted in ashes down the wind. He knew nought of the Skylark's ode, and nought of the Cor Cordium ; but the scene by the seashore had burned itself as though with flame into his mind, and he spoke of it a thousand times if once, sitting by the edge of the sea that had killed the singer.

"Will they burn me if I sing too well?" the child asked him this day, the words of Joconda being with her.

"Oh, that is sure," said Andreino, half in jest and half in earnest. "They burnt him because he sang better

than all of them. So they said. I do not know. I know
the resin ran out of the pinewood all golden and hissing
and his heart would not burn, all we could do. You are
a female thing, Musa; your heart will be the first to burn,
the first of all!"

"Will it?" said Musa seriously, but not any way
alarmed, for the thought of that flaming pile 'by the
seashore by night was a familiar image to her.

"Ay, for sure; you will be a woman!" said Andreino,
hammering into his boat.

"THOUGH there is not a soul here, still sometimes
they come—Lucchese, Pistoiese, what not—they
come as they go; they are a faithless lot; they love all
winter, and while the corn is in the ear it goes well, but
after harvest—phew!—they put their gains in their
pockets and they are off and away back to their mountains. There are broken hearts in Maremma when the,
threshing is done."

"Yes," said Musa again.

It was nothing to her, and she heeded but little.

"Yes, because men speak too lightly and women
hearken too quickly; that is how the mischief is born.
With the autumn the mountaineers come. They are
strong and bold; they are ruddy and brown; they work
all day, but in the long nights they dance and they sing;
then the girl listens. She thinks it is all true, though it
has all been said before in his own hills to other ears
The winter nights are long, and the devil is always near;
when the corn goes down and the heat is come there is
another sad soul the more, another burden to carry, and
he—he goes back to the mountains. What does he care?
Only when he comes down into the plains again he goes
to another place to work, because men do not love women's
tears. That is how it goes in Maremma."

"SO the saints will pluck her to themselves at last," thought Joconda ; and the dreariness, the loveless-ness, the hopelessness of such an existence did not occur to her, because age, which has learned the solace and sweetness of peace, never remembers that to youth peace seems only stagnation, inanition, death.

The exhausted swimmer, reaching the land, falls prone on it, and blesses it ; but the outgoing swimmer, full of strength, spurns the land, and only loves the high-crested wave, the abyss of the deep sea.

IMAGINATION without culture is crippled and moves slowly ; but it can be pure imagination, and rich also, as folk-lore will tell the vainest.

IT is this narrowness of the peasant mind which philo-sophers never fairly understand, and demagogues understand but too well, and warp to their own selfish purposes and profits.

FLYING, the flamingoes are like a sunset cloud ; walk-ing, they are like slender spirals of flame traversing the curling foam. When one looks on them across black lines of storm-blown weeds on a November morning in the marshes, as their long throats twist in the air with the flexile motion of the snake, the grace of a lily blown by wind, one thinks of Thebes, of Babylon, of the gorge-ous Persia of Xerxes, of the lascivious Egypt of the Ptolemies.

The world has grown grey and joyless in the twilight of age and fatigue, but these birds keep the colour of its morning. Eos has kissed them.

F OR want of a word lives often drift apart.

N AUSICAA, in the safe shelter of her father's halls,
had never tended Odysseus with more serenity and
purity than the daughter of Saturnino tended his fellow-
slave.

The sanctity of the tombs lay on them, the dead were
so near; neither profanity nor passion seemed to have
any place here in this mysterious twilight alive with the
memories of a vanished people. Her innocence was a
grand and noble thing, like any one of the largest white
lilies that rose up from the noxious mud of the marshes;
a cup of ivory wet with the dewdrops of dawn, blossoming
fair on fetid waters. And in him the languor of sickness
and of despair borrowed unconsciously for awhile the
liveries of chastity; and he spoke no word, he made no
gesture, that would have scared from its original calm
the soul of this lonely creature, who succoured him with
so much courage and so much compassion that they
awed him with the sense of an eternal, infinite, and over-
whelming obligation. It needs a great nature to bear
the weight of a great gratitude.

To a great nature it gives wings that bear it up to
heaven; a lower nature feels it always a clog that impatiently is dragged only so long as force compels.

H ER daily labours remained the same, but it seemed
to her as if she had the strength of those immortals
he told her she resembled. She felt as though she trod
on air, as though she drank the sunbeams and they gave
her force like wine; she had no sense of fatigue; she
might have had wings at her ankles, and nectar in her
veins. She was so happy, with that perfect happiness
which only comes where the world cannot enter, and the

free nature has lifted itself to the light, knowing nothing of, and caring nothing for, the bonds of custom and of prejudice with which men have paralysed and cramped themselves, calling the lower the higher law.

THE world was so far from her ; she knew not of it ; she was a law to herself, and her whole duty seemed to her set forth in one single word, perhaps the noblest word in human language—fidelity. When life is cast in solitary places, filled with high passions, and led aloof from men, the laws which are needful to curb the multitudes, but yet are poor conventional foolish things at their best, sink back into their true signification, and lose their fictitious awe.

MOREOVER, love is for ever measureless, and the deepest and most passionate love is that which survives the death of esteem.

Friendship needs to be rooted in respect, but love can live upon itself alone. Love is born of a glance, a touch, a murmur, a caress ; esteem cannot beget it, nor lack of esteem slay it. *Questi che mai da me non fia diviso,* shall be for ever its consolation amidst hell. One life alone is beloved, is beautiful, is needful, is desired : one life alone out of all the millions of earth. Though it fall, err, betray, be mocked of others and forsaken by itself, what does this matter ? This cannot alter love. The more it is injured by itself, derided of men, abandoned of God, the more will love still see that it has need of love, and to the faithless will be faithful.

HE stood mute and motionless awhile. Then as the truth was borne in on him, tears gushed from his eyes like rain, and he laughed long, and laughed loud as madmen do.

He never doubted her.

He sprang up the stone steps, and leapt into the open air : into that light of day which he had been forbidden to see so long.

To stand erect there, to look over the plains, to breathe, and move, and gaze, and stretch his arms out to the infinite spaces of the sea and sky—this alone was so intense a joy that he felt mad with it.

Never again to hide with the snake and the fox; never again to tremble as his shadow went beside him on the sand ; never to waste the sunlit hours hidden in the bowels of the earth ; never to be afraid of every leaf that stirred, of every bird that flew, of every moon-beam that fell across his path !—he laughed and sobbed with the ecstasy of his release.

"O God, Thou hast not forgotten !" he cried in that rapture of freedom.

All the old childish faiths that had been taught him by dim old altars in stately Mantuan churches came back to his memory and heart.

On the barren rock of Gorgona he had cursed and blasphemed the Creator and creation of a world that was hell ; he had been without hope : he had derided all the faiths of his youth as illusions woven by devils to make the disappointment of man the more bitter.

But now in the sweetness of his liberty, all the old happy beliefs rushed back to him ; he saw Deity in the smile of the seas, in the light upon the plains. He was free !

THE world has lost the secret of making labour a joy ; but nature has given it to a few. Where the maidens dance the *Saltarello* under the deep Sardinian forests, and the honey and the grapes are gathered beneath the snowy sides of Etna, and the oxen walk up to their loins in flowing grass where the long aisles of pines grow down the Adrian shore, this wood-magic is known still of the old simple charm of the pastoral life.

"DOES it vex you that I am not a boy?" said the girl— "why should it vex you? I can do all they can, I can row better than many, and sail and steer; I can drive too, and I know what to do with the nets; if I had a boat of my own you would see what I could do."

"All that is very well," said Joconda with a little nod. "I do not say it is not. But you have not a boat of your own, that is just it; that is what women always suffer from; they have to steer, but the craft is some one else's, and the haul too."

WILD bird of sea and cloud, you are a stormy petrel, but there may come a storm too many—and I am old. I have done my best, but that is little. If you were a lad one would not be so uneasy. I suppose the good God knows best—if one could be sure of that—I am a hard working woman, and I have done no great sin that I know of, but up in heaven they never take any thought of me. When I was young, I asked them at my marriage altar to help me, and when my boys were born, I did the same, but they never noticed; my man was drowned, and my beautiful boys got the fever and sickened one by one and died: that was all I got. Priests say it is best; priests are not mothers.

"THEY were greater than the men that live now," she said with a solemn tenderness.

"Perhaps; Why think so?"

"Because they were not afraid of their dead; they built them beautiful houses, and gave them beautiful things. Now, men are afraid or ashamed, or they have no remembrance. Their dead are huddled away in dust or mud as though they were hateful or sinful. That is what I think so cowardly, so thankless. If they will not bear the sight of death, it were better to let great ships go slowly out, far out to sea, and give the waves their lost ones."

MOTHS.

WHEN gardeners plant and graft, they know very well what will be the issue of their work ; they do not expect the rose from a bulb of garlic, or look for the fragrant olive from a slip of briar ; but the culturers of human nature are less wise, and they sow poison, yet rave in reproaches when it breeds and brings forth its like. "The rosebud garden of girls" is a favourite theme for poets, and the maiden in her likeness to a half-opened blossom, is as near purity and sweetness as a human creature can be, yet what does the world do with its opening buds?—it thrusts them in the forcing-house amidst the ordure, and then, if they perish prematurely, never blames itself. The streets absorb the girls of the poor ; society absorbs the daughters of the rich ; and not seldom one form of prostitution, like the other, keeps its captives "bound in the dungeon of their own corruption."

THE frivolous are always frightened at any strength or depth of nature, or any glimpse of sheer despair. Not to be consoled !

What can seem more strange to the shallow? What can seem more obstinate to the weak? Not to be con-

soled is to offend all swiftly forgetting humanity, most of
whose memories are writ on water.

IT is harder to keep true to high laws and pure instincts
in modern society than it was in days of martyrdom.
There is nothing in the whole range of life so dispiriting
and so unnerving as a monotony of indifference. Active
persecution and fierce chastisement are tonics to the
nerves; but the mere weary conviction that no one cares,
that no one notices, that there is no humanity that
honours, and no deity that pities, is more destructive of
all higher effort than any conflict with tyranny or with
barbarism.

YET as he thought, so he did not realise that he would
ever cease to be in the world—who does? Life
was still young in him, was prodigal to him of good gifts;
of enmity he only knew so much as made his triumph
finer, and of love he had more than enough. His life
was full—at times laborious—but always poetical and
always victorious. He could not realise that the day of
darkness would ever come for him, when neither woman
nor man would delight him, when no roses would have
fragrance for him, and no song any spell to rouse him.
Genius gives immortality in another way than in the
vulgar one of being praised by others after death; it
gives elasticity, unwearied sympathy, and that sense of
some essence stronger than death, of some spirit higher
than the tomb, which nothing can destroy. It is in this
sense that genius walks with the immortals.

A CRUEL story runs on wheels, and every hand oils the wheels as they run.

YOU may weep your eyes blind, you may shout your throat dry, you may deafen the ears of your world for half a lifetime, and you may never get a truth believed in, never have a simple fact accredited. But the lie flies like the swallow, multiplies itself like the caterpillar, is accepted everywhere, like the visits of a king; it is a royal guest for whom the gates fly open, the red carpet is unrolled, the trumpets sound, the crowds applaud.

SHE lived, like all women of her stamp and her epoch, in an atmosphere of sugared sophisms; she never reflected, she never admitted, that she did wrong; in her world nothing mattered much, unless, indeed, it were found out, and got into the public mouth.

Shifting as the sands, shallow as the rain-pools, drifting in all danger to a lie, incapable of loyalty, insatiably curious, still as a friend and ill as a foe, kissing like Judas, denying like Peter, impure of thought, even where by physical bias or political prudence still pure in act, the woman of modern society is too often at once the feeblest and the foulest outcome of a false civilisation. Useless as a butterfly, corrupt as a canker, untrue to even lovers and friends because mentally incapable of comprehending what truth means, caring only for physical comfort and mental inclination, tired of living, but afraid of dying; believing some in priests, and some in physiologists, but none at all in virtue; sent to sleep by chloral, kept awake by strong waters and raw meat; bored at twenty, and exhausted at thirty, yet dying in the harness of pleasure rather than drop out of the race

and live naturally; pricking their sated senses with the
spur of lust, and fancying it love ; taking their passions
as they take absinthe before dinner ; false in everything,
from the swell of their breast to the curls at their throat ;
—beside them the guilty and tragic figures of old, the
Medea, the Clytemnæstra, the Phædra, look almost pure,
seem almost noble.

When one thinks that they are the only shape of
womanhood which comes hourly before so many men,
one comprehends why the old Christianity which made
womanhood sacred dies out day by day, and why the new
Positivism, which would make her divine, can find no
lasting root.

The faith of men can only live by the purity of women,
and there is both impurity and feebleness at the core of
the dolls of Worth, as the canker of the phylloxera works
at the root of the vine.

"WHAT an actress was lost in your mother !" he added
with his rough laugh ; but he confused the talent
of the comedian of society with that of the comedian of
the stage, and they are very dissimilar. The latter almost
always forgets herself in her part ; the former never.

THE scorn of genius is the most arrogant and the most
boundless of all scorn.

THE fame of the singer can never be but a breath,
a sound through a reed. When our lips are once
shut, there is on us for ever eternal silence. Who can

remember a summer breeze when it has passed by, or
tell in any after-time how a laugh or a sigh sounded?"

"WHEN the soldier dies at his post, unhonoured and
unpitied, and out of sheer duty, is that unreal
because it is noble?" he said one night to his companions.
"When the sister of charity hides her youth and her sex
under a grey shroud, and gives up her whole life to woe
and solitude, to sickness and pain, is that unreal because
it is wonderful? A man paints a spluttering candle, a
greasy cloth, a mouldy cheese, a pewter can; 'How
real!' they cry. If he paint the spirituality of dawn, the
light of the summer sea, the flame of arctic nights, of
tropic woods, they are called unreal, though they exist
no less than the candle and the cloth, the cheese and the
can. Ruy Blas is now condemned as unreal because the
lovers kill themselves; the realists forget that there are
lovers still to whom that death would be possible, would
be preferable, to low intrigue and yet more lowering
falsehood. They can only see the mouldy cheese, they
cannot see the sunrise glory. All that is heroic, all that
is sublime, impersonal, or glorious, is derided as unreal.
It is a dreary creed. It will make a dreary world. Is
not my Venetian glass with its iridescent hues of opal as
real every whit as your pot of pewter? Yet the time is
coming when every one, morally and mentally at least,
will be allowed no other than a pewter pot to drink out
of, under pain of being 'writ down an ass'—or worse.
It is a dreary prospect."

"GOOD? bad? If there were only good and bad in
this world it would not matter so much," said

Corrèze a little recklessly and at random. "Life would
not be such a disheartening affair as it is. Unfortunately
the majority of people are neither one nor the other, and
have little inclination for either crime or virtue. It would
be almost as absurd to condemn them as to admire them.
They are like tracts of shifting sand, in which nothing
good or bad can take root. To me they are more des-
pairing to contemplate than the darkest depth of evil;
out of that may come such hope as comes of redemption
and remorse, but in the vast, frivolous, featureless mass
of society there is no hope."

"NO!" he said with some warmth: "I refuse to recognise the divinity of noise; I utterly deny the
majesty of monster choruses; clamour and clangour are
the death-knell of music as drapery and so-called realism
(which means, if it mean aught, that the dress is more
real than the form underneath it!) are the destruction of
sculpture. It is very strange. Every day art in every
other way becomes more natural and music more artificial.
Every day I wake up expecting to hear myself *dénigré*
and denounced as old-fashioned, because I sing as my
nature as well as my training teaches me to do. It is
very odd; there is such a cry for naturalism in other
arts—we have Millet instead of Claude; we have Zola
instead of Georges Sand; we have Dumas *fils* instead of
Corneille; we have Mercié instead of Canova; but in
music we have precisely the reverse, and we have the
elephantine creations, the elaborate and pompous com-
binations of Baireuth, and the Tone school, instead of
the old sweet strains of melody that went straight and
clear to the ear and the heart of man. Sometimes my
enemies write in their journals that I sing as if I were a
Tuscan peasant strolling through his corn—how proud

they make me ! But they do not mean to do so. I will not twist and emphasise. I trust to melody. I was taught music in its own country, and I will not sin against the canons of the Italians. They are right. Rhetoric is one thing, and song is another. Why confuse the two? Simplicity is the soul of great music ; as it is the mark of great passion. Ornament is out of place in melody which represents single emotions at their height, be they joy, or fear, or hate, or love, or shame, or vengeance, or whatsoever they will. Music is not a science any more than poetry is. It is a sublime instinct, like genius of all kinds. I sing as naturally as other men speak ; let me remain natural "——

CHILDHOOD goes with us like an echo always, a refrain to the ballad of our life. One always wants one's cradle-air.

"THE poor you have always with you," she said to a bevy of great ladies once. "Christ said so. You profess to follow Christ. How have you the poor with you? The back of their garret, the roof of their hovel, touches the wall of your palace, and the wall is thick. You have dissipations, spectacles, diversions that you call charities ; you have a tombola for a famine, you have a dramatic performance for a flood, you have a concert for a fire, you have a fancy fair for a leprosy. Do you never think how horrible it is, that mockery of woe? Do you ever wonder at revolutions? Why do you not say honestly that you care nothing? You do care nothing. The poor might forgive the avowal of indifference ; they will never forgive the insult of affected pity."

"WHY do you go to such a place?" he asked her as she stood on the staircase.

"There are poor there, and great misery," she answered him reluctantly ; she did not care to speak of these things at any time.

"And what good will you do? You will be cheated and robbed, and even if you are not, you should know that political science has found that private charity is the hotbed of all idleness."

"When political science has advanced enough to prevent poverty, it may have the right to prevent charity too," she answered him, with a contempt that showed thought on the theme was not new to her. "Perhaps charity—I dislike the word—may do no good ; but friendship from the rich to the poor must do good ; it must lessen class hatreds."

"Are you a socialist?" said Zouroff with a little laugh, and drew back and let her pass onward.

"MY dear ! I never say rude things ; but, if you wish me to be sincere, I confess I think everybody is a little vulgar now, except old women like me, who adhered to the Faubourg while you all were dancing and changing your dresses seven times a day at St. Cloud. There is a sort of vulgarity in the air ; it is difficult to escape imbibing it ; there is too little reticence, there is too much tearing about ; men are not well-mannered, and women are too solicitous to please, and too indifferent how far they stoop in pleasing. It may be the fault of steam ; it may be the fault of smoking ; it may come from that flood of new people of whom 'L'Etrangère' is the scarcely exaggerated sample ; but, whatever it comes from, there it is—a vulgarity that taints everything, courts and cabinets as well as society. Your daughter somehow or other has escaped it, and so you find her odd, and the world thinks her stiff. She is neither; but no dignified long-descended point-lace, you know, will ever let itself be twisted and twirled into a cascade and a *fouillis* like your Brétonne lace that is just the fashion of the hour, and worth nothing. I admire your Vera very greatly; she always makes me think of those dear old stately hotels with their grand gardens in which I saw, in my girlhood, the women who, in theirs, had known France before '30. These hotels and their gardens are gone, most of them, and there are stucco and gilt paint in their places. And here are people who think that a gain. I am not one of them."

UNDER TWO FLAGS.

THE old viscount, haughtiest of haughty nobles, would never abate one jot of his magnificence ; and his sons had but imbibed the teaching of all that surrounded them ; they did but do in manhood what they had been unconsciously moulded to do in boyhood, when they were sent to Eton at ten with gold dressing-boxes to grace their dame's tables, embryo dukes for their co-fags, and tastes that already knew to a nicety the worth of the champagnes at Christopher's. The old, old story —how it repeats itself ! Boys grow up amidst profuse prodigality, and are launched into a world where they can no more arrest themselves, than the feather-weight can pull in the lightning-stride of the two-year-old, who defies all check, and takes the flat as he chooses. They are brought up like young dauphins, and tossed into the costly whirl to float as best they can—on nothing. Then on the lives and deaths that follow ; on the graves where a dishonoured alien lies forgotten by the dark Austrian lake-side, or under the monastic shadow of some crumbling Spanish crypt ; where a red cross chills the lonely traveller in the virgin solitudes of Amazonian forest aisles, or the wild scarlet creepers of Australia trail over a nameless mound above the trackless stretch of sun-warmed waters—then, at them the world

"Shoots out its lips with scorn."

Not on *them* lies the blame.

HIS influence had done more to humanise the men he was associated with than any preachers or teachers could have done.

Almost insensibly they grew ashamed to be beaten by him, and strove to do like him as far as they could. They never knew him drunk, they never heard him swear, they never found him unjust, even to a poverty-stricken *indigène*, or brutal, even to a *fille de joie*. Insensibly his presence humanised them. Of a surety, the last part Bertie dreamed of playing was that of a teacher to any mortal thing. Yet—here in Africa—it might reasonably be questioned if a second Augustine or François Xavier would ever have done half the good among the devil-may-care Roumis that was wrought by the dauntless, listless, reckless soldier, who followed instinctively the one religion which has no cant in its brave, simple creed, and binds man to man in links that are as true as steel—the religion of a gallant gentleman's loyalty and honour.

THE child had been flung upward, a little straw floating in the gutter of Paris iniquities ; a little foambell, bubbling on the sewer waters of barrack vice ; the stick had been her teacher, the baggage-waggon her cradle, the camp-dogs her playfellows, the *caserne* oaths her lullaby, the *guidons* her sole guiding-stars, the *razzia* her sole fete-day : it was little marvel that the bright, bold, insolent little friend of the flag had nothing left of her sex save a kitten's mischief and coquette's archness. It said much rather for the straight, fair, sunlit instincts of the untaught nature, that Cigarette had gleaned, even out of such a life, two virtues that she would have held by to the death, if tried—a truthfulness that would have scorned a lie as only fit for cowards, and a loyalty that cleaved to France as a religion.

TIRED as over-worked cattle, and crouched or stretched like worn-out homeless dogs, they had never wakened as he had noiselessly harnessed himself, and he looked at them with that interest in other lives which had come to him through adversity; for if misfortune had given him strength, it had also given him sympathy.

AND he did her that injustice which the best amongst us are apt to do to those whom we do not feel interest enough in to study with that closeness which can alone give comprehension of the intricate and complex rebus, so faintly sketched, so marvellously involved, of human nature.

THE gleam of the dawn spread in one golden glow of the morning, and the day rose radiant over the world; they stayed not for its beauty or its peace; the carnage went on hour upon hour; men began to grow drunk with slaughter as with raki. It was sublimely grand; it was hideously hateful—this wild-beast struggle, that heaving tumult of striving lives that ever and anon stirred the vast war-cloud of smoke and broke from it as the lightning from the night. The sun laughed in its warmth over a thousand hills and streams, over the blue seas lying northward, and over the yellow sands of the south; but the touch of its heat only made the flame in their blood burn fiercer; and the fulness of its light only served to show them clearer where to strike, and how to slay.

S HE might be a careless young coquette, a lawless little brigand, a child of sunny caprices, an elf of dauntless mischief; but she was more than these. The divine fire of genius had touched her, and Cigarette would have perished for her country not less surely than Jeanne d'Arc. The holiness of an impersonal love, the glow of an imperishable patriotism, the melancholy of a passionate pity for the concrete and unnumbered sufferings of the people, were in her instinctive and inborn, as fragrance in the heart of flowers. And all these together moved her now, and made her young face beautiful as she looked down upon the crowding soldiery.

A FTER all, Diderot was in the right when he told Rousseau which side of the question to take. On my life, civilisation develops comfort, but I do believe it kills nobility. Individuality dies in it, and egotism grows strong and specious. Why is it that in a polished life a man, whilst becoming incapable of sinking to crime, almost always becomes also incapable of rising to greatness? Why is it that misery, tumult, privation, bloodshed, famine, beget, in such a life as this, such countless things of heroism, of endurance, of self-sacrifice—things mostly of demigods—in men who quarrel with the wolves for a wild-boar's carcase, for a sheep's offal?

A S for death—when it comes it comes. Every soldier carries it in his wallet, and it may jump out on him any minute. I would rather die young than old. Pardi! age is nothing else but death that is *conscious.*

IT is misery that is glory—the misery that toils with
bleeding feet under burning suns without complaint;
that lies half dead through the long night with but one
care, to keep the torn flag free from the conqueror's touch;
that bears the rain of blows in punishment rather than
break silence and buy release by betrayal of a comrade's
trust; that is beaten like the mule, and galled like the
horse, and starved like the camel, and housed like the
dog, and yet does the thing which is right, and the thing
which is brave, despite all; that suffers, and endures, and
pours out his blood like water to the thirsty sands whose
thirst is never stilled, and goes up in the morning sun to
the combat as though death were the Paradise of the
Arbico's dream, knowing the while that no Paradise waits
save the crash of the hoof through the throbbing brain, or
the roll of the gun-carriage over the writhing limb. *That*
is glory. The misery that is heroism because France
needs it, because a soldier's honour wills it. *That* is
glory. It is to-day in the hospital as it never is in the
Cour des Princes where the glittering host of the marshals
gather !

SPARE me the old world-worn, thread-bare formulas.
Because the flax and the colza blossom for use,
and the garden flowers grow trained and pruned,
must there be no bud that opens for mere love of the
sun, and swings free in the wind in its fearless fair
fashion? Believe me, it is the lives which follow no
previous rule that do the most good, and give the most
harvest.

" THE first thing I saw of Cigarette was this : She was
seven years old ; she had been beaten black and
blue ; she had had two of her tiny teeth knocked out. The

men were furious, she was a pet with them; and she
would not say who had done it, though she knew twenty
swords would have beaten him flat as a fritter if she had
given his name. I got her to sit to me some days after.
I pleased her with her own picture. I asked her to tell
me why she would not say who had ill-treated her. She
put her head on one side like a robin, and told me, in a
whisper: ' It was one of my comrades—because I would
not steal for him. I would not have the army know—it
would demoralise them. If a French soldier ever does a
cowardly thing, another French soldier must not betray
it.' That was Cigarette—at seven years. The *esprit du
corps* was stronger than her own wrongs."

A BETTER day's sport even the Quorn had never
had in all its brilliant annals, and faster things the
Melton men themselves had never wanted : both those
who love the "quickest thing you ever knew—thirty
minutes without a check—*such* a pace!" and care little
whether the *finale* be "killed" or "broke away," and those
of older fashion, who prefer "long day, you know, steady
as old time, the beauties stuck like wax through fourteen
parishes as I live ; six hours if it were a minute ; horses
dead beat ; positively walked, you know, no end of a
day!" but must have the fatal "who-whoop" as conclu-
sion—both of these, the "new style and the old," could
not but be content with the doings of the "Demoiselles"
from start to finish.

Was it likely that Cecil remembered the caustic lash of
his father's ironies while he was lifting Mother of Pearl
over the posts and rails, and sweeping on, with the halloo
ringing down the wintry wind as the grasslands flew beneath him ? Was it likely that he recollected the difficulties that hung above him while he was dashing down

the Gorse happy as a king, with the wild hail driving in
his face, and a break of stormy sunshine just welcoming
the gallant few who were landed at the death, as twilight
fell? Was it likely that he could unlearn all the lessons
of his life, and realise in how near a neighbourhood he
stood to ruin when he was drinking Regency sherry out
of his gold flask as he crossed the saddle of his second
horse, or, smoking, rode slowly homeward through the
leafless muddy lanes in the gloaming?

Scarcely ;—it is very easy to remember our difficulties
when we are eating and drinking them, so to speak, in
bad soups and worse wines in Continental impecuniosity,
sleeping on them as rough Australian shake-downs, or
wearing them perpetually in Californian rags and tatters,
it were impossible very well to escape from them then ;
but it is very hard to remember them when every touch
and shape of life is pleasant to us—when everything about
us is symbolical and redolent of wealth and ease—when
the art of enjoyment is the only one we are called on to
study, and the science of pleasure all we are asked to
explore.

It is well-nigh impossible to believe yourself a beggar
when you never want sovereigns for whist ; and it would
be beyond the powers of human nature to conceive your
ruin irrevocable, while you still eat turbot and terrapin
with a powdered giant behind your chair daily. Up in
his garret a poor wretch knows very well what he is, and
realises in stern fact the extremities of the last sou, the
last shirt, and the last hope ; but in these devil-may-
care pleasures—in this pleasant, reckless, velvet-soft rush
down-hill—in this club-palace, with every luxury that the
heart of man can devise and desire, yours to command
at your will—it is hard work, *then,* to grasp the truth that
the crossing-sweeper yonder, in the dust of Pall Mall, is
really not more utterly in the toils of poverty than you
are !

2 A

THE bell was clanging and clashing passionately, as
Cecil at last went down to the weights, all his
friends of the Household about him, and all standing
"crushers" on their champion, for their stringent *esprit
du corps* was involved, and the Guards are never backward in putting their gold down, as all the world knows.
In the inclosure, the cynosure of devouring eyes, stood
the King, with the *sang froid* of a superb gentleman,
amid the clamour raging round him, one delicate ear
laid back now and then, but otherwise indifferent to the
din, with his coat glistening like satin, the beautiful
tracery of vein and muscle, like the veins of vine-leaves,
standing out on the glossy, clear-carved neck that had
the arch of Circassia, and his dark antelope eyes gazing
with a gentle, pensive earnestness on the shouting
crowd.

His rivals, too, were beyond par in fitness and in
condition, and there were magnificent animals among
them. Bay Regent was a huge, raking chestnut, upwards
of sixteen hands, and enormously powerful, with very
fine shoulders, and an all-over-like-going head; he belonged to a Colonel in the Rifles, but was to be ridden
by Jimmy Delmar of the 10th Lancers, whose colours
were violet with orange hoops. Montacute's horse,
Pas de Charge, which carried all the money of the
Heavy Cavalry, Montacute himself being in the
Dragoon Guards, was of much the same order, a black
hunter with racing blood in him, loins and withers that
assured any amount of force, and no fault but that of a
rather coarse head, traceable to a slur on his 'scutcheon
on the distaff side from a plebeian great-grandmother,
who had been a cart mare, the only stain in his otherwise faultless pedigree. However, she had given him
her massive shoulders, so that he was in some sense a
gainer by her after all. Wild Geranium was a beautiful
creature enough, a bright bay Irish mare, with that rich

red gloss that is like the glow of a horse-chestnut, very
perfect in shape, though a trifle light perhaps, and with not
quite strength enough in neck or barrel; she would jump
the fences of her own paddock half a dozen times a day
for sheer amusement, and was game to anything. She
was entered by Cartouche of the Enniskillens, to be ridden
by "Baby Grafton," of the same corps, a feather-weight,
and quite a boy, but with plenty of science in him. These
were the three favourites; Day Star ran them close, the
property of Durham Vavassour, of the Scots Greys, and
to be ridden by his owner; a handsome, flea-bitten, grey
sixteen-hander, with ragged hips, and action that looked a
trifle string-halty, but noble shoulders, and great force in
the loins and withers; the rest of the field, though un-
usually excellent, did not find so many "sweet voices"
for them, and were not so much to be feared: each starter
was of course much backed by his party, but the betting
was tolerably even on these four:—all famous steeple-
chasers;—the King at one time, and Bay Regent at
another, slightly leading in the Ring.

Thirty-two starters were hoisted up on the telegraph
board, and as the field got at last under weigh, uncommonly handsome they looked, while the silk jackets of
all the colours of the rainbow glittered in the bright noon
sun. As Forest King closed in, perfectly tranquil still,
but beginning to glow and quiver all over with excitement, knowing as well as his rider the work that was
before him, and longing for it in every muscle and every
limb, while his eyes flashed fire as he pulled at the curb
and tossed his head aloft, there went up a general shout
of "Favourite!" His beauty told on the populace, and
even somewhat on the professionals, though the legs kept
a strong business prejudice against the working powers of
"the Guards' crack." The ladies began to lay dozens in
gloves on him; not altogether for his points, which perhaps they hardly appreciated, but for his owner and rider,

who, in the scarlet and gold, with the white sash across
his chest, and a look of serene indifference on his face,
they considered the handsomest man of the field. The
Household is usually safe to win the suffrages of the sex.

In the throng on the course Rake instantly bonneted
an audacious dealer who had ventured to consider that
Forest King was "light and curby in the 'ock." "You're
a wise 'un, you are!" retorted the wrathful and ever-
eloquent Rake, "there's more strength in his clean flat
legs, bless him! than in all the round, thick, mill-posts
of *your* half-breds, that have no more tendon than a bit
of wood, and are just as flabby as a sponge!" Which hit
the dealer home just as his hat was hit over his eyes;
Rake's arguments being unquestionable in their force.

The thoroughbreds pulled and fretted, and swerved in
their impatience; one or two over-contumacious bolted
incontinently, others put their heads between their knees
in the endeavour to draw their riders over their withers;
Wild Geranium reared straight upright, fidgeted all
over with longing to be off, passaged with the prettiest,
wickedest grace in the world, and would have given the
world to neigh if she had dared, but she knew it would
be very bad style, so, like an aristocrat as she was,
restrained herself; Bay Regent almost sawed Jimmy
Delmar's arms off looking like a Titan Bucephalus; while
Forest King, with his nostrils dilated till the scarlet
tinge on them glowed in the sun, his muscles quivering
with excitement as intense as the little Irish mare's, and
all his Eastern and English blood on fire for the fray,
stood steady as a statue for all that, under the curb of a
hand light as a woman's, but firm as iron to control, and
used to guide him by the slightest touch.

All eyes were on that throng of the first mounts in
the Service; brilliant glances by the hundred gleamed
down behind hot-house bouquets of their chosen colour,
eager ones by the thousand stared thirstily from the

crowded course, the roar of the Ring subsided for a
second, a breathless attention and suspense succeeded
it ; the Guardsmen sat on their drags, or lounged near
the ladies with their race-glasses ready, and their habitual
expression of gentle and resigned weariness in nowise
altered, because the Household, all in all, had from sixty
to seventy thousand on the event, and the Seraph murmured mournfully to his cheroot, "That chestnut's no
end *fit*," strong as his faith was in the champion of the
Brigades.

A moment's good start was caught—the flag dropped
—off they went, sweeping out for the first second like a
line of cavalry about to charge.

Another moment, and they were scattered over the first
field, Forest King, Wild Geranium, and Bay Regent leading for two lengths, when Montacute, with his habitual
"fast burst," sent Pas de Charge past them like lightning.
The Irish mare gave a rush and got alongside of him ;
the King would have done the same, but Cecil checked
him, and kept him in that cool swinging canter which
covered the grassland so lightly ; Bay Regent's vast
thundering stride was Olympian, but Jimmy Delmar saw
his worst foe in the "Guards' crack," and waited on him
warily, riding superbly himself.

The first fence disposed of half the field, they crossed
the second in the same order, Wild Geranium racing neck
to neck with Pas de Charge ; the King was all athirst to
join the duello, but his owner kept him gently back, saving
his pace and lifting him over the jumps as easily as a lap-
wing. The second fence proved a cropper to several,
some awkward falls took place over it, and tailing commenced ; after the third field, which was heavy plough, all
knocked off but eight, and the real struggle began in sharp
earnest : a good dozen who had shown a splendid stride
over the grass being done up by the terrible work on the
clods.

The five favourites had it all to themselves; Day Star pounding onward at tremendous speed, Pas de Charge giving slight symptoms of distress owing to the madness of his first burst, the Irish mare literally flying ahead of him, Forest King and the chestnut waiting on one another.

In the Grand Stand the Seraph's eyes strained after the Scarlet and White, and he muttered in his moustaches, "Ye gods, what's up? The world's coming to an end!— Beauty's turned cautious!"

Cautious, indeed,—with that giant of Pytchley fame running neck to neck by him; cautious,—with two-thirds of the course unrun, and all the yawners yet to come; cautious,—with the blood of Forest King lashing to boiling heat, and the wondrous greyhound stride stretching out faster and faster beneath him, ready at a touch to break away and take the lead: but he would be reckless enough by-and-by; reckless, as his nature was, under the indolent serenity of habit.

Two more fences came, laced high and stiff with the Shire thorn, and with scarce twenty feet between them, the heavy ploughed land leading to them, clotted, and black, and hard, with the fresh earthy scent steaming up as the hoofs struck the clods with a dull thunder. Pas de Charge rose to the first: distressed too early, his hind feet caught in the thorn, and he came down rolling clear of his rider; Montacute picked him up with true science, but the day was lost to the Heavy Cavalry men. Forest King went in and out over both like a bird, and led for the first time; the chestnut was not to be beat at fencing, and ran even with him; Wild Geranium flew still as fleet as a deer, true to her sex, she would not bear rivalry; but little Grafton, though he rode like a professional, was but a young one, and went too wildly—her spirit wanted cooler curb.

And now only, Cecil loosened the King to his full will and his full speed. Now only, the beautiful Arab head

was stretched like a racer's in the run-in for the Derby,
and the grand stride swept out till the hoofs seemed
never to touch the dark earth they skimmed over;
neither whip nor spur was needed, Bertie had only to
leave the gallant temper and the generous fire that were
roused in their might to go their way, and hold their
own. His hands were low; his head was a little back;
his face very calm; the eyes only had a daring, eager,
resolute will lighting in them; Brixworth lay before
him. He knew well what Forest King could do; but he
did not know how great the chestnut Regent's powers
might be.

The water gleamed before them, brown and swollen,
and deepened with the meltings of winter snows a month
before; the brook that has brought so many to grief
over its famous banks, since cavaliers leapt it with their
falcon on their wrist, or the mellow note of the horn
rang over the woods in the hunting days of Stuart reigns.
They knew it well, that long dark line, skimmering there
in the sunlight, the test that all must pass who go in for
the Soldiers' Blue Ribbon. Forest King scented water,
and went on with his ears pointed, and his greyhound
stride lengthening, quickening, gathering up all its force
and its impetus for the leap that was before—then like
the rise and the swoop of the heron he spanned the water,
and, landing clear, launched forward with the lunge of a
spear darted through air. Brixworth was passed—the
Scarlet and White, a mere gleam of bright colour, a mere
speck in the landscape, to the breathless crowds in the
stand, sped on over the brown and level grassland; two
and a quarter miles done in four minutes and twenty
seconds. Bay Regent was scarcely behind him; the
chestnut abhorred the water, but a finer trained hunter
was never sent over the Shires, and Jimmy Delmar rode
like Grimshaw himself. The giant took the leap in
magnificent style, and thundered on neck and neck with

the "Guards' crack." The Irish mare followed, and, with miraculous gameness, landed safely; but her hind-legs slipped on the bank, a moment was lost, and "Baby" Grafton scarce knew enough to recover it, though he scoured on nothing daunted.

Pas de Charge, much behind, refused the yawner; his strength was not more than his courage, but both had been strained too severely at first. Montacute struck the spurs into him with a savage blow over the head; the madness was its own punishment; the poor brute rose blindly to the jump, and missed the bank with a reel and a crash; Sir Eyre was hurled out into the brook, and the hope of the Heavies lay there with his breast and fore-legs resting on the ground, his hind-quarters in the water, and his back broken. Pas de Charge would never again see the starting-flag waved, or hear the music of the hounds, or feel the gallant life throb and glow through him at the rallying notes of the horn. His race was run.

Not knowing, or looking, or heeding what happened be-hind, the trio tore on over the meadow and the ploughed; the two favourites neck by neck, the game little mare hopelessly behind through that one fatal moment over Brixworth. The turning-flags were passed; from the crowds on the course a great hoarse roar came louder and louder, and the shouts rang, changing every second, "Forest King wins," "Bay Regent wins," "Scarlet and White's ahead," "Violet's up with him," "Violet's past him," "Scarlet recovers," "Scarlet beats," "A cracker on the King," "Ten to one on the Regent," "Guards are over the fence first," "Guards are winning," "Guards are losing," "Guards are beat!!"

Were they?

As the shout rose, Cecil's left stirrup leather snapped and gave way; at the pace they were going most men, ay, and good riders too, would have been hurled out of

their saddle by the shock ; he scarcely swerved ; a moment to ease the King and to recover his equilibrium,
then he took the pace up again as though nothing had
chanced. And his comrades of the Household, when
they saw this through their race-glasses, broke through
their serenity and burst into a cheer that echoed over
the grasslands and the coppices like a clarion, the grand
rich voice of the Seraph leading foremost and loudest—
a cheer that rolled mellow and triumphant down the
cold bright air like the blast of trumpets, and thrilled
on Bertie's ear where he came down the course a mile
away. It made his heart beat quicker with a victorious
headlong delight, as his knees pressed closer into Forest
King's flanks, and, half stirrupless like the Arabs, he
thundered forward to the greatest riding feat of his life.
His face was very calm still, but his blood was in tumult,
the delirium of pace had got on him, a minute of life
like this was worth a year, and he knew that he would
win or die for it, as the land seemed to fly like a black
sheet under him, and, in that killing speed, fence and
hedge and double and water all went by him like a
dream, whirling underneath him as the grey stretches,
stomach to earth, over the level, and rose to leap after
leap.

For that instant's pause, when the stirrup broke,
threatened to lose him the race.

He was more than a length behind the Regent, whose
hoofs as they dashed the ground up sounded like thunder,
and for whose herculean strength the plough has no terrors;
it was more than the lead to keep now, there was ground
to cover, and the King was losing like Wild Geranium.
Cecil felt drunk with that strong, keen, west wind that
blew so strongly in his teeth, a passionate excitation was
in him, every breath of winter air that rushed in its
bracing currents round him seemed to lash him like a
stripe—the Household to look on and see him beaten !

Certain wild blood that lay latent in Cecil under the tranquil gentleness of temper and of custom, woke, and had the mastery; he set his teeth hard, and his hands clenched like steel on the bridle. "Oh! my beauty, my beauty," he cried, all unconsciously half aloud as they clear the thirty-sixth fence; "kill me if you like, but don't *fail* me!"

As though Forest King heard the prayer and answered it with all his hero's heart, the splendid form launched faster out, the stretching stride stretched farther yet with lightning spontaneity, every fibre strained, every nerve struggled; with a magnificent bound like an antelope the grey recovered the ground he had lost, and passed Bay Regent by a quarter-length. It was a neck-to-neck race once more, across the three meadows with the last and lower fences that were between them and the final leap of all; that ditch of artificial water with the towering double hedge of oak rails and of blackthorn that was reared black and grim and well-nigh hopeless just in front of the Grand Stand. A roar like the roar of the sea broke up from the thronged course as the crowd hung breathless on the even race; ten thousand shouts rang as thrice ten thousand eyes watched the closing contest, as superb a sight as the Shires ever saw, while the two ran together, the gigantic chestnut, with every massive sinew swelled and strained to tension, side by side with the marvellous grace, the shining flanks, and the Arabian-like head of the Guards' horse.

Louder and wilder the shrieked tumult rose: "The Chestnut beats!" "The Grey beats!" "Scarlet's ahead!" "Bay Regent's caught him!" "Violet's winning, Violet's winning!" "The King's neck by neck!" "The King's beating!" "The Guards will get it!" "The Guards' crack has it!" "Not yet, not yet!" "Violet will thrash him at the jump!" "Now for it!" "The Guards, the

Guards, the Guards!" "Scarlet will win!" "The King has the finish!" "No, no, no, NO!"

Sent along at a pace that Epsom flat never saw eclipsed, sweeping by the Grand Stand like the flash of electric flame, they ran side to side one moment more, their foam flung on each other's withers, their breath hot in each other's nostrils, while the dark earth flew beneath their stride. The blackthorn was in front behind five bars of solid oak, the water yawning on its farther side, black and deep, and fenced, twelve feet wide if it were an inch, with the same thorn wall beyond it! a leap no horse should have been given, no steward should have set. Cecil pressed his knees closer and closer, and worked the gallant hero for the test; the surging roar of the throng, though so close, was dull on his ear; he heard nothing, knew nothing, saw nothing but that lean chestnut head beside him, the dull thud on the turf of the flying gallop, and the black wall that reared in his face. Forest King had done so much, could he have stay and strength for this?

Cecil's hands clenched unconsciously on the bridle, and his face was very pale—pale with excitation—as his foot where the stirrup was broken crushed closer and harder against the grey's flanks.

"Oh, my darling, my beauty—*now!*"

One touch of the spur—the first—and Forest King rose at the leap, all the life and power there were in him gathered for one superhuman and crowning effort; a flash of time, not half a second in duration, and he was lifted in the air higher, and higher, and higher in the cold, fresh, wild winter wind; stakes and rails, and thorn and water lay beneath him black and gaunt and shapeless, yawning like a grave; one bound, even in mid air, one last convulsive impulse of the gathered limbs, and Forest King was over!

And as he galloped up the straight run-in, he was alone.

Bay Regent had refused the leap.

As the grey swept to the judge's chair, the air was rent with deafening cheers that seemed to reel like drunken shouts from the multitude. "The Guards win, the Guards win;" and when his rider pulled up at the distance with the full sun shining on the scarlet and white, with the gold glisten of the embroidered "Cœur Vaillant se fait Royaume," Forest King stood in all his glory, winner of the Soldier's Blue Ribbon, by a feat without its parallel in all the annals of the Gold Vase.

OVER there in England, you know, sir, pipe-clay is the deuce-and-all; you've always got to have the stock on, and look as stiff as a stake, or it's all up with you; you're that tormented about little things that you get riled and kick the traces before the great 'uns come to try you. There's a lot of lads would be game as game could be in battle, ay, and good lads to boot, doing their duty right as a trivet when it came to anything like war, that are clean druv' out of the service in time o' peace, along with all them petty persecutions that worry a man's skin like mosquito-bites. Now here they know that, and Lord! what soldiers they do make through knowing of it! It's tight enough and stern enough in big things; martial law sharp enough, and obedience to the letter all through the campaigning; but that don't grate on a fellow; if he's worth his salt he's sure to understand that he must move like clockwork in a fight, and that he's to go to hell at double-quick march, and mute as a mouse, if his officers see fit to send him. *That's* all right, but they don't fidget

you here about the little fal-lals; you may stick your
pipe in your mouth, you may have your lark, you may
do as you like, you may spend your *décompte* how you
choose, you may settle your little duel as you will, you
may shout and sing and jump and riot on the march,
so long as you *march on;* you may lounge about half
dressed in any style as suits you best, so long as you're
up to time when the trumpets sound for you ; and that's
what a man likes. He's ready to be a machine when
the machine's wanted in working trim, but when it's run
off the line and the steam all let off, he do like to oil
his own wheels, and lie a bit in the sun at his fancy.
There aren't better stuff to make soldiers out of nowhere
than Englishmen, God bless 'em, but they're badgered,
they're horribly badgered, and that's why the service don't
take over there, let alone the way the country grudge
'em every bit of pay. In England you go in the ranks
—well, they all just tell you you're a blackguard, and
there's the lash, and you'd better behave yourself or
you'll get it hot and hot; they take for granted you're
a bad lot or you wouldn't be there, and in course you're
riled and go to the bad according, seeing that it's what's
expected of you. Here, contrariwise, you come in the
ranks and get a welcome, and feel that it just rests with
yourself whether you won't be a fine fellow or not; and
just along of feelin' that you're pricked to show the best
metal you're made on, and not to let nobody else beat
you out of the race like. Ah! it makes a wonderful
difference to a fellow—a wonderful difference—whether
the service he's come into look at him as a scamp that
never will be nothin' *but* a scamp, or as a rascal that's
maybe got in him, all rascal though he is, the pluck to
turn into a hero. It makes a wonderful difference, this
'ere, whether you're looked at as stuff that's only fit to be
shovelled into the sand after a battle ; or as stuff that'll
belike churn into a great man. And it's just that dif-

ference, sir, that France has found out, and England hasn't—God bless her all the same."

With which the soldier whom England had turned adrift, and France had won in her stead, concluded his long oration by dropping on his knees to refill his Corporal's chibouque.

"A army's just a machine, sir, in course," he concluded, as he rammed in the Turkish tobacco. "But then it's a live machine for all that; and each little bit of it feels for itself like the joints in an eel's body. Now, if only one of them little bits smarts, the whole crittur goes wrong—there's the mischief."

IT makes all the difference in life, whether hope is left, or—left out !

SHE had been ere now a child and a hero; beneath this blow which struck at him she changed—she became a woman and a martyr.

And she rode at full speed through the night, as she had done through the daylight, her eyes glancing all around in the keen instinct of a trooper, her hand always on the butt of her belt pistol. For she knew well what the danger was of these lonely, unguarded, untravelled leagues that yawned in so vast a distance between her and her goal. The Arabs, beaten, but only rendered furious by defeat, swept down on to those plains with the old guerilla skill, the old marvellous rapidity. She knew that with every second shot or steel might send her reeling from her saddle, that with every moment she might be surrounded by some desperate band who would spare neither her sex nor her youth. But that intoxica-

tion of peril, the wine-draught she had drunk from her
infancy, was all which sustained her in that race with
death. It filled her veins with their old heat, her heart
with its old daring, her nerves with their old matchless
courage: but for it she would have dropped, heart-sick
with terror and despair, ere her errand could be done;
under it she had the coolness, the keenness, the sagacity,
the sustained force, and the supernatural strength of
some young hunted animal. They might slay her so
that she left perforce her mission unaccomplished; but
no dread of such a fate had even an instant's power to
appal her or arrest her. While there should be breath
in her, she would go on to the end.

There were eight hours' hard riding before her, at the
swiftest pace her horse could make; and she was already
worn by the leagues already traversed. Although this
was nothing new that she did now, yet as time flew on
and she flew with it, ceaselessly, through the dim solitary
barren moonlit land, her brain now and then grew giddy,
her heart now and then stood still with a sudden numbing faintness. She shook the weakness off her with the
resolute scorn for it of her nature, and succeeded in its
banishment. They had put in her hand as she had
passed through the fortress gates a lance with a lantern
muffled in Arab fashion, so that the light was unseen
from before, while it streamed over her herself, to enable
her to guide her way if the moon should be veiled by
clouds. With that single starry gleam aslant on a level
with her eyes, she rode through the ghastly twilight of
the half-lit plains, now flooded with lustre as the moon
emerged, now engulfed in darkness as the stormy western
winds drove the cirri over it. But neither darkness nor
light differed to her; she noted neither; she was like
one drunk with strong wine, and she had but one dread
—that the power of her horse would give way under the
unnatural strain made on it, and that she would reach

too late, when the life she went to save would have fallen
for ever, silent unto death, as she had seen the life of
Marquise *fall*.

Hour on hour, league on league, passed away; she
felt the animal quiver under the spur, and she heard the
catch in his panting breath as he strained to give his
fleetest and best, that told her how, ere long, the racing
speed, the extended gallop at which she kept him, would
tell, and beat him down despite his desert strain. She
had no pity; she would have killed twenty horses under
her to reach her goal. She was giving her own life, she
was willing to lose it, if by its loss she did this thing, to
save even the man condemned to die with the rising of
the sun. She did not spare herself; and she would have
spared no living thing, to fulfil the mission that she
undertook. She loved with the passionate blindness of
her sex, with the absolute abandonment of the southern
blood. If to spare him she must have bidden thousands
fall, she would have given the word for their destruction
without a moment's pause.

Once from some screen of gaunt and barren rock a
shot was fired at her, and flew within a hair's-breadth of
her brain; she never even looked around to see whence
it had come; she knew it was from some Arab prowler
of the plains. Her single spark of light through the
half-veiled lantern passed as swiftly as a shooting-star
across the plateau. And as she felt the hours steal on
—so fast, so hideously fast—with that horrible relentless-
ness, "ohne Hast, ohne Rast," which tarries for no despair, as it hastens for no desire, her lips grew dry as
dust, her tongue clove to the roof of her mouth, the
blood beat like a thousand hammers on her brain.

What she dreaded came.

Midway in her course, when, by the stars, she knew
midnight was passed, the animal strained with hard-
drawn panting gasps to answer the demand made on

him by the spur and by the lance-shaft with which he
was goaded onward. In the lantern-light she saw his
head stretched out in the racing agony, his distended
eyeballs, his neck covered with foam and blood, his
heaving flanks that seem bursting with every throb that
his heart gave ; she knew that half a league more forced
from him, he would drop like a dead thing never to rise
again. She let the bridle drop upon the poor beast's
neck, and threw her arms above her head with a shrill
wailing cry, whose despair echoed over the noiseless
plains like the cry of a shot-stricken animal. She saw
it all ; the breathing of the rosy, golden day ; the stillness of the hushed camp ; the tread of the few picked
men ; the open coffin by the open grave ; the levelled
carbines gleaming in the first rays of the sun. . . . She
had seen it so many times—seen it to the awful end,
when the living man fell down in the morning light a
shattered, senseless, soulless, crushed-out mass.

That single moment was all the soldier's nature in
her gave to the abandonment of despair, to the paralysis
that seized her. With that one cry from the depths of
her breaking heart, the weakness spent itself : she knew
that action alone could aid him. She looked across,
southward and northward, east and west, to see if there
were aught near from which she could get aid. If there
were none, the horse must drop down to die, and with
his life the other life would perish as surely as the sun
would rise.

Her gaze, straining through the darkness, broken here
and there by fitful gleams of moonlight, caught sight in
the distance of some yet darker thing moving rapidly—
a large cloud skimming the earth. She let the horse,
which had paused the instant the bridle had touched his
neck, stand still awhile, and kept her eyes fixed on the
advancing cloud till, with the marvellous surety of her
desert-trained vision, she disentangled it from the float-

ing mists and wavering shadows, and recognised it, as it was, a band of Arabs.

If she turned eastward out of her route, the failing strength of her horse would be fully enough to take her into safety from their pursuit, or even from their perception, for they were coming straightly and swiftly across the plain. If she were seen by them she was certain of her fate; they could only be the desperate remnant of the decimated tribes, the foraging raiders of starving and desperate men, hunted from refuge to refuge, and carrying fire and sword in their vengeance wherever an unprotected caravan or a defenceless settlement gave them the power of plunder and of slaughter, that spared neither age nor sex. She was known throughout the length and the breadth of the land to the Arabs: she was neither child nor woman to them; she was but the soldier who had brought up the French reserve at Zaraila; she was but the foe who had seen them defeated, and ridden down with her comrades in their pursuit in twice a score of vanquished, bitter, intolerably shameful days. Some among them had sworn by their God to put her to a fearful death if ever they made her captive, for they held her in superstitious awe, and thought the spell of the Frankish successes would be broken if she were slain. She knew that; yet, knowing it, she looked at their advancing band one moment, then turned her horse's head and rode straight toward them.

"They will kill me, but that may save him," she thought. "Any other way he is lost."

So she rode directly toward them; rode so that she crossed their front, and placed herself in their path, standing quite still, with the cloth torn from the lantern, so that its light fell full about her, as she held it above her head. In an instant they knew her. They were the remnant who had escaped from the carnage of Zaraila; they knew her with all the rapid unerring surety of hate. They gave the shrill wild war-shout of their tribe, and the whole mass of gaunt, dark, mounted figures with their weapons whirling round their heads enclosed her: a cloud of kites settled down with their black wings and cruel beaks upon one young silvery-plumed gerfalcon.

She sat unmoved, and looked up at the naked blades that flashed above her: there was no fear upon her face, only a calm resolute proud beauty, very pale, very still in the light that gleamed on it from the lantern rays.

" I surrender," she said briefly. She had never thought to say these words of submission to her scorned foes ; she would not have been brought to utter them to spare her own existence. Their answer was a yell of furious delight, and their bare blades smote each other with a clash of brutal joy: they had her, the Frankish child who had brought shame and destruction on them at Zaraila, and they longed to draw their steel across the fair young throat, to plunge their lances into the bright bare bosom, to twine her hair round their spear handles, to rend her delicate limbs apart, as a tiger rends the antelope, to torture, to outrage, to wreak their vengeance on her. Their chief, only, motioned their violence back from her, and bade them leave her untouched. At him she looked, still with the same fixed, serene, scornful resolve: she had encountered these men so often in battle, she knew so well how rich a prize she was to him. But she had one thought alone with her ; and for it she subdued contempt, and hate, and pride, and every passion in her.

" I surrender," she said, with the same tranquillity. " I have heard that you have sworn by your God and your Prophet to tear me limb from limb because that I —a child, and a woman-child—brought you to shame and to grief on the day of Zaraila. Well, I am here ;

do it. You can slake your will on me. But that you
are brave men, and that I have ever met you in fair fight,
let me speak one word with you first."

Through the menaces and the rage around her, fierce
as the yelling of starving wolves around a frozen corpse,
her clear brave tones reached the ear of the chief in the
lingua-sabir that she used. He was a young man, and
his ear was caught by that tuneful voice, his eyes by that
youthful face. He signed upward the swords of his followers, and motioned them back as their arms were
stretched to seize her, and their shouts clamoured for her
slaughter.

"Speak on," he said briefly to her.

"You have sworn to take my body, sawn in two, to
Ben-Ihreddin?" she pursued, naming the Arab leader
whom her Spahis had driven off the field of Zaraila.
"Well, here it is; you can take it to him; and you will
receive the piastres, and the horse, and the arms that he
has promised to whosoever shall slay me. I have sur-
rendered; I am yours. But you are bold men, and the
bold are never mean; therefore I will ask one thing of
you. There is a man yonder, in my camp, condemned
to death with the dawn. He is innocent. I have ridden
from Algiers to-day with the order of his release. If it
is not there by sunrise, he will be shot; and he is guiltless as a child unborn. My horse is worn out; he could
not go another half-league. I knew that, since he had
failed, my comrade must die, unless I found a fresh
beast or a messenger to go in my stead. I saw your
band come across the plain. I knew that you would
kill me, because of your oath and of your Emir's bribe;
but I thought that you would have greatness enough in
you to save this man who is condemned, without crime,
and who must perish unless you, his foes, have pity on
him. Therefore I came. Take the paper that frees
him; send your fleetest and surest with it, under a flag

of truce, into our camp by the dawn ; let him tell them
there that I, Cigarette, gave it him—he must say no
word of what you have done to me, or his white flag
will not protect him from the vengeance of my army—
and then receive your reward from your chief, Ben-
Ihreddin, when you lay my head down for his horse's
hoofs to trample into the dust. Answer me—is the
compact fair ? Ride on with this paper northward, and
then kill me with what torments you choose."

She spoke with calm unwavering resolve, meaning
that which she uttered to its very uttermost letter. She
knew that these men had thirsted for her blood ; she
offered it to be shed to gain for him that messenger on
whose speed his life was hanging ; she knew that a price
was set upon her head, but she delivered herself over to
the hands of her enemies so that thereby she might
purchase his redemption.

As they heard, silence fell upon the brutal clamorous
herd around—the silence of amaze and of respect. The
young chief listened gravely ; by the glistening of his
keen black eyes, he was surprised and moved, though,
true to his teaching, he showed neither emotion as he
answered her :

"Who is this Frank for whom you do this thing ?"

"He is the warrior to whom you offered life on the
field of Zaraila, because his courage was as the courage
of gods."

She knew the qualities of the desert character ; knew
how to appeal to its reverence and to its chivalry.

"And for what does he perish ?" he asked.

"Because he forgot for once that he was a slave ; and
because he has borne the burden of a guilt that was not
his own."

They were quite still now, closed around her ; these
ferocious plunderers, who had been thirsty a moment
before to sheathe their weapons in her body, were spell-

bound by the sympathy of courageous souls, by some vague perception that there was a greatness in this little tigress of France, whom they had sworn to hunt down and slaughter, which surpassed all they had known or dreamed.

"And you have given yourself up to us that by your death you may purchase a messenger from us for this errand?" pursued their leader. He had been reared as a boy in the high tenets and the pure chivalries of the school of Abd-el-Kader; and they were not lost in him despite the crimes and the desperation of his life.

She held the paper out to him with a passionate entreaty breaking through the enforced calm of despair with which she had hitherto spoken.

"Cut me in ten thousand pieces with your swords, but save *him*, as you are brave men, as you are generous foes!"

With a single sign of his hand, their leader waved them back where they crowded around her, and leaped down from his saddle, and led the horse he had dismounted to her.

"Maiden," he said gently, "we are Arabs, but we are not brutes. We swore to avenge ourselves on an enemy; we are not vile enough to accept a martyrdom. Take my horse—he is the swiftest of my troop—and go you on your errand; you are safe from me."

She looked at him in stupor; the sense of his words was not tangible to her; she had had no hope, no thought, that they would ever deal thus with her; all she had ever dreamed of was so to touch their hearts and their generosity that they would spare one from among their troop to do the errand of mercy she had begged of them.

"You play with me;" she murmured, while her lips grew whiter and her great eyes larger in the intensity of her emotion. "Ah! for pity's sake, make haste and kill me, so that this only may reach him!"

The chief, standing by her, lifted her up in his sinewy arms, on to the saddle of his charger. His voice was very solemn, his glance was very gentle; all the nobility of the highest Arab nature was aroused in him at the heroism of a child, a girl, an infidel—one, in his sight, abandoned and shameful among her sex.

"Go in peace," he said simply; "it is not with such as thee that we war."

Then, and then only, as she felt the fresh reins placed in her hands, and saw the ruthless horde around her fall back and leave her free, did she understand his meaning, did she comprehend that she gave her back both liberty and life, and, with the surrender of the horse he loved, the noblest and most precious gift that the Arab ever bestows or ever receives. The unutterable joy seemed to blind her, and gleam upon her face like the blazing light of noon, as she turned her burning eyes full on him.

"Ah! now I believe that thine Allah rules thee, equally with Christians! If I live, thou shalt see me back ere another night; if I die, France will know how to thank thee!"

"We do not do the thing that is right for the sake that men may recompense us," he answered her gently. "Fly to thy friend, and hereafter do not judge that those who are in arms against thee must needs be as the brutes that seek out whom they shall devour."

Then, with one word in his own tongue, he bade the horse bear her southward, and, as swiftly as a spear launched from his hand, the animal obeyed him and flew across the plains. He looked after her awhile, through the dim tremulous darkness that seemed cleft by the rush of the gallop as the clouds are cleft by lightning, while his tribe sat silent on their horses in moody unwilling consent, savage in that they had been deprived of prey, moved in that they were sensible of this martyrdom which had been offered to them.

"Verily the courage of a woman has put the best among us unto shame," he said, rather to himself than them, as he mounted the stallion brought him from the rear and rode slowly northward, unconscious that the thing he had done was great, because conscious only that it was just.

And, borne by the fleetness of the desert-bred beast, she went away through the heavy bronze-hued dulness of the night. Her brain had no sense, her hands had no feeling, her eyes had no sight; the rushing as of waters was loud on her ears, the giddiness of fasting and of fatigue sent the gloom eddying round and round like a whirlpool of shadow. Yet she had remembrance enough left to ride on, and on, and on without once flinching from the agonies that racked her cramped limbs and throbbed in her beating temples; she had remembrance enough to strain her blind eyes toward the east and murmur, in her terror of that white dawn, that must soon break, the only prayer that had been ever uttered by the lips no mother's kiss had ever touched :

"*O God! keep the day back!*"

ONE of the most brilliant of Algerian autumnal days shone over the great camp in the south. The war was almost at an end for a time; the Arabs were defeated and driven desertwards; hostilities irksome, harassing, and annoying, like all guerilla warfare, would long continue, but peace was virtually established, and Zaraila had been the chief glory that had been added by the campaign to the flag of Imperial France. The kites

and the vultures had left the bare bones by thousands to
bleach upon the sands, and the hillocks of brown earth
rose in crowds where those more cared for in death
had been hastily thrust beneath the brown crust of the
earth. The dead had received their portion of reward—
in the jackall's teeth, in the crow's beak, in the worm's
caress. And the living received theirs in this glorious
rose-flecked glittering autumn morning, when the breath
of winter made the air crisp and cool, but the ardent
noon still lighted with its furnace glow the hillside and
the plain.

The whole of the Army of the South was drawn up
on the immense level of the plateau to witness the pre-
sentation of the Cross of the Legion of Honour.

It was full noon. The sun shone without a single cloud
on the deep sparkling azure of the skies. The troops
stretched east and west, north and south, formed up in
three sides of one vast massive square.

The red white and blue of the standards, the brass
of the eagle guidons, the grey tossed manes of the
chargers, the fierce swarthy faces of the soldiery, the
scarlet of the Spahis' cloaks, and the snowy folds of the
Demi-Cavalerie turbans, the shine of the sloped lances,
and the glisten of the carbine barrels, fused together in
one sea of blended colour, flashed into a million of
prismatic hues against the sombre bistre shadow of the
sunburnt plains and the clear blue of the skies.

It had been a sanguinary, fruitless, cruel campaign;
it had availed nothing except to drive the Arabs away
from some hundred leagues of useless and profitless soil;
hundreds of French soldiers had fallen by disease, and
drought, and dysentery, as well as by shot and sabre,
and were unrecorded save on the books of the bureaus,
unlamented save, perhaps, in some little nestling hamlet
among the great green woods of Normandy, or some
wooden hut among the olives and the vines of Provence,

where some woman toiling till sunset among the fields, or praying before some wayside saint's stone niche, would give a thought to the far-off and devouring desert that had drawn down beneath its sands the head that had used to lie upon her bosom, cradled as a child's, or caressed as a lover.

But the drums rolled out their long deep thunder over the wastes ; and the shot-torn standards fluttered gaily in the breeze blowing from the west, and the clear full music of the French bands echoed away to the dim distant terrible south, where the desert-scorch and the desert-thirst had murdered their bravest and best—and the Army was *en fête*. *En fête*, for it did honour to its darling. Cigarette received the Cross.

Mounted on her own little bright bay, Etoile-Filante, with tricolour ribbons flying from his bridle and among the glossy fringes of his mane, the Little One rode among her Spahis. A scarlet *képi* was set on her thick silken curls, a tricolour sash was knotted round her waist, her wine-barrel was slung on her left hip, her pistols thrust in her *ceinturon*, and a light carbine held in her hand with the butt-end resting on her foot. With the sun on her child-like brunette face, her eyes flashing like brown diamonds in the light, and her marvellous horsemanship, showing its skill in a hundred *désinvoltures* and daring tricks, the little Friend of the Flag had come hither among her half-savage warriors, whose red robes surrounded her like a sea of blood.

And on a sea of blood she, the Child of War, had floated, never sinking in that awful flood, but buoyant ever above its darkest waves, catching ever some ray of sunlight upon her fair young head, and being oftentimes like a star of hope to those over whom its dreaded waters closed. Therefore they loved her, these grim, slaughterous, and lustful warriors, to whom no other thing of womanhood was sacred, by whom in their wrath or their crime no friend and no brother was spared, whose law was license, and whose mercy was murder. They loved her, these brutes whose greed was like the tiger's, whose hate was like the devouring flame ; and any who should have harmed a single lock of her curling hair would have had the spears of the African Mussulmans buried by the score in his body. They loved her, with the one fond triumphant love these vultures of the army ever knew ; and to-day they gloried in her with fierce passionate delight. To-day she was to her wild wolves of Africa what Jeanne of Vaucouleurs was to her brethren of France. And to-day was the crown of her young life. It is given to most, if the desire of their soul ever become theirs, to possess it only when long and weary and fainting toil has brought them to its goal; when beholding the golden fruit so far off, through so dreary a pilgrimage, dulls its bloom as they approach ; when having so long centred all their thoughts and hopes in the denied possession of that one fair thing, they find but little beauty in it when that possession is granted to satiate their love. But thrice happy, and few as happy, are they to whom the dream of their youth is fulfilled *in* their youth, to whom their ambition comes in full sweet fruitage, while yet the colours of glory have not faded to the young, eager, longing eyes that watch its advent. And of these was Cigarette.

In the fair, slight, girlish body of the child-soldier there lived a courage as daring as Danton's, a patriotism as pure as Vergniaud's, a soul as aspiring as Napoleon's. Untaught, untutored, uninspired by poet's words or patriot's bidding, spontaneous as the rising and the blossoming of some wind-sown, sun-fed flower, there was, in this child of the battle and the razzia, the spirit of genius, the desire to live and to die greatly. It was unreasoned on, it was felt, not thought, it was often drowned in the gaiety of young laughter, and the ribaldry of military jest, it was often obscured by noxious influence, and stifled beneath the fumes of lawless pleasure; but there, ever, in the soul and the heart of Cigarette, dwelt the germ of a pure ambition—the ambition to do some noble thing for France, and leave her name upon her soldiers' lips, a watchword and a rallying-cry for ever-more. To be for ever a beloved tradition in the army of her country, to have her name remembered in the roll-call as "*Mort sur le champ d'honneur;*" to be once shrined in the love and honour of France, Cigarette—full of the boundless joys of life that knew no weakness and no pain, strong as the young goat, happy as the young lamb, careless as the young flower tossing on the summer breeze—Cigarette would have died contentedly. And now, living, some measure of this desire had been ful-filled to her, some breath of this imperishable glory had passed over her. France had heard the story of Zaraila; from the throne a message had been passed to her; what was far beyond all else to her, her own Army of Africa had crowned her, and thanked her, and adored her as with one voice, and wheresoever she passed the wild cheers rang through the roar of musketry, as through the silence of sunny air, and throughout the regiments every sword would have sprung from its scabbard in her defence if she had but lifted her hand and said one word—"Zaraila!"

The Army looked on her with delight now. In all that mute, still, immovable mass that stretched out so far, in such gorgeous array, there was not one man whose eyes did not turn on her, whose pride did not centre in her—their Little One who was so wholly theirs, and who had been under the shadow of their flag ever since the curls, so dark now, had been yellow as wheat in her infancy. The flag had been her shelter, her guardian, her plaything, her idol; the flutter of the striped folds had been the first thing at which her childish eyes had

laughed ; the preservation of its colours from the sacrilege
of an enemy's touch had been her religion, a religion
whose true following was, in her sight, salvation of the
worst and the most worthless life ; and that flag she
had saved, and borne aloft in victory at Zaraila.   There
was not one in all those hosts whose eyes did not turn
on her with gratitude, and reverence, and delight in her
as their own.

But she had scarce time even for that flash of pain to
quiver in impotent impatience through her.   The trumpets
sounded, the salvoes of artillery pealed out, the lances
and the swords were carried up in salute ; on to the
ground rode the Marshal of France, who represented the
imperial will and presence, surrounded by his staff, by
generals of division and brigade, by officers of rank, and
by some few civilian riders.   An *aide* galloped up to her
where she stood with the corps of her Spahis, and gave
her his orders.   The Little One nodded carelessly, and
touched Etoile-Filante with the prick of the spur.   Like
lightning the animal bounded forth from the ranks,
rearing and plunging, and swerving from side to side,
while his rider, with exquisite grace and address, kept
her seat like the little semi-Arab that she was, and with
a thousand curves and bounds cantered down the line of
the gathered troops, with the west wind blowing from
the far-distant sea, and fanning her bright cheeks till
they wore the soft scarlet flush of the glowing japonica
flower.   And all down the ranks a low, hoarse, strange,
longing murmur went—the buzz of the voices which, but
that discipline suppressed them, would have broken out
in worshipping acclamations.

As carelessly as though she reined up before the *café*
door of the *As de Pique*, she arrested her horse before
the great Marshal who was the impersonation of authority, and put her hand up in the salute, with her saucy
wayward laugh.   He was the impersonation of that vast,

silent, awful, irresponsible power which, under the name of the Second Empire, stretched its hand of iron across the sea, and forced the soldiers of France down into nameless graves, with the desert sand choking their mouths; but he was no more to Cigarette than any drummer-boy that might be present. She had all the contempt for the laws of rank of your thorough inborn democrat, all the gay *insouciant* indifference to station of the really free and untrammelled nature; and, in her sight, a dying soldier, lying quietly in a ditch to perish of shot-wounds without a word or a moan, was greater than all Messieurs les Maréchaux glittering in their stars and orders. As for impressing her, or hoping to impress her, with rank—pooh! You might as well have bid the sailing clouds pause in their floating passage because they came between royalty and the sun. All the sovereigns of Europe would have awed Cigarette not one whit more than a gathering of muleteers. "Allied sovereigns—bah!" she would have said, "what did that mean in '15? A chorus of magpies chattering over one stricken eagle!"

So she reined up before the Marshal and his staff, and the few great personages whom Algeria could bring around them, as indifferently as she had many a time reined up before a knot of grim Turcos, smoking under a barrack-gate. *He* was nothing to her; it was her Army that crowned her. "The Generalissimo is the poppy-head, the men are the wheat; lay every ear of the wheat low, and of what use is the towering poppy that blazed so grand in the sun?" Cigarette would say with metaphorical unction, forgetful, like most allegorists, that her fable was one sided and unjust in figure and deduction.

Nevertheless, despite her gay contempt for rank, her heart beat fast under its golden-laced jacket as she reined up Etoile and saluted. In that hot clear sun all

the eyes of that immense host were fastened on her, and
the hour of her longing desire was come at last. France
had recognised that she had done greatly, and France,
through the voice of this, its chief, spoke to her—France,
her beloved, and her guiding-star, for whose sake the
young brave soul within her would have dared and have
endured all things.   There was a group before her, large
and brilliant, but at them Cigarette never looked ; what
she saw were the sunburnt faces of her "children," of
men who, in the majority, were old enough to be her
grandsires, who had been with her through so many
darksome hours, and whose black and rugged features
lightened and grew tender whenever they looked upon
their Little One.   For the moment she felt giddy with
sweet fiery joy ; they were here to behold her thanked
in the name of France.

The Marshal, in advance of all his staff, touched his
plumed hat and bowed to his saddle-bow as he faced
her.   He knew her well by sight, this pretty child of
his Army of Africa, who had, before then, suppressed
mutiny like a veteran, and led the charge like a Murat
—this kitten with a lion's heart, this humming-bird with
an eagle's swoop.

"Mademoiselle," he commenced, while his voice,
well skilled to such work, echoed to the farthest end of
the long lines of troops, " I have the honour to discharge
to-day the happiest duty of my life.   In conveying to
you the expression of the Emperor's approval of your
noble conduct in the present campaign, I express the
sentiments of the whole Army.   Your action on the day
of Zaraila was as brilliant in conception as it was great
in execution ; and the courage you displayed was only
equalled by your patriotism.   May the soldiers of many
wars remember you and emulate you.   In the name of
France, I thank you.   In the name of the Emperor, I
bring to you the Cross of the Legion of Honour."

As the brief and soldierly words rolled down the ranks of the listening regiments, he stooped forward from his saddle and fastened the red ribbon on her breast; while from the whole gathered mass, watching, hearing, waiting breathlessly to give their tribute of applause to their darling also, a great shout rose as with one voice, strong, full, echoing over and over again across the plains in thunder that joined her name with the name of France and of Napoleon, and hurled it upward in fierce tumultuous idolatrous love to those cruel cloudless skies that shone above the dead. She was their child, their treasure, their idol, their young leader in war, their young angel in suffering; she was all their own, knowing with them one common mother—France. Honour to her was honour to them; they gloried with heart and soul in this bright young fearless life that had been among them ever since her infant feet had waded through the blood of slaughter-fields, and her infant lips had laughed to see the tricolour float in the sun above the smoke of battle.

And as she heard, her face became very pale, her large eyes grew dim and very soft, her mirthful mouth trembled with the pain of a too intense joy. She lifted her head, and all the unutterable love she bore her country and her people thrilled through the music of her voice:

"*Français!—ce n'était rien!*"

That was all she said; in that one first word of their common nationality, she spoke alike to the Marshal of the Empire and to the conscript of the ranks. "Français!" that one title made them all equal in her sight; whoever claimed it was honoured in her eyes, and was precious to her heart, and when she answered them that it was nothing, this thing which they glorified in her, she answered but what seemed the simple truth in her code. She would have thought it "nothing" to have perished by shot, or steel, or flame, in day-long torture, for that one fair sake of France.

Vain in all else, and to all else wayward, here she was docile and submissive as the most patient child ; here she deemed the greatest and the hardest thing that she could ever do far less than all that she would willingly have done. And as she looked upon the host whose thousand and ten thousand voices rang up to the noon-day sun in her homage, and in hers alone, a light like a glory beamed upon her face, that for once was white and still and very grave ;—none who saw her face then, ever forgot that look.

In that moment she touched the full sweetness of a proud and pure ambition, attained and possessed in all its intensity, in all its perfect splendour. In that moment she knew that divine hour which, born of a people's love and of the impossible desires of genius in its youth, comes to so few human lives—knew that which was known to the young Napoleon when, in the hot hush of the nights of July, France welcomed the Conqueror of Italy.

SHE longed to do as some girl of whom she had once been told by an old Invalide had done in the '89— a girl of the people, a fisher-girl of the Cannébière who had loved one above her rank, a noble who deserted her for a woman of his own order, a beautiful, soft-skinned, lily-like scornful aristocrat, with the silver ring of merci-less laughter, and the languid lustre of sweet contemp-tuous eyes. The Marseillaise bore her wrong in silence —she was a daughter of the south and of the populace, with a dark, brooding, burning beauty, strong and fierce, and braced with the salt lashing of the sea and with the keen breath of the stormy mistral. She held her peace while the great lady was wooed and won, while the

2 C

marriage joys came with the purple vintage time, while the people were made drunk at the bridal of their *châtelaine* in those hot, ruddy, luscious autumn days.

She held her peace ; and the Terror came, and the streets of the city by the sea ran blood, and the scorch of the sun blazed, every noon, on the scaffold. Then she had her vengeance. She stood and saw the axe fall down on the proud snow-white neck that never had bent till it bent there, and she drew the severed head into her own bronzed hands and smote the lips his lips had kissed, a cruel blow that blurred their beauty out, and twined a fish-hook in the long and glistening hair, and drew it, laughing as she went, through dust, and mire, and gore, and over the rough stones of the town, and through the shouting crowds of the multitudes, and tossed it out on to the sea, laughing still as the waves flung it out from billow to billow, and the fish sucked it down to make their feast. " *Voilà tes secondes noces !* " she cried where she stood, and laughed by the side of the gray angry water, watching the tresses of the floating hair sink downward like a heap of sea-tossed weed.

"THERE is only one thing worth doing—to die greatly !" thought the aching heart of the child-soldier, unconsciously returning to the only end that the genius and the greatness of Greece could find as issue to the terrible jest, the mysterious despair, of all existence.

A VERY old man—one who had been a conscript in the bands of Young France, and marched from his Pyrenéan village to the battle-tramp of the Marseillaise, and charged with the Enfans de Paris across the plains

of Gemappes ; who had known the passage of the Alps,
and lifted the long curls from the dead brow of Désaix,
at Marengo, and seen in the sultry noonday dust of a
glorious summer the Guard march into Paris, while the
people laughed and wept with joy, surging like the
mighty sea around one pale frail form, so young by
years, so absolute by genius.

A very old man ; long broken with poverty, with pain,
with bereavement, with extreme old age; and by a long
course of cruel accidents, alone, here in Africa, without
one left of the friends of his youth, or of the children
of his name, and deprived even of the charities due
from his country to his services—alone save for the
little Friend of the Flag, who, for four years, had kept
him on the proceeds of her wine trade, in this Moorish
attic, tending him herself when in town, taking heed
that he should want for nothing when she was campaigning.

She hid, as her lawless courage would not have
stooped to hide a sin, had she chosen to commit one,
this compassion which she, the young *condottiera* of
Algeria, showed with so tender a charity to the soldier
of Bonaparte. To him, moreover, her fiery imperious
voice was gentle as the dove, her wayward dominant will
was pliant as the reed, her contemptuous sceptic spirit
was reverent as a child's before an altar. In her sight
the survivor of the Army of Italy was sacred ; sacred
the eyes which, when full of light, had seen the sun
glitter on the breastplates of the Hussars of Murat, the
Dragoons of Kellerman, the Cuirassiers of Milhaud ;
sacred the hands which, when nervous with youth, had
borne the standard of the Republic victorious against the
gathered Teuton host in the Thermopylæ of Champagne ;
sacred the ears which, when quick to hear, had heard
the thunder of Arcola, of Lodi, of Rivoli, and, above
even the tempest of war, the clear, still voice of

Napoleon; sacred the lips which, when their beard was dark in the fulness of manhood, had quivered, as with a woman's weeping, at the farewell in the spring night in the moonlit Cour des Adieux.

Cigarette had a religion of her own; and followed it more closely than most disciples follow other creeds.

THE way was long; the road ill-formed, leading for the most part across a sere and desolate country, with nothing to relieve its barrenness except long stretches of the great spear-headed reeds. At noon the heat was intense; the little cavalcade halted for half an hour under the shade of some black towering rocks which broke the monotony of the district, and commenced a more hilly and more picturesque portion of the country. Cigarette came to the side of the temporary ambulance in which Cecil was placed. He was asleep—sleeping for once peacefully with little trace of pain upon his features, as he had slept the previous night. She saw that his face and chest had not been touched by the stinging insect-swarm; he was doubly screened by a shirt hung above him dexterously on some bent sticks.

"Who has done that?" thought Cigarette. As she glanced round she saw—without any linen to cover him, Zackrist had reared himself up and leaned slightly forward over against his comrade. The shirt that protected Cecil was his; and on his own bare shoulders and mighty chest the tiny armies of the flies and gnats were fastened, doing their will uninterrupted.

As he caught her glance, a sullen ruddy glow of shame shone through the black hard skin of his sunburnt visage—shame to which he had been never touched when discovered in any one of his guilty and barbarous actions.

" *Dame !*" he growled savagely; "he gave me his wine; one must do something in return. Not that I feel the insects—not I; my skin is leather, see you; they can't get through it; but his is *peau de femme*— white and soft—bah! like tissue paper !"

"I see, Zackrist; you are right. A French soldier can never take a kindness from an English fellow without outrunning him in generosity. Look—here is some drink for you."

She knew too well the strange nature with which she had to deal to say a syllable of praise to him for his self-devotion, or to appear to see that, despite his boast of his leather skin, the stings of the cruel winged tribes were drawing his blood and causing him alike pain and irritation which, under that sun, and added to the torment of his gunshot wound, were a martyrdom as great as the noblest saint ever endured.

" *Tiens! tiens!* I did him wrong," murmured Cigarette. "That is what they are—the children of France—even when they are at their worst, like that devil, Zackrist. Who dare say they are not the heroes of the world ?"

And all through the march she gave Zackrist a double portion of her water dashed with red wine, that was so welcome and so precious to the parched and aching throats; and all through the march Cecil lay asleep, and the man who had thieved from him, the man whose soul was stained with murder, and pillage, and rapine, sat erect beside him, letting the insects suck his veins and pierce his flesh.

It was only when they drew near the camp of the main army that Zackrist beat off the swarm and drew his old shirt over his head. "You do not want to say anything to him," he muttered to Cigarette. "I am of leather, you know; I have not felt it."

She nodded; she understood him. Yet his shoulders

and his chest were well-nigh flayed, despite the tough and horny skin of which he made his boast.

"*Dieu!* we are droll!" mused Cigarette. "If we do a good thing, we hide it as if it were a bit of stolen meat, we are so afraid it should be found out; but, if they do one in the world there, they bray it at the tops of their voices from the houses' roofs, and run all down the streets screaming about it for fear it should be lost. *Dieu!* we are droll!"

And she dashed the spurs into her mare and galloped off at the height of her speed into camp—a very city of canvas, buzzing with the hum of life, regulated with the marvellous skill and precision of French warfare, yet with the carelessness and the picturesqueness of the desert-life pervading it.

LIKE wave rushing on wave of some tempestuous ocean, the men swept out to meet her in one great surging tide of life, impetuous, passionate, idolatrous, exultant, with all the vivid ardour, all the uncontrolled emotion, of natures south-born, sun-nurtured. They broke away from their mid-day rest as from their military toil, moved as by one swift breath of fire, and flung themselves out to meet her, the chorus of a thousand voices ringing in deafening *vivas* to the skies. She was enveloped in that vast sea of eager, furious lives, in that dizzy tumult of vociferous cries, and stretching hands, and upturned faces. As her soldiers had done the night before, so these did now—kissing her hands, her dress, her feet, sending her name in thunder through the sun-lit air, lifting her from off her horse, and bearing her, in a score of stalwart arms, triumphant in their midst.

She was theirs—their own—the Child of the Army,

the Little One whose voice above their dying brethren
had the sweetness of an angel's song, and whose feet,
in their hours of revelry, flew like the swift and dazzling
flight of gold-winged orioles. And she had saved the
honour of their Eagles; she had given to them and to
France their god of Victory. They loved her—O
God, how they loved her!—with that intense, breathless,
intoxicating love of a multitude which, though it may
stone to-morrow what it adores to-day, has yet for those
on whom it has once been given thus a power no other
love can know—a passion unutterably sad, deliriously
strong.

That passion moved her strangely.

As she looked down upon them, she knew that not
one man breathed among that tumultuous mass but
would have died that moment at her word; not one
mouth moved among that countless host but breathed
her name in pride, and love, and honour.

She might be a careless young coquette, a lawless
little brigand, a child of sunny caprices, an elf of dauntless mischief; but she was more than these. The divine
fire of genius had touched her, and Cigarette would have
perished for her country not less surely than Jeanne
d'Arc. The holiness of an impersonal love, the glow of
an imperishable patriotism, the melancholy of a passionate pity for the concrete and unnumbered sufferings
of the people were in her, instinctive and inborn, as
fragrance in the heart of flowers. And all these together
moved her now, and made her young face beautiful as
she looked down upon the crowded soldiery.

"It was nothing," she answered them; "it was
nothing. It was for France."

For France! They shouted back the beloved word
with tenfold joy; and the great sea of life beneath her
tossed to and fro in stormy triumph, in frantic paradise
of victory, ringing her name with that of France upon

the air, in thunder-shouts like spears of steel smiting on shields of bronze.

But she stretched her hand out, and swept it backward to the desert-border of the south with a gesture that had awe for them.

"Hush!" she said softly, with an accent in her voice that hushed the riot of their rejoicing homage till it lulled like the lull in a storm. "Give me no honour while *they* sleep yonder. With the dead lies the glory!"

THOUGHTS are very good grain, but if they are not whirled round, round, round, and winnowed and ground in the millstones of talk, they remain little, hard, useless kernels, that not a soul can digest.

LOVE was all very well, so Cigarette's philosophy had always reckoned; a chocolate bonbon, a firework, a bagatelle, a draught of champagne, to flavour an idle moment. "*Vin et Vénus*" she had always been accustomed to see worshipped together, as became their alliterative; it was a bit of fun—that was all. A passion that had pain in it had never touched the Little One; she had disdained it with lightest, airiest contumely. "If your sweetmeat has a bitter almond in it, eat the sugar, and throw the almond away, you goose! that is simple enough, isn't it? Bah! I don't pity the people who eat the bitter almond; not I—*ce sont bien bêtes, ces gens!*" she had said once, when arguing with an officer on the absurdity of a melancholy love which possessed him, and whose sadness she rallied most unmercifully. Now, for once in her young life, the Child of France found that it was remotely possible to meet with almonds so bitter that the taste will remain and

taint all things, do what philosophy may to throw its
acridity aside.

THERE were before them death, deprivation, long days
of famine, long days of drought and thirst ; parching
sun-baked roads ; bitter chilly nights ; fiery furnace-
blasts of sirocco ; killing, pitiless, northern winds ; hunger, only sharpened by a snatch of raw meat or a handful of maize ; and the probabilities, ten to one, of being
thrust under the sand to rot, or left to have their skeletons
picked clean by the vultures. But what of that ? There
were also the wild delight of combat, the freedom of
lawless warfare, the joy of deep strokes thrust home,
the chance of plunder, of wine-skins, of cattle, of women ;
above all, that lust for slaughter which burns so deep
down in the hidden souls of men, and gives them such
brotherhood with wolf and vulture, and tiger, when once
its flames burst forth.

THE levelled carbines covered him ; he stood erect
with his face full toward the sun ; ere they could fire,
a shrill cry pierced the air—
"Wait! in the name of France."
Dismounted, breathless, staggering, with her arms
flung upward, and her face bloodless with fear, Cigarette
appeared upon the ridge of rising ground.
The cry of command pealed out upon the silence in
the voice that the Army of Africa loved as the voice of
their Little One. And the cry came too late ; the volley
was fired, the crash of sound thrilled across the words
that bade them pause, the heavy smoke rolled out upon
the air, the death that was doomed was dealt.

But beyond the smoke-cloud he staggered slightly, and then stood erect still, almost unharmed, grazed only by some few of the balls. The flash of fire was not so fleet as the swiftness of her love ; and on his breast she threw herself, and flung her arms about him, and turned her head backward with her old dauntless sunlit smile as the balls pierced her bosom, and broke her limbs, and were turned away by that shield of warm young life from him.

Her arms were gliding from about his neck, and her shot limbs were sinking to the earth as he caught her up where she dropped to his feet.

"O God ! my child ! they have killed you !"

He suffered more, as the cry broke from him, than if the bullets had brought him that death which he saw at one glance had stricken down for ever all the glory of her childhood, all the gladness of her youth.

She laughed—all the clear, imperious, arch laughter of her sunniest hours unchanged.

"Chut ! It is the powder and ball of France ! *that* does not hurt. If it were an Arbico's bullet now ! But wait ! Here is the Marshal's order. He suspends your sentence ; I have told him all. You are safe !— do you hear ?—you are safe ! How he looks ! Is he grieved to live ? *Mes Français !* tell him clearer than I can tell—here is the order. The General must have it. No—not out of my hand till the General sees it. Fetch him, some of you—fetch him to me."

"Great Heaven ! you have given your life for mine !"

The words broke from him in an agony as he held her upward against his heart, himself so blind, so stunned, with the sudden recall from death to life, and with the sacrifice whereby life was thus brought to him, that he could scarce see her face, scarce hear her voice, but only dimly, incredulously, terribly knew, in some vague sense, that she was dying, and dying thus for him.

She smiled up in his eyes, while even in that moment, when her life was broken down like a wounded bird's, and the shots had pierced through from her shoulder to her bosom, a hot scarlet flush came over her cheeks as she felt his touch and rested on his heart.

"A life! *Tiens!* what is it to give? We hold it in our hands every hour, we soldiers, and toss it in change for a draught of wine. Lay me down on the ground—at your feet—so! I shall live longest that way, and I have much to tell. How they crowd around me! *Mes soldats*, do not make that grief and that rage over me. They are sorry they fired; that is foolish. They were only doing their duty, and they could not hear me in time."

But the brave words could not console those who had killed the Child of the Tricolour; they flung their carbines away, they beat their breasts, they cursed themselves and the mother who had borne them; the silent, rigid, motionless phalanx that had stood there in the dawn to see death dealt in the inexorable penalty of the law was broken up into a tumultuous, breathless, heart-stricken, infuriated throng, maddened with remorse, convulsed with sorrow, turning wild eyes of hate on him as on the cause through which their darling had been stricken. He, laying her down with unspeakable gentleness as she had bidden him, hung over her, leaning her head against his arm, and watching in paralysed horror the helplessness of the quivering limbs, the slow flowing of the blood beneath the Cross that shone where that young heroic heart so soon would beat no more.

"Oh, my child, my child!" he moaned, as the full might and meaning of this devotion which had saved him at such cost rushed on him. "What am I worth that you should perish for me? Better a thousand times have left me to my fate! Such nobility, such sacrifice, such love!"

The hot colour flushed her face once more; she was strong to the last to conceal that passion for which she was still content to perish in her youth.

"Chut! we are comrades, and you are a brave man. I would do the same for any of my Spahis. Look you, I never heard of your arrest till I heard too of your sentence"——

She paused a moment, and her features grew white, and quivered with pain and with the oppression that seemed to lie like lead upon her chest. But she forced herself to be stronger than the anguish which assailed her strength; and she motioned them all to be silent as she spoke on while her voice still should serve her.

"They will tell you how I did it—I have not time. The Marshal gave his word you shall be saved; there is no fear. That is your friend who bends over me here? —is it not? A fair face, a brave face! You will go back to your land—you will live among your own people —and *she*, she will love you now—now she knows you are of her Order!"

Something of the old thrill of jealous dread and hate quivered through the words, but the purer, nobler nature vanquished it; she smiled up in his eyes, heedless of the tumult round them.

"You will be happy. That is well. Look you—it is nothing that I did. I would have done it for any one of my soldiers. And for this"—she touched the blood flowing from her side with the old, bright, brave smile —"it was an accident; they must not grieve for it. My men are good to me; they will feel such regret and remorse; but do not let them. I am glad to die."

The words were unwavering and heroic, but for one moment a convulsion went over her face; the young life was so strong in her, the young spirit was so joyous in her, existence was so new, so fresh, so bright, so dauntless a thing to Cigarette. She loved life: the darkness,

the loneliness, the annihilation of death were horrible to
her as the blackness and the solitude of night to a young
child. Death, like night, can be welcome only to the
weary, and she was weary of nothing on the earth that
bore her buoyant steps; the suns, the winds, the delights
of the sights, the joys of the senses, the music of her
own laughter, the mere pleasure of the air upon her
cheeks, or of the blue sky above her head, were all
so sweet to her. Her welcome of her death-shot was
the only untruth that had ever soiled her fearless lips.
Death was terrible; yet she was content—content to
have come to it for his sake.

There was a ghastly stricken silence round her. The
order she had brought had just been glanced at, but no
other thought was with the most callous there than the
heroism of her act, than the martyrdom of her death.

The colour was fast passing from her lips, and a
mortal pallor settling there in the stead of that rich
bright hue, once warm as the scarlet heart of the pomegranate. Her head leant back on Cecil's breast, and
she felt the great burning tears fall one by one upon her
brow as he hung speechless over her; she put her hand
upward and touched his eyes softly.

"Chut! What is it to die—just to die? You have
lived your martyrdom; I could not have done that.
Listen, just one moment. You will be rich. Take care
of the old man—he will not trouble long—and of Vole-
qui-veut and Etoile, and Boule Blanche, and the rat,
and all the dogs, will you? They will show you the
Château de Cigarette in Algiers. I should not like to
think that they would starve."

She felt his lips move with the promise he could not
find voice to utter; and she thanked him with that old
child-like smile that had lost nothing of its light.

"That is good; they will be happy with you. And
see here;—that Arab must have back his white horse:

he alone saved you. Have heed that they spare him.
And make my grave somewhere where my Army passes ;
where I can hear the trumpets, and the arms, and the passage of the troops—O God ! I forgot ! I shall not wake
when the bugles sound. It will all *end* now, will it not ?
That is horrible, horrible !"

A shudder shook her as, for the moment, the full
sense that all her glowing, redundant, sunlit, passionate
life was crushed out for ever from its place upon the
earth forced itself on and overwhelmed her. But she was
of too brave a mould to suffer any foe—even the foe that
conquers kings—to have power to appal her. She raised
herself, and looked at the soldiery around her, among
them the men whose carbines had killed her, whose
anguish was like the heartrending anguish of women.

"Mes Français ! That was a foolish word of mine.
How many of my bravest have fallen in death ; and
shall I be afraid of what they welcomed ? Do not grieve
like that. You could not help it ; you were doing your
duty. If the shots had not come to me, they would
have gone to him ; and he has been unhappy so long,
and borne wrong so patiently, he has earned the right
to live and enjoy. Now I—I have been happy all my
days, like a bird, like a kitten, like a foal, just from
being young and taking no thought. I should have
had to suffer if I had lived ; it is much best as it is "——

Her voice failed her when she had spoken the heroic
words ; loss of blood was fast draining all strength from
her, and she quivered in a torture she could not wholly
conceal ; he for whom she perished hung over her in an
agony greater far than hers ; it seemed a hideous dream
to him that this child lay dying in his stead.

"Can nothing save her ?" he cried aloud. "O God !
that you had fired one moment sooner !"

She heard ; and looked up at him with a look in
which all the passionate, hopeless, imperishable love she

had resisted and concealed so long spoke with an intensity she never dreamed.

"She is content," she whispered softly. "You did not understand her rightly ; that was all."

"*All !* O God ! how I have wronged you !"

The full strength, and nobility, and devotion of this passion he had disbelieved in and neglected rushed on him as he met her eyes ; for the first time he saw her as she was, for the first time he saw all of which the splendid heroism of this untrained nature would have been capable under a different fate. And it struck him suddenly, heavily, as with a blow ; it filled him with a passion of remorse.

"My darling !—my darling ! what have I done to be worthy of such love ?" he murmured, while the tears fell from his blinded eyes, and his head drooped until his lips met hers. At the first utterance of that word between them, at the unconscious tenderness of his kisses that had the anguish of a farewell in them, the colour suddenly flushed all over her blanched face ; she trembled in his arms ; and a great shivering sigh ran through her. It came too late, this warmth of love. She learned what its sweetness might have been only when her lips grew numb, and her eyes sightless, and her heart without pulse, and her senses without consciousness.

"Hush !" she answered, with a look that pierced his soul. "Keep those kisses for Miladi. She will have the right to love you ; she is of your '*aristocrates*,' she is not 'unsexed.' As for me,—I am only a little trooper who has saved my comrade ! My soldiers, come round me one instant ; I shall not long find words."

Her eyes closed as she spoke ; a deadly faintness and coldness passed over her ; and she gasped for breath. A moment, and the resolute courage in her conquered :

her eyes opened and rested on the war-worn faces of her "children"—rested in a long-lost look of unspeakable wistfulness and tenderness.

"I cannot speak as I would," she said at length, while her voice grew very faint. "But I have loved you. All is said!"

All was uttered in those four brief words. "She had loved them." The whole story of her young life was told in the single phrase. And the gaunt, battle-scarred, murderous, ruthless veterans of Africa who heard her could have turned their weapons against their own breasts, and sheathed them there, rather than have looked on to see their darling die.

"I have been too quick in anger sometimes—forgive it," she said gently. "And do not fight and curse among yourselves; it is bad amid brethren. Bury my Cross with me, if they will let you; and let the colours be over my grave, if you can. Think of me when you go into battle; and tell them in France"——

For the first time her own eyes filled with great tears as the name of her beloved land paused upon her lips; she stretched her arms out with a gesture of infinite longing, like a lost child that vainly seeks its mother.

"If I could only see France once more! France"——

It was the last word upon her utterance; her eyes met Cecil's in one fleeting upward glance of unutterable tenderness; then with her hands still stretched out westward to where her country was, and with the dauntless heroism of her smile upon her face like light, she gave a tired sigh as of a child that sinks to sleep, and in the midst of her Army of Africa the Little One lay dead.

STRATHMORE.

THE sun was setting, sinking downward beyond purple
bars of cloud, and leaving a long golden trail behind
it in its track—sinking slowly and solemnly towards the
west as the day declined, without rest, yet without haste,
as though to give to all the sons of earth warning and
time to leave no evil rooted, no bitterness unhealed, no
feud to ripen, and no crime to bring forth seed, when the
day should have passed away to be numbered with hours
irrevocable, and the night should cast its pall over the
dark deeds done, and seal their graves never to be unclosed. The sun was setting, and shedding its rich and
yellow light over the green earth, on the winding waters,
and the blue hills afar off, and down the thousand leafy
aisles close by; but to one place that warm radiance
wandered not, in one spot the rays did not play, the glory
did not enter. That place was the deer-pond of the old
Bois, where the dark plants brooding on the fetid waters,
which only stirred with noisome things, had washed
against the floating hair of lifeless women, and the sombre
branches of the crowding trees had been dragged earthward by the lifeless weight of the self-slain, till the air
seemed to be poisonous with death, and the grasses, as
they moved, to whisper to the winds dread secrets of the
Past. And here the light of the summer evening did not
come, but only through the leafless boughs of one seared
tree, which broke and parted the dark barrier of forest

2 D

growth, they saw the west, and the sun declining slowly
in its haze of golden air, sinking downward past the bars
of cloud.

All was quiet, save the dull sounds of the parting waters,
when some loathsome reptiles stirred among its brakes,
or the hot breeze moved its pestilential plants ; and in
the silence they stood fronting each other; in this silence
they had met, in it they would part.   And there, on their
right hand, through the break in the dank wall of leaves,
shone the sun, looking earthward, luminous, and blinding human sight like the gaze of God.

The light from the west fell upon Erroll, touching the
fair locks of his silken hair, and shining in his azure eyes
as they looked up at the sunny skies, where a bird was
soaring and circling in space, happy through its mere
sense and joy of life ; and on Strathmore's face the deep
shadows slanted, leaving it as though cast in bronze, chill
and tranquil as that of an Eastern Kabyl, each feature
set into the merciless repose of one immovable purpose.
Their faces were strangely contrasted, for the serenity of
the one was that of a man who fearlessly awaits an inevitable doom, the serenity of the other that of a man
who mercilessly deals out an implacable fate ; and while
in the one those present saw but the calmness of courage
and of custom, in the other they vaguely shrank from a
new and an awful meaning.   For beneath the suave
smile of the Duellist they read the intent of the Murderer.

The night was nigh at hand, and soon the day had to be
gathered to the past, such harvest garnered with it as men s
hands had sown throughout its brief twelve hours, which
are so short in span, yet are so long in sin.   "LET NOT
THE SUN GO DOWN UPON YOUR WRATH."   There, across
the west, in letters of flame, the warning of the Hebrew
scroll was written on the purple skies ; but he who
should have read them stood immutable yet insatiate,
with the gleam of a tiger's lust burning in his eyes—

the lust when it scents blood ; the lust that only slakes its thirst in life.

They fronted one another, those who had lived as brothers ; while at their feet babbled the poisonous waters, and on their right hand shone the evening splendour of the sun.

"One !"

The word fell down upon the silence, and the hiss of a shrill cicada echoed to it like a devil's laugh. Their eyes met, and in the gaze of the one was a compassionate pardon, but in the gaze of the other a relentless lust.

And the sun sank slowly downward beyond the barrier of purple cloud, passing away from earth.

"Two !"

Again the single word dropped out upon the stillness, marking the flight of the seconds ; again the hoot of the cicada echoed it, laughing hideously from its noisome marsh.

And the sun sank slowly, still slowly, nearer and nearer to its shroud of mist, bearing with it all that lingered of the day.

"Three !"

The white death-signal flickered in the breeze, and the last golden rays of the sun were still above the edge of the storm-cloud.

There was yet time.

But the warning was not read : there was the assassin's devilish greed within Strathmore's soul, the assassin's devilish smile upon his lips ; the calmness of his face never changed, the tranquil pulse of his wrist never quickened, the remorseless gleam of his eyes never softened. It was for him to fire first, and the doom written in his look never relaxed. He turned—in seeming carelessness, as you may turn to aim at carrion bird—but his shot sped home.

One moment Erroll stood erect, his fair hair blowing

in the wind, his eyes full open to the light; then—he reeled slightly backward, raised his right arm, and fired in the air ! The bullet flew far and harmless amidst the forest foliage, his arm dropped, and without sign or sound he fell down upon the sodden turf, his head strik-ing against the earth with a dull echo, his hands draw-ing up the rank herbage by the roots, as they closed convulsively in one brief spasm.

He was shot through the heart.

And the sun sank out of sight, leaving a dusky, sultry gloom to brood over the noxious brakes and sullen stag-nant waters, leaving the world to Night, as fitting watch and shroud of Crime ; and those who stood there were stricken with a ghastly horror, were paralysed by a vague and sudden awe, for they knew that they were in the presence of death, and that the hand which had dealt it was the hand of his chosen friend. But he, who had slain him, more coldly, more pitilessly than the merciful amongst us would slay a dog, stood unmoved in the shadow, with his ruthless calm, his deadly serenity, which had no remorse as it had had no mercy, while about his lips there was a cold and evil smile, and in his eyes gleamed the lurid flame of a tiger's triumph—the triumph when it has tasted blood, and slaked its thirst in life.

" *Voyez !—il est mort !* "

The words, uttered in his ear by Valdor, were hoarse and almost tremulous ; but he heard and assented to them unmoved. An exultant light shone and glittered in his eyes ; he had avenged himself and her ! Life was the sole price that his revenge had set ; his purpose had been as iron, and his soul was as bronze. He went nearer, leisurely, and stooped and looked at the work of his hand. In the gloom the dark-red blood could yet be clearly seen, slowly welling out and staining the clotted herbage as it flowed, while one stray gleam of light still stole across, as if in love and pity, and played about the long fair hair which trailed amidst the grass.

Life still lingered, faintly, flickeringly, as though loth to leave for ever that which one brief moment before had been instinct with all its richest glory ; the eyes opened wide once more, and looked up to the evening skies with a wild, delirious, appealing pain, and the lips which were growing white and drawn moved in a gasping prayer:

"Oh, God! I forgive — I forgive. He did not know"——

Then his head fell back, and his eyes gazed upward without sight or sense, and murmuring low a woman's name, "Lucille ! Lucille !" while one last breath shivered like a deep-drawn sigh through all his frame—he died. And his murderer stood by to see the shudder convulse the rigid limbs, and count each lingering pang—calm, pitiless, unmoved, his face so serene in its chill indifference, its brutal and unnatural tranquillity, whilst beneath the drooped lids his eyes watched with the dark glitter of a triumphant vengeance the last agony of the man whom he had loved, that the two who were with him in this ghastly hour shrank involuntarily from his side, awed more by the Living than the Dead. Almost unconsciously they watched him, fascinated basilisk-wise, as he stooped and severed a long flake of hair that was soiled by the dank earth and wet with the dew : unarrested they let him turn away with the golden lock in his hand and the fatal calm on his face, and move to the spot where his horse was waiting. The beat of the hoofs rang muffled on the turf, growing fainter and fainter as the gallop receded. Strathmore rode to her whose bidding had steeled his arm, and whose soft embrace would be his reward ; rode swift and hard, with his hand closing fast on the promised pledge of his vengeance ; while behind him, in the shadows of the falling night, lay a man whom he had once loved, whom he had now slain, with the light of

early stars breaking pale and cold, to shine upon the
oozing blood as it trailed slowly in its death-stream
through the grasses, staining red the arid turf.

And the sun had gone down upon his wrath.

M ES frères! it is well for us that we are no seers!
Were we cursed with prevision, could we know
how, when the idle trifle of the present hour shall have
been forged into a link of the past, it will stretch out and
bind captive the whole future in its bonds, we should be
paralysed, hopeless, powerless, old ere we were young!
It is well for us that we are no seers. Were we cursed
with second sight, we should see the white shroud breast-
high above the living man, the phosphor light of death
gleaming on the youthful radiant face, the feathery seed,
lightly sown, bearing in it the germ of the upas-tree; the
idle careless word, daily uttered, carrying in its womb the
future bane of a lifetime; we should see these things till
we sickened, and reeled, and grew blind with pain before
the ghastly face of the Future, as men in ancient days
before the loathsome visage of the Medusa!

C ONTRETEMPS generally have some saving crumbs
of consolation for those who laugh at fate, and look
good-humouredly for them; life's only evil to him who
wears it awkwardly, and philosophic resignation works
as many miracles as Harlequin; grumble, and you go
to the dogs in a wretched style; make *mots* on your own
misery, and you've no idea how pleasant a *trajet* even
drifting "to the bad" may become.

THE statue that Strathmore at once moulded and marred was his life : the statue which we all, as we sketch it, endow with the strength of the Milo, the glory of the Belvedere, the winged brilliance of the Perseus! which ever lies at its best; when the chisel has dropped from our hands, as they grow powerless and paralysed with death ; like the mutilated torso ; a fragment un-finished and broken, food for the ants and worms, buried in the sands that will quickly suck it down from sight or memory, with but touches of glory and of value left here and there, only faintly serving to show what *might have been,* had we had time, had we had wisdom !

WITH which satirical reflection on his times and his order drifting through his mind, Strathmore's thoughts floated onward to a piece of statecraft then numbered among the delicate diplomacies and intricate embroglie of Europe, whose moves absorbed him as the finesses of a problem absorb a skilful chess-player, and from thence stretched onwards to his future, in which he lived, like all men of dominant ambition, far more than he lived in his present. It was a future brilliant, secure, brightening in its lustre, and strengthening in its power, with each successive year ; a future which was not to him as to most wrapped in a chiaroscuro, with but points of luminance gleaming through the mist, but in whose cold glimmering light he seemed to see clear and distinct, as we see each object of the far-off landscape stand out in the air of a winter's noon, every thread that he should gather up, every distant point to which he should pass onward ; a future singular and characteristic, in which state-power was the single ambition marked out, from which the love of women was banished, in which pleasure and wealth were as little regarded as in Lacedæmon. in which age would be courted, not dreaded, since with it alone would come added dominion over the minds of men, and in which, as it stretched out before him, failure and alteration were alike impossible. What, if he lived, could destroy a future that would be solely dependent on, solely ruled by, himself? By his own hand alone would his future be fashioned; would he hew out any shape save the idol that pleased him? When we hold the chisel ourselves, are we not secure to have no error in the work? Is it likely that our hand will slip, that the marble we select will be dark-veined, and brittle, and impure, that the blows of the mallet will shiver our handiwork, and that when we plan a Milo—god of strength— we shall but mould and sculpture out a Laocoön of torture? Scarcely; and Strathmore held the chisel, and, certain of his own skill, was as sure of what he should make of life as Benvenuto, when he bade the molten metal pour into the shape that he, master-craftsman, had fashioned, and gave to the sight of the world the Winged Perseus. But Strathmore did not remember what Cellini did—that one flaw might mar the whole!

IN the little *millefleurs*-scented billet lay, unknown to its writer as to him, the turning-point of his life! God help us! what avail are experience, prescience, prudence, wisdom, in this world, when at every chance step the silliest trifle, the most commonplace meeting, an invitation to dinner, a turn down the wrong street, the dropping of a glove, the delay of a train, the introduction to an unnoticed stranger, will fling down every precaution, and build a fate for us of which we never dream? Of what avail for us to erect our sand-castle when every chance blast of air may blow it into nothing, and drift another into form that we have no power to move?

Life hinges upon hazard, and at every turn wisdom is
mocked by it, and energy swept aside by it, as the battled
dykes are worn away, and the granite walls beaten down
by the fickle ocean waves, which, never two hours together alike, never two instants without restless motion,
are yet as changeless as they are capricious, as omnipo-
tent as they are fickle, as cruel as they are countless !
Men and mariners may build their bulwarks, but hazard
and the sea will overthrow and wear away both alike at
their will—their wild and unreined will, which no fore-
sight can foresee, no strength can bridle.

Was it not the mere choice between the saddle and
the barouche that day when Ferdinand d'Orléans flung
down on second thoughts his riding-whip upon the console at the Tuileries, and ordered his carriage instead of
his horse, that cost himself his life, his son a throne, the
Bourbon blood their royalty, and France for long years
her progress and her peace ? Had he taken up his whip
instead of laying it aside, he might be living to-day with
the sceptre in his hand, and the Bee, crushed beneath
his foot, powerless to sting to the core of the Lily ! Of
all strange things in human life, there is none stranger
than the dominance of Chance.

HE landed and went into Silver-rest in the morning
light. Far as the eye could reach stretched the
deep still waters of the bay ; the white sails of his yacht
and of the few fishing skiffs in the offing stood out
distinct and glancing in the sun ; over the bluffs and in
all the clefts of rock the growing grass blew and flickered
in the breeze ; and as he crossed the sands the air was
fragrant with the scent of the wild flowers that grew
down to the water's edge. But to note these things a
man must be in unison with the world ; and to love them

he must be in unison with himself. Strathmore scarce
saw them as he went onward.

IF a military man's friend dies who had the step above
him, his first thought is "Promotion! deucedly lucky
for me!" His next, "Poor fellow, what a pity!" always
comes two seconds after. I understand Voltaire. If
your companion's existence at table makes you have a
dish dressed as you don't like it, you are naturally relieved
if an apoplectic fit empties his chair, and sets you free
to say, "*Point de sauce blanche!*" All men are egotists,
they only persuade themselves they are not selfish by
swearing so often, that at last they believe what they say.
No motive under the sun will stand the microscope;
human nature, like a faded beauty, must only have a
demi-lumièr; draw the blinds up, and the blotches
come out, the wrinkles show, and the paint peels off.
The beauty scolds the servants—men hiss the satirists—
who dare to let in daylight!

THE Frenchwoman prides herself on being thought
unfaithful to her husband; the Englishwoman
on being thought faithful to him; but though their
theories are different, their practice comes to much the
same thing.

FRIENDSHIP.

WHEN Zeus, half in sport and half in cruelty, made man, young Hermês, who, as all Olympus knew, was for ever at some piece of mischief, insisted on meddling with his father's work, and got leave to fashion the human ear out of a shell that he chanced to have by him, across which he stretched a fine cobweb that he stole from Arachne. But he hollowed and twisted the shell in such a fashion that it would turn back all sounds except very loud blasts that Falsehood should blow on a brazen horn, whilst the impenetrable web would keep out all such whispers as Truth could send up from the depths of her well.

Hermês chuckled as he rounded the curves of his ear, and fastened it on to the newly-made human creature.

"So shall these mortals always hear and believe the thing that is not," he said to himself in glee—knowing that the box he would give to Pandora would not bear more confused and complex woes to the hapless earth than this gift of an ear to man.

But he forgot himself so far that, though two ears were wanted, he only made one.

Apollo, passing that way, marked the blunder, and resolved to avenge the theft of his milk-white herds which had led him such a weary chase through Tempe.

Apollo took a pearl of the sea and hollowed it, and strung across it a silver string from his own lyre, and

with it gave to man one ear by which the voice of Truth
should reach the brain.

"You have spoilt all my sport," said the boy Hêrmes,
angry and weeping.

"Nay," said the elder brother with a smile. "Be
comforted. The brazen trumpets will be sure to drown
the whisper from the well, and ten thousand mortals to
one, be sure, will always turn by choice your ear instead
of mine."

WOMEN never like one another, except now and then
an old woman and a young woman like you and
me. They are good to one another amongst the poor,
you say ! Oh, that I don't know anything about. They
may be. Barbarians always retain the savage virtues.
In Society women hate one another—all the more because in Society they have to smile in each other's faces
every night of their lives. Only think what that is, my
dear !—to grudge each other's conquests, to grudge each
other's diamonds, to study each other's dress, to watch
each other's wrinkles, to outshine each other always on
every possible occasion, big or little, and yet always to
be obliged to give pet names to each other, and visit
each other with elaborate ceremonial—why, women *must*
hate each other ! Society makes them. Your poor folks,
I daresay, in the midst of their toiling and moiling, and
scrubbing and scraping, and starving and begging, do do
each other kindly turns, and put bread in each other's
mouths now and then, because they can scratch each
other's eyes out, and call each other hussies in the streets,
any minute they like, in the most open manner. But in
Society women's entire life is a struggle for precedence,
precedence in everything—beauty, money, rank, success,
dress, everything. We have to smother hate under
smiles, and envy under compliment, and while we are

dying to say "You hussy," like the women in the streets,
we are obliged, instead of boxing her ears, to kiss her on
both cheeks, and cry, "Oh, my dearest—how charming
of you—so kind!" Only think what all that repression
means. You laugh? Oh, you very clever people always
do laugh at these things. But you must study Society,
or suffer from it, sooner or later. If you don't always
strive to go out before everybody, life will end in everybody going out before you, everybody—down to the shoe-
black!

"READ!" echoed the old wise man with scorn. "O
child, what use is that? Read!—the inland
dweller reads of the sea, and thinks he knows it, and
believes it to be as a magnified duck-pond, and no more.
Can he tell anything of the light and the shade; of the
wave and the foam; of the green that is near, of the blue
that is far; of the opaline changes, now pure as a dove's
throat, now warm as a flame; of the great purple depths
and the fierce blinding storm; and the delight and the
fear, and the hurricane rising like a horse snorting for war,
and all that is known to man who goes down to the great
deep in ships? Passion and the sea are like one another.
Words shall not tell them, nor colour portray them.
The kiss that burns, and the salt spray that stings—let
the poet excel and the painter endeavour, yet the best
they can do shall say nothing to the woman without a
lover; and the landsman who knows not the sea. If
you would live—love. You will live in an hour a lifetime;
and you will wonder how you bore your life before. But
as an artist all will be over with you—that I think."

WHAT is the use of railing against Society? Society, after all, is only Humanity *en masse*, and the opinion of it must be the opinion of the bulk of human minds. Complaints against Society are like the lions' against the man's picture. No doubt the lions would have painted the combat as going just the other way, but then, so long as it is the man who has the knife or the gun, and the palette and the pencil, where is the use of the lions howling about injustice? Society has the knife and the pencil; that's the long and the short of it; and if people don't behave themselves they feel 'em both, and have to knock under. They're knifed first, and then caricatured—as the lions were.

"EXCELLING!—it is rather a Dead Sea apple, I fear. The effort is happiness, but the fruit always seems poor."

Lady Cardiff could not patiently hear such nonsense.

"There you are again, my dear feminine Alceste," she said irritably, "looking at things from your solitary standpoint on that rock of yours in the middle of the sea. *You* are thinking of the excelling of genius, of the possessor of an ideal fame, of the 'Huntress mightier than the moon,' and *I* am thinking of the woman who excels in Society—who has the biggest diamonds, the best *chef*, the most lovers, the most *chic* and *chien*, who leads the fashion, and condescends when she takes tea with an empress. But even from your point of view on your rock, I can't quite believe it. Accomplished ambition must be agreeable. To look back and say, 'I have achieved!'—what leagues of sunlight sever that proud boast from the weary sigh, 'I have failed!' Fame must console."

"Perhaps; but 'the world, at least, does its best that it should not. Its glory discs are of thorns."

"You mean that superiority has its attendant shadow, which is calumny? Always has had, since Apelles painted. What does it matter if everybody looks after you when you pass down a street, what they say when you pass?"

"A malefactor may obtain that sort of flattery. I do not see the charm of it."

"You are very perverse. Of course I talk of an un-sullied fame, not of an infamous notoriety."

"Fame nowadays is little else but notoriety," said Etoile with a certain scorn, "and it is dearly bought, per-haps too dearly, by the sacrifice of the serenity of obscur-ity, the loss of the peace of private life. Art is great and precious, but the pursuit of it is sadly embittered when we have become so the plaything of the public, through it, that the simplest actions of our lives are chronicled and misconstrued. You do not believe it, perhaps, but I often envy the women sitting at their cot-tage doors, with their little children on their knees; no one talks of *them!*"

"J'ai tant de gloire, ô roi, que j'aspire au fumier!"

said Lady Cardiff. "You are very thankless to Fate, my dear, but I suppose it is always so."

And Lady Cardiff took refuge in her cigar case, being a woman of too much experience not to know that it is quite useless to try and make converts to your opinions; and especially impossible to convince people dissatisfied with their good fortune that they ought to be charmed with it.

"It is very curious," she thought when she got into her own carriage, "really it makes one believe in that odd doctrine of, what is it, Compensations; but, certainly, people of great talent always are a little mad. If they're not flightily mad with eccentricity and brandy, they are morbidly mad with solitude and sentiment. Now she is a great creature, really a great creature ; might have the world at her feet if she liked ; and all she cares for is a big dog, a bunch of roses, and some artist or poet dead and gone three hundred or three thousand years ! It is very queer. It is just like that extraordinary possession of Victor Hugo's ; with powers that might have sufficed to make ten men brilliant and comfortable, he must vex and worry about politics that didn't concern him in the least, and go and live under a skylight in the middle of the sea. It is very odd. They are never happy; but when they are unhappy, and if you tell them that Addison could be a great writer, and yet live comfortably and enjoy the things of this world, they only tell you contemptuously that Addison had no genius, he had only a Style. I suppose he hadn't. I think if I were one of them and had to choose, I would rather have only a Style too."

WHEN passion and habit long lie in company it is only slowly and with incredulity that habit awakens to find its companion fled, itself alone.

A NEW acquaintance is like a new novel ; you open it with expectation, but what you find there seldom makes you care to take it off the shelf another time.

THE pity which is not born from experience is always cold. It cannot help being so. It does not understand.

THE house she lived in was very old, and had those charming conceits, those rich shadows and depth of shade, that play of light, that variety, and that character which seem given to a dwelling-place in ages when men asked nothing better of their God than to live where their fathers had lived, and leave the old roof-tree to their children's children.

The thing built yesterday, is a caravanserai: I lodge in it to-day, and you to-morrow; in an old house only can be made a home, where the blessings of the dead have rested and the memories of perfect faiths and lofty passions still abide.

THERE is so much mystery in this world, only people who lead humdrum lives will not believe it.

It is a great misfortune to be born to a romantic history. The humdrum always think that you are lying. In real truth romance is common in life, commoner, perhaps, than the commonplace. But the commonplace always looks more natural.

In Nature there are millions of gorgeous hues to a scarcity of neutral tints; yet the pictures that are painted in sombre semi-tones and have no one positive colour in them are always pronounced the nearest to nature. When a painter sets his palette, he dares not approach the gold of the sunset and dawn, or the flame of the pomegranate and poppy.

THIS age of Money, of Concessions, of Capitalists, and of Limited Liabilities, has largely produced the female financier, who thinks with M. de Camors, that "*l'humanité est composée des actionnaires.*" Other centuries have had their especial type of womanhood; the learned and graceful *hetaira*, the saintly and ascetic recluse, the warrior of Oriflamme or Red Rose, the *dame de beauté*, all loveliness and light, like a dewdrop, the philosophic *précieuse*, with sesquipedalian phrase, the

2 E

revolutionist, half nude of body and wholly nude of mind, each in their turn have given their sign and seal to their especial century, for better or for worse. The nineteenth century has some touch of all, but its own novelty of production is the female speculator.

The woman who, breathless, watches *la hausse* and *la baisse;* whose favour can only be won by some hint in advance of the newspapers ; whose heart is locked to all save golden keys ; who starts banks, who concocts companies, who keeps a broker, as in the eighteenth century a woman kept a monkey, and in the twelfth a knight ; whose especial art is to buy in at the right moments, and to sell out in the nick of time ; who is great in railways and canals, and new bathing-places, and shares in fashionable streets ; who chooses her lovers, thinking of concessions, and kisses her friends for sake of the secrets they may betray from their husbands—what other centuries may say of her who can tell ?

The Hôtel Rambouillet thought itself higher than heaven, and the generation of Catherine of Sienna believed her deal planks the sole highway to the throne of God.

PROUD women, and sensitive women, take hints and resent rebuffs, and so exile themselves from the world prematurely and haughtily. They abdicate the moment they see that any desire their discrowning. Abdication is grand, no doubt. But possession is more profitable. "A well-bred dog does not wait to be kicked out," says the old see-saw. But the well-bred dog thereby turns himself into the cold, and leaves the crumbs from under the table to some other dog with less good-breeding and more worldly wisdom. The sensible thing to do is to stay where you like best to be ; stay there with tooth and claw ready and a stout hide on which cudgels

break. People, after all, soon get tired of kicking a dog
that never will go.

High-breeding was admirable in days when the world
itself was high-bred. But those days are over. The
world takes high-breeding now as only a form of in-
solence.

" TO your poetic temper life is a vast romance, beautiful
and terrible, like a tragedy of Æschylus. You
stand amidst it entranced, like a child by the beauty
and awe of a tempest. And all the while the worldly-
wise, to whom the tempest is only a matter of the
machineries of a theatre—of painted clouds, electric
lights, and sheets of copper—the world-wise govern the
storm as they choose and leave you in it defenceless and
lonely as old Lear. To put your heart into life is the
most fatal of errors; it is to give a hostage to your
enemies whom you can only ransom at the price of your
ruin. But what is the use of talking? To you, life will
be always Alastor and Epipsychidion, and to us, it will
always be a Treatise on Whist. That's all !"

"A Treatise on Whist! No! It is something much
worse. It is a Book of the Bastile, with all entered as
criminal in it, who cannot be bought off by bribe or
intrigue, by a rogue's stratagem or a courtesan's vice!"

"The world is only a big Harpagon, and you and
such as you are Maître Jacques. '*Puisque vous l'avez
voulu!*' you say,—and call him frankly to his face,
'*Avare, ladre, vilain, fessemathieu!*' and Harpagon
answers you with a big stick and cries, '*Apprenez à
parler!*' Poor Maître Jacques! I never read of him
without thinking what a type he is of Genius. No offence
to you, my dear. He'd the wit to see he would never
be pardoned for telling the truth, and yet he told it ! The
perfect type of Genius."

THE untruthfulness of women communicates itself to
the man whose chief society they form, and the
perpetual necessities of intrigue end in corrupting the
temper whose chief pursuit is passion.

Women who environ a man's fidelity by ceaseless
suspicion and exaction, create the evil that they dread.

SOCIETY, after all, asks very little. Society only asks
you to wash the outside of your cup and platter :
inside you may keep any kind of nastiness that you like :
only wash the outside. Do wash the outside, says Society ;
and it would be a churl or an ass indeed who would
refuse so small a request.

A WOMAN who is ice to his fire, is less pain to a
man than the woman who is fire to his ice. There
is hope for him in the one, but only a dreary despair in
the other. The ardours that intoxicate him in the first
summer of his passion serve but to dull and chill him in
the later time.

A FROG that dwelt in a ditch spat at a worm that
bore a lamp.
"Why do you do that ?" said the glow-worm.
"Why do you shine ?" said the frog.

WHEN a name is in the public mouth the public
nostril likes to smell a foulness in it. It likes to
think that Byron committed incest ; that Milton was a
brute ; that Raffaelle's vices killed him ; that Pascal was

mad; that Lamartine lived and died a pauper; that
Scipio took the treasury moneys; that Thucydides and
Phidias stole; that Heloise and Hypatia were but loose
women after all—so the gamut runs over twice a thousand
years; and Rousseau is at heart the favourite of the
world because he was such a beast, with all his talent.

When the world is driven to tears and prayers by
Schiller, it hugs itself to remember that he could not
write a line without the smell of rotten apples near, and
that when he died there was not enough money in his
desk to pay his burial. They make him smaller, closer,
less divine—the apples and the pauper's coffin.

"GET a great cook; give three big balls a winter, and
drive English horses; you need never consider
Society then, it will never find fault with you, *ma très-
chère.*"

She did not quite understand, but she obeyed; and
Society never did. Society says to the members of it as
the Spanish monk to the tree that he pruned, and that
cried out under his hook:

"It is not beauty that is wanted of you, nor shade, but
olives."

Moral loveliness or mental depth, charm of feeling or
nobleness of instinct, beauty, or shade, it does not ask
for, but it does ask for olives—olives that shall round
off its dessert, and flavour its dishes, and tickle its sated
palate; olives that it shall pick up without trouble, and
never be asked to pay for; these are what it likes.

Now it is precisely in olives that the woman who
has one foot in Society and one foot out of it will be
profuse.

She must please, or perish.

She must content, or how will she be countenanced?

The very perilousness of her position renders her solicitous to attract and to appease.

Society follows a natural selfishness in its condonation of her ; she is afraid of it, therefore she must bend all her efforts to be agreeable to it ! it can reject her at any given moment, so that her court of it must be continual and expansive. No woman will take so much pains, give so much entertainment, be so willing to conciliate, be so lavish in hospitality, be so elastic in willingness, as the woman who adores Society, and knows that any black Saturday it may turn her out with a bundle of rods, and a peremptory dismissal.

Between her and Society there is a tacit bond.

"Amuse me, and I will receive you."

"Receive me, and I will amuse you."

OF all lay figures there is none on earth so useful as a wooden husband. You should get a wooden husband, my dear, if you want to be left in peace. It is like a comfortable slipper or your dressing - gown after a ball. It is like springs to your carriage. It is like a clever maid who never makes mistakes with your notes or comes without coughing discreetly through your dressing-room. It is like tea, cigarettes, postage-stamps, foot-warmers, eiderdown counterpanes — anything that smooths life, in fact. Young women do not think enough of this. An easy-going husband is the one indispensable comfort of life. He is like a set of sables to you. You may never want to put them on; still, if the north wind do blow—and one can never tell—how handy they are ! You pop into them in a second, and no cold wind can find you out, my dear. Couldn't find you out, if your shift were in rags underneath ! Without your husband's countenance, you have scenes. With

scenes, you have scandal. With scandal, you come to
a suit. With a suit, you most likely lose your settlements.
And without your settlements, where are you in Society?
With a husband you are safe. You need never think
about him in any way. His mere existence suffices. He
will always be at the bottom of your table, and the head
of your visiting-cards. That is enough. He will represent Respectability for you, without your being at the
trouble to represent Respectability for yourself. Respectability is a thing of which the shadow is more agreeable
than the substance. Happily for us, Society only requires
the shadow.

VERY well; if you dislike dancing, don't dance; though
if a woman don't, you know, they always think she
has got a short leg, or a cork leg, or something or other
that's dreadful. But why not show yourself at them?
At least show yourself. One goes to balls as one goes
to church. It's a social muster.

THE art of pleasing is more based on the art of seeming pleased than people think of, and she disarmed
the prejudices of her enemies by the unaffected delight
she appeared to take in themselves. You may think very
ill of a woman, but after all you cannot speak very ill of
her if she has assured you a hundred times that you are
amongst her dearest friends.

SOCIETY always had its fixed demands. It used to
exact birth. It used to exact manners. In a remote
and golden age there is a tradition that it was once contented with mind. Nowadays it exacts money, or rather

amusement, because if you don't let other folks have the
benefit of your money, Society will take no account of it
But have money and spend it well (that is, let Society
live on it, gorge with it, walk ankle-deep in it), and you
may be anything and do anything; you may have been
an omnibus conductor in the Strand, and you may marry
a duke's daughter; you may have been an oyster-girl
in New York, and you may entertain royalties. It is
impossible to exaggerate an age of anomaly and hyper-
bole. There never was an age when people were so
voracious of amusement, and so tired of it, both in one.
It is a perpetual carnival and a permanent yawn. If
you can do anything to amuse us you are safe—till
we get used to you—and then you amuse no longer,
and must go to the wall. Every age has its price : what
Walpole said of men must be true of mankind. Anybody
can buy the present age that will bid very high and pay
with tact as well as bullion. There is nothing it will
not pardon if it see its way to getting a new sensation
out of its leniency. Perhaps no one ought to complain.
A Society with an india-rubber conscience, no memory,
and an absolute indifference to eating its own words and
making itself ridiculous, is, after all, a convenient one to
live in—if you can pay for its suffrages.

IF you are only well beforehand with your falsehood all
will go upon velvet ; nobody ever listens to a recti-
fication. "Is it possible?" everybody cries with eager
zest ; but when they have only to say "Oh, wasn't it so?"
nobody feels any particular interest. It is the first state-
ment that has the swing and the success ; as for explana-
tion or retractation—pooh ! who cares to be bored?

THOSE people with fine brains and with generous souls will never learn that life is after all only a game—a game which will go to the shrewdest player and the coolest. They never see this; not they; they are caught on the edge of great passions, and swept away by them. They cling to their affections like commanders to sinking ships, and go down with them. They put their whole heart into the hands of others, who only laugh and wring out their lifeblood. They take all things too vitally in earnest. Life is to them a wonderful, passionate, pathetic, terrible thing that the gods of love and of death shape for them. They do not see that coolness and craft, and the tact to seize accident, and the wariness to obtain advantage, do in reality far more in hewing out a successful future than all the gods of Greek or Gentile. They are very unwise. It is of no use to break their hearts for the world; they will not change it. *La culte de l'humanité* is the one of all others which will leave despair as its harvest. Laugh like Rabelais, smile like Montaigne; that is the way to take the world. It only puts to death its Sebastians, and makes its Shelleys not sorrowful to see the boat is filling.

SOCIETY always adheres to its principles; just as a Moslem subscribes none the less to the Koran because he may just have been blowing the froth off his bumper of Mumm's before he goes to his mosque.

PLEASANTNESS is the soft note of this generation, just as scientific assassination is the harsh note of it. The age is compounded of the two. Half of it is chloroform; the other half is dynamite.

YOU make us think, and Society dislikes thinking. You call things by their right names, and Society hates that, though Queen Bess didn't mind it. You trumpet our own littleness in our ear, and we know it so well that we do not care to hear much about it. You shudder at sin, and we have all agreed that there is no such thing as sin, only mere differences of opinion, which, provided they don't offend us, we have no business with : adultery is a *liaison*, lying is gossip, debt is a momentary embarrassment, immorality is a little slip, and so forth : and when we have arranged this pretty little dictionary of convenient pseudonyms, it is not agreeable to have it sent flying by fierce, dreadful, old words, that are only fit for some book that nobody ever reads, like Milton or the Family Bible. We do not want to think. We do not want to hear. We do not care about anything. Only give us a good dinner and plenty of money, and let us outshine our neighbours. There is the Nineteenth Century Gospel. My dear, if Ecclesiasticus himself came he would preach in vain. You cannot convince people that don't want to be convinced. We call ourselves Christians—Heaven save the mark !—but we are only the very lowest kind of pagans. We do not believe in anything—except that nothing matters. Well, perhaps nothing does matter. Only one wonders why ever so many of us were all created, only just to find *that* out.

LOVE to the looker-on may be blind, unwise, unworthily bestowed, a waste, a sacrifice, a crime ; yet none the less is love, alone, the one thing that, come weal or woe, is worth the loss of every other thing ; the one supreme and perfect gift of earth, in which all common things of daily life become transfigured and divine. And perhaps of all the many woes that priesthoods have wrought upon humanity, none have been greater than this false teaching, that love can ever be a sin. To the sorrow and the harm of the world, the world's religions have all striven to make men and women shun and deny their one angel as a peril or a shame ; but religions cannot strive against nature, and when the lovers see each other's heaven in each other's eyes, they know the supreme truth that one short day together is worth a lifetime's glory.

GENIUS is like the nautilus, all sufficient for itself in its pretty shell, quite at home in the big ocean, with no fear from any storm. But if a wanton stone from a boat passing by break the shell, where is the nautilus then ? Drowned ; just like any common creature !

THERE are times when, even on the bravest temper, the ironical mockery, the cruel despotism of trifling circumstances, that have made themselves the masters of our lives, the hewers of our fate, must weigh with a sense of involuntary bondage, against which to strive is useless.

The weird sisters were forms of awe and magnitude proportionate to the woes they dealt out, to the destiny they wove. But the very littleness of the daily chances that actually shape fate is, in its discordance and its mockery, more truly terrible and most hideously solemn —it is the little child's laugh at a frisking kitten which brings down the avalanche, and lays waste the mountain side, or it is the cackle of the startled geese that saves the Capitol.

To be the prey of Atropos was something at the least ; and the grim *Deus vult perdere*, uttered in the delirium of pain, at the least made the maddened soul feel of some slender account in the sight of the gods and in the will of Heaven. But we, who are the children of mere accident and the sport of idlest opportunity, have no such consolation.

OF course they will stone you, as village bumpkins run out and stone an odd stray bird that they have never seen before; and the more beautiful the plumage looks, the harder rain the stones. If the bird were a sparrow the bumpkins would let it be.

LOVE that remembers aught save the one beloved may be affection, but it is not love.

ARIEL could not combat a leopardess; Ithuriel's spear glances pointless from a rhinoceros' hide. To match what is low and beat it, you must stoop, and soil your hands to cut a cudgel rough and ready. She did not see this; and seeing it, would not have lowered herself to do it.

WHICH is the truth, which is the madness?—when the artist, in the sunlit ice of a cold dreamland, scorns love and adores but one art; or when the artist, amidst the bruised roses of a garden of passion, finds all heaven in one human heart?

THERE is a story in an old poet's forgotten writings of a woman who was queen when the world was young, and reigned over many lands, and loved a captive, and set him free, and thinking to hurt him less by seeming lowly, came down from her throne and laid her sceptre in the dust, and passed amongst the common maidens that drew water at the well, or begged at the city gate, and seemed as one of them, giving him all and keeping nought herself : "so will he love me more," she thought; but he, crowned king, thought only of the sceptre and the throne, and having those, looked not amongst the women at the gate, and knew her not, because what he had loved had been a queen. Thus she, self-discrowned, lost both her lover and her kingdom. A wise man amongst the throng said to her, " Nay, you should have kept aloof upon your golden seat and made him feel your power to deal life or death, and fretted him long, and long kept him in durance and in doubt, you, meanwhile, far above. For men are light creatures as the moths are."

THEY had lived in London and Paris all their lives, and had, before this, heard patriotism used as a reason for a variety of things, from a minister's keeping in office against the will of the country, to a newspaper's writing a country into bloodshed and bankruptcy; they were quite aware of the word's elasticity.

IT was the true and perfect springtide of the year, when Love walks amongst the flowers, and comes a step nearer what it seeks with every dawn.

Without Love, spring is of all seasons cruel; more cruel than all frost and frown of winter.

IN the early days of an illicit passion concealment is charming ; every secret stairway of intrigue has a sweet surprise at its close ; to be in conspiracy with one alone against all the rest of humanity is the most seductive of seductions. Love lives best in this soft twilight, where it only hears its own heart and one other's beat in the solitude.

But when the reverse of the medal is turned ; when every step on the stairs has been traversed and tired of, when, instead of the heart's beat, there is but an upbraiding voice, when it is no longer *with* one but *from* one that concealment is needed, then the illicit passion is its own Nemesis, then nothing were ever drearier, wearier, more anxious, or more fatiguing than its devious paths become, and they seem to hold the sated wanderer in a labyrinth of which he knows, and knowing hates, every wind, and curve, and coil, yet out of which it seems to him he will never make his way back again into the light of wholesome day.

MY dear, the days of Fontenoy are gone out ; everybody nowadays only tries to get the first fire, by hook or by crook. Ours is an age of cowardice and cuirassed cannon ; chivalry is out of place in it.

WITH a woman, the vulgarity that lies in public adulation is apt to nauseate ; at least if she be so little of a woman that she is not vain, and so much of one that she cares for privacy. For the fame of our age is not glory but notoriety ; and notoriety is to a woman like the bull to Pasiphae—whilst it caresses it crushes.

HAD she your talent the world would have heard of her. As it is, she only enjoys herself. Perhaps the better part. Fame is a cone of smoke. Enjoyment is a loaf of sugar.

THERE is no such coward as the woman who toadies Society because she has outraged Society. The bully is never brave.

"Oignez vilain il vous poindra : poignez vilain il vous oindra," is as true of the braggart's soul still, as it used to be in the old days of Froissart, when the proverb was coined.

SHE was of opinion with Sganarelle, that "cinq ou six coups de bâton entre gens qui s'aiment ne font que ragaillarder l'affection."

But, like Sganarelle also, she always premised that the right to give the blows should be hers.

SHE was only like any other well-dressed woman after all, and humanity considers that when genius comes forth in the flesh the touch of the coal from the altar should have left some visible stigmata on the lips it has burned, as, of course anybody knows, it invariably leaves some smirch upon the character.

Humanity feels that genius ought to wear a livery, as Jews and loose women wore yellow in the old golden days of distinction.

"They don't even paint!" said one lady, and felt herself aggrieved.

CALUMNY is the homage of our contemp raries, as some South Sea Islanders spit on those they honour.

POPULARITY has been defined as the privilege of being cheered by the kind of people you would never allow to bow to you.

Fame may be said to be the privilege of being slandered at once by the people who do bow to you, as well as by the people who do not.

NOBODY there knew at all. So everybody averred they knew for certain. Nobody's story agreed with anybody else's, but that did not matter at all. The world, like Joseph's father, gives the favourite coat of many colours which the brethren rend.

"BE honey, and the flies will eat you," says the old saw, but, like most other proverbs, it will not admit of universal application. There is a way of being honey that is thoroughly successful and extremely popular, and constitutes a kind of armour that is bomb-proof.

THE longest absence is less perilous to love than the terrible trials of incessant proximity.

SHE forgot that love likes to preserve its illusions, and that it will bear better all the sharpest deprivations in the world than it will the cruel tests of an unlovely and unveiled intercourse.

She had committed the greatest error of all : she had

let him be disenchanted by familiarity. Passion will pardon rage, will survive absence, will forgive infidelity, will even thrive on outrage, and will often condone a crime ; but when it dies of familiarity it is dead for ever and aye.

SOCIETY will believe anything rather than ever believe that Itself can be duped.

If you have only assurance enough to rely implicitly on this, there is hardly anything you cannot induce it to accept.

HERE was the secret of her success. To her nothing was little.

This temper is always popular with Society. To enjoy yourself in the world, is, to the world, the prettiest of indirect compliments.

The chief offence of the poet, as of the philosopher, is that the world as it is fails to satisfy them.

Society, which is after all only a conglomerate of hosts, has the host's weakness—all its guests must smile.

The poet sighs, the philosopher yawns. Society feels that they depreciate it. Society feels more at ease without them.

To find every one acceptable to you is to make yourself acceptable to every one.

Hived bees get sugar because they will give back honey. All existence is a series of equivalents.

EVEN the discreetest friends will, like the closest-packed hold of a ship, leak occasionally. Salt water and secrets are alike apt to ooze.

2 F

THE simplicity of the artist is always the stumbling-block of the artist with the world.

A WOMAN need never dread the fiercest quarrel with her lover ; the tempest may bring sweeter weather than any it broke up, and after the thunder the singing of birds will sound lovelier than before. Anger will not extinguish love, nor will scorn trample it dead ; jealousy will fan its fires, and offences against it may but fasten closer the fetters that it adores beyond all liberty. But when love dies of a worn-out familiarity it perishes for ever and aye.

Jaded, disenchanted, wearied, indifferent, the tired passion expires of sheer listlessness and contemptuous disillusion.

The death is slow and unperceived, but it is sure ; and it is a death that has no resurrection.

THERE is nothing that you may not get people to believe in if you will only tell it them loud enough and often enough, till the welkin rings with it.

WHAT Raffaelle has left us must be to the glories he imagined as the weaver's dye to the sunset's fire.

A WOMAN'S violence is a mighty power ; before it reason recoils unnerved, justice quails appalled, and peace perishes like a burnt-up scroll ; it is a sand-storm, before which courage can do but little : the bravest man can but fall on his face and let it rage on above him.

A VERY trustful woman believes in her lover's fidelity with her heart; a very vain woman believes in it with her head.

FROM the moment that another life has any empire on ours, peace is gone.

Art spreads around us a profound and noble repose, but passion enters it, and then art grows restless and troubled as the deep sea at the call of the whirlwind.

WANDA.

A MAN cast forth from his home is like a ship cut loose from its anchor and rudderless. Whatever may have been his weakness, his offences, they cannot absolve you from your duty to watch over your husband's soul, to be his first and most faithful friend, to stand between him and his temptations and perils. That is the nobler side of marriage. When the light of love is faded, and its joys are over, its duties and its mercies remain. Because one of the twain has failed in these the other is not acquitted of obligation.

"CHOOSE some career; make yourself some aim in life; do not fold your talents in a napkin; in a napkin that lies on the supper-table at Bignon's. That idle, aimless life is very attractive, I daresay, in its way, but it must grow wearisome and unsatisfactory as years roll on. The men of my house have never been content with it; they have always been soldiers, statesmen, something or other beside mere nobles."

"But they have had a great position."

"Men make their own position; they cannot make a name (at least, not to my thinking). You have that good fortune; you have a great name; you only need, pardon me, to make your manner of life worthy of it."

"Cannot make a name? Surely in these days the

beggar rides on horseback in all the ministries and half the nobilities;"

"You mean that Hans, Pierre, or Richard becomes a count, an excellency, or an earl? What does that change? It alters the handle; it does not alter the saucepan. No one can be ennobled. Blood is blood; nobility can only be inherited; it cannot be conferred by all the heralds in the world. The very meaning and essence of nobility are descent, inherited traditions, instincts, habits, and memories—all that is meant by *noblesse oblige.*"

"MEN are always like Horace," said the princess. "They admire rural life, but they remain for all that with Augustus."

I READ the other day of some actresses dining off a truffled pheasant and a sack of bonbons. That is the sort of dinner we make all the year round, morally— metaphorically—how do you say it? It makes us thirsty, and perhaps—I am not sure—perhaps it leaves us half starved, though we nibble the sweetmeats, and don't know it.

"Your dinner must lack two things—bread and water."

"Yes; we never see either. It is all truffles and caramels and *vins frappés.*"

"There is your bread."

She glanced at the little children, two pretty, graceful little maids of six and seven years old.

"*Ouf!*" said the Countess Branka. "They are only little bits of puff paste, a couple of *petits fours* baked on the boulevards. If they be *chic,* and marry well, I for one shall ask no more of them. If ever you have children, I suppose you will rear them on science and the Antonines?"

"Perhaps on the open air and Homer."

CANNOT you make them understand that we are not public artists to need *réclames*, nor yet sovereigns to be compelled to submit to the microscope? Is this the meaning of civilisation—to make privacy impossible, to oblige every one to live under a lens?

THE world was much happier when distinctions and divisions were impassable. There are no sumptuary laws now. What is the consequence? That your *bourgeoise* ruins her husband in wearing gowns fit only for a duchess, and your prince imagines it makes him popular to look precisely like a cabman or a bailiff.

A GREAT love must be as exhaustless as the ocean in its mercy, and as profound in its comprehension.

WHAT was love if not one long forgiveness? What raised it higher than the senses if not its infinite patience and endurance of all wrong? What was its hope of eternal life if it had not gathered strength in it enough to rise above human arrogance and human vengeance?

THERE is an infinite sense of peace in those cool, vast, unworn mountain solitudes, with the rain-mists sweeping like spectral armies over the level lands below, and the sun-rays slanting heavenward, like the spears of

an angelic host. There is such abundance of rushing
water, of deep grass, of endless shade, of forest trees,
of heather and pine, of torrent and tarn; and beyond
these are the great peaks that loom through breaking
clouds, and the clear cold air, in which the vulture
wheels and the heron sails; and the shadows are so
deep, and the stillness is so sweet, and the earth seems
so green, and fresh, and silent, and strong. Nowhere
else can one rest so well; nowhere else is there so fit a
refuge for all the faiths and fancies that can find a home
no longer in the harsh and hurrying world; there is
room for them all in the Austrian forests, from the Erl-
King to Ariel and Oberon.

"YOU think any sin may be forgiven?" he said ir-
relevantly, with his face averted.

"That is a very wide question. I do not think St.
Augustine himself could answer it in a word or in a
moment. Forgiveness, I think, would surely depend
on repentance."

"Repentance in secret—would that avail?

"Scarcely—would it?—if it did not attain some
sacrifice. It would have to prove its sincerity to be
accepted."

"You believe in public penance?" said Sabran, with
some impatience and contempt.

"Not necessarily public," she said, with a sense of
perplexity at the turn his words had taken. "But of
what use is it for one to say he repents unless in some
measure he makes atonement?"

"But where atonement is impossible?"

"That could never be."

"Yes. There are crimes whose consequences can
never be undone. What then? Is he who did them
shut out from all hope?"

"I am no casuist," she said, vaguely troubled. "But if no atonement were possible I still think—nay, I am sure—a sincere and intense regret which is, after all, what we mean by repentance, must be accepted, must be enough."

"Enough to efface it in the eyes of one who had never sinned?"

"Where is there such a one? I thought you spoke of heaven."

"I spoke of earth. It is all we can be sure to have to do with; it is our one poor heritage."

"I hope it is but an antechamber which we pass through, and fill with beautiful things, or befoul with dust and blood, at our own will."

"Hardly at our own will. In your antechamber a capricious tyrant waits us all at birth. Some come in chained; some free."

"DO not compare the retreat of the soldier tired of his wounds, of the gambler wearied by his losses, with the poet or the saint who is at peace with himself and sees all his life long what he at least believes to be the smile of God. Loyola and Francis d'Assisi are not the same thing, are not on the same plane."

"What matter what brought them," she said softly, "if they reach the same goal?"

"YOU bade me do good at Romaris. Candidly, I see no way to do it except in saving a crew off a wreck, which is not an occasion that presents itself every week. I cannot benefit these people materially, since I am poor; I cannot benefit them morally, because I have not their faith in the things unseen, and I have not their morality

in the things tangible. They are God-fearing, infinitely
patient, faithful in their daily lives, and they reproach no
one for their hard lot, cast on an iron shore and forced
to win their scanty bread at the risk of their lives. They
do not murmur either at duty or mankind. What should
I say to them? I, whose whole life is one restless impatience, one petulant mutiny against circumstance?
If I talk with them I only take them what the world
always takes into solitude—discontent. It would be a
cruel gift, yet my hand is incapable of holding out any
other. It is a homely saying that no blood comes out of
a stone; so, out of a life saturated with the ironies, the
contempt, the disbelief, the frivolous philosophies, the
hopeless negations of what we call Society, there can be
drawn no water of hope and charity, for the well-head—
belief—is dried up at its source. Some pretend, indeed,
to find in humanity what they deny to exist as Deity, but
I should be incapable of the illogical exchange. It is to
deny that the seed sprang from a root; it is to replace a
grand and illimitable theism by a finite and vainglorious
bathos. Of all the creeds that have debased mankind,
the new creed that would centre itself in man seems to
me the poorest and the most baseless of all. If humanity
be but a *vibrion*, a conglomeration of gases, a mere mould
holding chemicals, a mere bundle of phosphorus and carbon, how can it contain the elements of worship? what
matter when or how each bubble of it bursts? This is
the weakness of all materialism when it attempts to ally
itself with duty. It becomes ridiculous. The *carpi diem*
of the classic sensualists, the morality of the 'Satyricon'
or the 'Decamerone,' are its only natural concomitants
and outcome; but as yet it is not honest enough to say
this. It affects the soothsayer's long robe, the sacer-
dotal frown, and is a hypocrite."

In answer she wrote back to him :

"I do not urge you to have my faith : what is the use?

Goethe was right. It is a question between a man and
his own heart. No one should venture to intrude there.
But taking life even as you do, it is surely a casket of
mysteries. May we not trust that at the bottom of it, as
at the bottom of Pandora's, there may be hope? I wish
again to think with Goethe that immortality is not an
inheritance, but a greatness to be achieved like any other
greatness, by courage, self-denial, and purity of purpose—
a reward allotted to the just. This is fanciful, may be, but
it is not illogical. And without being either a Christian or
a Materialist, without beholding either majesty or divinity
in humanity, surely the best emotion that our natures
know—pity—must be large enough to draw us to console
where we can, and sustain where we can, in view of the
endless suffering, the continual injustice, the appalling
contrasts, with which the world is full. Whether man
be the *vibrion* or the heir to immortality, the bundle of
carbon or the care of angels, one fact is indisputable : he
suffers agonies, mental and physical, that are wholly out
of proportion to the brevity of his life, while he is too often
weighted from infancy with hereditary maladies, both of
body and of character. This is reason enough, I think,
for us all to help each other, even though we feel, as you
feel, that we are as lost children, wandering in a great
darkness, with no thread or clue to guide us to the end."

"WE do not cultivate music one-half enough among
the peasantry. It lightens labour ; it purifies and
strengthens the home life ; it sweetens black bread. Do
you remember that happy picture of Jordaens' 'Where
the old sing, the young chirp,' where the old grandfather
and grandmother, and the baby in its mother's arms, and
the hale five-year-old boy, and the rough servant, are all
joining in the same melody, while the goat crops the
vine-leaves off the table? I should like to see every

cottage interior like that when the work was done. I
would hang up an etching from Jordaens where you
would hang up, perhaps, the programme of Proudhon."
Then she walked back with him through the green
sun-gleaming woods.
"I hope that I teach them content," she continued.
"It is the lesson most neglected in our day. '*Niemand
will ein Schuster sein; Jedermann ein Dichter.*' It is
true we are very happy in our surroundings. A moun-
taineer's is such a beautiful life, so simple, healthful,
hardy, and fine ; always face to face with nature. I try
to teach them what an inestimable joy that alone is. I
do not altogether believe in the prosaic views of rural
life. It is true that the peasant digging his trench sees
the clod, not the sky ; but then when he does lift his
head the sky is there, not the roof, not the ceiling. That
is so much in itself. And here the sky is an everlasting
grandeur ; clouds and domes of snow are blent together.
When the stars are out above the glaciers how serene the
night is, how majestic ! even the humblest creature feels
lifted up into that eternal greatness. Then you think of
the home-life in the long winters as dreary ; but it is not
so. Over away there, at Lahn, and other places on the
Hallstadtersee, they do not see the sun for five months ;
the wall of rock behind them shuts them from all light
of day ; but they live together, they dance, they work.
The young men recite poems, and the old men tell tales
of the mountains and the French war, and they sing
the homely songs of the *Schnader-hüpfeln*. Then when
winter passes, when the sun comes up again over the
wall of rocks, when they go out into the light once more,
what happiness it is ! One old man said to me, 'It is
like being born again !' and another said, 'Where it is
always warm and light I doubt they forget to thank God
for the sunshine ;' and quite a young child said, all of his
own accord, 'The primroses live in the dusk all the winter,

like us, and then when the sun comes up we and they run out together, and the Mother of Christ has set the water and the little birds laughing.' I would rather have the winter of Lahn than the winter of Belleville."

IF the Venus de Medici could be animated into life women would only remark that her waist was large.

TEDIUM is the most terrible and the most powerful foe love ever encounters.

" LIFE is after all like baccarat or billiards," he said to himself. "It is no use winning unless there be a *galerie* to look on and applaud."

TIME hung on his hands like a wearisome wallet of stones.

When all the habits of life are suddenly rent asunder, they are like a rope cut in two. They may be knotted together clumsily, or they may be thrown altogether aside and a new strand woven, but they will never be the same thing again.

THE greatness of a great race is a thing far higher than mere pride. Its instincts are noble and supreme, its obligations are no less than its privileges ; it is a great light which streams backward through the darkness of the ages, and if by that light you guide not your footsteps, then are you thrice accursed, holding as you do that lamp of honour in your hands.

EVEN to those who care nothing for Society, and dislike the stir and noise of the world about them, there is still always a vague sense of depression in the dispersion of a great party ; the house seems so strangely silent, the rooms seem so strangely empty, servants flitting noiselessly here and there, a dropped flower, a fallen jewel, an oppressive scent from multitudes of fading blossoms, a broken vase perhaps, or perhaps a snapped fan—these are all that are left of the teeming life crowded here one little moment ago. Though one may be glad they are gone, yet there is a certain sadness in it. *"Le lendemain de la fête"* keeps its pathos, even though the *fête* itself has possessed no poetry and no power to amuse.

IN every one of her villages she had her schools on this principle, and they throve, and the children with them. Many of these could not read a printed page, but all of them could read the shepherd's weather-glass in sky and flower ; all of them knew the worm that was harmful to the crops, the beetle that was harmless in the grass ; all knew a tree by a leaf, a bird by a feather, an insect by a grub.

Modern teaching makes a multitude of gabblers. She did not think it necessary for the little goat-herds, and dairymaids, and foresters, and charcoal-burners, and sennerins, and carpenters, and cobblers, to study the exact sciences or draw casts from the antique. She was of opinion, with Pope, that "a little learning is a dangerous thing," and that a smattering of it will easily make a man morose and discontented, whilst it takes a very deep and lifelong devotion to it to teach a man content with his lot. Genius, she thought, is too rare a thing to make it necessary to construct village schools for it, and whenever or wherever it comes upon earth, it will surely be its own master.

She did not believe in culture for little peasants who have to work for their daily bread at the plough-tail or with the reaping-hook. She knew that a mere glimpse of a Canaan of art and learning is cruelty to those who never can enter into and never even can have leisure to merely gaze on it. She thought that a vast amount of useful knowledge is consigned to oblivion whilst children are taught to waste their time in picking up the crumbs of a great indigestible loaf of artificial learning. She had her scholars taught their "ABC," and that was all. Those who wished to write were taught, but writing was not enforced. What they were made to learn was the name and use of every plant in their own country; the habits and ways of all animals; how to cook plain food well, and make good bread; how to brew simples from the herbs of their fields and woods, and how to discern the coming weather from the aspect of the skies, the shutting-up of certain blossoms, and the time of day from those "poor men's watches," the opening flowers. In all countries there is a great deal of useful household and out-of-door lore that is fast being choked out of existence under books and globes, and which, unless it passes by word of mouth from generation to generation, is quickly and irrevocably lost. All this lore she had cherished by her school-children. Her boys were taught in addition any useful trade they liked—boot-making, crampon-making, horse-shoeing, wheel-making, or carpentry. This trade was made a pastime to each. The little maidens learned to sew, to cook, to spin, to card, to keep fowls and sheep and cattle in good health, and to know all poisonous plants and berries by sight.

"I think it is what is wanted," she said. "A little peasant child does not need to be able to talk of the corolla and the spathe, but he does want to recognise at

a glance the flower that will give him healing and the
berries that will give him death. His sister does not in
the least require to know why a kettle boils, but she
does need to know when a warm bath will be good for
a sick baby or when hurtful. We want a new generation to be helpful, to have eyes, and to know the beauty
of silence. I do not mind much whether my children
reap or not. The labourer that reads turns Socialist,
because his brain cannot digest the hard mass of wonderful facts he encounters. But I believe every one of
my little peasants, being wrecked like Crusoe, would
prove as handy as he."

"CAN you inform me how it is that women possess
tenacity of will in precise proportion to the frivo-
lity of their lives? All these butterflies have a volition
of iron."

"It is egotism. Intensely selfish people are always
very decided as to what they wish. That is in itself a
great force; they do not waste their energies in con-
sidering the good of others."

"I AM not like you, my dear Olga," she wrote to her
relative the Countess Brancka. "I am not easily
amused. That *course effrénée* of the great world carries
you honestly away with it; all those incessant balls,
those endless visits, those interminable conferences on
your toilettes, that continual circling of human butterflies round you, those perpetual courtships of half a score
of young men; it all diverts you. You are never tired
of it; you cannot understand any life outside its pale.

All your days, whether they pass in Paris or Petersburgh, at Trouville, at Biarritz, or at Vienna or Scheveningen, are modelled on the same lines; you must have excitement as you have your cup of chocolate when you wake. What I envy you is that the excitement excites you. When I was amidst it I was not excited; I was seldom ever diverted. See the misfortune that it is to be born with a grave nature! I am as serious as Marcus Antoninus. You will say that it comes of having learned Latin and Greek. I do not think so; I fear I was born unamusable. I only truly care about horses and trees, and they are both grave things, though a horse can be playful enough sometimes when he is allowed to forget his servitude. Your friends, the famous tailors, send me admirably-chosen costumes which please that sense in me which Titians and Vandycks do (I do not mean to be profane); but I only put them on as the monks do their frocks. Perhaps I am very unworthy of them; at least, I cannot talk toilette as you can with ardour a whole morning and every whole morning of your life. You will think I am laughing at you; indeed I am not. I envy your faculty of sitting, as I am sure you are sitting now, in a straw chair on the shore, with a group of *boulevardiers* around you, and a crowd making a double hedge to look at you when it is your pleasure to pace the planks. My language is involved. I do not envy you the faculty of doing it, of course; I could do it myself to-morrow. I envy you the faculty of finding amusement in doing it, and finding flattery in the double hedge."

"NO doubt a love of nature is a triple armour against self-love. How can I say how right I think your system with these children? You seem not to believe me. There is only one thing in which I differ with you;

you think the 'eyes that see' bring content. Surely not! surely not !"

" It depends on what they see. When they are wide open in the woods and fields, when they have been taught to see how the tree-bee forms her cell and the mole her fortress, how the warbler builds his nest for his love and the water-spider makes his little raft, how the leaf comes forth from the hard stem and the fungi from the rank mould, then I think that sight is content—content in the simple life of the woodland place, and in such delighted wonder that the heart of its own accord goes up in peace and praise to the Creator. The printed page may teach envy, desire, coveteousness, hatred, but the Book of Nature teaches resignation, hope, willingness to labour and live, submission to die. The world has gone farther and farther from peace since larger and larger have grown its cities, and its shepherd kings are no more."

SHE remained still, her hands folded on her knees, her face set as though it were cast in bronze. The great bedchamber, with its hangings of pale blue plush and its silver-mounted furniture, was dim and shadowy in the greyness of a midwinter afternoon. Doors opened, here to the bath and dressing chambers, there to the oratory, yonder to the apartments of Sabran. She looked across to the last, and a shudder passed over her ; a sense of sickness and revulsion came on her.

She sat still and waited ; she was too weak to go farther than this room. She was wrapped in a long loose gown of white satin, lined and trimmed with sable. There were black bearskins beneath her feet ; the atmosphere was warmed by hot air, and fragrant with some bowls full of forced roses, which her women had placed there at noon. The grey light of the fading afternoon touched the silver scrollwork of the bed, and the silver frame of one large mirror, and fell on her folded hands and on the glister of their rings. Her head leaned backward against the high carved ebony of her chair. Her face was stern and bitterly cold, as that of Maria Theresa when she signed the loss of Silesia.

He approached from his own apartments, and came timidly and with a slow step forward. He did not dare to salute her, or go near to her; he stood like a banished man, disgraced, a few yards from her seat.

Two months had gone by since he had seen her. When he entered he read on her features that he must leave all hope behind.

Her whole frame shrank within her as she saw him there, but she gave no sign of what she felt. Without looking at him she spoke, in a voice quite firm, though it was faint from feebleness.

"I have but little to say to you, but that little is best said, not written."

He did not reply; his eyes were watching her with a terrible appeal, a very agony of longing. They had not rested on her for two months. She had been near the gates of the grave, within the shadow of death. He would have given his life for a word of pity, a touch, a regard—and he dared not approach her!

She dared not look at him. After that first glance, in which there had been so much of horror, of revulsion, she did not once look towards him. Her face had the immutability of a mask of stone; so many wretched days and haunted nights had she spent nerving herself for this inevitable moment that no emotion was visible in her; into her agony she had poured her pride, and it sustained her, as the plaster poured into the dry bones at Pompeii makes the skeleton stand erect, the ashes speak.

"After that which you have told me," she said, after a moment's silence in which he fancied she must hear the throbbing of his heart, "you must know that my life cannot be lived out beside yours. The law gives you many rights, no doubt, but I believe you will not be so base as to enforce them."

"I have no rights!" he muttered. "I am a criminal before the law. The law will free you from me, if you choose."

"I do not choose," she said coldly; "you understand me ill. I do not carry my wrongs or my woes to others. What you have told me is known only to Prince Vásárhely and to the Countess Brancka. He will be silent; he has the power to make her so. The world need know nothing. Can you think that I shall be its informant?"

"If you divorce me"——— he murmured.

A quiver of bitter anger passed over her features, but she retained her self-control.

"Divorce? What could divorce do for me? Could it destroy the past? Neither Church or Law can undo what you have done. Divorce would make me feel that in the past I had been your mistress, not your wife, that is all."

She breathed heavily, and again pressed her hand on her breast.

"Divorce!" she repeated. "Neither priest nor judge can efface a past as you clean a slate with a sponge! No power, human or divine, can free *me*, purify *me*, wash your dishonoured blood from your children's veins."

She almost lost her self-control; her lips trembled, her eyes were full of flame, her brow was black with passion. With a violent effort she restrained herself; invective or reproach seemed to her low and coarse and vile.

He was silent; his greatest fear, the torture of which had harassed him sleeping and waking ever since he had placed his secret in her hands, was banished at her words. She would seek no divorce—the children would not be disgraced—the world of men would not learn his shame; and yet as he heard a deeper despair than any he had ever known came over him. She was but as those sovereigns of old who scorned the poor tribunals of man's justice because they held in their own might the power of so much heavier chastisement.

"I shall not seek for a legal separation," she resumed; "that is to say, I shall not, unless you force me to do so to protect myself from you. If you fail to abide by the conditions I shall prescribe, then you will compel me to resort to any means that may shelter me from your demands. But I do not think you will endeavour to force on me conjugal rights which you obtained over me by a fraud."

All that she desired was to end quickly the torture of this interview, from which her courage had not permitted her to shrink. She had to defend herself because she would not be defended by others, and she only sought to strike swiftly and unerringly so as to spare herself and him all needless or lingering throes. Her speech was brief, for it seemed to her that no human language held expression deep and vast enough to measure the wrong done to her, could she seek to give it utterance.

She would not have made a sound had any murderer stabbed her body; she would not now show the death-wound of her soul and honour to this man who had stabbed both to the quick. Other women would have made their moan aloud, and cursed him. The daughter of the Szalras choked down her heart in silence, and spoke as a judge speaks to one condemned by man and God.

"I wish no words between us," she said, with renewed calmness. "You know your sin; all your life has been a lie. I will keep me and mine back from vengeance; but do not mistake—God may pardon you, I never! What I desired to say to you is that henceforth you shall wholly abandon the name you stole; you shall assign the land of Romaris to the people; you shall be known only as you have been known here of late, as the Count von Idrac. The title was mine to give, I gave it you; no wrong is done save to my fathers, who were brave men."

He remained silent; all excuse he might have offered seemed as if from him to her it would be but added outrage. He was her betrayer, and she had the power to avenge betrayal; naught that she could say or do could seem unjust or undeserved beside the enormity of her irreparable wrongs.

"The children?" he muttered faintly, in an unuttered supplication.

"They are mine," she said, always with the same unchanging calm that was cold as the frozen earth without. "You will not, I believe, seek to enforce your title to dispute them with me?"

He gave a gesture of denial.

He, the wrong-doer, could not realise the gulf which his betrayal had opened betwixt himself and her. On him all the ties of their past passion were sweet, precious, unchanged in their dominion. He could not realise that to her all these memories were abhorred, poisoned, stamped with ineffable shame; he could not believe that she, who had loved the dust that his feet had brushed, could now regard him as one leprous and accursed. He was slow to understand that his sin had driven him out of her life for evermore.

Commonly it is the woman on whom the remembrance of love has an enthralling power when love itself is traitor; commonly it is the man on whom the past has little influence, and to whom its appeal is vainly made; but here the position was reversed. He would have pleaded by it; she refused to acknowledge it, and remained as adamant before it. His nerve was too broken, his conscience was too heavily weighted, for him to attempt to rebel against her decisions or sway her judgment. If she had bidden him go out and slay himself he would gladly have obeyed.

"Once you said," he murmured timidly, "that repentance washes out all crimes. Will you count my remorse as nothing?"

"You would have known no remorse had your secret never been discovered!"

He shrank as from a blow.

"That is not true," he said wearily. "But how can I hope you will believe me?"

She answered nothing.

"Once you told me that there was no sin you would not pardon me!" he muttered.

She replied:

"We pardon sin; we do not pardon baseness."

She paused and put her hand to her heart; then she spoke again in that cold, forced, measured voice, which seemed on his ear as hard and pitiless as the strokes of an iron hammer, beating life out beneath it.

"You will leave Hohenszalras; you will go where you will; you have the revenues of Idrac. Any other financial arrangements that you may wish to make I will direct my lawyers to carry out. If the revenues of Idrac be insufficient to maintain you"——

"Do not insult me—so," he murmured, with a suffocated sound in his voice, as though some hand were clutching at his throat.

"Insult *you!*" she echoed with a terrible scorn.

She resumed with the same inflexible calmness.

"You must live as becomes the rank due to my hus-

band. The world need suspect nothing. There is no
obligation to make it your confidante. If any one were
wronged by the usurpation of the name you took it would
be otherwise, but as it is you will lose nothing in the
eyes of men; Society will not flatter you the less. The
world will only believe that we are tired of one another,
like so many. The blame will be placed on me. You
are a brilliant comedian, and can please and humour it.
I am known to be a cold, grave, eccentric woman, a
recluse, of whom it will deem it natural that you are
weary. Since you allow that I have the right to separate
from you—to deal with you as with a criminal—you will
not seek to recall your existence to me. You will meet
my abstinence by the only amends you can make to me.
Let me forget—as far as I am able—let me forget that
ever you have lived!"

He staggered slightly, as if under some sword-stroke
from an unseen hand. A great faintness came upon him.
He had been prepared for rage, for reproach, for bitter
tears, for passionate vengeance; but this chill, passionless, disdainful severance from him for all eternity he had
never dreamed of; it crept like the cold of frost into his
very marrow; he was speechless and mute with shame.
If she had dragged him through all the tribunals of the
world she would have hurt him and humiliated him far
less. Better all the hooting gibes of the whole earth
than this one voice, so cold, so inflexible, so full of utter
scorn!

Despite her bodily weakness she rose to her full height,
and for the first time looked at him.

"You have heard me," she said; "now go!"

But instead, blindly, not knowing what he did, he fell
at her feet.

"But you loved me," he cried, "you loved me so
well!"

The tears were coursing down his cheeks.

She drew the sables of her robe from his touch.

"Do not recall *that*," she said, with a bitter smile. "Women of my race have killed men before now for less outrage than yours has been to me."

"Kill me!" he cried to her. "I will kiss your hand."

She was mute.

He clung to her gown with an almost convulsive supplication.

"Believe, at least, that *I* loved *you!*" he cried, beside himself in his misery and impotence. "Believe that, at the least!"

She turned from him.

"Sir, I have been your dupe for ten long years; I can be so no more!"

Under that intolerable insult he rose slowly, and his eyes grew blind, and his limbs trembled, but he walked from her, and sought not again either her pity or her pardon.

On the threshold he looked back once. She stood erect, one hand resting upon the carved work of her high oak chair; cold, stately, motionless, the furred velvets falling to her feet like a queen's robes.

He looked, then passed the threshold and closed the door behind him.

THE END.

Printed in the United States
108525LV00001B/97/A

9 780548 600252